Earl of Beaconsfield

**Novels and Tales by the Earl of Beaconsfield**

Vol. IV

Earl of Beaconsfield

**Novels and Tales by the Earl of Beaconsfield**
*Vol. IV*

ISBN/EAN: 9783337039431

Printed in Europe, USA, Canada, Australia, Japan

Cover: Foto ©ninafisch / pixelio.de

More available books at **www.hansebooks.com**

Hughenden Edition

# ALROY
## IXION IN HEAVEN
## THE INFERNAL MARRIAGE
## POPANILLA

BY THE

EARL OF BEACONSFIELD

Hughenden Manor
NORTH FRONT

LONDON
LONGMANS, GREEN, AND CO.
1881

# PREFACE

TO

# ALROY.

Being at Jerusalem in the year 1831, and visiting the traditionary tombs of the Kings of Israel, my thoughts recurred to a personage whose marvellous career had, even in boyhood, attracted my attention, as one fraught with the richest materials of poetic fiction. And I then commenced these pages that should commemorate the name of ALROY.

In the twelfth century, when he arose, this was the political condition of the East:

The Caliphate was in a state of rapid decay. The Seljukian Sultans, who had been called to the assistance of the Commanders of the Faithful, had become, like the Mayors of the palace in France, the real sovereigns of the Empire. Out of the dominions of the successors of the Prophet, they had carved four kingdoms, which conferred titles on four Seljukian Princes, to wit, the Sultan of Bagdad, the Sultan of Persia, the Sultan of Syria, and the Sultan of Roum, or Asia Minor

But these warlike princes, in the relaxed discipline and doubtful conduct of their armies, began themselves to evince the natural effects of luxury and indulgence. They were no longer the same invincible and irresistible warriors who had poured forth from the shores of the Caspian over the fairest regions of the East; and although they still contrived to preserve order in their dominions, they witnessed with ill-concealed apprehension the rising power of the Kings of Karasmé, whose conquests daily made their territories more contiguous.

With regard to the Hebrew people, it should be known that, after the destruction of Jerusalem, the Eastern Jews, while they acknowledged the supremacy of their conquerors, gathered themselves together for all purposes of jurisdiction, under the control of a native ruler, a reputed descendant of David, whom they dignified with the title of 'The Prince of the Captivity.' If we are to credit the enthusiastic annalists of this imaginative people, there were periods of prosperity when the Princes of the Captivity assumed scarcely less state and enjoyed scarcely less power than the ancient Kings of Judah themselves. Certain it is that their power increased always in an exact proportion to the weakness of the Caliphate, and, without doubt, in some of the most distracted periods of the Arabian rule, the Hebrew Princes rose into some degree of local and temporary importance. Their chief residence was Bagdad, where they remained until the eleventh century, an age fatal in Oriental history, and from the disasters of which the Princes of the Captivity were not exempt. They are heard of even in the twelfth century. I have ventured to place one at Hamadan, which was a favourite residence of the Hebrews, from being the burial-place of Esther and Mordecai.

With regard to the supernatural machinery of this romance, it is Cabalistical and correct. From the Spirits of the Tombs to the sceptre of Solomon, authority may be found in the traditions of the Hebrews for the introduction of all these spiritual agencies.

GROSVENOR GATE:
*July*, 1845.

# ALROY.

## PART I.

### CHAPTER I

THE CORNETS sounded a final flourish as the Prince of the Captivity dismounted from his white mule; his train shouted as if they were once more a people; and, had it not been for the contemptuous leer which played upon the countenances of the Moslem bystanders, it might have been taken for a day of triumph rather than of tribute.

'The glory has not departed!' exclaimed the venerable Bostenay, as he entered the hall of his mansion. 'It is not as the visit of Sheba unto Solomon; nevertheless the glory has not yet departed. You have done well, faithful Caleb.' The old man's courage waxed more vigorous, as each step within his own walls the more assured him against the recent causes of his fear, the audible curses and the threatened missiles of the unbelieving mob.

'It shall be a day of rejoicing and thanksgiving!' continued the Prince; 'and look, my faithful Caleb, that the trumpeters be well served. That last flourish was bravely done. It was not as the blast before Jericho; nevertheless, it told that the Lord of Hosts was for us. How the accursed Ishmaelites started! Did you mark, Caleb, that tall Turk in green upon my left? By the sceptre of Jacob, he turned pale! Oh! it shall be a day of rejoicing and thanksgiving! And spare not the wine, nor the flesh-pots for the people. Look you to this, my child, for the people shouted bravely and with a stout voice. It was not as the great shout in the camp when the ark returned; nevertheless, it was boldly done, and showed that the glory had not yet departed. So spare not the wine, my son, and drink to the desolation of Ishmael in the juice which he dare not quaff.'

'It has indeed been a great day for Israel!' exclaimed Caleb, echoing his master's exultation.

'Had the procession been forbidden,' continued Bostenay, 'had it been reserved for me of all the princes to have dragged the accursed tribute upon foot, without trumpets and without guards, by this sceptre, my good Caleb, I really think that, sluggishly as this old blood now runs, I would —— But it is needless now to talk; the God of our fathers hath been our refuge.'

'Verily, my lord, we were as David in the wilderness of Ziph; but now we are as the Lord's anointed in the stronghold of Engedi!'

'The glory truly has not yet utterly departed,' resumed the Prince in a more subdued tone; 'yet if.—— I tell you what, Caleb; praise the Lord that you are young.'

'My Prince too may yet live to see the good day.'

'Nay, my child, you misinterpret me. Your Prince has lived to see the evil day. 'Twas not of the coming that I thought when I bid you praise the Lord because you were young, the more my sin. I was thinking, Caleb, that if your hair was as mine, if you could recollect, like me, the days that are gone by, the days when it needed no bribe to prove we were princes, the glorious days when we led captivity captive; I was thinking, I say, my son, what a gainful heritage it is to be born after the joys that have passed away.'

'My father lived at Babylon,' said Caleb.

'Oh! name it not! name it not!' exclaimed the old chieftain. 'Dark was the day that we lost that second Sion! We were then also slaves to the Egyptian; but verily we ruled over the realm of Pharaoh. Why, Caleb, Caleb, you who know all, the days of toil, the nights restless as a love-sick boy's, which it has cost your Prince to gain permission to grace our tribute-day with the paltry presence of half-a-dozen guards; you who know all my difficulties, who have witnessed all my mortifications, what would you say to the purse of dirhems, surrounded by seven thousand scimetars?'

'Seven thousand scimetars!'

'Not one less; my father flourished one.'

'It was indeed a great day for Israel!'

'Nay, that is nothing. When old Alroy was prince, old David Alroy, for thirty years, good Caleb, thirty long years we paid *no* tribute to the Caliph.'

'No tribute! no tribute for thirty years! What marvel then, my Prince, that the Philistines have of late exacted interest?'

'Nay, that is nothing,' continued old Bostenay, unmindful of his servant's ejaculations. 'When Moctador was Caliph, he sent to the same Prince David, to know why the dirhems were not brought up, and David immediately called to horse, and, attended by all the chief people, rode to the palace, and told the Caliph that tribute was an acknowledgment made from the weak to the strong to insure protection and support; and, inasmuch as he and his people had garrisoned the city for ten years against the Seljuks, he held the Caliph in arrear.'

'We shall yet see an ass mount a ladder,'¹ exclaimed Caleb, with uplifted eyes of wonder.

'It is true, though,' continued the Prince; 'often have I heard my father tell the tale. He was then a child, and his mother held him up to see the procession return, and all the people shouted "The sceptre has not gone out of Jacob."'

'It was indeed a great day for Israel.'

'Nay, that is nothing. I could tell you such things! But we prattle; our business is not yet done. You to the people; the widow and the orphan are waiting. Give freely, good Caleb, give freely; the spoils of the Canaanite are no longer ours, nevertheless the Lord is still our God, and, after all, even this is a great day for Israel. And,

Caleb, Caleb, bid my nephew, David Alroy, know that I would speak with him.'

'I will do all promptly, good master! We wondered that our honoured lord, your nephew, went not up with the donation this day.'

'Who bade you wonder? Begone, sir! How long are you to idle here? Away!'

'They wonder he went not up with the tribute to-day. Ay! surely, a common talk. This boy will be our ruin, a prudent hand to wield our shattered sceptre. I have observed him from his infancy; he should have lived in Babylon. The old Alroy blood flows in his veins, a stiff-necked race. When I was a youth, his grandsire was my friend; I had some fancies then myself. Dreams, dreams! we have fallen on evil days, and yet we prosper. I have lived long enough to feel that a rich caravan, laden with the shawls of India and the stuffs of Samarcand, if not exactly like dancing before the ark, is still a goodly sight. And our hard-hearted rulers, with all their pride, can they subsist without us? Still we wax rich. I have lived to see the haughty Caliph sink into a slave viler far than Israel. And the victorious and voluptuous Seljuks, even now they tremble at the dim mention of the distant name of Arslan. Yet I, Bostenay, and the frail remnant of our scattered tribes, still we exist, and still, thanks to our God! we prosper. But the age of power has passed; it is by prudence now that we must flourish. The gibe and jest, the curse, perchance the blow, Israel now must bear, and with a calm or even smiling visage. What then? For every gibe and jest, for every curse, I'll have a dirhem; and for every blow, let him look to it who is my debtor, or wills to be so. But see, he comes, my nephew! His grandsire was my friend. Methinks I look upon him now: the same Alroy that was the partner of my boyish hours. And yet that fragile form and girlish face but ill consort with the dark passions and the dangerous fancies, which, I fear, lie hidden in that tender breast. Well, sir?'

'You want me, uncle?'

'What then? Uncles often want what nephews seldom offer.'

'I at least can refuse nothing; for I have nought to give.'

'You have a jewel which I greatly covet.'

'A jewel! See my chaplet! You gave it me, my uncle; it is yours.'

'I thank you. Many a blazing ruby, many a soft and shadowy pearl, and many an emerald glowing like a star in the far desert, I behold, my child. They are choice stones, and yet I miss a jewel far more precious, which, when I gave you this rich chaplet, David, I deemed you did possess.'

'How do you call it, sir?'

'Obedience.'

'A word of doubtful import; for to obey, when duty is disgrace, is not a virtue.'

'I see you read my thought. In a word, I sent for you to know, wherefore you joined me not to-day in offering our, our ——'

'Tribute.'

'Be it so: tribute. Why were you absent?'

'Because it was a tribute; I pay none.'

'But that the dreary course of seventy winters has not erased the memory of my boyish follies, David, I should esteem you mad. Think you, because I am old, I am enamoured of disgrace, and love a house of bondage? If life were a mere question between freedom and slavery, glory and dishonour, all could decide. Trust me, there needs but little spirit to be a moody patriot in a sullen home, and vent your heroic spleen upon your fellow-sufferers, whose sufferings you cannot remedy. But of such stuff your race were ever made. Such deliverers ever abounded in the house of Alroy. And what has been the result? I found you and your sister orphan infants, your sceptre broken, and your tribes dispersed. The tribute, which now at least we pay like princes, was then exacted with the scourge and offered in chains. I collected our scattered people, I re-established our ancient throne, and this day, which you look upon as a day of humiliation and of mourning, is rightly considered by all a day of triumph and of feasting; for, has it not proved, in the very teeth of the Ishmaelites, that the sceptre has not yet departed from Jacob?'

'I pray you, uncle, speak not of these things. I would not willingly forget you are my kinsman, and a kind one. Let there not be strife between us. What my feelings are is nothing. They are my own: I cannot change them. And for my ancestors, if they pondered much, and achieved little, why then 'twould seem our pedigree is pure, and I am their true son. At least one was a hero.'

'Ah! the great Alroy; you may well be proud of such an ancestor.'

'I am ashamed, uncle, ashamed, ashamed.'

'His sceptre still exists. At least, I have not betrayed him. And this brings me to the real purport of our interview. That sceptre I would return.'

'To whom?'

'To its right owner, to yourself.'

'Oh! no, no, no; I pray you, I pray you not. I do entreat you, sir, forget that I have a right as utterly as I disclaim it. That sceptre, you have wielded it wisely and well; I beseech you keep it. Indeed, good uncle, I have no sort of talent for all the busy duties of this post.'

'You sigh for glory, yet you fly from toil.'

'Toil without glory is a menial's lot.'

'You are a boy; you may yet live to learn that the sweetest lot of life consists in tranquil duties and well-earned repose.'

'If my lot be repose, I'll find it in a lair.'

'Ah! David, David, there is a wildness in your temper, boy, that makes me often tremble. You are already too much alone, child. And for this, as well as weightier reasons, I am desirous that you should at length assume the office you inherit. What my poor experience can afford to aid you, as your counsellor, I shall ever proffer; and, for the rest, our God will not desert you, an orphan child, and born of royal blood.'

'Pr'ythee, no more, kind uncle. I have but little heart

to mount a throne, which only ranks me as the first of slaves.'

'Pooh, pooh, you are young. Live we like slaves? Is this hall a servile chamber? These costly carpets, and these rich divans, in what proud harem shall we find their match? I feel not like a slave. My coffers are full of dirhems. Is that slavish? The wealthiest company of the caravan is ever Bostenay's. Is that to be a slave? Walk the bazaar of Bagdad, and you will find my name more potent than the Caliph's. Is that a badge of slavery?'

'Uncle, you toil for others.'

'So do we all, so does the bee, yet he is free and happy.'

'At least he has a sting.'

'Which he can use but once, and when he stings ——'

'He dies, and like a hero. Such a death is sweeter than his honey.'

'Well, well, you are young, you are young. I once, too, had fancies. Dreams all, dreams all. I willingly would see you happy, child. Come, let that face brighten; after all, to-day is a great day. If you had seen what I have seen, David, you too would feel grateful. Come, let us feast. The Ishmaelite, the accursed child of Hagar, he does confess to-day that you are a prince; this day also you complete your eighteenth year. The custom of our people now requires that you should assume the attributes of manhood. To-day, then, your reign commences; and at our festival I will present the elders to their prince. For a while farewell, my child. Array that face in smiles. I shall most anxiously await your presence.'

'Farewell, sir.'

He turned his head and watched his uncle as he departed: the bitter expression of his countenance gradually melted away as Bostenay disappeared: dejection succeeded to sarcasm; he sighed, he threw himself upon a couch and buried his face in his hands.

Suddenly he arose and paced the chamber with an irregular and moody step. He stopped, and leant against a column. He spoke in a tremulous and smothered voice.

'Oh! my heart is full of care, and my soul is dark with sorrow! What am I? What is all this? A cloud hangs heavy o'er my life. God of my fathers, let it burst!

'I know not what I feel, yet what I feel is madness. Thus to be is not to live, if life be what I sometimes dream, and dare to think it might be. To breathe, to feed, to sleep, to wake and breathe again, again to feel existence without hope; if this be life, why then these brooding thoughts that whisper death were better?

'Away! The demon tempts me. But to what? What nameless deed shall desecrate this hand? It must not be: the royal blood of twice two thousand years, it must not die, die like a dream. Oh! my heart is full of care, and my soul is dark with sorrow!

'Hark! the trumpets that sound our dishonour. Oh, that they but sounded to battle! Lord of Hosts, let me conquer or die! Let me conquer like David; or die, Lord, like Saul!

'Why do I live? Ah! could the thought that lurks within my secret heart but answer, not that trumpet's blast could speak as loud or clear. The votary of a false idea, I linger in this shadowy life, and feed on silent images which no eye but mine can gaze upon, till at length they are invested with all the terrible circumstance of life, and breathe, and act, and form a stirring world of fate and beauty, time, and death, and glory. And then, from out this dazzling wilderness of deeds, I wander forth and wake, and find myself in this dull house of bondage, even as I do now. Horrible! horrible!

'God of my fathers! for indeed I dare not style thee God of their wretched sons; yet, by the memory of Sinai, let me tell thee that some of the antique blood yet beats within these pulses, and there yet is one who fain would commune with thee face to face, commune and conquer.

'And if the promise unto which we cling be not a cheat, why, let him come, come, and come quickly, for thy servant Israel, Lord, is now a slave so infamous, so woe-begone, and so contemned, that even when our fathers hung their harps by the sad waters of the Babylonian stream, why, it was paradise compared with what we suffer.

'Alas! they do not suffer; they endure and do not feel. Or by this time our shadowy cherubim would guard again the ark. It is the will that is the father to the deed, and he who broods over some long idea, however wild, will find his dream was but the prophecy of coming fate.

'And even now a vivid flash darts through the darkness of my mind. Methinks, methinks: ah! worst of woes to dream of glory in despair. No, no; I live and die a most ignoble thing; beauty and love, and fame and mighty deeds, the smile of women and the gaze of men, and the ennobling consciousness of worth, and all the fiery course of the creative passions, these are not for me, and I, Alroy, the descendant of sacred kings, and with a soul that pants for empire, I stand here extending my vain arm for my lost sceptre, a most dishonoured slave! And do I still exist? Exist! ay, merrily. Hark! Festivity holds her fair revel in these light-hearted walls. We are gay to-day; and yet, ere yon proud sun, whose mighty course was stayed before our swords that now he even does not deign to shine upon; ere yon proud sun shall, like a hero from a glorious field, enter the bright pavilion of his rest, there shall a deed be done.

'My fathers, my heroic fathers, if this feeble arm cannot redeem your heritage; if the foul boar must still wallow in thy sweet vineyard, Israel, at least I will not disgrace you. No! let me perish. The house of David is no more; no more our sacred seed shall lurk and linger, like a blighted thing, in this degenerate earth. If we cannot flourish, why then we will die!'

'Oh! say not so, my brother!'

He turns, he gazes on a face beauteous as a starry night; his heart is full, his voice is low.

'Ah, Miriam! thou queller of dark spirits! is it thou? Why art thou here?'

'Why am I here? Are you not here? and need I urge a stronger plea? Oh! brother dear, I pray you come, and mingle in our festival! Our walls are hung with flowers you love;² I culled them by the fountain's side; the holy lamps are trimmed and set, and you must raise their earliest flame. Without the gate, my maidens wait, to offer you a robe of state. Then, brother dear, I pray you come and mingle in our festival.'

'Why should we feast?'

'Ah! is it not in thy dear name these lamps are lit, these garlands hung? To-day to us a prince is given, to-day——'

'A prince without a kingdom.'

'But not without that which makes kingdoms precious, and which full many a royal heart has sighed for, willing subjects, David.'

'Slaves, Miriam, fellow-slaves.'

'What we are, my brother, our God has willed; and let us bow and tremble.'

'I will not bow, I cannot tremble.'

'Hush, David, hush! It was this haughty spirit that called the vengeance of the Lord upon us.'

'It was this haughty spirit that conquered Canaan.'

'Oh, my brother, my dear brother! they told me the dark spirit had fallen on thee, and I came, and hoped that Miriam might have charmed it. What we have been, Alroy, is a bright dream; and what we may be, at least as bright a hope; and for what we are, thou art my brother. In thy love I find present felicity, and value more thy chance embraces and thy scanty smiles than all the vanished splendour of our race, our gorgeous gardens, and our glittering halls.'

'Who waits without there?'

'Caleb.'

'Caleb?'

'My Lord.'

'Go tell my uncle that I will presently join the banquet. Leave me a moment, Miriam. Nay, dry those tears.'

'Oh, Alroy! they are not tears of sorrow.'

'God be with thee! Thou art the charm and consolation of my life. Farewell! farewell!'

'I do observe the influence of women very potent over me. 'Tis not of such stuff that they make heroes. I know not love, save that pure affection which doth subsist between me and this girl, an orphan and my sister. We are so alike, that when, last Passover, in mimicry she twined my turban round her head, our uncle called her David.

'The daughters of my tribe, they please me not, though they are passing fair. Were our sons as brave as they are beautiful, we still might dance on Sion. Yet have I often thought that, could I pillow this moody brow upon some snowy bosom that were my own, and dwell in the wilderness, far from the sight and ken of man, and all the care and toil and wretchedness that groan and sweat and sigh about me, I might haply lose this deep sensation of overwhelming woe that broods upon by being. No matter! Life is but a dream, and mine must be a dull one.'

## CHAPTER II.

WITHOUT the gates of Hamadan, a short distance from the city, was an enclosed piece of elevated ground, in the centre of which rose an ancient sepulchre, the traditionary tomb of Esther and Mordecai.[3] This solemn and solitary spot was an accustomed haunt of Alroy, and thither, escaping from the banquet, about an hour before sunset, he this day repaired.

As he unlocked the massy gate of the burial-place, he heard behind him the trampling of a horse; and before he had again secured the entrance, some one shouted to him.

He looked up, and recognised the youthful and voluptuous Alschiroch, the governor of the city, and brother of the sultan of the Seljuks. He was attended only by a single running footman, an Arab, a detested favourite, and notorious minister of his pleasures.

'Dog!' exclaimed the irritated Alschiroch, 'art thou deaf, or obstinate, or both? Are we to call twice to our slaves? Unlock that gate!'

'Wherefore?' inquired Alroy.

'Wherefore! By the holy Prophet he bandies questions with us! Unlock that gate, or thy head shall answer for it!'

'Who art thou,' inquired Alroy, 'whose voice is so loud? Art thou some holiday Turk, who hath transgressed the orders of thy Prophet, and drunken aught but water? Go to, or I will summon thee before thy Cadi;' and, so saying, he turned towards the tomb.

'By the eyes of my mother, the dog jeers us! But that we are already late, and this horse is like an untamed tiger, I would impale him on the spot. Speak to the dog, Mustapha! manage him!'

'Worthy Hebrew,' said the silky Mustapha, advancing, apparently you are not aware that this is our Lord Alschiroch. His highness would fain walk his horse through the burial-ground of thy excellent people, as he is obliged to repair, on urgent matters, to a holy Santon, who sojourns on the other side of the hill, and time presses.'

'If this be our Lord Alschiroch, thou doubtless art his faithful slave, Mustapha.'

'I am, indeed, his poor slave. What then, young master?'

'Deem thyself lucky that the gate is closed. It was but yesterday thou didst insult the sister of a servant of my house. I would not willingly sully my hands with such miserable blood as thine, but away, wretch, away!'

'Holy Prophet! who is this dog?' exclaimed the astonished governor.

''Tis the young Alroy,' whispered Mustapha, who had not at first recognised him; 'he they call their Prince; a most headstrong youth. My lord, we had better proceed.'

'The young Alroy! I mark him. They must have a prince too! The young Alroy! Well, let us away, and, dog!' shouted Alschiroch, rising in his stirrups, and shaking his hand with a threatening air, 'dog! remember thy tribute!'

Alroy rushed to the gate, but the massy lock was slow to

open; and ere he could succeed, the fiery steed had borne Alschiroch beyond pursuit.

An expression of baffled rage remained for a moment on his countenance; for a moment he remained with his eager eye fixed on the route of his vanished enemy, and then he walked slowly towards the tomb; but his excited temper was now little in unison with the still reverie in which he had repaired to the sepulchre to indulge. He was restless and disquieted, and at length he wandered into the woods, which rose on the summit of the burial-place.

He found himself upon a brow crested with young pine-trees, in the midst of which rose a mighty cedar. He threw himself beneath its thick and shadowy branches, and looked upon a valley small and green; in the midst of which was a marble fountain, the richly-carved cupola,[4] supported by twisted columns, and banded by a broad inscription in Hebrew characters. The bases of the white pillars were covered with wild flowers, or hidden by beds of variegated gourds. The transparent sunset flung over the whole scene a soft but brilliant light.

The tranquil hour, the beauteous scene, the sweetness and the stillness blending their odour and serenity, the gentle breeze that softly rose, and summoned forth the languid birds to cool their plumage in the twilight air, and wave their radiant wings in skies as bright —— Ah! what stern spirit will not yield to the soft genius of subduing Eve?

And Alroy gazed upon the silent loneliness of earth, and a tear stole down his haughty cheek.

' 'Tis singular! but when I am thus alone at this still hour, I ever fancy I gaze upon the Land of Promise. And often, in my dreams, some sunny spot, the bright memorial of a roving hour, will rise upon my sight, and, when I wake, I feel as if I had been in Canaan. Why am I not? The caravan that bears my uncle's goods across the Desert would bear me too. But I rest here, my miserable life running to seed in the dull misery of this wretched city, and do nothing. Why! the old captivity was empire to our inglorious bondage. We have no Esther now to share their thrones, no politic Mordecai, no purple-vested Daniel. O Jerusalem, Jerusalem! I do believe one sight of thee would nerve me to the sticking-point. And yet to gaze upon thy fallen state, my uncle tells me that of the Temple not a stone remains. 'Tis horrible. Is there no hope?'

'THE BRICKS ARE FALLEN, BUT WE WILL REBUILD WITH MARBLE; THE SYCAMORES ARE CUT DOWN, BUT WE WILL REPLACE THEM WITH CEDARS.'

'The chorus of our maidens, as they pay their evening visit to the fountain's side.[5] The burden is prophetic.

'Hark again! How beautifully, upon the soft and flowing air, their sweet and mingled voices blend and float!'

'YET AGAIN I WILL BUILD THEE, AND THOU SHALT BE BUILT, O VIRGIN OF ISRAEL! YET AGAIN SHALT THOU DECK THYSELF WITH THY TABRETS, AND GO FORTH IN THE DANCE OF THOSE THAT MAKE MERRY. YET AGAIN SHALT THOU PLANT VINEYARDS ON THE MOUNTAINS OF SAMARIA.'

'See! their white forms break through the sparkling foliage of the sunny shrubs as they descend, with measured step, that mild declivity. A fair society in bright procession: each one clothed in solemn drapery, veiling her shadowy face with modest hand, and bearing on her graceful head a graceful vase. Their leader is my sister.

'And now they reach the fountain's side, and dip their vases in the water, pure and beauteous as themselves. Some repose beneath the marble pillars; some, seated 'mid the flowers, gather sweets, and twine them into garlands; and that wild girl, now that the order is broke, touches with light fingers her moist vase, and showers startling drops of glittering light on her serener sisters. Hark! again they sing.'

'O VINE OF SIBMAH! UPON THY SUMMER FRUITS, AND UPON THY VINTAGE, A SPOILER HATH FALLEN!'

A scream, a shriek, a long wild shriek, confusion, flight,

despair! Behold! from out the woods a turbaned man rushes, and seizes the leader of the chorus. Her companions fly on all sides, Miriam alone is left in the arms of Alschiroch.

The water column wildly rising from the breast of summer ocean, in some warm tropic clime, when the sudden clouds too well discover that the holiday of heaven is over, and the shrieking sea-birds tell a time of fierce commotion, the column rising from the sea, it was not so wild as he, the young Alroy.

Pallid and mad, he swift upsprang, and he tore up a tree by its lusty roots, and down the declivity, dashing with rapid leaps, panting and wild, he struck the ravisher on the temple with the mighty pine. Alschiroch fell lifeless on the sod, and Miriam fainting into her brother's arms.

And there he stood, fixed and immovable, gazing upon his sister's deathly face, and himself exhausted by passion and his exploit, supporting her cherished but senseless body.

One of the fugitive maidens appeared reconnoitring in the distance. When she observed her mistress in the arms of one of her own people, her courage revived, and, desirous of rallying her scattered companions, she raised her voice, and sang:

'HASTE, DAUGHTERS OF JERUSALEM; O! HASTE, FOR THE LORD HAS AVENGED US, AND THE SPOILER IS SPOILED.'

And soon the verse was responded to from various quarters of the woods, and soon the virgins re-assembled, singing,

'WE COME, O DAUGHTER OF JERUSALEM! WE COME; FOR THE LORD HAS AVENGED US, AND THE SPOILER IS SPOILED.'

They gathered round their mistress, and one loosened her veil, and another brought water from the fountain, and sprinkled her reviving countenance. And Miriam opened her eyes, and said, 'My brother!' And he answered, 'I am here.' And she replied in a low voice, 'Fly, David, fly; for the man you have stricken is a prince among the people.'

'He will be merciful, my sister; and, doubtless, since he first erred, by this time he has forgotten my offence.'

'Justice and mercy! Oh, my brother, what can these foul tyrants know of either! Already he has perhaps doomed you to some refined and procrastinated torture, already—— Ah! what unutterable woe is mine! fly, my brother, fly!'

'FLY, FLY, FLY!'

'There is no fear, my Miriam; would all his accursed race could trouble us as little as their sometime ruler. See, he sleeps soundly. But his carcass shall not defile our fresh fountain, and our fragrant flowers. I'll stow it in the woods, and stroll here at night to listen to the jackals at their banquet.'

'You speak wildly, David. What! No! It is impossible! He is not dead! You have not slain him! He sleeps, he is afraid. He mimics death, that we may leave his side, and he may rise again in safety. Girls, look to him. David, you do not answer. Brother, dear brother, surely he has swooned! I thought he had fled. Bear water, maidens, to that terrible man. I dare not look upon him.'

'Away! I'll look on him, and I'll triumph. Dead! Alschiroch dead! Why, but a moment since, this clotted carcass was a prince, my tyrant! So we can rid ourselves of them, eh? If the prince fall, why not the people? Dead, absolutely dead, and I his slayer! Hah! at length I am a man. This, this indeed is life. Let me live slaying!'

'Woe! woe! our house is fallen! The wildness of his gestures frightens me. David, David, I pray thee cease. He hears me not; my voice, perchance, is thin. I am very faint. Maidens, kneel to your Prince, and soothe the madness of his passion.'

'SWEET IS THE VOICE OF A SISTER IN THE SEASON OF SORROW, AND WISE IS THE COUNSEL OF THOSE WHO LOVE US'

'Why, this is my Goliath! a pebble or a stick, it is the same. The Lord of Hosts is with us. Rightly am I called David.'

'DELIVER US FROM OUR ENEMIES, O LORD! FROM THOSE WHO RISE UP AGAINST US, AND THOSE WHO LIE IN WAIT FOR US.'

'Were but this blow multiplied, were but the servants of my uncle's house to do the same, why we should see again the days of Elah! The Philistine, the foul, lascivious, damnable Philistine! and he must touch my sister! Oh! that all his tribe were here, all, all! I'd tie such firebrands to their foxes' tails, the blaze should light to freedom!'

While he spoke, a maiden, who had not yet rejoined the company, came running towards them swiftly with an agitated countenance.

'Fly,' she exclaimed, 'they come, they come!'

Miriam was reclining in an attendant's arms, feeble and faint, but the moment her quick ear caught these words she sprang up, and seized her brother's arm.

'Alroy! David! brother, dear brother! I beseech thee, listen, I am thy sister, thy Miriam; they come, they come, the hard-hearted, wicked men, they come, to kill, perhaps to torture thee, my tender brother. Rouse thyself, David; rouse thyself from this wild, fierce dream: save thyself, fly!'

'Ah! is it thou, Miriam? Thou seest he sleepeth soundly. I was dreaming of noble purposes and mighty hopes. 'Tis over now. I am myself again. What wouldst thou?'

'They come, the fierce retainers of this fallen man; they come, to seize thee. Fly, David!'

'And leave thee?'

'I and my maidens, we have yet time to escape by the private way we entered, our uncle's garden. When in his house, we are for a moment safe, as safe as our poor race can ever be. Bostenay is so rich, so wise, so prudent, so learned in man's ways, and knows so well the character and spirit of these men, all will go right; I fear nothing. But thou, if thou art here, or to be found, thy blood alone will satiate them. If they be persuaded that thou hast escaped, as I yet pray thou mayest, their late master here, whom they could scarcely love, why, give me thy arm an instant, sweet Beruna. So, that's well. I was saying, if well bribed, and they may have all my jewels, why, very soon, he will be as little in their memories as he is now in life. I can scarcely speak; I feel my words wander, or seem to wander; I could

c

swoon, but will not; nay! do not fear. I will reach home. These maidens are my charge. 'Tis in these crises we should show the worth of royal blood. I'll see them safe, or die with them.'

'O! my sister, methinks I never knew I was a brother until this hour. My precious Miriam, what is life? what is revenge, or even fame and freedom without thee? I'll stay.'

'SWEET IS THE VOICE OF A SISTER IN THE SEASON OF SORROW, AND WISE IS THE COUNSEL OF THOSE WHO LOVE US.'

'Fly, David, fly!'
'Fly! whither and how?'
The neigh of a horse sounded from the thicket.
'Ah! they come!' exclaimed the distracted Miriam.

'ALL THIS HAS COME UPON US, O LORD! YET HAVE WE NOT FORGOTTEN THEE, NEITHER HAVE WE DEALT FALSELY IN THY COVENANT.'

'Hark! again it neighs! It is a horse that calleth to its rider. I see it. Courage, Miriam! it is no enemy, but a very present friend in time of trouble. It is Alschiroch's courser. He passed me on it by the tomb ere sunset. I marked it well, a very princely steed.'

'BEHOLD, BEHOLD, A RAM IS CAUGHT IN THE THICKET BY HIS HORNS.'

'Our God hath not forgotten us! Quick, maidens, bring forth the goodly steed. What! do you tremble? I'll be his groom.'

'Nay! Miriam, beware, beware. It is an untamed beast, wild as the whirlwind. Let me deal with him.'

He ran after her, dashed into the thicket, and brought forth the horse.

Short time I ween that stately steed had parted from his desert home; his haughty crest, his eye of fire, the glory of his snorting nostril, betokened well his conscious pride, and pure nobility of race. His colour was like the sable night shining with a thousand stars, and he pawed the ground with his delicate hoof, like an eagle flapping its wing.

Alroy vaulted on his back, and reined him with a master's hand.

'Hah!' he exclaimed, 'I feel more like a hero than a fugitive. Farewell, my sister; farewell, ye gentle maidens; fare ye well, and cherish my precious Miriam. One embrace, sweet sister,' and he bent down and whispered, 'Tell the good Bostenay not to spare his gold, for I have a deep persuasion that, ere a year shall roll its heavy course, I shall return, and make our masters here pay for this hurried ride and bitter parting. Now for the desert!'

# PART II.

### CHAPTER I.

Speed, fleetly speed, thou courser bold, and track the desert's trackless way. Beneath thee is the boundless earth, above thee is the boundless heaven, an iron soil and brazen sky. Speed, swiftly speed, thou courser bold, and track the desert's trackless way.

Ah! dost thou deem these salty plains [6] lead to thy Yemen's happy groves, and dost thou scent on the hot breeze the spicy breath of Araby? A sweet delusion, noble steed, for this briny wilderness leads not to the happy groves of Yemen, and the breath thou scentest on the coming breeze is not the spicy breath of Araby.

The day has died, the stars have risen, with all the splendour of a desert sky, and now the Night descending brings solace on her dewy wings to the fainting form and pallid cheek of the youthful Hebrew Prince.

Still the courser onward rushes, still his mighty heart supports him. Season and space, the glowing soil, the burning ray, yield to the tempest of his frame; the thunder of his nerves, and lightning of his veins.

Food or water they have none. No genial fount, no graceful tree, rise with their pleasant company. Never a beast or bird is there, in that hoary desert bare. Nothing breaks the almighty stillness. Even the jackal's felon cry might seem a soothing melody. A grey wild rat, with snowy whiskers, out of a withered bramble stealing, with a youthful snake in its ivory teeth, in the moonlight grins with glee. This is their sole society.

Morn comes, the fresh and fragrant morn, for which even

the guilty sigh. Morn comes, and all is visible. And light falls like a signet on the earth, and its face is turned like wax beneath a seal. Before them and also on their right was the sandy desert; but in the night they had approached much nearer to the mountainous chain, which bounded the desert on the left, and whither Alroy had at first guided the steed.

The mountains were a chain of the mighty Elburz; and, as the sun rose from behind a lofty peak, the horse suddenly stopped and neighed, as if asking for water. But Alroy, himself exhausted, could only soothe him with caresses. And the horse, full of courage, understood his master, and neighed again more cheerfully.

For an hour or two the Prince and his faithful companion proceeded slowly, but, as the day advanced, the heat became so oppressive, and the desire to drink so overwhelming, that Alroy again urged on the steed towards the mountains, where he knew that he should find a well. The courser dashed willingly forward, and seemed to share his master's desire to quit the arid and exhausting wilderness.

More than once the unhappy fugitive debated whether he should not allow himself to drop from his seat and die; no torture that could await him at Hamadan, but seemed preferable to the prolonged and inexpressible anguish which he now endured. As he rushed along, leaning on his bearer's neck, he perceived a patch of the desert that seemed of a darker colour than the surrounding sand. Here, he believed, might perhaps be found water. He tried to check the steed, but with difficulty he succeeded, and with still greater difficulty dismounted. He knelt down, and feebly raked up the sand with his hands. It was moist. He nearly fainted over his fruitless labour. At length, when he had dug about a foot deep, there bubbled up some water. He dashed in his hand, but it was salt as the ocean. When the horse saw the water his ears rose, but, when he smelt it, he turned away his head, and neighed most piteously.

'Alas, poor beast!' exclaimed Alroy, 'I am the occasion of thy suffering, I, who would be a kind master to thee, if the world would let me. Oh, that we were once more by my own fair fountain! The thought is madness. And Miriam too! I fear I am sadly tender-hearted.' He leant against his horse's back, with a feeling of utter exhaustion, and burst into hysteric sobs.

And the steed softly moaned, and turned its head, and gently rubbed its face against his arm, as if to solace him in his suffering. And strange, but Alroy was relieved by having given way to his emotion, and, charmed with the fondness of the faithful horse, he leant down and took water, and threw it over its feet to cool them, and wiped the foam from its face, and washed it, and the horse again neighed.

And now Alroy tried to remount, but his strength failed him, and the horse immediately knelt down and received him. And the moment that the Prince was in his seat, the horse rose, and again proceeded at a rapid pace in their old direction. Towards sunset they were within a few miles of the broken and rocky ground into which the mountains descended; and afar off Alroy recognised the cupola of the long-expected well. With re-animated courage and rallied energies he patted his courser's neck, and pointed in the direction of the cupola, and the horse pricked up its ears, and increased its pace.

Just as the sun set, they reached the well. Alroy jumped off the horse, and would have led it to the fountain, but the animal would not advance. It stood shivering with a glassy eye, and then with a groan fell down and died.

## CHAPTER II.

NIGHT brings rest; night brings solace; rest to the weary, solace to the sad. And to the desperate night brings despair.

The moon has sunk to early rest; but a thousand stars are in the sky. The mighty mountains rise severe in the

clear and silent air. In the forest all is still. The tired
wind no longer roams, but has lightly dropped on its leafy
couch, and sleeps like man. Silent all but the fountain's
drip. And by the fountain's side a youth is lying.

Suddenly a creature steals through the black and broken
rocks. Ha, ha! the jackal smells from afar the rich corruption of the courser's clay. Suddenly and silently it
steals, and stops, and smells. Brave banqueting I ween
to-night for all that goodly company. Jackal, and fox,
and marten-cat, haste ye now, ere morning's break shall
call the vulture to his feast and rob you of your prey.

The jackal lapped the courser's blood, and moaned with
exquisite delight. And in a moment, a faint bark was
heard in the distance. And the jackal peeled the flesh from
one of the ribs, and again burst into a shriek of mournful
ecstasy.

Hark, their quick tramp! First six, and then three,
galloping with ungodly glee. And a marten-cat came rushing down from the woods; but the jackals, fierce in their
number, drove her away, and there she stood without the
circle, panting, beautiful, and baffled, with her white teeth
and glossy skin, and sparkling eyes of rabid rage.[7]

Suddenly as one of the half-gorged jackals retired from
the main corpse, dragging along a stray member by some
still palpitating nerves, the marten-cat made a spring at
her enemy, carried off his prey, and rushed into the woods.

Her wild scream of triumph woke a lion from his lair.
His mighty form, black as ebony, moved on a distant eminence, his tail flowed like a serpent. He roared, and the
jackals trembled, and immediately ceased from their banquet, turning their heads in the direction of their sovereign's
voice. He advanced; he stalked towards them. They retired; he bent his head, examined the carcass with condescending curiosity, and instantly quitted it with royal dis-
dain. The jackals again collected around their garbage.
The lion advanced to the fountain to drink. He beheld a
man. His mane rose, his tail was wildly agitated, he bent
over the sleeping Prince, he uttered an awful roar, which
awoke Alroy.

## CHAPTER III.

He awoke; his gaze met the flaming eyes of the enormous beast fixed upon him with a blended feeling of desire and surprise. He awoke, and from a swoon; but the dreamless trance had refreshed the exhausted energies of the desolate wanderer; in an instant he collected his senses, remembered all that had passed, and comprehended his present situation. He returned the lion a glance as imperious, and fierce, and scrutinising, as his own. For a moment, their flashing orbs vied in regal rivalry; but at length the spirit of the mere animal yielded to the genius of the man. The lion, cowed, slunk away, stalked with haughty timidity through the rocks, and then sprang into the forest.

## CHAPTER IV.

Morn breaks; a silver light is shed over the blue and starry sky. Pleasant to feel is the breath of dawn. Night brings repose, but day brings joy.

The carol of a lonely bird singing in the wilderness! A lonely bird that sings with glee! Sunny and sweet, and light and clear, its airy notes float through the sky, and trill with innocent revelry.

The lonely youth on the lonely bird upgazes from the fountain's side. High in the air it proudly floats, balancing its crimson wings, and its snowy tail, long, delicate, and thin, shines like a sparkling meteor in the sun.

The carol of a lonely bird singing in the wilderness! Suddenly it downward dashes, and thrice with circling grace it flies around the head of the Hebrew Prince. Then by his side it gently drops a bunch of fresh and fragrant dates.

'Tis gone, 'tis gone! that cheerful stranger, gone to the palmy land it loves; gone like a bright and pleasant dream. A moment since and it was there, glancing in the sunny air, and now the sky is without a guest. Alas, alas! no more is heard the carol of that lonely bird singing in the wilderness.

## CHAPTER V.

'As thou didst feed Elijah, so also hast thou fed me, God of my fathers!' And Alroy arose, and he took his turban and unfolded it, and knelt and prayed. And then he ate of the dates, and drank of the fountain, and, full of confidence in the God of Israel, the descendant of David pursued his flight.

He now commenced the ascent of the mountainous chain, a wearisome and painful toil. Two hours past noon he reached the summit of the first ridge, and looked over a wild and chaotic waste full of precipices and ravines, and dark unfathomable gorges. The surrounding hills were ploughed in all directions by the courses of dried-up cataracts, and here and there a few savage goats browsed on an occasional patch of lean and sour pasture. This waste extended for many miles; the distance formed by a more elevated range of mountains, and beyond these, high in the blue sky, rose the loftiest peaks of Elburz,[8] shining with sharp glaciers of eternal snow.

It was apparent that Alroy was no stranger in the scene of his flight. He had never hesitated as to his course, and now, after having rested for a short time on the summit, he descended towards the left by a natural but intricate path, until his progress was arrested by a black ravine. Scarcely half a dozen yards divided him from the opposite precipice by which it was formed, but the gulf beneath, no one could shoot a glance at its invisible termination without drawing back with a cold shudder.

The Prince knelt down and examined the surrounding ground with great care. At length he raised a small square stone which covered a metallic plate, and, taking from his vest a carnelian talisman covered with strange characters, he knocked thrice upon the plate with the signet. A low solemn murmur sounded around. Presently the plate flew off, and Alroy pulled forth several yards of an iron chain, which he threw over to the opposite precipice. The chain fastened without difficulty to the rock, and was evidently constrained by some magnetic influence. The Prince, seizing the chain with both his hands, now swung across the ravine. As he landed, the chain parted from the rock, swiftly disappeared down the opposite aperture, and its covering closed with the same low, solemn murmur as before.

## CHAPTER VI.

ALROY proceeded for about a hundred paces through a natural cloister of basalt until he arrived at a large uncovered court of the same formation, which a stranger might easily have been excused for believing to have been formed and smoothed by art. In its centre bubbled up a perpetual spring, icy cold; the stream had worn a channel through the pavement, and might be traced for some time wandering among the rocks, until at length it leaped from a precipice into a gorge below, in a gauzy shower of variegated spray. Crossing the court, Alroy now entered a vast cavern.

The cavern was nearly circular in form, lighted from a large aperture in the top. Yet a burning lamp, in a distant and murky corner, indicated that its inhabitant did not trust merely to this natural source of the great blessing of existence. In the centre of the cave was a circular and brazen table, sculptured with strange characters and mysterious figures: near it was a couch, on which lay several volumes.[9] Suspended from the walls were a shield, some bows and arrows, and other arms.

As the Prince of the Captivity knelt down and kissed the vacant couch, a figure advanced from the extremity of the cavern into the light. He was a man of middle age, considerably above the common height, with a remarkably athletic frame, and a strongly-marked but majestic countenance. His black beard descended to his waist, over a dark red robe, encircled by a black girdle embroidered with yellow characters, like those sculptured on the brazen table. Black also was his turban, and black his large and luminous eye.

The stranger advanced so softly, that Alroy did not perceive him, until the Prince again rose up.

'Jabaster!' exclaimed the Prince.

'Sacred seed of David,' answered the Cabalist,[10] 'thou art expected. I read of thee in the stars last night. They spoke of trouble.'

'Trouble or triumph, Time must prove which it is, great master. At present I am a fugitive and exhausted. The bloodhounds track me, but methinks I have baffled them now. I have slain an Ishmaelite.'

# PART III.

## CHAPTER I.

It was midnight. Alroy slept upon the couch: his sleep was troubled. Jabaster stood by his side motionless, and gazing intently upon his slumbering guest.

'The only hope of Israel,' murmured the Cabalist, 'my pupil and my prince! I have long perceived in his young mind the seed of mighty deeds, and o'er his future life have often mused with a prophetic hope. The blood of David, the sacred offspring of a solemn race. There is a magic in his flowing veins my science cannot reach.

'When, in my youth, I raised our standard by my native Tigris, and called our nation to restore their ark, why, we were numerous, wealthy, potent; we were a people then, and they flocked to it boldly. Did we lack counsel? Did we need a leader? Who can aver that Jabaster's brain or arm was ever wanting? And yet the dream dissolved, the glorious vision! Oh! when I struck down Marvan, and the Caliph's camp flung its blazing shadow over the bloody river, ah! then indeed I lived. Twenty years of vigil may gain a pardon that I then forgot we lacked the chief ingredient in the spell, the blood that sleeps beside me.

'I recall the glorious rapture of that sacred strife amid the rocks of Caucasus. A fugitive, a proscribed and outlawed wretch, whose life is common sport, and whom the vilest hind may slay without a bidding. I, who would have been Messiah!

'Burn thy books, Jabaster; break thy brazen tables; forget thy lofty science, Cabalist, and read the stars no longer.'11 But last night, I stood upon the gulf which girds my dwelling: in one hand, I held my sacred talisman, that bears the name ineffable; in the other, the mystic record of our holy race. I remembered that I had evoked spirits, that I had communed with the great departed, and that the glowing heavens were to me a natural language. I recalled, as consolation to my gloomy soul, that never had my science been exercised but for a sacred or a noble purpose. And I remembered Israel, my brave, my chosen, and my antique race, slaves, wretched slaves. I was strongly tempted to fling me down this perilous abyss, and end my learning and my life together.

'But, as I gazed upon the star of David, a sudden halo rose around its rays, and ever and anon a meteor shot from out the silver veil. I read that there was trouble in the holy seed; and now comes this boy, who has done a deed which ——'

'The ark, the ark! I gaze upon the ark!'

'The slumberer speaks; the words of sleep are sacred.'

'Salvation only from the house of David.'

'A mighty truth; my life too well has proved it.'

'He is more calm. It is the holy hour. I'll steal into the court, and gaze upon the star that sways the fortunes of his royal house.'

## CHAPTER II.

THE moonbeam fell upon the fountain; the pavement of the court was a flood of light; the rocks rose dark around. Jabaster, seated by the spring, and holding his talisman in his left hand, shaded his sight with the other as he gazed upon the luminous heavens.

A shriek! his name was called. Alroy, wild and panting, rushed into the court with extended arms. The Cabalist started up, seized him, and held him in his careful grasp, foaming and in convulsions.

'Jabaster, Jabaster!'

'I am here, my child.'

'The Lord hath spoken.'

'The Lord is our refuge. Calm thyself, son of David, and tell me all.'

'I have been sleeping, master; is it not so?'

'Even so, my child. Exhausted by his flight and the exciting narrative of his exploit, my Prince lay down upon the couch and slumbered; but I fear that slumber was not repose.'

'Repose and I have nought in common now. Farewell for ever to that fatal word. I am the Lord's anointed.'

'Drink of the fountain, David: it will restore thee.'

'Restore the covenant, restore the ark, restore the holy city.'

'The Spirit of the Lord hath fallen upon him. Son of David, I adjure thee tell me all that hath passed. I am a Levite; in my hand I hold the name ineffable.'

'Take thy trumpet then, summon the people, bid them swiftly raise again our temple. "The bricks have fallen, but we will rebuild with marble." Didst hear that chorus, sir?'

'Unto thy chosen ear alone it sounded.'

'Where am I? This is not our fountain. Yet thou didst say, "the fountain." Think me not wild. I know thee, I know all. Thou art not Miriam. Thou art Jabaster; I am Alroy. But thou didst say, "the fountain," and it distracted me, and called back my memory to ——'

'God of Israel, lo, I kneel before thee! Here, in the solitude of wildest nature, my only witness here this holy man, I kneel and vow, Lord! I will do thy bidding. I am young, O God! and weak; but thou, Lord, art all-powerful! What God is like to thee? Doubt not my courage, Lord; and fill me with thy spirit! but remember, remember her, O Lord! remember Miriam. It is the only worldly thought I have, and it is pure.'

'Still of his sister, calm thyself, my son.'

'Holy master, thou dost remember when I was thy pupil in this cavern. Thou hast not forgotten those days of tranquil study, those sweet, long wandering nights of sacred science! I was dutiful, and hung upon each accent of thy lore with the devotion that must spring from love.'

'I cannot weep, Alroy; but, were it in my power, I would yield a tear of homage to the memory of those days.'

'How calmly have we sat on some high brow, and gazed upon the stars!'

''Tis very true, sweet child.'

'And if thou e'er didst chide me, 'twas half in jest, and only for my silence.'

'What would he now infer? No matter, he grows calmer. How solemn is his visage in the moonlight! And yet not Solomon, upon his youthful throne, could look more beautiful.'

'I never told thee an untruth, Jabaster.'

'My life upon thy faith.'

'Fear not the pledge, and so believe me, on the mountain brow watching the starry heavens with thyself, I was not calmer than I feel, sir, now.'

'I do believe thee.'

'Then, Jabaster, believe as fully I am the Lord's anointed.'

'Tell me all, my child.'

'Know, then, that sleeping on the couch within, my sleep was troubled. Many dreams I had, indefinite and broken. I recall none of their images, except I feel a dim sensation 'twas my lot to live in brighter days than now rise on our race. Suddenly I stood upon a mountain tall and grey, and gazed upon the stars. And, as I gazed, a trumpet sounded. Its note thrilled through my soul. Never have I heard a sound so awful. The thunder, when it broke over the cavern here, and shivered the peak, whose ruins lie around us, was but a feeble worldly sound to this almighty music. My cheek grew pale, I panted even for breath. A flaming light spread over the sky, the stars melted away, and I beheld, advancing from the bursting radiancy, the foremost body of a mighty host.

'Oh! not when Saul led forth our fighting men against

the Philistine, not when Joab numbered the warriors of my great ancestor, did human vision gaze upon a scene of so much martial splendour. Chariots and cavalry, and glittering trains of plumed warriors too robust to need a courser's solace; streams of shining spears, and banners like a sunset; reverend priests swinging their perfumed censers, and prophets hymning with their golden harps a most triumphant future.

'"Joy, joy," they say, "to Israel, for he cometh, he cometh in his splendour and his might, the great Messiah of our ancient hopes."

'And, lo! a mighty chariot now appeared, drawn by strange beasts, whose forms were half obscured by the bright flames on which they seemed to float. In that glorious car a warrior stood, proud and immovable his form, his countenance; hold my hand, Jabaster, while I speak, that chieftain was myself!'

'Proceed, proceed, my son.'

'I started in my dream, and I awoke. I found myself upsitting on my couch. The pageantry had vanished. Nought was seen but the bright moonlight and the gloomy cave. And, as I sighed to think I e'er had wakened, and mused upon the strangeness of my vision, a still small voice descended from above and called, "Alroy!" I started, but I answered not. Methought it was my fancy. Again my name was called, and now I murmured, "Lord, I am here, what wouldst thou?" Nought responded, and soon great dread came over me, and I rushed out and called to thee, my master.'

'It was "the Daughter of the Voice"[12] that spake. Since the Captivity 'tis the only mode by which the saints are summoned. Oft have I heard of it, but never in these sad degenerate days has its soft aspiration fallen upon us. These are strange times and tidings. The building of the temple is at hand. Son of David, my heart is full. Let us to prayer!'

## CHAPTER III.

DAY dawned upon Jabaster, still musing in solitude among his rocks. Within the cavern, Alroy remained in prayer.

Often and anxiously the Cabalist shot a glance at his companion, and then again relapsed into reverie.

'The time is come that I must to this youth reveal the secrets of my early life. Much will he hear of glory, much of shame. Nought must I conceal, and nought gloss over.

'I must tell how in the plains of Tigris I upraised the sacred standard of our chosen race, and called them from their bondage; how, despairing of his recreant fathers, and inspired by human power alone, I vainly claimed the mighty office for his sacred blood alone reserved. God of my fathers, grant that future service, the humble service of a contrite soul, may in the coming glory that awaits us, atone for past presumption!

'But for him great trials are impending. Not lightly must that votary be proved, who fain would free a people. The Lord is faithful to his promise, but the Lord will choose his season and his minister. Courage, and faith, and deep humility, and strong endurance, and the watchful soul temptation cannot sully, these are the fruits we lay upon his altar, and meekly watch if some descending flame will vouchsafe to accept and brightly bless them.

'It is written in the dread volume of our mystic lore, that not alone the Saviour shall spring from out our house of princes, but that none shall rise to free us, until, alone and unassisted, he have gained the sceptre which Solomon of old wielded within his cedar palaces.

'That sceptre must he gain. This fragile youth, untried and delicate, unknowing in the ways of this strange world, where every step is danger, how much hardship, how much peril, what withering disappointment, what dull care, what long despondency, what never-ending lures, now lie in ambush for this gentle boy! O my countrymen, is this your hope? And I, with all my lore, and all my courage, and all my deep intelligence of man; unhappy Israel, why am I not thy Prince?

'I check the blasphemous thought. Did not his great ancestor, as young and as untried, a beardless stripling, with but a pebble, a small smoothed stone, level a mailed giant with the ground, and save his people?

'He is clearly summoned. The Lord is with him. Be he with the Lord, and we shall prosper.'

## CHAPTER IV.

IT was at sunset, on the third day after the arrival of Alroy at the cave of the Cabalist, that the Prince of the Captivity commenced his pilgrimage in quest of the sceptre of Solomon.

Silently the pilgrim and his master took their way to the brink of the ravine, and there they stopped to part, perhaps for ever.

'It is a bitter moment, Alroy. Human feelings are not for beings like us, yet they will have their way. Remember all. Cherish the talisman as thy life; nay! welcome death with it pressing against thy heart, rather than breathe without it. Be firm, be pious. Think of thy ancestors, think of thy God.'

'Doubt me not, dear master; if I seem not full of that proud spirit, which was perhaps too much my wont, ascribe it not to fear, Jabaster, nor even to the pain of leaving thee, dear friend. But ever since that sweet and solemn voice summoned me so thrillingly, I know not how it is, but a change has come over my temper; yet I am firm, oh! firmer far than when I struck down the Ishmaelite. Indeed, indeed, fear not for me. The Lord, that knoweth all things, knows full well I am prepared even to the death. Thy prayers, Jabaster, and ——'

'Stop, stop. I do remember me. See this ring: 'tis a choice emerald. Thou mayst have wondered I should wear a bauble. Alroy, I had a brother once: still he may live. When we parted, this was the signal of his love: a love, my child, strong, though we greatly differed. Take it. The hour may come that thou mayst need his aid. It will command it. If he live, he prospers. I know his temper well. He was made for what the worldly deem prosperity. God be with thee, sacred boy: the God of our great fathers, the God of Abraham, of Isaac, and of Jacob!'

They embraced.

'We linger,' exclaimed the Cabalist, 'we linger. Oh! in vain we quell the feelings of our kind. God, God bless and be with thee! Art sure thou hast all? thy dagger and thy wallet? That staff has seen some service. I cut it on the Jordan. Ah! that I could be thy mate! 'Twould be nothing then. At the worst to die together. Such a fate seems sweeter now than parting. I'll watch thy star, my child. Thou weepest! And I too. Why! what is this? Am I indeed Jabaster? One more embrace, and so —— we'll not say farewell, but only think it.'

# PART IV.

## CHAPTER I.

TRADITION taught that the sceptre of Solomon could be found only in the unknown sepulchres of the ancient Hebrew monarchs, and that none might dare to touch it but one of their descendants. Armed with the cabalistic talisman, which was to guide him in his awful and difficult researches, Alroy commenced his pilgrimage to the Holy City. At this time, the love of these sacred wanderings was a reigning passion among the Jews as well as the Christians.

The Prince of the Captivity was to direct his course into the heart of those great deserts which, in his flight from Hamadan, he had only skirted. Following the track of the caravan, he was to make his way to Babylon, or Bagdad. From the capital of the caliphs, his journey to Jerusalem was one comparatively easy; but to reach Bagdad he must encounter hardship and danger, the prospect of which would have divested any one of hope, who did not conceive himself the object of an omnipotent and particular Providence.

Clothed only in a coarse black frock, common among the Kourds, girded round his waist by a cord which held his dagger, his head shaven, and covered with a large white turban, which screened him from the heat, his feet protected only by slippers, supported by his staff, and bearing on his shoulders a bag of dried meat and parched corn, and a leathern skin of water, behold, toiling over the glowing sands of Persia, a youth whose life had hitherto been a long unbroken dream of domestic luxury and innocent indulgence.

He travelled during the warm night or the early starlit

morn. During the day he rested: happy if he could recline by the side of some charitable well, shaded by a palm-tree, or frighten a gazelle from its resting-place among the rough bushes of some wild rocks. Were these resources wanting, he threw himself upon the sand, and made an awning with his staff and turban.

Three weeks had elapsed since he quitted the cavern of the Cabalist. Hitherto he had met with no human being. The desert became less arid. A scanty vegetation sprang up from a more genial soil; the ground broke into gentle undulations; his senses were invigorated with the odour of wild plants, and his sight refreshed by the glancing form of some wandering bird, a pilgrim like himself, but more at ease.

Soon sprang up a grove of graceful palm-trees, with their tall thin stems, and bending feathery crowns, languid and beautiful. Around, the verdant sod gleamed like an emerald: silver streams, flowing from a bubbling parent spring, wound their white forms within the bright green turf. From the grove arose the softening song of doves, and showers of gay and sparkling butterflies, borne on their tinted wings of shifting light, danced without danger in the liquid air. A fair and fresh Oasis!

## CHAPTER II.

ALROY reposed in this delicious retreat for two days, feeding on the living dates, and drinking of the fresh water. Fain would he have lingered, nor indeed, until he rested, had he been sufficiently conscious of his previous exertion. But the remembrance of his great mission made him restless, and steeled him to the sufferings which yet awaited him.

At the dawn of the second day of his journey from the Oasis he beheld, to his astonishment, faintly but distinctly traced on the far horizon, the walls and turrets of an extensive city.[13] Animated by this unexpected prospect, he continued his progress for several hours after sunrise. At length, utterly exhausted, he sought refuge from the overpowering heat beneath the cupola of the ruined tomb of some Moslem saint. At sunset he continued his journey, and in the morning found himself within a few miles of the city. He halted, and watched with anxiety for some evidence of its inhabitants. None was visible. No crowds or cavalcades issued from the gates. Not a single human being, not a solitary camel, moved in the vicinity.

The day was too advanced for the pilgrim to proceed, but so great was his anxiety to reach this unknown settlement, and penetrate the mystery of its silence, that ere sunset Alroy entered the gates.

A magnificent city, of an architecture with which he was unacquainted, offered to his entranced vision its gorgeous ruins and deserted splendour; long streets of palaces, with their rich line of lessening pillars, here and there broken by some fallen shaft, vast courts surrounded by ornate and solemn temples, and luxurious baths adorned with rare mosaics, and yet bright with antique gilding; now an arch of triumph, still haughty with its broken friezes; now a granite obelisk covered with strange characters, and proudly towering over a prostrate companion; sometimes a void and crumbling theatre, sometimes a long and elegant aqueduct, sometimes a porphyry column, once breathing with the heroic statue that now lies shivered at its base, all suffused with the warm twilight of an eastern eve.

He gazed with wonder and admiration upon the strange and fascinating scene. The more he beheld, the more his curiosity was excited. He breathed with difficulty; he advanced with a blended feeling of eagerness and hesitation. Fresh wonders successively unfolded themselves. Each turn developed a new scene of still and solemn splendour. The echo of his step filled him with awe. He looked around him with an amazed air, a fluttering heart, and a changing countenance. All was silent: alone the Hebrew Prince stood amid the regal creation of the Macedonian captains. Empires and dynasties flourish and pass away; the proud metropolis becomes a solitude, the conquering kingdom even a desert; but Israel still remains, still a descendant of the most ancient kings breathed amid those royal ruins, and still the eternal sun could never rise without gilding the towers of living Jerusalem. A word, a deed, a single day, a single man, and we might be a nation.

A shout! he turns, he is seized; four ferocious Kourdish bandits grapple and bind him.

## CHAPTER III.

THE bandits hurried their captive through a street which appeared to have been the principal way of the city. Nearly at its termination, they turned by a small Ionian temple, and, clambering over some fallen pillars, entered a quarter of the city of a more ruinous aspect than that which Alroy had hitherto visited. The path was narrow, often obstructed, and around were signs of devastation for which the exterior of the city had not prepared him.

The brilliant but brief twilight of the Orient was fast fading away; a sombre purple tint succeeded to the rosy flush; the distant towers rose black, although defined, in the clear and shadowy air; and the moon, which, when he first entered, had studded the heavens like a small white cloud, now glittered with deceptive light.

Suddenly, before them rose a huge pile. Oval in shape, and formed by tiers of arches, it was evidently much dilapidated, and one enormous, irregular, and undulating rent, extending from the top nearly to the foundation, almost separated the side to which Alroy and his companions advanced.

Clambering up the remainder of this massive wall, the robbers and their prisoner descended into an immense amphitheatre, which seemed vaster in the shadowy and streaming moonlight. In it were groups of men, horses, and camels. In the extreme distance, reclining or squatting on mats and carpets, was a large assembly, engaged in a rough but merry banquet. A fire blazed at their side, its red and uncertain flame mingling with the white and steady moonbeam, and throwing a flickering light over their ferocious countenances, their glistening armour, ample drapery, and shawled heads.

'A spy,' exclaimed the captors, as they dragged Alroy before the leader of the band.

'Hang him, then,' said the chieftain, without even looking up.

'This wine, great Scherirah, is excellent, or I am no true Moslem,' said a principal robber; 'but you are too cruel; I hate this summary punishment. Let us torture him a little, and extract some useful information.'

'As you like, Kisloch,' said Scherirah; 'it may amuse us. Fellow, where do you come from? He cannot answer. Decidedly a spy. Hang him up.'

The captors half untied the rope that bound Alroy, that it might serve him for a further purpose, when another of the gentle companions of Scherirah interfered.

'Spies always answer, captain. He is more probably a merchant in disguise.'

'And carries hidden treasure,' added Kisloch; 'these rough coats often cover jewels. We had better search him.'

'Ah! search him,' said Scherirah, with his rough brutal voice; 'do what you like, only give me the bottle. This Greek wine is choice booty. Feed the fire, men. Are you asleep? And then Kisloch, who hates cruelty, can roast him if he likes.'

The robbers prepared to strip their captive. 'Friends, friends!' exclaimed Alroy, 'for there is no reason why you should not be friends, spare me, spare me. I am poor, I am young, I am innocent. I am neither a spy nor a merchant. I have no plots, no wealth. I am a pilgrim.'

'A decided spy,' exclaimed Scherirah; 'they are ever pilgrims.'

'He speaks too well to speak truth,' exclaimed Kisloch.

'All talkers are liars,' exclaimed Scherirah.

'That is why Kisloch is the most eloquent of the band.'

'A jest at the banquet may prove a curse in the field,' replied Kisloch.

'Pooh!' exclaimed Scherirah. 'Fellows, why do you hesitate? Search the prisoner, I say!'

They advanced, they seized him. In vain he struggled.

'Captain,' exclaimed one of the band, 'he wears upon his breast a jewel!'

'I told you so,' said the third robber.

'Give it me,' said Scherirah.

But Alroy, in despair at the thought of losing the talisman, remembering the injunctions of Jabaster, and animated by supernatural courage, burst from his searchers, and, seizing a brand from the fire, held them at bay.

'The fellow has spirit,' said Scherirah, calmly. ''Tis pity it will cost him his life.'

'Bold man,' exclaimed Alroy, 'for a moment hear me! I am a pilgrim, poorer than a beggar. The jewel they talk of is a holy emblem, worthless to you, to me invaluable, and to be forfeited only with my life. You may be careless of that. Beware of your own. The first man who advances dies. I pray you humbly, chieftain, let me go.'

'Kill him,' said Scherirah.

'Stab him!' exclaimed Kisloch.

'Give me the jewel,' said the third robber.

'The God of David be my refuge, then!' exclaimed Alroy.

'He is a Hebrew, he is a Hebrew,' exclaimed Scherirah, jumping up. 'Spare him, my mother was a Jewess.'

The assailants lowered their arms, and withdrew a few paces. Alroy still remained upon his guard.

'Valiant pilgrim,' said Scherirah, advancing, with a softened voice, 'are you for the holy city?'

'The city of my fathers.'

'A perilous journey. And whence from?'

'Hamadan.'

'A dreary way. You need repose. Your name?'

'David.'

'David, you are among friends. Rest, and repose in safety. You hesitate. Fear not! The memory of my mother is a charm that always changes me!' Scherirah unsheathed his dagger, punctured his arm,[14] and, throwing away the weapon, offered the bleeding member to Alroy. The Prince of the Captivity touched the open vein with his lips.

'My troth is pledged,' said the bandit; 'I can never betray him in whose veins my own blood is flowing.' So saying, he led Alroy to his carpet.

## CHAPTER IV.

'Eat, David,' said Scherirah.

'I will eat bread,' answered Alroy.

'What! have you had so much meat lately that you will refuse this delicate gazelle that I brought down this morning with my own lance? 'Tis food for a caliph.'

'I pray you give me bread.'

'Oh! bread if you like. But that a man should prefer bread to meat, and such meat as this, 'tis miraculous.'

'A thousand thanks, good Scherirah; but with our people the flesh of the gazelle is forbidden. It is unclean. Its foot is *cloven*.'

'I have heard of these things,' replied Scherirah, with a thoughtful air. My mother was a Jewess, and my father was a Kourd. Whichever be right, I hope to be saved.'

'There is but one God, and Mahomed is his prophet!' exclaimed Kisloch; 'though I drink wine. Your health, Hebrew.'

'I will join you,' said the third robber. 'My father was a Guebre, and sacrificed his property to his faith; and the consequence is, his son has got neither.'

'As for me,' said a fourth robber, of very dark complexion and singularly small bright eyes, 'I am an Indian, and I believe in the great golden figure with carbuncle eyes, in the temple of Delhi.'

'I have no religion,' said a tall negro in a red turban, grinning with his white teeth; 'they have none in my country; but if I had heard of your God before, Calidas, I would have believed in him.'

'I almost wish I had been a Jew,' exclaimed Scherirah, musing. 'My mother was a good woman.'

'The Jews are very rich,' said the third robber.

'When you get to Jerusalem, David, you will see the Christians,' continued Scherirah.

'The accursed Giaours,' exclaimed Kisloch, 'we are all against them.'

'With their white faces,' exclaimed the negro.

'And their blue eyes,' said the Indian.

'What can you expect of men who live in a country without a sun?' observed the Guebre.

## CHAPTER V.

ALROY awoke about two hours after midnight. His companions were in deep slumber. The moon had set, the fire had died away, a few red embers alone remaining; dark masses of shadow hung about the amphitheatre. He arose and cautiously stepped over the sleeping bandits. He was not in strictness a prisoner; but who could trust to the caprice of these lawless men? To-morrow might find him their slave, or their companion in some marauding expedition, which might make him almost retrace his steps to the Caucasus, or to Hamadan. The temptation to ensure his freedom was irresistible. He clambered up the ruined wall, descended into the intricate windings that led to the Ionic fane, that served him as a beacon, hurried through the silent and starry streets, gained the great portal, and rushed once more into the desert.

A vague fear of pursuit made him continue his course many hours without resting. The desert again became sandy, the heat increased. The breeze that plays about the wilderness, and in early spring is often scented with the wild fragrance of aromatic plants, sank away. A lurid brightness suffused the heavens. An appalling stillness pervaded nature; even the insects were silent. For the first time in his pilgrimage, a feeling of deep despondency fell over the soul of Alroy. His energy appeared suddenly to have deserted him. A low hot wind began to rise, and fan his cheek with pestiferous kisses, and enervate his frame with its poisonous embrace. His head and limbs ached with a dull sensation, more terrible than pain; his sight was dizzy, his tongue swollen. Vainly he looked around for aid; vainly he extended his forlorn arms, and wrung them to the remorseless heaven. Almost frantic with thirst, the boundless horizon of the desert disappeared, and the unhappy victim, in the midst of his torture, found himself apparently surrounded by bright and running streams, the fleeting waters of the false mirage!

The sun became blood-red, the sky darker, the sand rose in fierce eddies, the moaning wind burst into shrieks and exhaled more ardent and still more malignant breath. The pilgrim could no longer sustain himself.[15] Faith, courage, devotion deserted him with his failing energies. He strove no longer with his destiny, he delivered himself up to despair and death. He fell upon one knee with drooping head, supporting himself by one quivering hand, and then, full of the anguish of baffled purposes and lost affections, raising his face and arm to heaven, thus to the elements he poured his passionate farewell.

'O life! once vainly deemed a gloomy toil, I feel thy sweetness now! Farewell, O life, farewell my high resolves and proud conviction of almighty fame. My days, my short unprofitable days, melt into the past; and death, with which I struggle, horrible death, arrests me in this wilderness. O my sister, could thy voice but murmur in my ear one single sigh of love; could thine eye with its soft radiance but an instant blend with my dim fading vision, the pang were nothing. Farewell, Miriam! my heart is with thee by thy fountain's side. Fatal blast, bear her my dying words, my blessing. And ye too, friends, whose too neglected love I think of now, farewell! Farewell, my uncle; farewell, pleasant home, and Hamadan's serene and shadowy bowers! Farewell, Jabaster, and the mighty lore of which thou wert the priest and I the pupil! Thy talisman throbs on my faithful heart. Green earth and golden sun, and all the beautiful and glorious sights ye fondly lavish on unthinking man, farewell, farewell! I die in the desert: 'tis bitter. No more, oh! never more for me the hopeful day shall break, and the fresh breeze rise on its cheering wings of health and joy. Heaven and earth, water and air, my chosen country and my antique creed, farewell, farewell! And thou, too, city of my soul, I cannot name thee, unseen Jerusalem——'

Amid the roar of the wind, the bosom of the earth heaved and opened, swift columns of sand sprang up to the lurid sky, and hurried towards their victim. With the clang of universal chaos, impenetrable darkness descended on the desert.

# PART V.

## CHAPTER I.

'Now our dreary way is over, now the desert's toil is past. Soon the river broadly flowing, through its green and palmy banks, to our wearied limbs shall offer baths which caliphs cannot buy. Allah-illah, Allah-hu. Allah-illah, Allah-hu.'

'Blessed the man who now may bear a relic from our Prophet's tomb; blessed the man who now unfolds the treasures of a distant mart, jewels of the dusky East, and silks of farthest Samarcand. Allah-illah, Allah-hu. Allah-illah, Allah-hu.'

'Him the sacred mosque shall greet with a reverence grave and low; him the busy Bezestein shall welcome with confiding smile. Holy merchant, now receive the double triumph of thy toil. Allah-illah, Allah-hu. Allah-illah, Allah-hu.'

'The camel jibs, Abdallah! See, there is something in the track.'

'By the holy stone,[16] a dead man. Poor devil! One should never make a pilgrimage on foot. I hate your humble piety. Prick the beast and he will pass the corpse.'

'The Prophet preaches charity, Abdallah. He has favoured my enterprise, and I will practise his precept. See if he be utterly dead.'

It was the Mecca caravan returning to Bagdad. The pilgrims were within a day's journey of the Euphrates, and welcomed their approach to fertile earth with a triumphant chorus. Far as the eye could reach, the long line of their straggling procession stretched across the wilderness, thousands of camels in strings, laden with bales of merchandise, and each company headed by an animal of superior size, leading with tinkling bells; groups of horsemen, clusters of litters; all the pilgrims armed to their teeth, the van formed by a strong division of Seljukian cavalry, and the rear protected by a Kourdish clan, who guaranteed the security of the pious travellers through their country.

Abdallah was the favourite slave of the charitable merchant Ali. In obedience to his master's orders, he unwillingly descended from his camel, and examined the body of the apparently lifeless Alroy.

'A Kourd by his dress,' exclaimed Abdallah, with a sneer; 'what does he here?'

'It is not the face of a Kourd,' replied Ali; 'perchance a pilgrim from the mountains.'

'Whatever he be, he is dead,' answered the slave: 'I doubt not an accursed Giaour.'

'God is great,' exclaimed Ali; 'he breathes; the breast of his caftan heaved.'

''Twas the wind,' said Abdallah.

''Twas the sigh of a human heart,' answered Ali.

Several pilgrims who were on foot now gathered around the group.

'I am a Hakim,'[17] observed a dignified Armenian. 'I will feel his pulse; 'tis dull, but it beats.'

'There is but one God,' exclaimed Ali.

'And Mahomed is his Prophet,' responded Abdallah. 'You do not believe in him, you Armenian infidel.'

'I am a Hakim,' replied the dignified Armenian. 'Although an infidel, God has granted me skill to cure true believers. Worthy Ali, believe me, the boy may yet live.'

'Hakim, you shall count your own dirhems if he breathe in my divan in Bagdad,' answered Ali; 'I have taken a fancy to the boy. God has sent him to me. He shall carry my slippers.'

'Give me a camel, and I will save his life.'

'We have none,' said the servant.

'Walk, Abdallah,' said the master.

'Is a true believer to walk to save the life of a Kourd? Master slipper-bearer shall answer for this, if there be any sweetness in the bastinado,' murmured Abdallah.

The Armenian bled Alroy; the blood flowed slowly but surely. The Prince of the Captivity opened his eyes.

'There is but one God,' exclaimed Ali.

'The evil eye fall on him!' muttered Abdallah.

The Armenian took a cordial from his vest, and poured it down his patient's throat. The blood flowed more freely.

'He will live, worthy merchant,' said the physician.

'And Mahomed is his Prophet,' continued Ali.

'By the stone of Mecca, I believe it is a Jew,' shouted Abdallah.

'The dog!' exclaimed Ali.

'Pah!' said a negro-slave, drawing back with disgust.

'He will die,' said the Christian physician, not even binding up the vein.

'And be damned,' said Abdallah, again jumping on his camel.

The party rode on, the caravan proceeded. A Kourdish horseman galloped forward. He curbed his steed as he passed Alroy bleeding to death.

'What accursed slave has wounded one of my clan?'

The Kourd leaped off his horse, stripped off a slip of his blue shirt, stanched the wound, and carried the unhappy Alroy to the rear.

The desert ceased, the caravan entered upon a vast but fruitful plain. In the extreme distance might be descried a long undulating line of palm-trees. The vanguard gave a shout, shook their tall lances in the air, and rattled their scimetars in rude chorus against their small round iron shields. All eyes sparkled, all hands were raised, all voices sounded, save those that were breathless from overpowering joy. After months wandering in the sultry wilderness, they beheld the great Euphrates.

Broad and fresh, magnificent and serene, the mighty waters rolled through the beautiful and fertile earth. A vital breeze rose from their bosom. Every being responded to their genial influence. The sick were cured, the desponding became sanguine, the healthy and light-hearted broke into shouts of laughter, jumped from their camels, and embraced the fragrant earth, or, wild in their renovated strength, galloped over the plain, and threw their wanton jerreeds in the air,[18] as if to show that suffering and labour had not deprived them of that skill and strength, without which it were vain again to enter the haunts of their less adventurous brethren.

The caravan halted on the banks of the broad river, glowing in the cool sunset. The camp was pitched, the plain glittered with tents. The camels, falling on their knees, crouched in groups, the merchandise piled up in masses by their sides. The unharnessed horses rushed neighing about the plain, tossing their glad heads, and rolling in the unaccustomed pasture. Spreading their mats, and kneeling towards Mecca, the pilgrims performed their evening orisons. Never was thanksgiving more sincere. They arose: some rushed into the river, some lighted lamps, some pounded coffee.[19] Troops of smiling villagers arrived with fresh provisions, eager to prey upon such light hearts and heavy purses. It was one of those occasions when the accustomed gravity of the Orient disappears. Long through the night the sounds of music and the shouts of laughter were heard on the banks of that starry river; long through the night you might have listened with enchantment to the wild tales of the storier, or gazed with fascination on the wilder gestures of the dancing girls.[20]

## CHAPTER II.

THE great bazaar of Bagdad afforded an animated and sumptuous spectacle on the day after the arrival of the caravan. All the rare and costly products of the world were collected in that celebrated mart: the shawls of Cashmere and the silks of Syria, the ivory, and plumes, and gold of Afric, the jewels of Ind, the talismans of Egypt, the perfumes and manuscripts of Persia, the spices and gums of Araby, beautiful horses, more beautiful slaves, cloaks of sable, pelisses of ermine, armour alike magnificent in ornament and temper, rare animals, still rarer birds, blue apes in silver collars, white gazelles bound by a golden chain, greyhounds, peacocks, paroquets. And everywhere strange, and busy, and excited groups; men of all nations, creeds, and climes: the sumptuous and haughty Turk, the graceful and subtle Arab, the Hebrew with his black cap and anxious countenance; the Armenian Christian, with his dark flowing robes, and mild demeanour, and serene visage. Here strutted the lively, affected, and superfine Persian; and there the Circassian stalked with his long hair and chain cuirass. The fair Georgian jostled the ebony form of the merchant of Dongola or Sennaar.

Through the long, narrow, arched, and winding streets of the bazaar, lined on each side with loaded stalls, all was bustle, bargaining, and barter. A passenger approached, apparently of no common rank. Two pages preceded him, beautiful Georgian boys, clothed in crimson cloth, and caps of the same material, sitting tight to their heads, with long golden tassels. One bore a blue velvet bag, and the other a clasped and richly bound volume. Four footmen, armed, followed their master, who rode behind the pages on a milk-white mule. He was a man of middle age, eminently handsome. His ample robes concealed the only fault in his appearance, a figure which indulgence had rendered somewhat too exuberant. His eyes were large, and soft, and dark; his nose aquiline, but delicately moulded; his mouth small, and beautifully proportioned; his lip full and red; his teeth regular and dazzling white. His ebony beard flowed, but not at too great a length, in graceful and natural curls, and was richly perfumed; a delicate mustachio shaded his upper lip, but no whisker was permitted to screen the form and shroud the lustre of his oval countenance and brilliant complexion. Altogether, the animal perhaps predominated too much in the expression of the stranger's countenance; but genius beamed from his passionate eye, and craft lay concealed in that subtle lip. The dress of the rider was sumptuous. His turban, formed by a scarlet Cashmere shawl, was of great breadth, and, concealing half of his white forehead, increased by the contrast the radiant height of the other. His under-vest was of white Damascus silk, stiff with silver embroidery, and confined by a girdle formed by a Brusa scarf of gold stuff, and holding a dagger, whose hilt appeared blazing with brilliants and rubies. His loose and exterior robe was of crimson cloth. His white hands sparkled with rings, and his ears glittered with pendulous gems.

'Who is this?' asked an Egyptian merchant, in a low whisper, of the dealer whose stuffs he was examining.

''Tis the Lord Honain,' replied the dealer.

'And who may he be?' continued the Egyptian. 'Is he the Caliph's son?'

'A much greater man; his physician.'

The white mule stopped at the very stall where this conversation was taking place. The pages halted, and stood on each side of their master, the footmen kept off the crowd.

'Merchant,' said Honain, with a gracious smile of condescension, and with a voice musical as a flute, 'Merchant, did you obtain me my wish?'

'There is but one God,' replied the dealer, who was the charitable Ali, 'and Mahomed is his Prophet. I succeeded, please your highness, in seeing at Aleppo the accursed Giaour, of whom I spoke, and behold, that which you desired is here.' So saying, Ali produced several Greek manuscripts, and offered them to his visitor.

'Hah!' said Honain, with a sparkling eye, ''tis well; their cost?'

'The infidel would not part with them under five hundred dirhems,' replied Ali.

'Ibrahim, see that this worthy merchant receive a thousand.'

'As many thanks, my Lord Honain.'

The Caliph's physician bowed gracefully

'Advance, pages,' continued Honain; 'why this stoppage? Ibrahim, see that our way be cleared. What is all this?'

A crowd of men advanced, pulling along a youth, who, almost exhausted, still singly struggled with his ungenerous adversaries.

'The Cadi, the Cadi,' cried the foremost of them, who was Abdallah, 'drag him to the Cadi.'

'Noble lord,' cried the youth, extricating himself by a sudden struggle from the grasp of his captors, and seizing the robe of Honain, 'I am innocent and injured. I pray thy help.'

'The Cadi, the Cadi,' exclaimed Abdallah; the knave has stolen my ring, the ring given me by my faithful Fatima on our marriage-day, and which I would not part with for my master's stores.'

The youth still clung to the robe of Honain, and, mute from exhaustion, fixed upon him his beautiful and imploring eye.

'Silence,' proclaimed Honain, 'I will judge this cause.'

'The Lord Honain, the Lord Honain, listen to the Lord Honain!'

'Speak, thou brawler; of what hast thou to complain?' said Honain to Abdallah.

'May it please your highness,' said Abdallah, in a whining voice, 'I am the slave of your faithful servant, Ali: often have I had the honour of waiting on your highness. This young knave here, a beggar, has robbed me, while slumbering in a coffee-house, of a ring; I have my witnesses to prove my slumbering. 'Tis a fine emerald, may it please your highness, and doubly valuable to me as a love-token from my Fatima. No consideration in the world could induce me to part with it; and so, being asleep, here are three honest men who will prove the sleep, comes this little vagabond, may it please your highness, who while he pretends to offer me my coffee, takes him my finger, and slips off this precious ring, which he now wears upon his beggarly paw, and will not restore to me without the bastinado.'

'Abdallah is a faithful slave, may it please your highness, and a Hadgee,' said Ali, his master.

'And what sayest thou, boy?' inquired Honain.

'That this is a false knave, who lies as slaves ever will.'

'Pithy, and perhaps true,' said Honain.

'You call me a slave, you young scoundrel?' exclaimed Abdallah; 'shall I tell you what you are? Why, your highness, do not listen to him a moment. It is a shame to bring such a creature into your presence; for, by the holy stone, and I am a Hadgee, I doubt little he is a Jew.'

Honain grew somewhat pale, and bit his lip. He was perhaps annoyed that he had interfered so publicly in behalf of so unpopular a character as a Hebrew, but he was unwilling to desert one whom a moment before he had resolved to befriend, and he inquired of the youth where he had obtained the ring.

'The ring was given to me by my dearest friend when I first set out upon an arduous pilgrimage not yet completed. There is but one person in the world, except the donor, to whom I would part with it, and with that person I am unacquainted. All this may seem improbable, but all this is true. I have truth alone to support me. I am destitute and friendless; but I am not a beggar, nor will any suffering induce me to become one. Feeling, from various circumstances, utterly exhausted, I entered a coffee-house and lay down, it may have been to die. I could not sleep, although my eyes were shut, and nothing would have roused me from a tremulous trance, which I thought was dying, but this plunderer here, who would not wait until death had permitted him quietly to possess himself of a jewel I value more than life.'

'Show me the jewel.'

The youth held up his hand to Honain, who felt his pulse, and then took off the ring.

'O, my Fatima!' exclaimed Abdallah.

'Silence, sir!' said Honain. 'Page, call a jeweller.'

Honain examined the ring attentively. Whether he were near-sighted, or whether the deceptive light of the covered bazaar prevented him from examining it with ease, he certainly raised his hand to his brow, and for some moments his countenance was invisible.

The jeweller arrived, and, pressing his hand to his heart, bowed before Honain.

'Value this ring,' said Honain, in a low voice.

The jeweller took the ring, viewed it in all directions with a scrutinising glance, held it to the light, pressed it to his tongue, turned it over and over, and finally declared that he could not sell such a ring under a thousand dirhems.

'Whatever be the justice of the case,' said Honain to Abdallah, 'art thou ready to part with this ring for a thousand dirhems?'

'Most certainly,' said Abdallah.

'And thou, lad, if the decision be in thy favour, wilt thou take for the ring double the worth at which the jeweller prizes it?'

'My lord, I have spoken the truth. I cannot part with that ring for the palace of the Caliph.'

'The truth for once is triumphant,' said Honain. 'Boy, the ring is thine; and for thee, thou knave,' turning to Abdallah, 'liar, thief, and slanderer!—for thee the bastinado,[21] which thou destinedst for this innocent youth. Ibrahim, see that he receives five hundred. Young pilgrim, thou art no longer destitute or friendless. Follow me to my palace.'

## CHAPTER III.

The arched chamber was of great size and beautiful proportion. The ceiling, encrusted with green fretwork, and studded with silver stars, rested upon clustered columns of white and green marble. In the centre of a variegated pavement of the same material, a fountain rose and fell into a green porphyry basin, and by the side of the fountain, upon a couch of silver, reposed Honain.

He raised his eyes from the illuminated volume on which he had been long intent; he clapped his hands, and a Nubian slave advanced, and, folding his arms upon his breast, bowed in silence before his lord.

'How fares the Hebrew boy, Analschar?'

'Master, the fever has not returned. We gave him the potion; he slumbered for many hours, and has now awakened, weak but well.'

'Let him rise and attend me.

The Nubian disappeared.

'There is nothing stranger than sympathy,' soliloquised the physician of the Caliph, with a meditative air; 'all resolves itself into this principle, and I confess this learned doctor treats it deeply and well. An erudite spirit truly, and an eloquent pen; yet he refines too much. 'Tis too scholastic. Observation will teach us more than dogma. Meditating upon my passionate youth, I gathered wisdom. I have seen so much that I have ceased to wonder. However we doubt, there is a mystery beyond our penetration. And yet 'tis near our grasp. I sometimes deem a step, a single step, would launch us into light. Here comes my patient. The rose has left his cheek, and his deep brow is wan and melancholy. Yet 'tis a glorious visage, Meditation's throne; and Passion lingers in that languid eye. I know not why, a strong attraction draws me to this lone child.

'Gentle stranger, how fares it with thee?'

'Very well, my lord. I come to thank thee for all thy goodness. My only thanks are words, and those too weak; and yet the orphan's blessing is a treasure.'

'You are an orphan, then?'

'I have no parent but my father's God.'

'And that God is ——'

'The God of Israel.'

'So I deemed. He is a Deity we all must honour; if he be the great Creator whom we all allow.'

'He is what he is, and we are what we are, a fallen people, but faithful still.'

'Fidelity is strength.'

'Thy words are truth, and strength must triumph.'

'A prophecy!'

'Many a prophet is little honoured, till the future proves his inspiration.'

'You are young and sanguine.'

'So was my ancestor within the vale of Elah. But I speak unto a Moslem, and this is foolishness.'

'I have read something, and can take your drift. As for my faith, I believe in truth, and wish all men to do the same. By the bye, might I inquire the name of him who is the inmate of my house?'

'They call me David.'

'David, you have a ring, an emerald cut with curious characters, Hebrew, I believe.'

''Tis here.'

'A fine stone, and this inscription means ——.'

'A simple legend, "*Parted, but one;*" the kind memorial of a brother's love.'

'Your brother?'

'I never had a brother.'

'I have a silly fancy for this ring: you hesitate. Search my palace, and choose the treasure you deem its match.'

'Noble sir, the gem is little worth; but were it such might deck a Caliph's brow, 'twere a poor recompense for all thy goodness. This ring is a trust rather than a possession, and strange to say, although I cannot offer it to thee who mayst command, as thou hast saved, the life of its unhappy wearer, some stranger may cross my path to-morrow, and almost claim it as his own.'

'And that stranger is ——'

'The brother of the donor.'

'The brother of Jabaster?'

'Jabaster!'

'Even so. I am that parted brother.'

'Great is the God of Israel! Take the ring. But what is this? the brother of Jabaster a turbaned chieftain! a Moslem! Say, but say that thou has not assumed their base belief; say, but say, that thou hast not become a traitor to our covenant, and I will bless the fortunes of this hour.'

'I am false to no God. Calm thyself, sweet youth. These are higher questions than thy faint strength can master now. Another time we'll talk of this, my boy; at present of my brother and thyself. He lives and prospers?'

'He lives in faith; the pious ever prosper.'

'A glorious dreamer! Though our moods are different, I ever loved him. And thyself? Thou art not what thou seemest. Tell me all. Jabaster's friend can be no common mind. Thy form has heralded thy fame. Trust me.'

'I am Alroy.'

'What! the Prince of our Captivity?'

'Even so.'

'The slayer of Alschiroch?'

'Ay!'

My sympathy was prophetic. I loved thee from the first. And what dost thou here? A price is set upon thy head: thou knowest it?'

'For the first time; but I am neither astonished nor alarmed. I am upon the Lord's business.'

'What wouldst thou?'

'Free his people.'

'The pupil of Jabaster: I see it all. Another victim to his reveries. I'll save this boy. David, for thy name must not be sounded within this city, the sun is dying. Let us to the terrace, and seek the solace of the twilight breeze.'

---

## CHAPTER IV.

'What is the hour, David?'

'Near to midnight. I marvel if thy brother may read in the stars our happy meeting.'

'Men read that which they wish. He is a learned Cabalist.'

'But what we wish comes from above.'

'So they say. We make our fortunes, and we call them Fate.'

'Yet the Voice sounded, the Daughter of the Voice that summoned Samuel.'

'You have told me strange things; I have heard stranger solved.'

'My faith is a rock.'

'On which you may split.'

'Art thou a Sadducee?'

'I am a man who knows men.'

'You are learned, but different from Jabaster.'

'We are the same, though different. Day and Night are both portions of Time.'

'And thy portion is ——'

'Truth.'

'That is, light.'

'Yes; so dazzling that it sometimes seems dark.'

'Like thy meaning.'

'You are young.'

'Is youth a defect?'

'No, the reverse. But we cannot eat the fruit while the tree is in blossom.'

'What fruit?'

'Knowledge.'

'I have studied.'

'What?'

'All sacred things.'

'How know you that they are sacred?'

'They come from God.'

'So does everything. Is everything sacred?'

'They are the deep expression of his will.'

'According to Jabaster. Ask the man who prays in yonder mosque, and he will tell you that Jabaster's wrong.'

'After all, thou art a Moslem?'

'No.'

'What then?'
'I have told you, a man.'
'But what dost thou worship?'
'What is worship?'
'Adoration due from the creature to the Creator.'
'Which is he?'
'Our God.'
'The God of Israel?'
'Even so.'
'A frail minority, then, burn incense to him.'
'We are the chosen people.'
'Chosen for scoffs, and scorns, and contumelies. Commend me to such choice.'
'We forgot him, before he chastened us'
'Why did we?'
'Thou knowest the records of our holy race.
'Yes, I know them; like all records, annals of blood.
'Annals of victory, that will dawn again.'
'If redemption be but another name for carnage, I envy no Messiah.'
'Art thou Jabaster's brother?'
'So our mother was wont to say: a meek and blessed woman.'
'Lord Honain, thou art rich, and wise, and powerful. Thy fellow-men speak of thee only with praise or fear, and both are cheering. Thou hast quitted our antique ark; why; no matter. We'll not discuss it. 'Tis something, if a stranger, at least thou art not a renegade. The world goes well with thee, my Lord Honain. But if, instead of bows and blessings, thou, like thy brethren, wert greeted only with the cuff and curse; if thou didst rise each morning only to feel existence to be dishonour, and to find thyself marked out among surrounding men as something foul and fatal; if it were thy lot, like theirs, at best to drag on a mean and dull career, hopeless and aimless, or with no other hope or aim but that which is degrading, and all this too with a keen sense of thy intrinsic worth, and a deep conviction of superior race; why then, per-

chance, Honain might even discover 'twere worth a struggle to be free and honoured.'

'I pray your pardon, sir; I thought you were Jabaster's pupil, a dreaming student. I see you have a deep ambition.'

'I am a prince; and I fain would be a prince without my fetters.'

'Listen to me, Alroy,' said Honain in a low voice, and he placed his arm around him, 'I am your friend. Our acquaintance is very brief: no matter, I love you; I rescued you in injury, I tended you in sickness, even now your life is in my power, I would protect it with my own. You cannot doubt me. Our affections are not under our own control; and mine are yours. The sympathy between us is entire. You see me, you see what I am; a Hebrew, though unknown; one of that despised, rejected, persecuted people, of whom you are the chief. I too would be free and honoured. Freedom and honour are mine, but I was my own messiah. I quitted in good time our desperate cause, but I gave it a trial. Ask Jabaster how I fought. Youth could be my only excuse for such indiscretion. I left this country; I studied and resided among the Greeks. I returned from Constantinople, with all their learning, some of their craft. No one knew me. I assumed their turban, and I am, the Lord Honain. Take my experience, child, and save yourself much sorrow. Turn your late adventure to good account. No one can recognise you here. I will introduce you amongst the highest as my child by some fair Greek. The world is before you. You may fight, you may love, you may revel. War, and women, and luxury are all at your command. With your person and talents you may be grand vizir. Clear your head of nonsense. In the present disordered state of the empire, you may even carve yourself out a kingdom, infinitely more delightful than the barren land of milk and honey. I have seen it, child; a rocky wilderness, where I would not let my courser graze.'

He bent down, and fixed his eyes upon his companion

with a scrutinising glance. The moonlight fell upon the resolved visage of the Prince of the Captivity.

'Honain,' he replied, pressing his hand, 'I thank thee. Thou knowest not me, but still I thank thee.'

'You are resolved, then, on destruction.'

'On glory, eternal glory.'

'Is it possible to succeed?'

'Is it possible to fail?'

'You are mad.'

'I am a believer.'

'Enough. You have yet one chance. My brother has saddled your enterprise with a condition, and an impossible one. Gain the sceptre of Solomon, and I will agree to be your subject. You will waste a year in this frolic. You are young, and can afford it. I trust you will experience nothing worse than a loss of time, which is, however, valuable. My duty will be, after all your sufferings, to send you forth on your adventures in good condition, and to provide you means for a less toilsome pilgrimage than has hitherto been your lot. Trust me you will return to Bagdad to accept my offers. At present, the dews are descending, and we will return to our divan, and take some coffee.'

## CHAPTER V.

Some few days after this conversation on the terrace, as Alroy was reclining in a bower, in the beautiful garden of his host, meditating on the future, some one touched him on the back. He looked up. It was Honain.

'Follow me,' said the brother of Jabaster.

The Prince rose, and followed him in silence. They entered the house, and, passing through the saloon already described, they proceeded down a long gallery, which terminated in an arched flight of broad steps leading to the river. A boat was fastened to the end of the stairs, floating on the blue line of the Tigris, bright in the sun.

Honain now gave to Alroy a velvet bag, which he requested him to carry, and then they descended the steps and entered the covered boat; and, without any directions to the rower, they were soon skimming over the water. By the sound of passing vessels, and the occasional shouts of the boatmen, Alroy, although he could observe nothing, was conscious that for some time their course lay through a principal thoroughfare of the city; but by degrees the sounds became less frequent, and in time entirely died away, and all that caught his ear was the regular and monotonous stroke of their own oar.

At length, after the lapse of nearly an hour from their entrance, the boat stopped, and was moored against a quay. The curtains were withdrawn, and Honain and his companion disembarked.

A low but extensive building, painted in white and gold arabesque, and irregular but picturesque in form, with many small domes, and tall thin towers, rose amid groves of cypress on the bank of the broad and silent river. The rapid stream had carried them far from the city, which was visible but distant. Around was no habitation, no human being. The opposite bank was occupied by enclosed gardens. Not even a boat passed.

Honain, beckoning to Alroy to accompany him, but still silent, advanced to a small portal, and knocked. It was instantly opened by a single Nubian, who bowed reverently as the visitors passed him. They proceeded along a low and gloomy passage, covered with arches of fretwork, until they arrived at a door of tortoiseshell and mother of pearl.[22] Here Honain, who was in advance, turned round to Alroy, and said, 'Whatever happen, and whoever may address you, as you value your life and mine, do not speak.'

The door opened, and they found themselves in a vast and gorgeous hall. Pillars of many-coloured marbles rose from a red and blue pavement of the same material, and supported a vaulted, circular, and highly-embossed roof of purple, scarlet, and gold.[23] Around a fountain, which rose fifty feet in height from an immense basin of lapis-lazuli, and reclining on small yellow Barbary mats, was a group of Nubian eunuchs, dressed in rich habits of scarlet and gold,[24] and armed with ivory battle-axes, the white handles worked in precious arabesque finely contrasting with the blue and brilliant blades.

The commander of the eunuch-guard rose on seeing Honain, and, pressing his hand to his head, mouth, and heart, saluted him. The physician of the Caliph, motioning Alroy to remain, advanced somes paces in front of him, and entered into a whispering conversation with the eunuch. After a few minutes, this officer resumed his seat, and Honain, beckoning to Alroy to rejoin him, crossed the hall.

Passing through an open arch, they entered a quadrangular court of roses,[25] each bed of flowers surrounded by a stream of sparkling water, and floating like an enchanted islet upon a fairy ocean. The sound of the water and the sweetness of the flowers blended together, and produced a lulling sensation, which nothing but his strong and strange curiosity might have enabled Alroy to resist. Proceeding along a cloister of light airy workmanship which connected the hall with the remainder of the buildings, they stood before a lofty and sumptuous portal.

It was a monolith gate, thirty feet in height, formed of one block of green and red jasper, and cut into the fanciful undulating arch of the Saracens. The consummate artist had seized the advantage afforded to him by the ruddy veins of the precious stone, and had formed them in bold relief into two vast and sinuous serpents, which shot forth their crested heads and glittering eyes at Honain and his companion.

The physician of the Caliph, taking his dagger from his girdle, struck the head of one of the serpents thrice. The massy portal opened with a whirl and a roar, and before them stood an Abyssinian giant,[26] holding in his leash a roaring lion.

'Hush, Haroun!' said Honain to the animal, raising at the same time his arm; and the beast crouched in silence.

'Worthy Morgargon, I bring you a remembrance.' The Abyssinian showed his tusks, larger and whiter than the lion's, as he grinningly received the tribute of the courtly Honain; and he uttered a few uncouth sounds, but he could not speak, for he was a mute.

The jasper portal introduced the companions to a long and lofty and arched chamber, lighted by high windows of stained glass, hung with tapestry of silk and silver, covered with prodigious carpets, and surrounded by immense couches. And thus through similar chambers they proceeded, in some of which were signs of recent habitation, until they arrived at another quadrangle nearly filled by a most singular fountain which rose from a basin of gold encrusted with pearls, and which was surrounded by figures of every rare quadruped[27] in the most costly materials. Here a golden tiger, with flaming eyes of ruby and flowing stripes of opal, stole, after some bloody banquet, to the refreshing brink; a cameleopard raised its slender neck of silver from the centre of a group of every inhabitant of the forest; and brilliant bands of monkeys, glittering with precious stones, rested, in every variety of fantastic posture, on the margin of the basin.

The fountain itself was a tree of gold and silver[28] spreading into innumerable branches, covered with every variety of curious birds, their plumage appropriately imitated by the corresponding tints of precious stones, and which warbled in beautiful melody as they poured forth from their bills the musical and refreshing element.

It was with difficulty that Alroy could refrain from an admiring exclamation, but Honain, ever quick, turned to him, with his finger pressed on his mouth, and quitting the quadrangle, they entered the gardens.

Lofty terraces, dark masses of cypress, winding walks of acacia, in the distance an interminable paradise, and here and there a glittering pavilion and bright kiosk! Its appearance on the river had not prepared Alroy for the extent of the palace itself. It seemed infinite, and it was evident that he had only viewed a small portion of it.

While they were moving on, there suddenly arose a sound
of trumpets. The sound grew nearer and nearer, louder
and louder: soon was heard the tramp of an approaching
troop. Honain drew Alroy aside. A procession appeared
advancing from a dark grove of cypress. Four hundred
men led as many white bloodhounds with collars of gold
and rubies.[29] Then came one hundred men, each with a
hooded hawk; then six horsemen in rich dresses; after
them a single horseman, mounted on a steed, marked on its
forehead with a star.[30] The rider was middle-aged, handsome, and dignified. He was plainly dressed, but the staff
of his hunting-spear was entirely of diamonds and the
blade of gold. He was followed by a company of Nubian
eunuchs, with their scarlet dresses and ivory battle-axes,
and the procession closed.

'The Caliph,' whispered Honain, when they had passed,
placing at the same time his finger on his lip to prevent
any inquiry. This was the first intimation that had reached
Alroy of what he had already suspected, that he was a
visitor to the palace of the Commander of the Faithful.

The companions turned down a wild and winding walk,
which, after some time, brought them to a small and gently
sloping lawn, surrounded by cedar-trees of great size. Upon
the lawn was a kiosk, a long and many-windowed building,
covered with blinds, and further screened by an overhang-
ing roof. The kiosk was built of white and green marble,
the ascent to it was by a flight of steps the length of the
building, alternately of white and green marble, and nearly
covered with rose-trees. Honain went up these steps alone,
and entered the kiosk. After a few minutes he looked out
from the blinds and beckoned to Alroy. David advanced,
but Honain, fearful of some indiscretion, met him, and said
to him in a low whisper between his teeth, 'Remember you
are deaf, a mute, and a eunuch.' Alroy could scarcely
refrain from smiling, and the Prince of the Captivity and
the physician of the Caliph entered the kiosk together.
Two women, veiled, and two eunuchs of the guard, received

F

them in an antechamber. And then they passed into a room which ran nearly the whole length of the kiosk, opening on one side to the gardens, and on the other supported by an ivory wall, with niches painted in green fresco, and in each niche a rose-tree. Each niche, also, was covered with an almost invisible golden grate, which confined a nightingale, and made him constant to the rose he loved. At the foot of each niche was a fountain, but, instead of water, each basin was replenished with the purest quicksilver.[31] The roof of the kiosk was of mother-of-pearl inlaid with tortoise-shell; the pavement, a mosaic of rare marbles and precious stones, representing the most delicious fruits and the most beautiful flowers. Over this pavement, a Georgian page flung at intervals refreshing perfumes. At the end of this elegant chamber was a divan of light green silk, embroidered with pearls, and covered with cushions of white satin and gold. Upon one of these cushions, in the middle of the divan, sat a lady, her eyes fixed in abstraction upon a volume of Persian poetry lying on her knees, one hand playing with a rosary of pearls and emeralds,[32] and the other holding a long gold chain, which imprisoned a white gazelle.

The lady looked up as Honain and his companion entered. She was very young, as youthful as Alroy. Her long light brown hair, drawn off a high white forehead covered with blue veins, fell braided with pearls over each shoulder. Her eyes were large and deeply blue; her nose small, but high and aquiline. The fairness of her face was dazzling, and, when she looked up and greeted Honain, her lustrous cheeks broke into dimples, the more fascinating from their contrast with the general expression of her countenance, which was haughty and derisive. The lady was dressed in a robe of crimson silk girded round her waist by a green shawl, from which peeped forth the diamond hilt of a small poniard.[33] Her round white arms looked infinitely small, as they occasionally flashed forth from their large loose hanging sleeves. One was covered with jewels, and the right arm was quite bare.

Honain advanced, and, bending, kissed the lady's proffered hand. Alroy fell into the background.

'They told me that the Rose of the World drooped this morning,' said the Physician, bending again as he smiled, 'and her slave hastened at her command to tend her.'

'It was a south wind. The wind has changed, and the Rose of the World is better,' replied the lady laughing.

Honain touched her pulse.

'Irregular,' said the Physician.

'Like myself,' said the lady. 'Is that a new slave?'

'A recent purchase, and a great bargain. He is good-looking, has the advantage of being deaf and dumb, and is harmless in every respect.'

''Tis a pity,' replied the lady; 'it seems that all good-looking people are born to be useless. I, for instance.'

'Yet rumour whispers the reverse,' remarked the Physician.

'How so?' inquired the lady.

'The young King of Karasmé.'

'Poh! I have made up my mind to detest him. A barbarian!'

'A hero!'

'Did you ever see him?'

'I have.'

'Handsome?'

'An archangel.'

'And sumptuous?'

'Is he not a conqueror? All the plunder of the world will be yours.'

'I am tired of magnificence. I built this kiosk to forget it.'

'It is not in the least degree splendid,' said Honain, looking round with a smile.

'No,' answered the lady, with a self-satisfied air: 'here, at least, one can forget one has the misfortune to be a princess.'

'It is certainly a great misfortune,' said the Physician.

'And yet it must be the only tolerable lot,' replied the lady.

'Assuredly,' replied Honain.

'For our unhappy sex at least.'

'Very unhappy.'

'If I were only a man!'

'What a hero you would be!'

'I should like to live in endless confusion.'

'I have not the least doubt of it.'

'Have you got me the books?' eagerly inquired the Princess.

'My slave bears them,' replied Honain.

'Let me see them directly.'

Honain took the bag from Alroy, and unfolded its contents; the very volumes of Greek romances which Ali, the merchant, had obtained for him.

'I am tired of poetry, said the Princess, glancing over the costly volumes, and tossing them away; 'I long to see the world.'

'You would soon be tired of that,' replied the Physician.

'I suppose common people are never tired,' said the Princess.

'Except with labour,' said the Physician; 'care keeps them alive.'

'What is care?' asked the Princess, with a smile.

'It is a god,' replied the Physician, 'invisible, but omnipotent. It steals the bloom from the cheek and lightness from the pulse; it takes away the appetite, and turns the hair grey.'

'It is no true divinity, then,' replied the Princess, but an idol we make ourselves. I am a sincere Moslem, and will not worship it. Tell me some news, Honain.'

'The young King of Karasmé ——'

'Again! the barbarian! You are in his pay. I'll none of him. To leave one prison, and to be shut up in another, why do you remind me of it? No, my dear Hakim, if I marry at all, I will marry to be free.'

'An impossibility,' said Honain.

'My mother was free till she was a queen and a slave. I intend to end as she began. You know what she was.'

Honain knew well, but he was too politic not to affect ignorance.

'The daughter of a bandit,' continued the Princess, 'who fought by the side of her father. That is existence!' I must be a robber. 'Tis in the blood. I want my fate foretold, Honain. You are an astrologer; do it.'

'I have already cast your nativity. Your star is a comet.'

'That augurs well; brilliant confusion and erratic splendour. I wish I were a star,' added the Princess in a deep rich voice, and with a pensive air; 'a star in the clear blue sky, beautiful and free. Honain, Honain, the gazelle has broken her chain, and is eating my roses.'

Alroy rushed forward and seized the graceful truant. Honain shot him an anxious look; the Princess received the chain from the hand of Alroy, and cast at him a scrutinising glance.

'What splendid eyes the poor beast has got!' exclaimed the Princess.

'The gazelle?' inquired the Physician.

'No, your slave,' replied the Princess.

'Why, he blushes. Were he not deaf as well as dumb, I could almost believe he understood me.'

'He is modest,' replied Honain, rather alarmed; 'and is frightened at the liberty he has taken.'

'I like modesty,' said the Princess; 'it is interesting. I am modest; you think so?'

'Certainly,' said Honain.

'And interesting?'

'Very.'

'I detest an interesting person. After all, there is nothing like plain dulness.'

'Nothing,' said Honain.

'The day flows on so serenely in such society.'

'It does,' said Honain.

'No confusion; no scenes.'

'None.'

'I make it a rule only to have ugly slaves.'

'You are quite right.'

'Honain, will you ever contradict me? You know very well I have the handsomest slaves in the world.'

'Every one knows it.'

'And do you know, I have taken a great fancy to your new purchase, who, according to your account, is eminently qualified for the post. Why, do you not agree with me?'

'Why, yes; I doubt not your Highness would find him eminently qualified, and certainly few things would give me greater pleasure than offering him for your acceptance; but I got into such disgrace by that late affair of the Circassian, that ——'

'Oh! leave it to me,' said the Princess.

'Certainly,' said the Physician, turning the conversation; 'and when the young King of Karasmé arrives at Bagdad, you can offer him to his majesty as a present.'

'Delightful! and the king is really handsome and young as well as brave; but has he any taste?'

'You have enough for both.'

'If he would but make war against the Greeks!'

'Why so violent against the poor Greeks?'

'You know they are Giaours. Besides, they might beat him, and then I should have the pleasure of being taken prisoner.'

'Delightful!'

'Charming! to see Constantinople, and marry the Emperor.'

'Marry the Emperor!'

'To be sure. Of course he would fall in love with me.'

'Of course.'

'And then, and then, I might conquer Paris!'

'Paris!'

'You have been at Paris?'[34]

'Yes.'

'The men are shut up there,' said the Princess with a smile, 'are they not? and the women do what they like?'

'You will always do what you like,' said Honain, rising.

'You are going?'

'My visits must not be too long.'

'Farewell, dear Honain!' said the Princess, with a melancholy air. 'You are the only person who has an idea in all Bagdad, and you leave me. A miserable lot is mine, to feel everything, and be nothing. These books and flowers, these sweet birds, and this fair gazelle: ah! poets may feign as they please, but how cheerfully would I resign all these elegant consolations of a captive life for one hour of freedom! I wrote some verses on myself yesterday; take them, and get them blazoned for me by the finest scribe in the city; letters of silver on a violet ground with a fine flowing border; I leave the design to you. Adieu! Come hither, mute.' Alroy advanced to her beckon, and knelt. 'There, take that rosary for thy master's sake, and those dark eyes of thine.'

The companions withdrew, and reached their boat in silence. It was sunset. The musical and sonorous voice of the Muezzin resounded from the innumerable minarets of the splendid city. Honain threw back the curtains of the barque. Bagdad rose before them in huge masses of sumptuous dwellings, seated amid groves and gardens. An infinite population, summoned by the invigorating twilight, poured forth in all directions. The glowing river was covered with sparkling caiques, the glittering terraces with showy groups. Splendour, and power, and luxury, and beauty were arrayed before them in their most captivating forms, and the heart of Alroy responded to their magnificence.

'A glorious vision!' said the Prince of the Captivity.

'Very different from Hamadan,' said the physician of the Caliph.

'To-day I have seen wonders,' said Alroy.

'The world is opening to you,' said Honain.

Alroy did not reply; but after some minutes he said, in a hesitating voice, 'Who was that lady?'

'The Princess Schirene,' replied Honain, 'the favourite daughter of the Caliph. Her mother was a Georgian and a Giaour.'

## CHAPTER VI.

The moonlight fell upon the figure of Alroy lying on a couch; his face was hidden by his arm. He was motionless, but did not sleep.

He rose and paced the chamber with agitated steps; sometimes he stopped, and gazed on the pavement, fixed in abstraction. He advanced to the window, and cooled his feverish brow in the midnight air.

An hour passed away, and the young Prince of the Captivity remained fixed in the same position. Suddenly he turned to a tripod of porphyry, and, seizing a rosary of jewels, pressed it to his lips.

'The Spirit of my dreams, she comes at last; the form for which I have sighed and wept; the form which rose upon my radiant vision when I shut my eyes against the jarring shadows of this gloomy world.

'Schirene! Schirene! here in this solitude I pour to thee the passion long stored up: the passion of my life, no common life, a life full of deep feeling and creative thought. O beautiful! O more than beautiful! for thou to me art as a dream unbroken: why art thou not mine? why lose a moment in our glorious lives, and balk our destiny of half its bliss?

'Fool, fool, hast thou forgotten? The rapture of a prisoner in his cell, whose wild fancy for a moment belies his fetters! The daughter of the Caliph and a Jew!

'Give me my fathers' sceptre.

'A plague on talismans! Oh! I need no inspiration but her memory, no magic but her name. By heavens! I will enter this glorious city a conqueror, or die.

'Why, what is Life? for meditation mingles ever with my passion: why, what is Life? Throw accidents to the dogs, and tear off the painted mask of false society! Here am I a hero; with a mind that can devise all things, and a heart of superhuman daring, with youth, with vigour, with a glorious lineage, with a form that has made full many a lovely maiden of our tribe droop her fair head by Hamadan's sweet fount, and I am, nothing.

'Out on Society! 'twas not made for me. I'll form my own, and be the deity I sometimes feel.

'We make our fortunes, and we call them Fate.' Thou saidst well, Honain. Most subtle Sadducee! The saintly blood flowed in my fathers' veins, and they did nothing; but I have an arm formed to wield a sceptre, and I will win one.

'I cannot doubt my triumph. Triumph is a part of my existence. I am born for glory, as a tree is born to bear its fruit, or to expand its flowers. The deed is done. 'Tis thought of, and 'tis done. I will confront the greatest of my diademed ancestors, and in his tomb. Mighty Solomon! he wedded Pharaoh's daughter. Hah! what a future dawns upon my hope. An omen, a choice omen!

'Heaven and earth are mingling to form my fortunes. My mournful youth, which I have so often cursed, I hail thee: thou wert a glorious preparation; and when, feeling no sympathy with the life around me, I deemed myself a fool, I find that I was a most peculiar being. By heavens, I am joyful; for the first time in my life I am joyful. I could laugh, and fight, and drink. I am new-born; I am another being; I am mad!

'O Time, great Time! the world belies thy fame. It calls thee swift. Methinks thou art wondrous slow. Fly on, great Time, and on thy coming wings bear me my sceptre!

'All is to be. It is a lowering thought. My fancy, like a bright and wearied bird, will sometimes flag and fall, and then I am lost. The young King of Karasmé, a youthful hero! Would he had been Alschiroch! My heart is sick even at the very name. Alas! my trials have not yet begun. Jabaster warned me: good, sincere Jabaster! His talisman presses on my frantic heart, and seems to warn me. I am in danger. Braggart to stand here, filling the careless air with idle words, while all is unaccomplished. I grow dull. The young King of Karasmé! Why, what am I compared to this same prince? Nothing, but in my thoughts. In the full bazaar, they would not deem me worthy even to hold his stirrup or his slipper—— Oh! this contest, this constant, bitter, never-ending contest between my fortune and my fancy! Why do I exist? or, if existing, why am I not recognised as I would be?

'Sweet voice, that in Jabaster's distant cave descendedst from thy holy home above, and whispered consolation, breathe again! Again breathe thy still summons to my lonely ear, and chase away the thoughts that hover round me; thoughts dark and doubtful, like fell birds of prey hovering around a hero in expectation of his fall, and gloating on their triumph over the brave. There is something fatal in these crowded cities. Faith flourishes in solitude.'

He threw himself upon the couch, and, leaning down his head, seemed lost in meditation. He started up, and, seizing his tablets, wrote upon them these words:

'Honain, I have been the whole night like David in the wilderness of Ziph; but, by the aid of the Lord, I have conquered. I fly from this dangerous city upon his business, which I have too much neglected. Attempt not to discover me, and accept my gratitude.'

# PART VI.

## CHAPTER I.

A scorching sun, a blue and burning sky, on every side lofty ranges of black and barren mountains, dark ravines, deep caverns, unfathomable gorges!

A solitary being moved in the distance. Faint and toiling, a pilgrim slowly clambered up the steep and stony track.

The sultry hours moved on; the pilgrim at length gained the summit of the mountain, a small and rugged table-land, strewn with huge masses of loose and heated rock. All around was desolation: no spring, no herbage; the bird and the insect were alike mute. Still it was the summit: no loftier peaks frowned in the distance; the pilgrim stopped, and breathed with more facility, and a faint smile played over his languid and solemn countenance.

He rested a few minutes; he took from his wallet some locusts and wild honey, and a small skin of water. His meal was short as well as simple. An ardent desire to reach his place of destination before nightfall urged him to proceed. He soon passed over the table-land, and commenced the descent of the mountain. A straggling olive-tree occasionally appeared, and then a group, and soon the groups swelled into a grove. His way wound through the grateful and unaccustomed shade. He emerged from the grove, and found that he had proceeded down more than half the side of the mountain. It ended precipitously in a dark and narrow ravine, formed on the other side by an opposite mountain, the lofty steep of which was crested by a city gently rising on a gradual slope.

Nothing could be conceived more barren, wild, and

terrible than the surrounding scenery, unillumined by a single trace of culture. The city stood like the last gladiator in an amphitheatre of desolation.

It was surrounded by a lofty turreted wall, of an architecture to which the pilgrim was unaccustomed: gates with drawbridge and portcullis, square towers, and loopholes for the archer. Sentinels, clothed in steel and shining in the sunset, paced, at regular intervals, the cautious wall, and on a lofty tower a standard waved, a snowy standard, with a red, red cross!

The Prince of the Captivity at length beheld the lost capital of his fathers.[35]

## CHAPTER II.

A FEW months back, and such a spectacle would have called forth all the latent passion of Alroy; but time and suffering, and sharp experience, had already somewhat curbed the fiery spirit of the Hebrew Prince. He gazed upon Jerusalem, he beheld the City of David garrisoned by the puissant warriors of Christendom, and threatened by the innumerable armies of the Crescent. The two great divisions of the world seemed contending for a prize, which he, a lonely wanderer, had crossed the desert to rescue. If his faith restrained him from doubting the possibility of his enterprise, he was at least deeply conscious that the world was a very different existence from what he had fancied amid the gardens of Hamadan and the rocks of Caucasus, and that if his purpose could be accomplished, it could only be effected by one means. Calm, perhaps somewhat depressed, but full of pious humiliation, and not deserted by holy hope, he descended into the Valley of Jehoshaphat, and so, slaking his thirst at Siloah, and mounting the opposite height, David Alroy entered Jerusalem by the gate of Sion.[36]

He had been instructed that the quarter allotted to his

people was near this entrance. He inquired the direction of the sentinel, who did not condescend to answer him. An old man, in shabby robes, who was passing, beckoned to him.

'What want you, friend?' inquired Alroy.

'You were asking for the quarter of our people. You must be a stranger, indeed, in Jerusalem, to suppose that a Frank would speak to a Jew. You were lucky to get neither kicked nor cursed.'

'Kicked and cursed! Why, these dogs——'

'Hush! hush! for the love of God,' said his new companion, much alarmed. 'Have you lent money to their captain that you speak thus? In Jerusalem our people speak only in a whisper.'

'No matter: the cure is not by words. Where is our quarter.'

'Was the like ever seen! Why he speaks as if he were a Frank. I save him from having his head broken by a gauntlet, and——'

'My friend, I am tired. Our quarter?'

'Whom may you want?'

'The Chief Rabbi.'

'You bear letters to him?'

'What is that to you?'

'Hush! hush! You do not know what Jerusalem is, young man. You must not think of going on in this way. Where do you come from?'

'Bagdad.'

'Bagdad! Jerusalem is not Bagdad. A Turk is a brute, but a Christian is a demon.'

'But our quarter, our quarter?'

'Hush! you want the Chief Rabbi?'

'Ay! ay!

'Rabbi Zimri?'

'It may be so. I neither know nor care.'

'Neither knows nor cares! This will never do: you must not go on in this way at Jerusalem. You must not think of it.'

'Fellow, I see thou art a miserable prattler. Show me our quarter, and I will pay thee well, or be off.'

'Be off! Art thou a Hebrew? to say 'be off' to any one. You come from Bagdad! I tell you what, go back to Bagdad. You will never do for Jerusalem.'

'Your grizzled beard protects you. Old fool, I am a pilgrim just arrived, wearied beyond expression, and you keep me here listening to your flat talk!'

'Flat talk! Why! what would you?'

'Lead me to the Rabbi Zimri, if that be his name.'

'If that be his name! Why, every one knows Rabbi Zimri, the chief rabbi of Jerusalem, the successor of Aaron. We have our temple yet, say what they like. A very learned doctor is Rabbi Zimri.'

'Wretched driveller. I am ashamed to lose my patience with such a dotard.

'Driveller! dotard! Why, who are you?'

'One you cannot comprehend. Without another word lead me to your chief.'

'Chief! you have not far to go. I know no one of the nation who holds his head higher than I do here, and they call me Zimri.'

'What, the Chief Rabbi, that very learned doctor?'

'No less; I thought you had heard of him.'

'Let us forget the past, good Zimri. When great men play the incognito, they must sometimes hear rough phrases. It is the Caliph's lot as well as yours. I am glad to make the acquaintance of so great a doctor. Though young, and roughly habited, I have seen the world a little, and may offer next Sabbath in the synagogue more dirhems than you would perhaps suppose. Good and learned Zimri, I would be your guest.'

'A very worshipful young man! And he speaks low and soft now! But it was lucky I was at hand. Good, what's your name?'

'David.'

'A very honest name, good David. It was lucky I was at hand when you spoke to the sentinel, though. A Jew speak to a Frank, and a sentinel too! Hah! hah! hah! that is good. How Rabbi Maimon will laugh! Faith it was very lucky, now, was not it?'

'Indeed, most fortunate.'

'Well, that is candid! Here! this way. 'Tis not far. We number few, sir, of our brethren here, but a better time will come, a better time will come.'

'I think so. This is your door?'

'An humble one. Jerusalem is not Bagdad, but you are welcome.'

## CHAPTER III.

'KING PIRGANDICUS [37] entered them,' said Rabbi Maimon, 'but no one since.'

'And when did he live?' inquired Alroy.

'His reign is recorded in the Talmud,' answered Rabbi Zimri, 'but in the Talmud there are no dates.'

'A long while ago?' said Alroy.

'Since the Captivity,' answered Rabbi Maimon.

'I doubt that,' said Rabbi Zimri, 'or why should he be called king?'

'Was he of the house of David?' said Alroy.

'Without doubt,' said Rabbi Maimon; 'he was one of our greatest kings, and conquered Julius Cæsar.' [38]

'His kingdom was in the northernmost parts of Africa,' said Rabbi Zimri, 'and exists to this day, if we could but find it.'

'Ay, truly,' added Rabbi Maimon, 'the sceptre has never departed out of Judah; and he rode always upon a white elephant.'

'Covered with cloth of gold,' added Rabbi Zimri.

'And he visited the Tombs of the Kings?' [39] inquired Alroy.

'Without doubt,' said Rabbi Maimon. 'The whole account is in the Talmud.'

'And no one can now find them?'

'No one,' replied Rabbi Zimri; 'but, according to that

learned doctor, Moses Hallevy, they are in a valley in the mountains of Lebanon, which was sealed up by the Archangel Michael.'

'The illustrious Doctor Abarbanel, of Babylon,' said Rabbi Maimon, 'gives one hundred and twenty reasons in his commentary on the Gemara to prove that they sunk under the earth at the taking of the Temple.'

'No one reasons like Abarbanel of Babylon,' said Rabbi Zimri.

'The great Rabbi Akiba, of Pundebita, has answered them all,' said Rabbi Maimon, 'and holds that they were taken up to heaven.'

'And which is right?' inquired Rabbi Zimri.

'Neither,' said Rabbi Maimon.

'One hundred and twenty reasons are strong proof,' said Rabbi Zimri.

'The most learned and illustrious Doctor Aaron Mendola, of Granada,' said Rabbi Maimon, 'has shown that we must look for the Tombs of the Kings in the south of Spain.'

'All that Mendola writes is worth attention,' said Rabbi Zimri.

'Rabbi Hillel,[40] of Samaria, is worth two Mendolas any day,' said Rabbi Maimon.

''Tis a most learned doctor,' said Rabbi Zimri; 'and what thinks he?'

'Hillel proves that there are two Tombs of the Kings,' said Rabbi Maimon, 'and that neither of them are the right ones.'

'What a learned doctor!' exclaimed Rabbi Zimri.

'And very satisfactory,' remarked Alroy.

'These are high subjects,' continued Maimon, his blear eyes twinkling with complacency. 'Your guest, Rabbi Zimri, must read the treatise of the learned Shimei, of Damascus, on "Effecting Impossibilities."'

'That is a work!' exclaimed Zimri.

'I never slept for three nights after reading that work,' said Rabbi Maimon. 'It contains twelve thousand five hundred and thirty-seven quotations from the Pentateuch, and not a single original observation.'

'There were giants in those days,' said Rabbi Zimri; 'we are children now.'

'The first chapter makes equal sense, read backward or forward,' continued Rabbi Maimon.

'Ichabod!' exclaimed Rabbi Zimri.

'And the initial letter of every section is a cabalistical type of a king of Judah.'

'The temple will yet be built,' said Rabbi Zimri.

'Ay, ay! that is learning!' exclaimed Rabbi Maimon; 'but what is the great treatise on "Effecting Impossibilities" to that profound, admirable, and —— '

'Holy Rabbi!' said a youthful reader of the synagogue, who now entered, 'the hour is at hand.'

'You don't say so! Learned Maimon, I must to the synagogue. I could sit here all day listening to you. Come, David, the people await us.'

Zimri and Alroy quitted the house, and proceeded along the narrow hilly streets to the chief temple of the Hebrews.

'It grieves the venerable Maimon much that he cannot join us,' said Rabbi Zimri. 'You have doubtless heard of him at Bagdad; a most learned doctor.'

Alroy bowed in silence.

'He bears his years well. You would hardly believe that he was my master.'

'I perceive that you inherit much of his erudition.'

'You are kind. If he have breathed one year, Rabbi Maimon will be a hundred and ten next Passover.'

'I doubt it not.'

'When he is gathered to his fathers, a great light will be extinguished in Israel. You wanted to know something about the Tombs of the Kings; I told you he was your man. How full he was! His mind, sir, is an egg.'

'A somewhat ancient one. I fear his guidance will hardly bring me the enviable fortune of King Pirgandicus.'

'Between ourselves, good David, talking of King Pirgandicus, I cannot help fancying that the learned

Maimon made a slight mistake. I hold Pirgandicus was only a prince. It was after the Captivity, and I know no authority for any of our rulers since the destruction assuming a higher title. Clearly a prince, eh? But, though I would whisper it to no one but you, I think our worthy friend grows a little old. We should remember his years, sir. A hundred and ten next Passover. 'Tis a great burden.'

'Ay! with his learning added, a very fearful burden indeed!'

'You have been a week in Jerusalem, and have not yet visited our synagogue. It is not of cedar and ivory, but it is still a temple. This way. Is it only a week that you have been here? Why, you look another man! I shall never forget our first meeting: you did not know me. That was good, eh? And when I told you I was the chief Rabbi Zimri, how you changed! You have quite regained your appetite. Ah! 'tis pleasant to mix once more with our own people. To the left. So! we must descend a little. We hold our meetings in an ancient cemetery. You have a finer temple, I warrant me, in Bagdad. Jerusalem is not Bagdad. But this has its conveniences. 'Tis safe, and we are not very rich, nor wish to seem so.'

## CHAPTER IV.

A LONG passage brought them to a number of small, square, low chambers[41] leading into each other. They were lighted by brass lamps, placed at intervals in vacant niches, that once held corpses, and which were now soiled by the smoky flame. Between two and three hundred individuals were assembled in these chambers, at first scarcely distinguishable by those who descended from the broad daylight; but by degrees the eyesight became accustomed to the dim and vaporous atmosphere, and Alroy recognised in the final and more illumined chamber a high cedar cabinet, the type of the ark, and which held the sacred vessels and the sanctified copy of the law.

Standing in lines, with their heads mystically covered,[42] the forlorn remnant of Israel, captives in their ancient city, avowed, in spite of all their sufferings, their fidelity to their God, and, notwithstanding all the bitterness of hope delayed, their faith in the fulfilment of his promises. Their simple service was completed, their prayers were read, their responses made, their law exhibited, and their charitable offerings announced by their high priest. After the service, the venerable Zimri, opening a volume of the Talmud, and fortified by the opinions of all those illustrious and learned doctors, the heroes of his erudite conversations with the aged Maimon, expounded the law to the congregation of the people.[43]

'It is written,' said the Rabbi, ' " Thou shalt have none other God but me." Now know ye what our father Abraham said when Nimrod ordered him to worship fire? "Why not water," answered Abraham, "which can put out fire? why not the clouds, which can pour forth water? why not the winds, which can produce clouds? why not God, which can create winds?"'

A murmur of approbation sounded throughout the congregation.

'Eliezer,' said Zimri, addressing himself to a young Rabbi, 'it is written, that he took a rib from Adam when he was asleep. Is God then a robber?'

The young Rabbi looked puzzled, and cast his eyes on the ground. The congregation was perplexed and a little alarmed.

'Is there no answer?' said Zimri.

'Rabbi,' said a stranger, a tall, swarthy African pilgrim, standing in a corner, and enveloped in a red mantle, over which a lamp threw a flickering light; 'Rabbi, some robbers broke into my house last night, and stole an earthen pipkin, but they left a golden vase in its stead.'

'It is well said; it is well said,' exclaimed the congregation. The applause was loud.

'Learned Zimri,' continued the African, 'it is written in the Gemara, that there was a youth in Jerusalem who fell in love with a beautiful damsel, and she scorned him. And the youth was so stricken with his passion that he could not speak; but when he beheld her, he looked at her imploringly, and she laughed. And one day the youth, not knowing what to do with himself, went out into the desert; and towards night he returned home, but the gates of the city were shut. And he went down into the valley of Jehoshaphat, and entered the tomb of Absalom and slept; and he dreamed a dream; and next morning he came into the city smiling. And the maiden met him, and she said, "Is that thou; art thou a laugher?" and he answered, "Behold, yesterday being disconsolate, I went out of the city into the desert, and I returned home, and the gates of the city were shut, and I went down into the valley of Jehoshaphat, and I entered the tomb of Absalom, and I slept, and I dreamed a dream, and ever since then I have laughed." And the damsel said, "Tell me thy dream." And he answered and said, "I may not tell my dream only to my wife, for it regards her honour." And the maiden grew sad and curious, and said, "I am thy wife, tell me thy dream." And straightway they went and were married, and ever after they both laughed. Now, learned Zimri, what means this tale, an idle jest for a master of the law, yet it is written by the greatest doctor of the Captivity?'

'It passeth my comprehension,' said the chief Rabbi.

Rabbi Eliezer was silent; the congregation groaned.

'Now hear the interpretation,' said the African. 'The youth is our people, and the damsel is our lost Sion, and the tomb of Absalom proves that salvation can only come from the house of David. Dost thou hear this, young man?' said the African, coming forward and laying his hand on Alroy. 'I speak to thee, because I have observed a deep attention in thy conduct.'

The Prince of the Captivity started, and shot a glance at the dark visage before him, but the glance read nothing. The upper part of the countenance of the African was half concealed by masses of dark matted hair, and the lower by his uncouth robes. A flashing eye was its only characteristic, which darted forth like lightning out of a black cloud.

'Is my attention the only reason that induces you to address me?' inquired Alroy.

'Whoever gave all his reasons?' replied the African, with a laughing sneer.

'I seek not to learn them. Suffice it, stranger, that how much soever you may mean, as much I can understand.'

''Tis well. Learned Zimri, is this thy pupil? I congratulate thee. I will match him against the hopeful Eliezer.' So saying, the lofty African stalked out of the chamber. The assembly also broke up. Alroy would willingly have immediately followed the African, and held some further and more private conversation with him; but some minutes elapsed, owing to the officious attentions of Zimri, before he could escape; and, when he did, his search after the stranger was vain. He inquired among the congregation, but none knew the African. He was no man's guest and no man's debtor, and apparently had never before been seen.

## CHAPTER V.

THE trumpet was sounding to close the gates, as Alroy passed the Sion entrance. The temptation was irresistible. He rushed out, and ran for more than one hundred yards without looking back, and when he did, he had the satisfaction of ascertaining that he was fairly shut out for the night. The sun had set, still the Mount of Olives was flushed with the reflection of his dying beams, but Jehoshaphat at its feet was in deep shadow.

He wandered among the mountains for some time, beholding Jerusalem from a hundred different points of view, and watching the single planets and clustering constellations that gradually burst into beauty, or gathered into light. At length, somewhat exhausted, he descended into the vale. The scanty rill of Siloah [45] looked like a thread of silver winding in the moonlight. Some houseless wretches were slumbering under the arch of its fountain. Several isolated tombs of considerable size [46] rose at the base of Olivet, and the largest of these Alroy entered. Proceeding through a narrow passage, he entered a small square chamber. On each side was an empty sarcophagus of granite, one with its lid broken. Between these the Prince of the Captivity laid his robe, and, wearied by his ramble, soon soundly slept.

After some hours he woke. He fancied that he had been wakened by the sound of voices. The chamber was not quite dark. A straggling moonbeam fought its way through an open fretwork pattern in the top of the tomb, and just revealed the dim interior. Suddenly a voice spoke, a strange and singular voice.

'Brother, brother, the sounds of the night begin.'
Another voice answered,
'Brother, brother, I hear them, too.'
'The woman in labour!'
'The thief at his craft!'
'The sentinel's challenge!'
'The murderer's step!'
'Oh! the merry sounds of the night!'
'Brother, brother, let us come forth and wander about the world.'
'We have seen all things. I'll lie here and listen to the baying hound. 'Tis music for a tomb.'
'Choice and rare. You are idle. I like to sport in the starry air. Our hours are few, they should be fair.'
'What shall we see, Heaven or Earth?'
'Hell for me, 'tis more amusing.'
'As for me, I am sick of Hades.'
'Let us visit Solomon!'
'In his unknown metropolis?'
'That will be rare.'

'But where, oh! where?'
'Even a spirit cannot tell. But they say, but they say, 1 dare not whisper what they say.'
'Who told you?'
'No one. I overheard an Afrite whispering to a female Ghoul he wanted to seduce.'
'Hah, hah! hah, hah! choice pair, choice pair! We are more ethereal.'
'She was a beauty in her way. Her eyes were luminous, though somewhat dank, and her cheek tinged with carnation caught from infant blood.'
'Oh! gay; oh! gay; what said they?'
'He was a deserter without leave from Solomon's bodyguard. The trull wriggled the secret out.'
'Tell me, kind brother.'
'I'll show, not tell.'
'I pr'ythee tell me.'
'Well, then, well. In Genthesma's gloomy cave there is a river none has reached, and you must sail, and you must sail —— Brother!'
'Ay.'
'Methinks I smell something too earthly.'
'What's that?'
'The breath of man.'
'Scent more fatal than the morning air! Away, away!'

## CHAPTER VI.

IN the range of mountains that lead from Olivet to the river Jordan is the great cavern of Genthesma, a mighty excavation formed by the combined and immemorial work of Nature and of Art; for on the high basaltic columns are cut strange characters and unearthly forms,[47] and in many places the natural ornaments have been completed by the hands of the sculptor into symmetrical entablatures and fanciful capitals, the work, they say, of captive Dives and conquered Afrites, for the great king.

It was midnight; the cold full moon showered its brilliancy upon this narrow valley, shut in on all sides by black and barren mountains. A single being stood at the entrance of the cave.

It was Alroy. Desperate and determined, after listening to the spirits in the tomb, he resolved to penetrate the mysteries of Genthesma. He took from his girdle a flint and steel, with which he lighted a torch and then he entered.

The cavern narrowed as he cautiously advanced, and soon he found himself at the head of an evidently artificial gallery. A crowd of bats rushed forward and extinguished his torch.[48] He leant down to relight it, and in so doing observed that he trod upon an artificial pavement.

The gallery was of great extent, with a gradual declination.[49] Being in a straight line with the mouth of the cavern, the moonlit scene was long visible, but Alroy, on looking round, now perceived that the exterior was shut out by the eminence that he had left behind him. The sides of the gallery were covered with strange and sculptured forms.

The Prince of the Captivity proceeded along this gallery for nearly two hours. A distant murmur of falling water, which might have been distinguished nearly from the first, increased in sound as he advanced, and now, from the loud roar and dash at hand, he felt that he was on the brink of some cataract. It was very dark. His heart trembled. He felt his footing ere he ventured to advance. The spray suddenly leaped forward and extinguished his torch. His imminent danger filled him with terror, and he receded some paces, but in vain endeavoured to re-illumine his torch, which was soaked with water.

His courage deserted him. Energy and exertion seemed hopeless. He was about to deliver himself up to despair, when an expanding lustre attracted his attention in the opposing gloom.

A small and bright red cloud seemed sailing towards

him. It opened, discharged from its bosom a silvery star, and dissolved again into darkness. But the star remained, the silvery star, and threw a long line of tremulous light upon the vast and raging rapid, which now, fleet and foaming, revealed itself on all sides to the eye of Alroy.

The beautiful interposition in his favour re-animated the adventurous pilgrim. A dark shadow in the foreground, breaking the line of light shed by the star upon the waters, attracted his attention. He advanced, regained his former footing, and more nearly examined it. It was a boat, and in the boat, mute and immovable, sat one of those vast, singular, and hideous forms, which he had observed sculptured on the walls of the gallery.

David Alroy, committing his fortunes to the God of Israel, leapt into the boat.

## CHAPTER VII.

AND at the same moment the Afrite, for it was one of those dread beings,[50] raised the oars, and the boat moved. The falling waters suddenly parted in the long line of the star's reflection, and the barque glided through their high and severed masses.

In this wise they proceeded for a few minutes, until they entered a beautiful and moonlit lake. In the distance was a mountainous country. Alroy examined his companion with a feeling of curiosity not unmixed with terror. It was remarkable that Alroy could never succeed in any way in attracting his notice. The Afrite seemed totally unconscious of the presence of his passenger. At length the boat reached the opposite shore of the lake, and the Prince of the Captivity disembarked.

He disembarked at the head of an avenue of colossal lions of red granite,[51] extending far as the eye could reach, and ascending the side of the mountain, which was cut into a flight of magnificent steps. The easy ascent was in consequence soon accomplished, and Alroy, proceeding along the avenue of lions, soon gained the summit of the mountain.

To his infinite astonishment he beheld Jerusalem. That strongly-marked locality could not be mistaken: at his feet were Jehoshaphat, Kedron, Siloah; he stood upon Olivet; before him was Sion. But in all other respects, how different was the landscape from the one that he had gazed upon a few days back, for the first time! The surrounding hills sparkled with vineyards, and glowed with summer palaces, and voluptuous pavilions, and glorious gardens of pleasure. The city, extending all over Mount Sion, was encompassed with a wall of white marble, with battlements of gold; a gorgeous mass of gates and pillars, and gardened terraces; lofty piles of rarest materials, cedar, and ivory, and precious stones; and costly columns of the richest workmanship and the most fanciful orders, capitals of the lotus and the palm, and flowing friezes of the olive and the vine.

And in the front a mighty Temple rose, with inspiration in its very form; a Temple so vast, so sumptuous, that there needed no priest to tell us that no human hand planned that sublime magnificence!

'God of my fathers!' said Alroy, 'I am a poor, weak thing, and my life has been a life of dreams and visions, and I have sometimes thought my brain lacked a sufficient master; where am I? Do I sleep or live? Am I a slumberer or a ghost? This trial is too much.' He sank down, and hid his face in his hands: his over-exerted mind appeared to desert him: he wept.

Many minutes elapsed before Alroy grew composed. His wild bursts of weeping sank into sobs, and the sobs died off into sighs. And at length, calm from exhaustion, he again looked up, and lo! the glorious city was no more! Before him was a moon-lit plain, over which the avenue of lions still advanced, and appeared to terminate only in the mountainous distance.

This limit the Prince of the Captivity at length reached,

and stood before a stupendous portal, cut out of the solid
rock, four hundred feet in height, and supported by clusters
of colossal Caryatides.[52] Upon the portal were engraven
some Hebrew characters, which upon examination proved
to be the same as those upon the talisman of Jabaster.
And so, taking from his bosom that all-precious and long-
cherished deposit, David Alroy, in obedience to his instructions, pressed the signet against the gigantic portal.

The portal opened with a crash of thunder louder than
an earthquake. Pale, panting, and staggering, the Prince
of the Captivity entered an illimitable hall, illumined by
pendulous balls of glowing metal. On each side of the
hall, sitting on golden thrones, was ranged a line of kings,
and, as the pilgrim entered, the monarchs rose, and took off
their diadems, and waved them thrice, and thrice repeated,
in solemn chorus. 'All hail, Alroy! Hail to thee, brother
king! Thy crown awaits thee!'

The Prince of the Captivity stood trembling, with his
eyes fixed upon the ground, and leaning breathless against
a column. And when at length he had a little recovered
himself, and dared again to look up, he found that the
monarchs were re-seated; and, from their still and vacant
visages, apparently unconscious of his presence. And this
emboldened him, and so, staring alternately at each side
of the hall, but with a firm, perhaps desperate step, Alroy
advanced.

And he came to two thrones which were set apart from
the others in the middle of the hall. On one was seated a
noble figure, far above the common stature, with arms
folded and down-cast eyes. His feet rested upon a broken
sword and a shivered sceptre, which told that he was a
monarch, in spite of his discrowned head.

And on the opposite throne was a venerable personage,
with a long flowing beard, and dressed in white raiment.
His countenance was beautiful, although ancient. Age had
stolen on without its imperfections, and time had only invested it with a sweet dignity and solemn grace. The countenance of the king was upraised with a seraphic gaze,

and, as he thus looked up on high, with eyes full of love, and thanksgiving, and praise, his consecrated fingers seemed to touch the trembling wires of a golden harp.

And further on, and far above the rest, upon a throne that stretched across the hall, a most imperial presence straightway flashed upon the startled vision of Alroy. Fifty steps of ivory, and each step guarded by golden lions,[53] led to a throne of jasper. A dazzling light blazed forth from the glittering diadem and radiant countenance of him who sat upon the throne, one beautiful as a woman, but with the majesty of a god. And in one hand he held a seal, and in the other a sceptre.

And when Alroy had reached the foot of the throne, he stopped, and his heart misgave him. And he prayed for some minutes in silent devotion, and, without daring to look up, he mounted the first step of the throne, and the second, and the third, and so on, with slow and faltering feet, until he reached the forty-ninth step.

The Prince of the Captivity raised his eyes. He stood before the monarch face to face. In vain Alroy attempted to attract his attention, or to fix his gaze. The large dark eyes, full of supernatural lustre, appeared capable of piercing all things, and illuminating all things, but they flashed on without shedding a ray upon Alroy.

Pale as a spectre, the pilgrim, whose pilgrimage seemed now on the point of completion, stood cold and trembling before the object of all his desires and all his labours. But he thought of his country, his people, and his God; and, while his noiseless lips breathed the name of Jehovah, solemnly he put forth his arm, and with a gentle firmness grasped the unresisting sceptre of his great ancestor.

And, as he seized it, the whole scene vanished from his sight!

## CHAPTER VIII.

Hours or years might have passed away, so far as the sufferer was concerned, when Alroy again returned to self-consciousness. His eyes slowly opened, he cast around a vacant stare, he was lying in the cavern of Genthesma. The moon had set, but the morn had not broken. A single star glittered over the brow of the black mountains. He faintly moved his limbs; he would have raised his hand to his bewildered brain, but found that it grasped a sceptre. The memory of the past returned to him. He tried to rise, and found that he was reposing in the arms of a human being. He turned his head; he met the anxious gaze of Jabaster!

# PART VII.

## CHAPTER I.

'Your pace is troubled, uncle.'

'So is my mind.'

'All may go well.'

'Miriam, we have seen the best. Prepare yourself for sorrow, gentle girl. I care not for myself, for I am old, and age makes heroes of us all. I have endured, and can endure more. As we approach our limit, it would appear that our minds grow callous. I have seen my wealth, raised with the labours of a thoughtful life, vanish in a morn: my people, a fragile remnant, nevertheless a people, dispersed, or what is worse. I have wept for them, although no tear of selfish grief has tinged this withered cheek. And, were I but alone, ay! there's the pang. The solace of my days is now my sorrow.'

'Weep not for me, dear uncle. Rather let us pray that our God will not forsake us.'

'We know not when we are well. Our hours stole tranquilly along, and then we murmured. Prospering, we murmured, and now we are rightly stricken. The legend of the past is Israel's bane. The past is a dream; and, in the waking present, we should discard the enervating shadow. Why should we be free? We murmured against captivity. This *is* captivity: this damp, dim cell, where we are brought to die.

'O! youth, rash youth, thy being is destruction. But yesterday a child, it seems but yesterday I nursed him in these arms, a thoughtless child, and now our house has fallen by his deeds. I will not think of it; 'twill make me mad.'

'Uncle, dearest uncle, we have lived together, and we

will die together, and both in love; but, I pray you, speak no harsh word of David.'

'Shall I praise him?'

'Say nothing. What he has done, if done in grief, has been done all in honour. Would you that he had spared Alschiroch?'

'Never! I would have struck him myself. Brave boy, he did his duty; and I, I, Miriam, thy uncle, at whom they wink behind his back and call him niggard, was I wanting in that hour of trial? Was my treasure spared to save my people? Did I shrink from all the toil and trouble of that time? A trying time, my Miriam, but compared with this, the building of the Temple ——'

'You were then what you have ever been, the best and wisest. And since our fathers' God did not forsake us, even in that wilderness of wildest woe, I offer gratitude in present faith, and pay him for past mercies by my prayers for more.'

'Well, well, life must end. The hour approaches when we must meet our rulers and mock trial; precious justice that begins in threats and ends in torture. You are silent, Miriam.'

'I am speaking to my God.'

'What is that noise? A figure moves behind the dusky grate. Our gaoler. No, no, it is Caleb! Faithful child, I fear you have perilled much.'

'I enter with authority, my lord, and bear good tidings.'

'He smiles! Is't possible? Speak on, speak on!'

'Alroy has captured the harem of our Governor, as they journeyed from Badgad to this city, guarded by his choicest troops. And he has sent to offer that they shall be exchanged for you and for your household. And Hassan has answered that his women shall owe their freedom to nothing but his sword. But, in the meantime, it is agreed between him and the messenger of your nephew, that both companies of prisoners shall be treated with all becoming courtesy. You, therefore, are remanded to your palace, and the trumpet is now sounding before the great mosque to summon all the host against Alroy, whom Hassan has vowed to bring to Hamadan dead or alive.'

'The harem of the Governor, guarded too by his choicest troops! 'Tis a great deed. He did remember us. Faithful boy! The harem of the Governor! his choicest troops! 'Tis a very great deed. Methinks the Lord is with him. He has his great father's heart. Only think of David, a child! I nursed him, often. Caleb! Can this be David, our David, a child, a girl? Yet he struck Alschiroch! Miriam! where is she? Worthy Caleb, look to your mistress; she has fallen. Quite gone! Fetch water. 'Tis not very pure, but we shall be in our palace soon. The harem of the Governor! I can't believe it. Sprinkle, sprinkle. David take them prisoners! Why, when they pass, we are obliged to turn our heads, and dare not look. More water: I'll rub her hand. 'Tis warmer! Her eyes open! Miriam, choice news, my child! The harem of the Governor! I'll not believe it!'

## CHAPTER II.

'ONCE more within our walls, Caleb. Life is a miracle. I feel young again. This is home; and yet I am a prisoner. You said the host were assembling; he can have no chance. Think you, Caleb, he has any chance? I hope he will die. I would not have him taken. I fear their tortures. We will die too; we will all die. Now I am out of that dungeon, methinks I could even fight. Is it true that he has joined with robbers?'

'I saw the messenger, and learnt that he first repaired to some bandits in the ruins in the desert. He had become acquainted with them in his pilgrimage. They say their leader is one of our people.'

'I am glad of that. He can eat with him. I would not have him eat unclean things with the Ishmaelites.'

'Lord, sir! our people gather to him from all quarters. 'Tis said that Jabaster, the great Cabalist, has joined him from the mountains with ten thousand men.'

'The great Jabaster! then there is some chance. I know Jabaster well. He is too wise to join a desperate cause. Art sure about Jabaster? 'Tis a great name, a very potent spirit. I have heard such things of that Jabaster, sir, would make you stare like Saul before the spirit! Only think of our David, Caleb, making all this noise! I am full of hope. I feel not like a prisoner. He beat the Harem guard, and, now he has got Jabaster, he will beat them all.'

'The messenger told me he captured the Harem, only to free his uncle and his sister.'

'He ever loved me; I have done my duty to him; I think I have. Jabaster! why, man, the name is a spell! There are men at Bagdad who will get up in the night to join Jabaster. I hope David will follow his counsels in all things. I would I had seen his servant, I could have sent him a message.'

'Lord, sir! the Prince Alroy has no great need of counsellors, I can tell you. 'Tis said he bears the sceptre of great Solomon, which he himself obtained in the unknown tombs of Palestine.'

'The sceptre of Solomon! could I but believe it! 'Tis an age of wonders! Where are we? Call for Miriam, I'll tell her this. Only think of David, a mere child, our David with the sceptre of Solomon! and Jabaster too! I have great faith. The Lord confound his enemies!'

---

## CHAPTER III.

'GENTLE Rachel, I fear I trouble you; sweet Beruna, I thank you for your zeal. I am better now; the shock was great. These are strange tidings, maidens.'

'Yes, dear lady! who would have thought of your brother turning out a Captain?'

'I am sure I always thought he was the quietest person in the world,' said Beruna, 'though he did kill Alschiroch.'

'One could never get a word out of him,' said Rachel.

'He was always moping alone,' said Beruna.

'And when one spoke to him he always turned away,' said Leah.

'Or blushed,' added Imra.

'Well, for my part,' said the beautiful Bathsheba, 'I always thought Prince David was a genius. He had such beautiful eyes!'

'I hope he will conquer Hassan,' said Rachel.

'So do I,' said Beruna.

'I wonder what he has done with the Harem,' said Leah.

'I don't think he will dare to speak to them,' said Imra.

'You are very much mistaken,' said Bathsheba.

'Hark!' said Miriam.

''Tis Hassan,' said Bathsheba; 'may he never return!'

The wild drum of the Seljuks sounded, then a flourish of their fierce trumpets, and soon the tramp of horse. Behind the blinds of their chamber, Miriam and her maidens beheld the magnificent troop of turbaned horsemen, who, glittering with splendid armour and bright shawls, and proudly bounding on their fiery steeds, now went forth to crush and conquer the only hope of Israel. Upon an Arab, darker than night, rode the superb Hassan, and, as he passed the dwelling of his late prisoners, whether from the exulting anticipation of coming triumph, or from a soft suspicion that, behind that lattice, bright eyes and brilliant faces were gazing on his state, the haughty but handsome Seljuk flourished his scimetar over his head, as he threw his managed steed into attitudes that displayed the skill of its rider.

'He is handsomer than Alschiroch,' said Rachel.

'What a shawl!' said Beruna.

'His scimetar was like lightning,' said Leah.

'And his steed like thunder,' said Imra.

'The evil eye fall on him!' said Bathsheba.
'Lord,' exclaimed Miriam, 'remember David and all his afflictions!'

## CHAPTER IV.

THE deserted city of the wilderness presented a very different appearance from that which met the astonished gaze of Alroy, when he first beheld its noble turrets, and wandered in its silent streets of palaces.

Without the gates was pitched a numerous camp of those low black tents common among the Kourds and Turkmans; the principal street was full of busy groups engaged in all the preparations of warfare, and all the bustling expedients of an irregular and adventurous life; steeds were stalled in ruined chambers, and tall camels raised their still visages among the clustering columns, or crouched in kneeling tranquillity amid fallen statues and prostrate obelisks.

Two months had scarcely elapsed since Alroy and Jabaster had sought Scherirah in his haunt, and announced to him their sacred mission. The callous heart of him, whose 'mother was a Jewess,' had yielded to their inspired annunciations. He embraced their cause with all the fervour of conversion, and his motley band were not long sceptical of a creed which, while it assuredly offered danger and adventure, held out the prospects of wealth and even empire. From the city of the wilderness the new Messiah sent forth his messengers to the neighbouring cities, to announce his advent to his brethren in captivity. The Hebrews, a proud and stiff-necked race, ever prone to rebellion, received the announcement of their favourite prince with transport. The descendant of David, and the slayer of Alschiroch, had double claims upon their confidence and allegiance, and the flower of the Hebrew youth in the neighbouring cities of the Caliphate repaired in crowds to pay their homage to the recovered sceptre of Solomon.

The affair was at first treated by the government with contempt, and the sultan of the Seljuks contented himself with setting a price upon the head of the murderer of his brother; but, when several cities had been placed under contribution, and more than one Moslem caravan stopped, and plundered in the name of the God of Abraham, of Isaac, and of Jacob, orders were despatched from Bagdad to the new governor of Hamadan, Hassan Subah, to suppress the robbers, or the rebels, and to send David Alroy dead or alive to the capital.

The Hebrew malcontents were well apprised by their less adventurous but still sympathising brethren of everything that took place at the head-quarters of the enemy. Spies arrived on the same day at the city of the wilderness, who informed Alroy that his uncle was thrown into a dungeon at Hamadan, and that a body of chosen troops were about to escort a royal harem from Bagdad into Persia.

Alroy attacked the escort in person, utterly discomfited them, and captured their charge. It proved to be the harem of the Governor of Hamadan, and if for a moment the too sanguine fancy of the captor experienced a passing pang of disappointment, the prize at least obtained, as we have seen, the freedom and security of his dear though distant friends. This exploit precipitated the expedition which was preparing at Hamadan for his destruction. The enraged Hassan Subah started from his divan, seized his scimetar, and without waiting for the auxiliaries he had summoned from the neighbouring chieftains, called to horse, and at the head of two thousand of the splendid Seljuk cavalry, hurried to vindicate his love and satiate his revenge.

Within the amphitheatre which he first entered as a prisoner, Alroy sat in council. On his right was Jabaster, Scherirah on his left. A youth, little his senior, but tall as a palm-tree, and strong as a young lion, was the fourth captain. In the distance, some standing, some reclining, were about fifty men completely armed.

'Are the people numbered, Abner?' inquired Alroy of the youth.

'Even so; three hundred effective horsemen, and two thousand footmen; but the footmen lack arms.'

'The Lord will send them in good time,' said Jabaster; 'meanwhile let them continue to make javelins.'

'Trust in the Lord,' murmured Scherirah, bending his head, with his eyes fixed on the ground.

A loud shout was heard throughout the city. Alroy started from his carpet. The messenger had returned. Pale and haggard, covered with sweat and sand, the faithful envoy was borne into the amphitheatre almost upon the shoulders of the people. In vain the guard endeavoured to stem the passage of the multitude. They clambered up the tiers of arches, they filled the void and crumbling seats of the antique circus, they supported themselves upon each other's shoulders, they clung to the capitals of the lofty columns. The whole multitude had assembled to hear the intelligence; the scene recalled the ancient purpose of the building, and Alroy and his fellow-warriors seemed like the gladiators of some old spectacle.

'Speak,' said Alroy, 'speak the worst. No news can be bitter to those whom the Lord will avenge.'

'Ruler of Israel! thus saith Hassan Subah,' answered the messenger: 'My harem shall owe their freedom to nothing but my sword. I treat not with rebels, but I war not with age or woman; and between Bostenay and his household on one side, and the prisoners of thy master on the other, let there be peace. Go, tell Alroy I will seal it in his best blood. And lo! thy uncle and thy sister are again in their palace.'

Alroy placed his hand for a moment to his eyes, and then instantly resuming his self-possession, he enquired as to the movements of the enemy.

'I have crossed the desert on a swift dromedary [54] lent to me by Shelomi of the Gate, whose heart is with our cause. I have not tarried, neither have I slept. Ere to-morrow's sunset the Philistines will be here, led by Hassan Subah himself. The Lord of Hosts be with us! Since we conquered Canaan, Israel hath not struggled with such a power!'

A murmur ran through the assembly. Men exchanged enquiring glances, and involuntarily pressed each other's arms.

'The trial has come,' said a middle-aged Hebrew, who had fought twenty years ago with Jabaster.

'Let me die for the Ark!' said a young enthusiast of the band of Abner.

'I thought we should get into a scrape,' whispered Kisloch the Kourd to Calidas the Indian. 'What could have ever induced us to give up robbing in a quiet manner?'

'And turn Jews!' said the Guebre, with a sneer.

'Look at Scherirah,' said the Negro, grinning. 'If he is not kissing the sceptre of Solomon!'

'I wish to heaven he had only hung Alroy the first time he met him,' said Calidas.

'Sons of the Covenant!' exclaimed Alroy, 'the Lord hath delivered them into our hands. To-morrow eve we march to Hamadan!'

A cheer followed this exclamation.

'It is written,' said Jabaster, opening a volume, 'Lo! I will defend this city, to save it, for mine own sake, and for my servant David's sake.'

'And it came to pass that night that the angel of the Lord went out, and smote in the camp of the Assyrians, an hundred four score and five thousand; and when they arose early in the morning, behold! they were all dead corpses.'

'Now, as I was gazing upon the stars this morn, and reading the celestial alphabet known to the true Cabalist,[55] behold! the star of the house of David and seven other stars moved, and met together, and formed into a circle. And the word they formed was a mystery to me; but lo! I have opened the book, and each star is the initial letter of each line of the Targum that I have now read to you. Therefore the fate of Sennacherib is the fate of Hassan Subah!'

'TRUST IN HIM AT ALL TIMES, YE PEOPLE; POUR OUT YOUR HEART BEFORE HIM: GOD IS A REFUGE FOR US. SELAH!'

At this moment a female form appeared on the very top of the amphitheatre, upon the slight remains of the uppermost tier of which a solitary arch alone was left. The chorus instantly died away, every tongue was silent, every eye fixed. Hushed, mute, and immovable, even Kisloch and his companions were appalled as they gazed upon Esther the Prophetess.

Her eminent position, her imposing action, the flashing of her immense eyes, her beautiful but awful countenance, her black hair, that hung almost to her knees, and the white light of the moon, just rising over the opposite side of the amphitheatre, and which threw a silvery flash upon her form, and seemed to invest her with some miraculous emanation, while all beneath her was in deep gloom, these circumstances combined to render her an object of universal interest and attention, while in a powerful but high voice she thus addressed them.

'They come, they come! But will they go? Lo! hear ye this, O house of Jacob, which are called by the name of Israel, and are come forth out of the waters of Judah! I hear their drum in the desert, and the voice of their trumpets is like the wind of eve, but a decree hath gone forth, and it says, that a mortal shall be more precious than fine gold, yea, a man than the rich ore of Ophir.

'They come, they come! But will they go? I see the flash of their scimetars, I mark the prancing of their cruel steeds; but a decree hath gone forth, and it says, a gleaning shall be left among them, as in the shaking of the olive-tree; two or three berries on the top of the uppermost bough; four or five on the straggling branches.

'They come, they come! But will they go? Lo! a decree hath gone forth, and it says, Hamadan shall be to thee for a spoil, and desolation shall fall upon Babylon. And there shall the wild beasts of the desert lodge, and howling monsters shall fill their houses, and there shall the daughters of the ostrich dwell, and there shall the screech-owl pitch her tent, and there shall the night-raven lay her eggs, and there shall the satyrs hold their revels. And wolves shall howl to one another in their palaces, and dragons in their voluptuous pavilions. Her time is near at hand; her days shall not be prolonged; the reed and the lotus shall wither in her rivers; and the meadows by her canals shall be as the sands of the desert. For, is it a light thing that the Lord should send his servant to raise up the tribes of Jacob, and to restore the preserved of Israel? Sing, O heavens, and be joyful, O earth, and break forth into singing, O mountains, for the Lord hath comforted his people, and will have mercy upon his afflicted!'

She ceased; she descended the precipitous side of the amphitheatre with rapid steps, vaulting from tier to tier, and bounding with wonderful agility from one mass of ruin to another. At length she reached the level; and then foaming and panting, she rushed to Alroy, threw herself upon the ground, embraced his feet, and wiped off the dust from his sandals with her hair.

The assembly broke into long and loud acclamations of supernatural confidence and sanguine enthusiasm. They beheld their Messiah wave his miraculous sceptre. They thought of Hassan Subah and his Seljuks only as of victims, and of to-morrow only as of a day which was to commence a new era of triumph, freedom, and empire!

## CHAPTER V.

HASSAN SUBAH, after five days' forced marches pitched his sumptuous pavilion in that beautiful Oasis, which had afforded such delightful refreshment to Alroy when a solitary pilgrim. Around for nearly a mile, were the tents of his warriors, and of the numerous caravan that had accompanied him, laden with water and provisions for his troops. Here, while he reposed, he also sought information as to the position of his enemy.

A party of observation, which he had immediately despatched, returned almost instantly with a small caravan that had been recently plundered by the robbers. The merchant, a venerable and pious Moslem, was ushered into the presence of the Governor of Hamadan.

'From the robbers' haunt?' inquired Hassan.

'Unfortunately so,' answered the merchant.

'Is it far?'

'A day's journey.'

'And you quitted it?'

'Yesterday morn.'

'What is their force?'

The merchant hesitated.

'Do they not make prisoners?' enquired the Governor, casting a scrutinising glance at his companion.

'Holy Prophet! what a miserable wretch am I!' exclaimed the venerable merchant, bursting into tears. 'A faithful subject of the Caliph, I am obliged to serve rebels, a devout Moslem, I am forced to aid Jews! Order me to be hanged at once, my lord,' continued the unfortunate merchant, wringing his hands. 'Order me to be hanged at once. I have lived long enough.'

'What is all this?' enquired Hassan; 'speak, friend, without fear.'

'I am a faithful subject of the Caliph,' answered the merchant; 'I am a devout Moslem, but I have lost ten thousand dirhems.'

'I am sorry for you, sir; I also have lost something, but my losses are nothing to you, nor yours to me.'

'Accursed be the hour when these dogs tempted me! Tell me, is it sin to break faith with a Jew?'

'On the contrary, I could find you many reverend Mollahs, who will tell you that such a breach is the highest virtue. Come! come, I see how it is: you have received your freedom on condition of not betraying your merciful plunderers. Promises exacted by terror are the bugbears of fools. Speak, man, all you know. Where are they? What is their force? Are we supposed to be at hand?'

'I am a faithful subject of the Caliph, and I am bound to serve him,' replied the merchant; 'I am a devout Moslem, and 'tis my duty to destroy all Giaours, but I am also a man, and I must look after my own interest. Noble Governor, the long and the short is, these scoundrels have robbed me of ten thousand dirhems, as my slaves will tell you: at least, goods to that amount. No one can prove that they be worth less. It is true that I include in that calculation the fifty per cent. I was to make on my shawls at Hamadan, but still to me it is as good as ten thousand dirhems. Ask my slaves if such an assortment of shawls was ever yet beheld.'

'To the point, to the point. The robbers?'

'I am at the point. The shawls is the point. For when I talked of the shawls and the heaviness of my loss, you must know that the captain of the robbers ——'

'Alroy?'

'A fierce young gentleman, I do not know how they call him: said the captain to me, "Merchant, you look gloomy." "Gloomy," I said, "you would look gloomy if you were a prisoner, and had lost ten thousand dirhems." "What, is this trash worth ten thousand dirhems?" said he. "With the fifty per cent. I was to make at Hamadan." "Fifty per cent.," said he; "you are an old knave." "Knave! I should like to hear any one call me knave at Bagdad." "Well, knave or not, you may get out of this scrape." "How?" "Why you are a respectable-looking man," said he, "and are a good Moslem into the bargain, I warrant." "That I am," said I, "although you be a Jew: but how the faith is to serve me here I am sure I don't know, unless the angel Gabriel, as in the fifty-fifth verse of the twenty-seventh chapter of the Koran ——"'

'Tush, tush!' exclaimed Hassan; 'to the point.'

'I always am at the point, only you put me out. However, to make it as short as possible, the captain knows all about your coming, and is frightened out of his wits, although he did talk big; I could easily see that. And he let me go, you see, with some of my slaves, and gave me an order for five thousand dirhems on one Bostenay, of Hamadan, (perhaps you know him; is he a good man?) on condition that I would fall in with you, and, Mohammed forgive me, tell you a lie!'

'A lie!'

'Yes, a lie; but these Jewish dogs do not understand what a truly religious man is, and when I began to tell the lie, I was soon put out. Now, noble Hassan, if a promise to a Jew be not binding on a true believer, and you will see me straight with the five thousand dirhems, I will betray everything at once.'

'Be easy about the five thousand dirhems, good man, and tell me all.'

'You will see me paid?'

'My honour upon it.'

''Tis well! Know then, the infamous dogs are very weak, and terrified at the news of your progress: one, whom I think they call Jabaster, has departed with the great majority of the people into the interior of the desert, about seven hundred strong. I heard so; but mind, I do not know it. The young man, whom you call Alroy, being wounded in a recent conflict, could not depart with them, but remains among the ruins with some female prisoners, some treasure, and about a hundred companions hidden in sepulchres. He gave me my freedom on condition that I should fall in with you, and assure you that the dogs, full five thousand strong, had given you the go-by in the night, and marched towards Hamadan. They wanted me to frighten you; it was a lie, and I could not tell it. And now you know the plain truth; and if it be a sin to break faith with an infidel, you are responsible for it, as well as for the five thousand dirhems, which, by the bye, ought to have been ten.'

'Where is your order?'

''Tis here,' said the merchant, drawing it from his vest, 'a very business-like document, drawn upon one Bostenay, whom they described as very rich, and who is here enjoined to pay me five thousand dirhems, if, in consequence of my information, Hassan Subah, that is yourself, return forthwith to Hamadan without attacking them.'

'Old Bostenay's head shall answer for this.'

'I am glad of it. But were I you, I would make him pay me first.'

'Merchant,' said Hassan, 'have you any objection to pay another visit to your friend Alroy?'

'Allah forbid!'

'In my company?'

'That makes a difference.'

'Be our guide. The dirhems shall be doubled.'

'That will make up for the fifty per cent. I hardly like it; but in your company that makes a difference. Lose no time. If you push on, Alroy must be captured. Now or never! The Jewish dogs, to rifle a true believer!'

'Oglu,' said Hassan to one of his officers. 'To horse! You need not strike the tents. Can we reach the city by sunset, merchant?'

'An hour before, if you be off at once.'

'Sound the drums. To horse! to horse!'

## CHAPTER VI.

THE Seljuks halted before the walls of the deserted city. Their commander ordered a detachment to enter and reconnoitre. They returned and reported its apparent desolation. Hassan Subah, then directing that a guard should surround the walls to prevent any of the enemy from escaping, passed with his warriors through the vast portal into the silent street.

The still magnificence of the strange and splendid scene influenced the temper even of this ferocious cavalry. They gazed around them with awe and admiration. The fierceness of their visages was softened, the ardour of their impulse stilled. A supernatural feeling of repose stole over their senses. No one brandished his scimetar, the fiery courser seemed as subdued as his lord, and no sound was heard but the melancholy, mechanical tramp of the disciplined march, unrelieved by martial music, inviolate by oath or jest, and unbroken even by the ostentatious caracoling of any showy steed.

It was sunset; the star of eve glittered over the white
Ionian fane that rose serene and delicate in the flashing and
purple sky.

'This way, my lord!' said the merchant guide, turning
round to Hassan Subah, who, surrounded by his officers,
led the van. The whole of the great way of the city was
filled with the Seljukian warriors. Their ebon steeds, their
snowy turbans, adorned with plumes of the black eagle and
the red heron, their dazzling shawls, the blaze of their
armour in the sunset, and the long undulating perspective
of beautiful forms and brilliant colours, this regiment of
heroes in a street of palaces. War had seldom afforded a
more imposing or more picturesque spectacle.

'This way, my lord!' said the merchant, pointing to the
narrow turning that, at the foot of the temple, led through
ruined streets to the amphitheatre.

'Halt!' exclaimed a wild shrill voice. Each warrior
suddenly arrested his horse.

'Who spoke?' exclaimed Hassan Subah.

'I!' answered a voice. A female form stood in the portico of the temple, with uplifted arms.

'And who art thou?' enquired Hassan Subah, not a little
disconcerted.

'Thine evil genius, Seljuk!'

Hassan Subah, pale as his ivory battle-axe, did not answer; every man within hearing shuddered; still the dread
woman remained immovable within the porch of the
temple.

'Woman, witch, or goddess,' at length exclaimed Hassan
Subah, 'what wouldst thou here?'

'Seljuk! behold this star. 'Tis a single drop of light,
yet who even of thy wild band can look upon it without
awe? And yet thou worse than Sisera, thou comest to
combat against those, for whom even "the stars in their
courses fought."'

'A Jewish witch!' exclaimed the Seljuk.

'A Jewish witch! Be it so; behold, then, my spell falls
upon thee, and that spell is Destruction.

'Awake, awake, Deborah: awake, awake, utter a song; arise Barak, and lead thy captivity captive, thou son of Abinoam!'

Immediately the sky appeared to darken, a cloud of arrows and javelins broke from all sides upon the devoted Seljuks: immense masses of stone and marble were hurled from all directions, horses were stabbed by spears impelled by invisible hands, and riders fell to the ground without a struggle, and were trampled upon by their disordered and affrighted brethren.

'We are betrayed,' exclaimed Hassan Subah, hurling a javelin at the merchant, but the merchant was gone. The Seljuks raised their famous war cry.

'Oglu, regain the desert,' ordered the chieftain.

But no sooner had the guard without the walls heard the war cry of their companions, than, alarmed, for their safety, they rushed to their assistance. The retreating forces of Subah, each instant diminishing as they retreated, were baffled in their project by the very eagerness of their auxiliaries. The unwilling contention of the two parties increased the confusion; and when the Seljuks, recently arrived, having at length formed into some order, had regained the gate, they found to their dismay that the portal was barricadoed and garrisoned by the enemy. Uninspired by the presence of their commander, who was in the rear, the puzzled soldiers were seized with a panic, and spurring their horses, dispersed in all directions of the city. In vain Hassan Subah endeavoured to restore order. The moment was past. Dashing with about thirty men to an open ground, which his quick eye had observed in his progress down the street, and dealing destruction with every blow, the dreaded Governor of Hamadan, like a true soldier, awaited an inevitable fate, not wholly despairing that some chance might yet turn up to extricate him from his forlorn situation.

And now, as it were by enchantment, wild armed men seemed to arise from every part of the city. From every mass of ruin, from every crumbling temple and mouldering mansion, from every catacomb and cellar, from behind every column and every obelisk, upstarted some desperate warrior with a bloody weapon. The massacre of the Seljuks was universal. The horsemen dashed wildly about the ruined streets, pursued by crowds of footmen; sometimes, formed in small companies, the Seljuks charged and fought desperately; but, however stout might be their resistance to the open foe, it was impossible to withstand their secret enemies. They had no place of refuge, no power of gaining even a moment's breathing time. If they retreated to a wall it instantly bristled with spears; if they endeavoured to form in a court, they sank under the falling masses which were showered upon them. Strange shouts of denunciation blended with the harsh braying of horns, and the clang and clash of cymbals and tambours sounded in every quarter of the city.

'If we could only mount the walls, Ibrahim, and leap into the desert!' exclaimed Hassan Subah to one of his few remaining comrades; ''tis our only chance. We die here like dogs! Could I but meet Alroy!'

Three of the Seljuks dashed swiftly across the open ground in front, followed by several Hebrew horsemen.

'Smite all, Abner. Spare none, remember Amalek,' exclaimed their youthful leader, waving his bloody scimetar.

'They are down; one, two, there goes the third. My javelin has done for him.'

'Your horse bleeds freely. Where's Jabaster?'

'At the gates; my arm aches with slaughter. The Lord hath delivered them into our hands. Could I but meet their chieftain!'

'Turn, bloodhound, he is here,' exclaimed Hassan Subah.

'Away, Abner, this affair is mine.'

'Prince, you have already slain your thousands.'

'And Abner his tens of thousands. Is it so? This business is for me only. Come on, Turk.'

'Art thou Alroy?'

'The same.'

'The slayer of Alschiroch?'

'Even so.'

'A rebel and a murderer.'

'What you please. Look to yourself.'

The Hebrew Prince flung a javelin at the Seljuk. It glanced from the breastplate; but Hassan Subah staggered in his seat. Recovering, he charged Alroy with great force. Their scimetars crossed, and the blade of Hassan shivered.

'He who sold me that blade told me it was charmed, and could be broken only by a caliph,' said Hassan Subah. 'He was a liar.'

'As it may be,' said Alroy, and he cut the Seljuk to the ground. Abner had dispersed his comrades. Alroy leaped from his fainting steed, and, mounting the ebon courser of his late enemy, dashed again into the thickest of the fight.

The shades of night descended, the clamour gradually decreased, the struggle died away. A few unhappy Moslemin who had quitted their saddles and sought concealment among the ruins, were occasionally hunted out, and brought forward and massacred. Long ere midnight the last of the Seljuks had expired.[56]

The moon shed a broad light upon the street of palaces crowded with the accumulated slain and the living victors. Fires were lit, torches illumined, the conquerors prepared the eager meal as they sang hymns of praise and thanksgiving.

A procession approached. Esther the prophetess, clashing her cymbals, danced before the Messiah of Israel, who leant upon his victorious scimetar, surrounded by Jabaster, Abner, Scherirah, and his chosen chieftains. Who could now doubt the validity of his mission? The wide and silent desert rang with the acclamations of his enthusiastic votaries.

## CHAPTER VII.

HEAVILY the anxious hours crept on in the Jewish quarter of Hamadan. Again and again the venerable Bostenay discussed the chances of success with the sympathising but desponding elders. Miriam was buried in constant prayer. Their most sanguine hopes did not extend beyond the escape of their Prince.

A fortnight had elapsed, and no news had been received of the progress of the expedition, when suddenly, towards sunset, a sentinel on a watch-tower announced the appearance of an armed force in the distance. The walls were instantly lined with the anxious inhabitants, the streets and squares filled with curious crowds. Exultation sat on the triumphant brow of the Moslemin; a cold tremor stole over the fluttering heart of the Hebrew.

'There is but one God,' said the captain of the gate.

'And Mohammed is His prophet,' responded a sentinel.

'To-morrow we will cut off the noses of all these Jewish dogs.'

'The sceptre has departed,' exclaimed the despairing Bostenay.

'Lord remember David!' whispered Miriam, as she threw herself upon the court of the palace, and buried her face in ashes.

The Mollahs in solemn procession advanced to the ramparts, to shed their benediction on the victorious Hassan Subah. The Muezzin ascended the minarets to watch the setting sun, and proclaim the power of Allah with renewed enthusiasm.

'I wonder if Alroy be dead or alive,' said the captain of the gate.

'If he be alive, he will be impaled,' responded a sentinel.

'If dead, the carcass will be given to the dogs,' rejoined the captain; 'that is the practice.'

'Bostenay will be hung,' said the sentinel.

'And his niece, too,' answered the captain.

'Hem!' said the sentinel. 'Hassan Subah loves a black eye.'

'I hope a true Moslem will not touch a Jewess,' exclaimed an indignant black eunuch.

'They approach. What a dust!' said the captain of the gate.

'I see Hassan Subah!' said the sentinel.

'So do I,' said the eunuch, 'I know his black horse.'

'I wonder how many dirhems old Bostenay is worth,' said the captain.

'Immense!' said the sentinel.

'No plunder, I suppose?' said the eunuch.

'We shall see,' said the captain; 'at any rate, I owe a thousand to old Shelomi. We need not pay now, you know.'

'Certainly not,' said the black eunuch. 'The rebels!'

A body of horsemen dashed forward. Their leader in advance reined in his fiery charger beneath the walls.

'In the name of the Prophet, who is that?' exclaimed the captain of the gate, a little confused.

'I never saw him before,' said the sentinel, 'although he is in the Seljuk dress. 'Tis some one from Bagdad, I guess.'

A trumpet sounded.

'Who keeps the gate?' called out the warrior.

'I am the captain of the gate,' answered our friend.

'Open it, then, to the King of Israel.'

'To whom?' enquired the astonished captain.

'To King David. The Lord hath delivered Hassan Subah and his host into our hands, and of all the proud Seljuks none remaineth. Open thy gates, I say, and lose no time. I am Jabaster, a lieutenant of the Lord; this scimetar is my commission. Open thy gates, and thou and thy people shall have that mercy which they have never shown; but if thou delayest one instant, thus saith the King our master, "I will burst open your portal, and smite, and utterly destroy all that you have, and spare them not; but slay both man and woman, infant and suckling, ox and sheep, camel and ass." '

'Call forth the venerable Lord Bostenay,' said the captain of the gate, with chattering teeth. 'He will intercede for us.'

'And the gentle Lady Miriam,' said the sentinel. 'She is ever charitable.'

'I will head the procession,' said the black eunuch; 'I am accustomed to women.'

The procession of Mollahs shuffled back to their college with profane precipitation; the sun set, and the astounded Muezzin stood with their mouths open, and quite forgot to announce the power of their Deity, and the validity of their Prophet. The people all called out for the venerable Lord Bostenay and the gentle Lady Miriam, and ran in crowds to see who could first kiss the hem of their garments.

The principal gate of Hamadan opened into the square of the great mosque. Here the whole population of the city appeared assembled. The gates were thrown open; Jabaster and his companions mounted guard. The short twilight died away, the shades of night descended. The minarets were illumined,[57] the houses hung with garlands, the ramparts covered with tapestry and carpets.

A clang of drums, trumpets, and cymbals announced the arrival of the Hebrew army. The people shouted, the troops without responded with a long cheer of triumph. Amid the blaze of torches, a youth waving his scimetar, upon a coal-black steed, bounded into the city, at the head of his guards, the people fell upon their knees, and shouted 'Long live Alroy!'

A venerable man, leading a beauteous maiden with downcast eyes, advanced. They headed a deputation of the chief inhabitants of the city. They came to solicit mercy and protection. At the sight of them, the youthful warrior leaped from his horse, flung away his scimetar, and clasping the maiden in his arms, exclaimed, 'Miriam, my sister, this, this indeed is triumph!'

## CHAPTER VIII.

'Drink,' said Kisloch the Kourd to Calidas the Indian; 'you forget, comrade, we are no longer Moslemin.'

'Wine, methinks, has a peculiarly pleasant flavour in a golden cup,' said the Guebre. 'I got this little trifle to-day in the Bazaar,' he added, holding up a magnificent vase studded with gems.

'I thought plunder was forbidden,' grinned the Negro.

'So it is,' replied the Guebre; 'but we may purchase what we please, upon credit.'

'Well, for my part, I am a moderate man,' exclaimed Calidas the Indian, 'and would not injure even these accursed dogs of Turks. I have not cut my host's throat, but only turned him into my porter, and content myself with his harem, his baths, his fine horses, and other little trifles.'

'What quarters we are in! There is nothing like a true Messiah!' exclaimed Kisloch, devoutly.

'Nothing,' said Calidas; 'though to speak truth, I did not much believe in the efficacy of Solomon's sceptre, till his Majesty clove the head of the valliant Seljuk with it.'

'But now there's no doubt of it,' said the Guebre.

'We should indeed be infidels if we doubted now,' replied the Indian.

'How lucky,' grinned the Negro, 'as I had no religion before, that I have now fixed upon the right one!'

'Most fortunate!' said the Guebre. 'What shall we do to amuse ourselves to-night?'

'Let us go to the coffee-houses and make the Turks drink wine,' said Calidas the Indian.

'What say you to burning down a mosque?' said Kisloch the Kourd.

'I had great fun with some Dervishes this morning,' said the Guebre. 'I met one asking alms with a wire run through his cheek,[58] so I caught another, bored his nose, and tied them both together!'

'Hah! hah! hah!' burst the Negro.

## CHAPTER IX.

ASIA resounded with the insurrection of the Jews and the massacre of the Seljuks. Crowds of Hebrews, from the rich cities of Persia and the populous settlements on the Tigris and the Euphrates, hourly poured into Hamadan.

The irritated Moslemin persecuted the brethren of the successful rebel, and this impolicy precipitated their flight. The wealth of Bagdad flowed into the Hebrew capital. Seated on the divan of Hassan Subah, and wielding the sceptre of Solomon, the King of Israel received the homage of his devoted subjects, and despatched his envoys to Syria and to Egypt. The well-stored magazines and arsenals of Hamadan soon converted the pilgrims into warriors. The city was unable to accommodate the increased and increasing population. An extensive camp, under the command of Abner, was formed without the walls, where the troops were daily disciplined, and where they were prepared for greater exploits than a skirmish in a desert.

Within a month after the surrender of Hamadan, the congregation of the people assembled in the square of the great mosque, now converted into a synagogue. The multitude was disposed in ordered ranks, and the terrace of every house was crowded. In the centre of the square was an altar of cedar and brass, and on each side stood a company of priests guarding the victims, one young bullock, and two rams without blemish.

Amid the flourish of trumpets, the gates of the synagogue opened, and displayed to the wondering eyes of the Hebrews a vast and variegated pavilion planted in the court. The holy remnant, no longer forlorn, beheld that tabernacle of which they had so long dreamed, once more shining in the sun, with its purple and scarlet hangings, its curtains of rare skins, and its furniture of silver and gold.

A procession of priests advanced, bearing, with staves of cedar, run through rings of gold, a gorgeous ark, the work of the most cunning artificers of Persia. Night and day had they laboured, under the direction of Jabaster, to produce this wondrous spectacle. Once more the children of Israel beheld the cherubim. They burst into a triumphant hymn of thanksgiving, and many drew their swords, and cried aloud to be led against the Canaanites.

From the mysterious curtains of the tabernacle, Alroy came forward, leading Jabaster. They approached the altar. And Alroy took robes from the surrounding priests, and put them upon Jabaster, and a girdle, and a breast-plate of jewels. And Alroy took a mitre, and placed it upon the head of Jabaster, and upon the mitre he placed a crown; and, pouring oil upon his head, the pupil anointed the master High Priest of Israel.

The victims were slain, the sin-offering burnt. Amid clouds of incense, bursts of music, and the shouts of a devoted people; amid odour, and melody, and enthusiasm; Alroy mounted his charger, and at the head of twenty thousand men, departed to conquer Media.

## CHAPTER X.

The extensive and important province of Aderbijan, of which Hamadan was the capital, was formed of the ancient Media. Its fate was decided by one battle. On the plain of Nehauend, Alroy met the hastily-raised levies of the Atabek of Kermanshah, and entirely routed them. In the course of a month, every city of the province had acknowledged the supremacy of the new Hebrew monarch, and, leaving Abner to complete the conquest of Louristan, Alroy entered Persia.

The incredible and irresistible progress of Alroy roused Togrul, the Turkish Sultan of Persia, from the luxurious indolence of the palaces of Nishabur. He summoned his emirs to meet him at the imperial city of Rhey, and crush, by one overwhelming effort, the insolent rebel.

Religion, valour, and genius, alike inspired the arms of Alroy, but he was, doubtless, not a little assisted by the strong national sympathy of his singular and scattered people, which ever ensured him prompt information of all the movements of his enemy. Without any preparation, he found agents in every court, and camp, and cabinet; and, by their assistance, he anticipated the designs of his adversaries, and turned even their ingenuity to their confusion. The imperial city of Rhey was surprised in the night, sacked, and burnt to the ground. The scared and baffled emirs who escaped, flew to the Sultan Togrul, tearing their beards, and prophesying the approaching termination of the world. The palaces of Nishabur resounded with the imprecations of their master, who, cursing the Jewish dogs, and vowing a pilgrimage to Mecca, placed himself at the head of a motley multitude of warriors, and rushed upon the plains of Irak, to exterminate Alroy.

The Persian force exceeded the Hebrew at least five times in number. Besides a large division of Seljuks, the Caucasus had poured forth its strange inhabitants to swell the ranks of the Faithful. The wild tribes of the Bactiari were even enlisted, with their fatal bows, and the savage Turkmans, tempted by the sultan's gold, for a moment yielded their liberty, and shook their tall lances in his ranks.

But what is a wild Bactiari, and what is a savage Turkman, and what even a disciplined and imperious Seljuk, to the warriors of the God of Abraham, of Isaac, and of Jacob? At the first onset, Alroy succeeded in dividing the extended centre of Togrul, and separating the greater part of the Turks from their less disciplined comrades. At the head of his Median cavalry, the Messiah charged and utterly routed the warriors of the Caucasus. The wild tribes of the Bactiari discharged their arrows and fled, and the savage Turkmans plundered the baggage of their own commander.

The Turks themselves fought desperately; but, deserted by their allies, and surrounded by an inspired foe, their efforts were unavailing, and their slaughter terrible. Togrul was slain while heading a desperate and fruitless charge, and, after his fall, the battle resembled a massacre rather than a combat. The plain was glotted with Seljuk gore. No quarter was given or asked. Twenty thousand chosen troops fell on the side of the Turks; the rest dispersed and gained the mountains. Leaving Scherirah to restore order, Alroy the next morning pushed on to Nishabur at the head of three thousand horsemen, and summoned the city ere the inhabitants were apprised of the defeat and death of their sultan. The capital of Persia escaped the fate of Rhey by an inglorious treaty and a lavish tribute. The treasures of the Chosroes and the Gasnevides were despatched to Hamadan, on which city day dawned, only to bring intelligence of a victory or a conquest.

While Alroy dictated peace on his own terms in the palaces of Nishabur, Abner, having reduced Louristan, crossed the mountains, and entered Persia with the reinforcements he had received from Jabaster. Leaving the government and garrisoning of his new conquests to this valiant captain, Alroy, at the head of the conquerors of Persia, in consequence of intelligence received from Hamadan, returned by forced marches to that city.

## CHAPTER XI.

LEAVING the army within a day's march of the capital, Alroy, accompanied only by his staff, entered Hamadan in the evening, and, immediately repairing to the citadel, summoned Jabaster to council. The night was passed by the king and the high priest in deep consultation. The next morning, a decree apprised the inhabitants of the return of their monarch, of the creation of the new 'Kingdom of the Medes and Persians,' of which Hamadan was declared the capital, and Abner the viceroy, and of the intended and immediate invasion of Syria, and re-conquest of the Land of Promise.

The plan of this expedition had been long matured, and the preparations to effect it were considerably advanced. Jabaster had not been idle during the absence of his pupil. One hundred thousand warriors were now assembled[59] at the capital of the kingdom of the Medes and Persians; of these the greater part were Hebrews, but many Arabs, wearied of the Turkish yoke, and many gallant adventurers from the Caspian, easily converted from a vague idolatry to a religion of conquest, swelled the ranks of the army of the Lord of Hosts.

The plain of Hamadan was covered with tents, the streets were filled with passing troops, the bazaars loaded with military stores; long caravans of camels laden with supplies every day arrived from the neighbouring towns; each instant some high-capped Tartar with despatches[60] rushed into the city and galloped his steed up the steep of the citadel. The clang of arms, the prance of horses, the flourish of warlike music, resounded from all quarters. The business and the treasure of the world seemed, as it were in an instant, to have become concentrated in Hamadan. Every man had some great object; gold glittered in every hand. All great impulses were stirring; all the causes of human energy were in lively action. Every eye sparkled, every foot trod firm and fast. Each man acted as if the universal fate depended upon his exertions; as if the universal will sympathised with his particular desire. A vast population influenced by a high degree of excitement is the most sublime of spectacles.

The commander of the Faithful raised the standard of the Prophet on the banks of the Tigris. It was the secret intelligence of this intended event that had recalled Alroy so suddenly from Persia. The latent enthusiasm of the

Moslemin was excited by the rare and mystic ceremony, and its effects were anticipated by previous and judicious preparations. The Seljuks of Bagdad alone amounted to fifty thousand men; the Sultan of Syria contributed the warriors who had conquered the Arabian princes of Damascus and Aleppo; while the ancient provinces of Asia Minor, which formed the rich and powerful kingdom of Seljukian Roum, poured forth a myriad of that matchless cavalry, which had so often baffled the armies of the Cæsars. Never had so imposing a force been collected on the banks of the Tigris since the reign of Haroun Alraschid. Each day some warlike Atabek, at the head of his armed train, poured into the capital of the caliphs,[61] or pitched his pavilion on the banks of the river; each day the proud emir of some remote principality astonished or affrighted the luxurious Babylonians by the strange or uncouth warriors that had gathered round his standard in the deserts of Arabia, or on the shores of the Euxine. For the space of twenty miles, the banks of the river were, on either side, far as the eye could reach, covered with the variegated pavilions, the glittering standards, the flowing streamers and twinkling pennons of the mighty host, of which Malek, the Grand Sultan of the Seljuks, and Governor of the Caliph's palace, was chief commander.

Such was the power assembled on the plains of Asia to arrest the progress of the Hebrew Prince, and to prevent the conquest of the memorable land promised to the faith of his fathers, and forfeited by their infidelity. Before the walls of Hamadan, Alroy reviewed the army of Israel, sixty thousand heavy-armed footmen, thirty thousand archers and light troops, and twenty thousand cavalry. Besides these, there had been formed a body of ten thousand picked horsemen, styled the 'Sacred Guard,' all of whom had served in the Persian campaign. In their centre, shrouded in a case of wrought gold, studded with carbuncles, and carried on a lusty lance of cedar, a giant, for the height of Elnebar exceeded that of common men by three feet, bore the sceptre of Solomon. The

Sacred Guard was commanded by Asriel, the brother of Abner.

The army was formed into three divisions. All marched in solemn order before the throne of Alroy, raised upon the ramparts, and drooped their standards and lances as they passed their heroic leader. Bostenay, and Miriam, and the whole population of the city witnessed the inspiring spectacle from the walls. That same eve, Scherirah, at the head of forty thousand men, pushed on towards Bagdad, by Kermanshah; and Jabaster, who commanded in his holy robes, and who had vowed not to lay aside his sword until the rebuilding of the temple, conducted his division over the victorious plain of Nehauend. They were to concentrate at the pass of Kerrund, which conducted into the province of Bagdad, and await the arrival of the king.

At the dawn of day, the royal division and the Sacred Guard, the whole under the command of Asriel, quitted the capital. Alroy still lingered, and for some hours the warriors of his staff might have been observed lounging about the citadel, or practising their skill in throwing the jerreed as they exercised their impatient chargers before the gates.

The king was with the lady Miriam, walking in the garden of their uncle. One arm was wound round her delicate waist, and with the other he clasped her soft and graceful hand. The heavy tears burst from her downcast eyes, and stole along her pale and pensive cheek. They walked in silence, the brother and the sister, before the purity of whose surpassing love even ambition vanished. He opened the lattice gate. They entered into the valley small and green; before them was the marble fountain with its columns and cupola, and in the distance the charger of Alroy and his single attendant.

They stopped, and Alroy gathered flowers, and placed them in the hair of Miriam. He would have softened the bitterness of parting with a smile. Gently he relaxed his embracing arm, almost insensibly he dropped her quivering hand.

'Sister of my soul,' he whispered, 'when we last parted here, I was a fugitive, and now I quit you a conqueror.'

She turned, she threw herself upon his neck, and buried her face in his breast.

'My Miriam, we shall meet at Bagdad.'

He beckoned to her distant maidens; they advanced, he delivered Miriam into their arms. He pressed her hand to his lips, and, rushing to his horse, mounted and disappeared.

## CHAPTER XII.

A BODY of irregular cavalry feebly defended the pass of Kerrund. It was carried, with slight loss, by the vanguard of Scherirah, and the fugitives prepared the host of the caliph for the approach of the Hebrew army.

Upon the plain of the Tigris the enemy formed into battle array. The centre was commanded by Malek, the Grand Sultan of the Seljuks himself, the right wing, headed by the Sultan of Syria, was protected by the river; and the left, under the Sultan of Roum, was posted upon the advantageous position of some irregular and rising ground. Thus proud in the number, valour, discipline, and disposition of his forces, Malek awaited the conqueror of Persia.

The glittering columns of the Hebrews might even now be perceived defiling from the mountains, and forming at the extremity of the plain. Before nightfall the camp of the invaders was pitched within hearing of that of Malek. The moving lights in the respective tents might plainly be distinguished; and ever and anon the flourish of hostile music fell with an ominous sound upon the ears of the opposed foemen. A few miles only separated those mighty hosts. Upon to-morrow depended, perhaps, the fortunes of ages. How awful is the eve of battle!

Alroy, attended by a few chieftains, personally visited the tents of the soldiery, promising them on the morrow a triumph, before which the victories of Nehauend and Nishabur would sink into insignificance. Their fiery and excited visages proved at once their courage and their faith. The sceptre of Solomon was paraded throughout the camp in solemn procession. On the summit of a huge tumulus, perhaps the sepulchre of some classic hero, Esther, the prophetess, surrounded by the chief zealots of the host, poured forth her exciting inspirations. It was a grand picture, that beautiful wild girl, the groups of stern devoted warriors, the red flame of the watch-fires mixing with the silver shadows of the moon as they illumined the variegated turbans and gleaming armour of her votaries!

In the pavilion of Alroy, Jabaster consulted with his pupil on the conduct of the morrow.

'This is a different scene from the cavern of the Caucasus,' said Alroy, as the high priest rose to retire.

'It has one great resemblance, sire; the God of our fathers is with us.'

'Ay! the Lord of Hosts. Moses was a great man. There is no career except conquest.'

'You muse.'

'Of the past. The present is prepared. Too much thought will mar it.'

'The past is for wisdom, the present for action, but for joy the future. The feeling that the building of the temple is at hand, that the Lord's anointed will once again live in the house of David, absorbs my spirit; and, when I muse over our coming glory, in my fond ecstacy I almost lose the gravity that doth beseem my sacred office.'

'Jerusalem; I have seen it. How many hours to dawn?'

'Some three.'

'' Tis strange I could sleep. I remember, on the eve of battle I was ever anxious. How is this, Jabaster?'

'Your faith, sire, is profound.'

'Yes, I have no fear. My destiny is not complete. Good night, Jabaster. See, Asriel, valiant priest. Pharez!'

'My lord!'

'Rouse me at the second watch. Good night, boy.'

'Good night, my lord.'

'Pharez! Be sure you rouse me at the second watch. Think you it wants three hours to dawn?'

'About three hours, my lord.'

'Well! at the second watch, remember; good night.'

## CHAPTER XIII.

'It is the second watch, my lord.'

'So soon! Have I slept? I feel fresh as an eagle. Call Scherirah, boy.'

' 'Tis strange I never dream now. Before my flight my sleep was ever troubled. Say what they like, man is made for action. My life is now harmonious, and sleep has now become what nature willed it, a solace, not a contest. Before, it was a struggle of dark passions and bright dreams, in whose creative fancy and fair vision my soul sought refuge from the dreary bale of daily reality.

'I will withdraw the curtains of my tent. O most majestic vision! And have I raised this host! Over the wide plain, far as my eye can range, their snowy tents studding the purple landscape, embattled legions gather round their flags to struggle for my fate. It is the agony of Asia.

'A year ago, upon this very spot, I laid me down to die, an unknown thing, or known and recognised only to be despised, and now the sultans of the world come forth to meet me. I have no fear. My destiny is not complete. And whither tends it? Let that power decide which hitherto has fashioned all my course.

'Jerusalem, Jerusalem! ever harping on Jerusalem. With all his lore, he is a narrow-minded zealot whose dreaming memory would fondly make a future like the past. O Bagdad, Bagdad, within thy glittering halls, there is a charm worth all his Cabala!

'Hah! Scherirah! The dawn is near at hand; the

stars still shining. The air is very pleasant. To-morrow will be a great day, Scherirah, for Israel and for you. You lead the attack. A moment in my tent, my brave Scherirah!'

## CHAPTER XIV.

The dawn broke; a strong column of the Hebrews, commanded by Scherirah, poured down upon the centre of the army of the caliph. Another column, commanded by Jabaster, attacked the left wing, headed by the Sultan of Roum. No sooner had Alroy perceived that the onset of Scherirah had succeeded in penetrating the centre of the Turks, than he placed himself at the head of the Sacred Guard, and by an irresistible charge completed their disorder and confusion. The division of the Sultan of Syria, and a great part of the centre, were entirely routed and driven into the river, and the remainder of the division of Malek was effectually separated from his left wing.

But while to Alroy the victory seemed already decided, a far different fate awaited the division of Jabaster. The Sultan of Roum, posted in an extremely advantageous position, and commanding troops accustomed to the discipline of the Romans of Constantinople, received the onset of Jabaster without yielding, and not only repelled his attack, but finally made a charge which completely disordered and dispersed the column of the Hebrews. In vain Jabaster endeavoured to rally his troops, in vain he performed prodigies of valour, in vain he himself struck down the standard-bearer of the sultan, and once even penetrated to the pavilion of the monarch. His division was fairly routed. The eagerness of the Sultan of Roum to effect the annihilation of his antagonists prevented him from observing the forlorn condition of the Turkish centre. Had he, after routing the division of Jabaster, only attacked Alroy in the rear, the fortune of the day might have been widely different. As it was, the eagle eye of Alroy soon detected his inadvertence, and profited by his indiscretion. Leaving Ithamar to keep the centre in check, he charged the Sultan of Roum with the Sacred Guard, and afforded Jabaster an opportunity of rallying some part of his forces. The Sultan of Roum perceiving that the day was lost by the ill-conduct of his colleagues, withdrew his troops, retreated in haste, but in good order to Bagdad, carried off the caliph, his harem, and some of his treasure, and effected his escape into Syria. In the meantime the discomfiture of the remaining Turkish army was complete. The Tigris was dyed with their blood, and the towns through which the river flowed were apprised of the triumph of Alroy by the floating corpses of his enemies. Thirty thousand Turks were slain in battle: among them the Sultans of Bagdad and Syria, and a vast number of atabeks, emirs, and chieftains. A whole division, finding themselves surrounded, surrendered on terms, and delivered up their arms. The camps and treasures of the three sultans were alike captured, and the troops that escaped so completely dispersed, that they did not attempt to rally, but, disbanded and desperate, prowled over and plundered the adjoining provinces. The loss of the division of Jabaster was also severe, but the rest of the army suffered little. Alroy himself was slightly wounded. The battle lasted barely three hours. Its results were immense. David Alroy was now master of the East.

## CHAPTER XV.

THE plain was covered with the corpses of men and horses, arms and standards, and prostrate tents. Returning from the pursuit of the Sultan of Roum, Alroy ordered the trumpets to sound to arms, and, covered with gore and dust, dismounted from his charger, and stood before the pavilion of Malek, leaning on his bloody scimetar, and surrounded by his victorious generals.

'Ah, Jabaster!' said the conqueror, giving his hand to the

pontiff, ''twas well your troops had such a leader. No one but you could have rallied them. You must drill your lads a little before they again meet the Cappadocian cavalry. Brave Scherirah, we shall not forget our charge. Asriel, tell the guard, from me, that the victory of the Tigris was owing to their scimetars. Ithamar, what are our freshest troops?'

'The legion of Aderbijan, sire.'

'How strong can they muster?'

'It counts twelve thousand men: we might collect two-thirds.'

'Valiant Ithamar, take the Aderbijans and a division of the guards, push on towards Bagdad, and summon the city. If his sultanship of Roum offer battle, take up a position, and he shall quickly have his desire. For the present, after these hasty marches and sharp fighting, the troops must rest. I guess he will not tarry. Summon the city, and say that if any resistance be offered, I will make it as desolate as old Babylon. Treat with no armed force. Where is the soldier that saved me a cracked skull; his name Benaiah?'

'I wait your bidding, sire.'

'You're a captain. Join the division of Ithamar, and win fresh laurels ere we meet again. Gentle Asriel, let your brother know our fortune.'

'Sire, several Tartars have already been despatched to Hamadan.'

''Tis well. Send another with these tablets to the Lady Miriam. Despatch the pavilion of Malek as a trophy for the town. Elnebar, Goliath of the Hebrews, you bore our sacred standard like a hero! How fares the prophetess? I saw her charging in our ranks, waving a sabre with her snowy arm, her long, dark hair streaming like a storm, from which her eyes flashed lightning.'

'The king bleeds,' said Jabaster.

'Slightly. It will do me service. I am somewhat feverish. A kingdom for a draught of water! And now for our wounded friends. Asriel, do you marshal the camp. It is the Sabbath eve.[62] Time presses.'

K

## CHAPTER XVI.

The dead were plundered, and thrown into the river, the encampment of the Hebrews completed. Alroy, with his principal officers, visited the wounded, and praised the valiant. The bustle which always succeeds a victory was increased in the present instance by the anxiety of the army to observe with grateful strictness the impending Sabbath.

When the sun set, the Sabbath was to commence. The undulating horizon rendered it difficult to ascertain the precise moment of his fall. The crimson orb sunk behind the purple mountains, the sky was flushed with a rich and rosy glow. Then might be perceived the zealots, proud in their Talmudical lore, holding a skein of white silk in their hands, and announcing the approach of the Sabbath by their observation of its shifting tints. While the skein was yet golden, the forge of the armourer still sounded, the fire of the cook still blazed, still the cavalry led their steeds to the river, and still the busy footmen braced up their tents, and hammered at their palisades. The skein of silk became rosy, the armourer worked with renewed energy, the cook puffed with increased zeal, the horsemen scampered from the river, the footmen cast an anxious glance at the fading twilight.

The skein of silk became blue; a dim, dull, sepulchral, leaden tinge fell over its purity. The hum of gnats arose, the bat flew in circling whirls over the tents, horns sounded from all quarters, the sun had set, the Sabbath had commenced. The forge was mute, the fire extinguished, the prance of horses and the bustle of men in a moment ceased. A deep, a sudden, an all-pervading stillness dropped over that mighty host. It was night; the sacred lamp of the Sabbath sparkled in every tent of the camp, which vied in silence and in brilliancy with the mute and glowing heavens.

Morn came; the warriors assembled around the altar and the sacrifice. The high priest and his attendant Levites

proclaimed the unity and the omnipotence of the God of
Israel, and the sympathetic responses of his conquering and
chosen people re-echoed over the plain. They retired again
to their tents, to listen to the expounding of the law; even
the distance of a Sabbath walk was not to exceed that space
which lies between Jerusalem and the Mount of Olives.
This was the distance between the temple and the tabernacle;
it had been nicely measured, and every Hebrew who ventured
forth from the camp this day might be observed counting
the steps of a Sabbath-day's journey. At length the sun
again set, and on a sudden fires blazed, voices sounded, men
stirred, in the same enchanted and instantaneous manner
that had characterised the stillness of the preceding eve.
Shouts of laughter, bursts of music, announced the festivity
of the coming night; supplies poured in from all the
neighbouring villages, and soon the pious conquerors com-
memorated their late triumph in a round of banqueting.

On the morrow, a Tartar arrived from Ithamar, informing
Alroy that the Sultan of Roum had retreated into Syria,
that Bagdad was undefended, but that he had acceded to
the request of the inhabitants that a deputation should wait
upon Alroy before the troops entered the city, and had
granted a safe conduct for their passage.

## CHAPTER XVII.

On the morrow, messengers announced the approach of
the deputation. All the troops were under arms. Alroy
directed that the suppliants should be conducted through
the whole camp before they arrived at the royal pavilion,
on each side of which the Sacred Guard was mustered in
array. The curtains of his tent withdrawn, displayed the
conqueror himself, seated on a sumptuous divan. On his
right hand stood Jabaster in his priestly robes, on his left
Scherirah. Behind him, the giant Elnebar supported the
sacred sceptre. A crowd of chieftains was ranged on each
side of the pavilion.

Cymbals sounded, muffled kettle-drums, and the faint flourish of trumpets; the commencement of the procession might be detected in the long perspective of the tented avenue. First came a company of beauteous youths, walking two by two, and strewing flowers, then a band of musicians in flowing robes of cloth of gold, plaintively sounding their silver trumpets. After these followed slaves of all climes, bearing a tribute of the most rare and costly productions of their countries: Negroes with tusks and teeth of the elephant, plumes of ostrich feathers, and caskets of gold dust; Syrians with rich armour; Persians with vases of atar-gul, and Indians with panniers of pearls of Ormuz, and soft shawls of Cashmere. Encircled by his children, each of whom held alternately a white or fawn-coloured gazelle, an Arab, clothed in his blue bornouz, led by a thick cord of crimson silk a tall and tawny giraffe. Fifty stout men succeeded two by two, carrying in company a silver shield laden with gold coin, or chased goblets studded with gems.

The clash of cymbals announced the presence of the robes of honour,[63] culled from the wardrobe of the commander of the Faithful; the silk of Aleppo and the brocade of Damascus, lined with the furs of the sable and the ermine, down from the breast of the swan, and the skins of white foxes.

After these followed two grey dromedaries, with furniture of silver, and many caparisoned horses, each led by a groom in rich attire. The last of these was a snow-white steed, upon whose front was the likeness of a ruby star, a courser of the sacred stud of Solomon, and crossed only by the descendants of the Prophet.

The muffled kettle-drums heralded the company of black eunuchs, with their scarlet vests and ivory battle-axes. They surrounded, and shrouded from the vulgar gaze, fourteen beautiful Circassian girls, whose brilliant visages and perfect forms were otherwise concealed by their long veils and ample drapery.

The gorgeous procession, as they approached the conqueror, bowed humbly to Alroy, and formed in order on each side of the broad avenue. The deputation appeared;

twelve of the principal citizens of Bagdad, with folded arms, and downcast eyes, and disordered raiment. Meekly and mutely each touched the earth with his hand, and kissed it in token of submission, and then, moving aside, made way for the chief envoy and orator of the company, Honain!

## CHAPTER XVIII.

HUMBLY, but gracefully, the physician of the caliph bowed before the conqueror of the East. His appearance and demeanour afforded a contrast to the aspect of his brother envoys; not less calm or contented his countenance, not less sumptuous or studied his attire, than when he first rescued Alroy in the Bazaar of Bagdad from the gripe of the false Abdallah.

He spoke, and every sound was hushed before the music of his voice.

'Conqueror of the world, that destiny with which it is in vain to struggle, has placed our lives and fortunes in your power. Your slaves offer for your approbation specimens of their riches; not as tribute, for all is yours; but to show you the products of security and peace, and to induce you to believe that mercy may be a policy as profitable to the conqueror as to the conquered; that it may be better to preserve than to destroy; and wiser to enjoy than to extirpate.

'Fate ordained that we should be born the slaves of the caliph; that same fate has delivered his sceptre into your hands. We offer you the same devotion that we yielded to him, and we entreat the same protection which he granted to us.

'Whatever may be your decision, we must bow to your decree with the humility that recognises superior force. Yet we are not without hope. We cannot forget that it is our good fortune not to be addressing a barbarous chieftain, unable to sympathise with the claims of civilisation, tho creations of art, and the finer impulses of humanity. We acknowledge your irresistible power, but we dare to hope everything from a prince whose genius all acknowledge and admire, who has spared some portion of his youth from the cares of government and the pursuits of arms to the ennobling claims of learning, whose morality has been moulded by a pure and sublime faith, and who draws his lineage from a sacred and celebrated race, the unrivalled antiquity of which even the Prophet acknowledges.'

He ceased: a buzz of approbation sounded throughout the pavilion, which was hushed instantly as the lips of the conqueror moved.

'Noble emir,' replied Alroy, 'return to Bagdad, and tell your fellow-subjects that the King of Israel grants protection to their persons, and security to their property.'

'And for their faith?' enquired the envoy, in a lower voice.

'Toleration,' replied Alroy, turning to Jabaster.

'Until further regulations,' added the high priest.

'Emir,' said Alroy, 'the person of the caliph will be respected.'

'May it please your highness,' replied Honain, 'the Sultan of Roum has retired with our late ruler.'

'And his harem?'

'And his harem.'

'It was needless. We war not with women.'

'Men, as well as women, must acknowledge the gracious mercy of your highness.'

'Benomi,' said Alroy, addressing himself to a young officer of the guard, 'command the guard of honour that will attend this noble emir on his return. We soldiers deal only in iron, sir, and cannot vie with the magnificence of Bagdad, yet wear this dagger for the donor's sake:' and Alroy held out to Honain a poniard flaming with gems.

The Envoy of Bagdad advanced, took the dagger, pressed it to his lips, and placed it in his vest.[64]

'Scherirah,' continued Alroy, 'this noble emir is your charge. See that a choice pavilion of the host be for his use, and that his train complain not of the rough customs of our camp.'

'May it please your highness,' replied Honain, 'I have fulfilled my office, and, with your gracious permission, would at once return. I have business only less urgent than the present, because it concerns myself.'

'As you will, noble emir. Benomi, to your post. Farewell, sir.'

The deputation advanced, bowed, and retired. Alroy turned to Jabaster.

'No common person that, Jabaster?'

'A very gracious Turk, sire.'

'Think you he is a Turk?'

'By his dress.'

'It may be so. Asriel, break up the camp. We'll march at once to Bagdad.'

## CHAPTER XIX.

THE chiefs dispersed to make the necessary arrangements for the march. The news that the army was immediately to advance to Bagdad soon circulated throughout the camp, and excited the most lively enthusiasm. Every hand was at work, striking the tents, preparing the arms and horses. Alroy retired to his pavilion. The curtains were drawn. He was alone, and plunged in profound meditation.

'Alroy!' a voice sounded.

He started, and looked up. Before him stood Esther the prophetess.

'Esther! is it thou?'

'Alroy! enter not into Babylon.'

'Indeed.'

'As I live, the Lord hath spoken it. Enter not into Babylon.'

'Not enjoy my fairest conquest, maiden?'

'Enter not into Babylon.'

'What affrights thee?'

'Enter not into Babylon.'

'I shall surely change the fortunes of my life without a cause!'

'The Lord hath spoken. Is not that a cause?'

'I am the Lord's anointed. His warning has not reached me.'

'Now it reaches thee. Doth the king despise the prophetess of the Lord? It is the sin of Ahab.'

'Despise thee! despise the mouth that is the herald of my victories! 'Twere rank blasphemy. Prophecy triumph, Esther, and Alroy will never doubt thy inspiration.'

'He doubts it now. I see he doubts it now. O my king, I say again, enter not into Babylon.'

'Beauteous maiden, those eyes flash lightning. Who can behold their wild and liquid glance, and doubt that Esther is inspired! Be calm, sweet girl, some dream disturbs thy fancy.'

'Alroy, Alroy, enter not into Babylon!'

'I have no fear, I bear a charmed life.'

'Ah me! he will not listen. All is lost!'

'All is gained, my beautiful.'

'I would we were upon the Holy Mount, and gazing on the stars of sacred Zion.'

'Esther,' said Alroy, advancing, and gently taking her hand, 'the capital of the East will soon unfold its marvels to thy sight. Prepare thyself for wonders. Girl, we are no longer in the desert. Forget thy fitful fancies. Come, choose a husband from my generals, child, and I will give a kingdom for thy dower. I would gladly see a crown upon that imperial brow. It well deserves one.'

The prophetess turned her dark eyes full upon Alroy. What passed in her mind was neither evident nor expressed. She gazed intently upon the calm and inscrutable countenance of the conqueror, she flung away his hand, and rushed out of the pavilion.

# PART VIII.

## CHAPTER I.

The waving of banners, the flourish of trumpets, the neighing of steeds, and the glitter of spears! On the distant horizon they gleam like the morning, when the gloom of the night shivers bright into day.

Hark! the tramp of the foemen, like the tide of the ocean, flows onward and onward, and conquers the shore. From the brow of the mountain, like the rush of a river, the column defiling melts into the plain.

Warriors of Judah! holy men that battle for the Lord! The land wherein your fathers wept, and touched their plaintive psaltery; the haughty city where your sires bewailed their cold and distant hearth; your steeds are prancing on its plain, and you shall fill its palaces. Warriors of Judah! holy men that battle for the Lord!

March, onward march, ye valiant tribes, the hour has come, the hour has come! All the promises of ages, all the signs of sacred sages, meet in this ravishing hour. Where is now the oppressor's chariot, where your tyrant's purple robe? The horse and the rider are both overthrown, the horse and the rider are both overthrown!

Rise, Rachel, from thy wilderness, arise, and weep no more. No more thy lonely palm-tree's shade need shroud thy secret sorrowing. The Lord hath heard the widow's sigh, the Lord hath stilled the widow's tear. Be comforted, be comforted, thy children live again!

Yes! yes! upon the bounding plain fleet Asriel glances like a star, and stout Scherirah shakes his spear by stern Jabaster's scimetar. And He is there, the chosen one, hymned by prophetic harps, whose life is like the morning dew on Sion's holy hill: the chosen one, the chosen one, that leads his race to victory; warriors of Judah! holy men that battle for the Lord!

They come, they come, they come!

The ramparts of the city were crowded with the inhabitants, the river sparkled with ten thousand boats, the bazaars were shut, the streets lined with the populace, and the terrace of every house covered with spectators. In the morning, Ithamar had entered with his division and garrisoned the city. And now the vanguard of the Hebrew army, after having been long distinguished in the distance, approached the walls. A large body of cavalry dashed forward at full speed from the main force. Upon a milk-white charger, and followed by a glittering train of warriors, amid the shouts of the vast multitude, Alroy galloped up to the gates.

He was received by Ithamar and the members of the deputation, but Honain was not there. Accompanied by his staff and a strong detachment of the Sacred Guard, Alroy was conducted through the principal thoroughfares of the city, until he arrived at the chief entrance of the serail, or palace, of the caliph. The vast portal conducted him into a large quadrangular court, where he dismounted, and where he was welcomed by the captain of the eunuch guard. Accompanied by his principal generals and his immediate attendants, Alroy was then ushered through a suite of apartments which reminded him of his visit with Honain, until he arrived at the grand council-chamber of the caliphs.

The conqueror threw himself upon the gorgeous divan of the commander of the Faithful.

'An easy seat after a long march,' said Alroy, as he touched with his lips the coffee, which the chief of the eunuchs presented to him in a cup of transparent pink porcelain, studded with pearls.[65] 'Ithamar, now for your report. What is the temper of the city? Where is his sultanship of Roum?'

'The city, sire, is calm, and I believe content. The sultan and the caliph are still hovering on the borders of the province.'

'So I supposed. Scherirah will settle that. Let the troops be encamped without the walls, the garrison, ten thousand strong, must be changed monthly. Ithamar, you are governor of the city: Asriel commands the forces. Worthy Jabaster, draw up a report of the civil affairs of the capital. Your quarters are the College of the Dervishes. Brave Scherirah, I cannot afford you a long rest. In three days you must have crossed the river with your division. It will be quick work. I foresee that they will not fight. Meet me all here in council by to-morrow's noon. Farewell.'

The chieftains retired, the high priest lingered.

'Were it not an intrusion, sire, I would fain entreat a moment's audience.'

'My own Jabaster, you have but to speak.'

'Sire, I would speak of Abidan, as valiant a warrior as any in the host. It grieves me much, that by some fatality, his services seem ever overlooked.'

'Abidan! I know him well, a valiant man, but a dreamer, a dreamer.'

'A dreamer, sire! Believe me, a true son of Israel, and one whose faith is deep.'

'Good Jabaster, we are all true sons of Israel. Yet let me have men about me who see no visions in a mid-day sun. We must beware of dreamers.'

'Dreams are the oracles of God.'

'When God sends them. Very true, Jabaster. But this Abidan, and the company with whom he consorts, are filled with high-flown notions, caught from old traditions, which, if acted on, would render government impracticable, in a word, they are dangerous men.'

'The very flower of Israel! Some one has poisoned your sacred ear against them.'

'No one, worthy Jabaster. I have no counsellor except yourself. They may be the flower of Israel, but they are not the fruit. Good warriors, bad subjects: excellent means, by which we may accomplish greater ends. I'll have no dreamers in authority. I must have practical men about me, practical men. See how Abner, Asriel, Ithamar, Medad, see how these conform to what surrounds them, yet invincible captains, invincible captains. But then they are practical men, Jabaster; they have eyes and use them. They know the difference of times and seasons. But this Abidan, he has no other thought but the rebuilding of the temple: a narrow-souled bigot, who would sacrifice the essence to the form. The rising temple soon would fall again with such constructors. Why, sir, what think you, this same Abidan preached in the camp against my entry into what the quaint fanatic chooses to call "Babylon," because he had seen what he calls a vision.'

'There was a time your Majesty thought not so ill of visions.'

'Am I Abidan, sir? Are other men to mould their conduct or their thoughts by me? In this world I stand alone, a being of a different order from yourselves, incomprehensible even to you. Let this matter cease. I'll hear no more, and have heard too much. To-morrow at council.'

The high priest withdrew in silence.

'He is gone; at length I am alone. I cannot bear the presence of these men, except in action. Their words, even their looks, disturb the still creation of my brooding thought. I am once more alone, and loneliness hath been the cradle of my empire. Now I do feel inspired. There needs no mummery now to work a marvel.'

'The sceptre of Solomon! It may be so. What then? Here's now the sceptre of Alroy. What's that without his mind? The legend said that none should free our people but he who bore the sceptre of great Solomon. The legend knew that none could gain that sceptre, but with a mind to whose supreme volition the fortunes of the world would bow like fate. I gained it; I confronted the spectre monarchs in their sepulchre; and the same hand that grasped their shadowy rule hath seized the diadem of the mighty caliphs by the broad rushing of their imperial river.

'The world is mine: and shall I yield the prize, the universal and heroic prize, to realise the dull tradition of some dreaming priest, and consecrate a legend? He conquered Asia, and he built the temple. Are these my annals? Shall this quick blaze of empire sink to a glimmering and a twilight sway over some petty province, the decent patriarch of a pastoral horde? Is the Lord of hosts so slight a God, that we must place a barrier to His sovereignty, and fix the boundaries of Omnipotence between the Jordan and the Lebanon? It is not thus written; and were it so, I'll pit my inspiration against the prescience of my ancestors. I also am a prophet, and Bagdad shall be my Sion. The daughter of the Voice! Well, I am clearly summoned. I am the Lord's servant, not Jabaster's. Let me make His worship universal as His power; and where's the priest shall dare impugn my faith, because His altars smoke on other hills than those of Judah?

'I must see Honain. That man has a great mind. He alone can comprehend my purpose. Universal empire must not be founded on sectarian prejudices and exclusive rights. Jabaster would massacre the Moslemin like Amalek; the Moslemin, the vast majority, and most valuable portion, of my subjects. He would depopulate my empire, that it might not be said that Ishmael shared the heritage of Israel. Fanatic! I'll send him to conquer Judah. We must conciliate. Something must be done to bind the conquered to our conquering fortunes. That bold Sultan of Roum: I wish Abner had opposed him. To run off with the harem! I have half a mind to place myself at the head of the pursuing force, and—— Passion and policy alike combine: and yet Honain is the man; I might send him on a mission. Could we make terms? I detest treaties. My fancy flies from all other topics. I must see him. Could I but tell him all I think! This door, whither leads it? Hah! methinks I do remember yon glittering gallery! No one in attendance. The discipline of our palace is somewhat lax. My warriors are no courtiers. What an admirable marshal of the palace Honain would make! Silence everywhere. So! 'tis well. These saloons I have clearly passed through before. Could I but reach the private portal by the river side, unseen or undetected! 'Tis not impossible. Here are many dresses. I will disguise myself. Trusty scimetar, thou hast done thy duty, rest awhile. 'Tis lucky I am beardless. I shall make a capital eunuch. So! a handsome robe. One dagger for a pinch, slippers powdered with pearls,[66] a caftan of cloth of gold, a Cashmere girdle, and a pelisse of sables. One glance at the mirror. Good! I begin to look like the conqueror of the world!'

## CHAPTER II.

It was twilight: a small and solitary boat, with a single rower, glided along the Tigris, and stopped at the archway of a house that descended into the river. It stopped, the boatman withdrew the curtains, and his single passenger disembarked, and ascended the stairs of the archway.

The stranger reached the landing-place, and, unfastening a golden grate, proceeded along a gallery, and entered a beautiful saloon of white and green marble, opening into gardens. No one was in the apartment; the stranger threw himself upon a silver couch, placed at the side of a fountain that rose from the centre of the chamber and fell into a porphyry basin. A soft whisper roused the stranger from his reverie, a soft whisper, that faintly uttered the word 'Honain.' The stranger looked up, a figure, enveloped in a veil, that touched the ground, advanced from the gardens.

'Honain!' said the advancing figure, throwing off the veil. 'Honain! Ah! the beautiful mute returned!'

A woman more lovely than the rosy morn, beheld an unexpected guest. They stood, the lady and the stranger, gazing on each other in silence. A man, with a light, entered the extremity of the hall. Carefully he closed the portal, slowly he advanced, with a subdued step; he approached the lady and the stranger.

'Alroy!' said the astonished Honain, the light fell from his hand.

'Alroy!' exclaimed the lady, with a bewildered air: she turned pale, and leant against a column.

'Daughter of the caliph!' said the leader of Israel; and he advanced, and fell upon his knee, and stole her passive hand. 'I am indeed that Alroy to whom destiny has delivered the empire of thy sire; but the Princess Schirene can have nothing to fear from one who values above all his victories this memorial of her goodwill;' and he took from his breast a rosary of pearls and emeralds, and, rising slowly, left it in her trembling hand.

The princess turned and hid her face in her arm, which reclined against the column.

'My kind Honain,' said Alroy, 'you thought me forgetful of the past; you thought me ungrateful. My presence here proves that I am not so. I come to enquire all your wishes. I come to gratify and to fulfil them, if that be in my power.'

'Sire,' replied Honain, who had recovered from the emotion in which he rarely indulged, and from the surprise which seldom entrapped him, 'Sire, my wishes are slight. You see before you the daughter of my master. An interview, for which I fear I shall not easily gain that lady's pardon, has made you somewhat acquainted with her situation and her sentiments. The Princess Schirene seized the opportunity of the late convulsions to escape from a mode of life long repugnant to all her feelings, and from a destiny at which she trembled. I was her only counsellor, and she may feel assured, a faithful, although perhaps an indiscreet one. The irresistible solicitation of the inhabitants that I should become their deputy to their conqueror, prevented us from escaping as we had intended. Since then, from the movement of the troops, I have deemed it more prudent that we should remain at present here, although I have circulated the intelligence of my departure. In the kiosk of my garden, the princess is now a willing prisoner. At twilight she steals forth for the poor relaxation of my society, to listen to the intelligence which I acquire during the day in disguise. The history, sire, is short and simple. We are in your power: but instead of deprecating your interference, I now solicit your protection.'

'Dear Honain, 'tis needless. The Princess Schirene has only to express a wish that it may be fulfilled. I came to speak with you on weighty matters, Honain, but I retire, for I am an intruder now. To-morrow, if it please you, at this hour, and in this disguise, I will again repair hither. In the meantime, this lady may perchance express to you her wishes, and you will bear them to me. If an escort to any country, if any palace or province for her rule and residence—— But I will not offer to one who should command. Lady! farewell. Pardon the past! To-morrow, good Honain! pr'ythee let us meet. Good even!'

## CHAPTER III.

'THE royal brow was clouded,' said Ithamar to Asriel, as, departing from the council, they entered their magnificent barque.

'With thought; he has so much upon his mind, 'tis wondrous how he bears himself.'

'I have seen him gay on the eve of battle, and lively though calm, with weightier matters than now oppress him. His brow was clouded, but not, methinks, with *thought*; one might rather say with *temper*. Mark you, how he rated Jabaster?'

'Roundly! The stern priest writhed under it; and as he signed the ordinance, shivered his reed in rage. I never saw a man more pale.'

'Or more silent. He looked like an embodied storm. I tell you what, Asriel, that stern priest loves not us.'

'Have you just discovered that secret, Ithamar? We are not of his school. Nor, in good faith, is our ruler. I am glad to see the king is so staunch about Abidan. Were he in council he would support Jabaster.'

'Oh! his mere tool. What think you of Scherirah?'

'I would not trust him. As long as there is fighting, he will meddle with nothing else; but, mark my words, Ithamar: in quiet times he will support the priest.'

'Medad will have a place in council. He is with us.'

'Heart and soul. I would your brother were here, Asriel: he alone could balance Jabaster. Alroy loves your brother like himself. Is it true that he marries the Lady Miriam?'

'So the king wishes. 'Twill be a fine match for Abner.'

'The world is all before us. I wonder who will be viceroy of Syria.'

'When we conquer it. Not Scherirah. Mark my words, Ithamar: he never will have a government. You or I perchance. For my own part, I would rather remain as I am.'

'Yours is a good post; the best.'

'With the command of the city. It should go with the guard.'

'Well then help me in getting Syria, and you can ask for my command.'

'Agreed. Jabaster will have it that, in a Hebrew monarchy, the chief priest is in fact the grand vizir.'

'Alroy will be his own minister.'

'I am not so sure of that. He may choose to command the Syrian expedition in person; he must leave some head at Bagdad. Jabaster is no general.'

'Oh! none at all. Alroy will be glad to leave him at home. The Sultan of Roum may not be always so merciful.'

'Hah! hah! that was an escape!'

'By heavens! I thought it was all over. You made a fine charge.'

'I shall never forget it. I nearly ran over Jabaster.'

'Would that you had!'

L

## CHAPTER IV.

It is the tender twilight hour, when maidens in their lonely bower, sigh softer than the eve! The languid rose her head upraises, and listens to the nightingale, while his wild and thrilling praises, from his trembling bosom gush: the languid rose her head upraises, and listens with a blush.

In the clear and rosy air, sparkling with a single star, the sharp and spiry cypress-tree rises like a gloomy thought, amid the flow of revelry. A singing bird, a single star, a solemn tree, an odorous flower, are dangerous in the tender hour, when maidens in their twilight bower, sigh softer than the eve!

The daughter of the caliph comes forth to breathe the air: her lute her only company. She sits her down by a fountain's side, and gazes on the waterfall. Her cheek reclines upon her arm, like fruit upon a graceful bough. Very pensive is the face of that bright and beauteous lady. She starts; a warm voluptuous lip presses her soft and idle hand. It is her own gazelle. With his large and lustrous eyes, more eloquent than many a tongue, the fond attendant mutely asks the cause of all her thoughtfulness.

'Ah! bright gazelle! ah! bright gazelle!' the princess cried, the princess cried; 'thy lips are softer than the swan, thy lips are softer than the swan; but his breathed passion, when they pressed, my bright gazelle! my bright gazelle!'

'Ah! bright gazelle! ah! bright gazelle!' the princess cried, the princess cried; 'thine eyes are like the stars of night, thine eyes are like the stars of night; but his glanced passion when they gazed, my bright gazelle! my bright gazelle!'

She seized her lute, she wildly threw her fingers o'er its thrilling cords, and, gazing on the rosy sky, to borrow all its poetry, thus, thus she sang; thus, thus she sang:

1.

He rose in beauty like the morn
That brightens in our Syrian skies;
Dark passion glittered in his eye,
And Empire sparkled in his form!

2.

My soul! thou art the dusky earth,
On which his sunlight fell;
The dusky earth, that dim no longer,
Now breathes with light, now beams with love!

3.

He rose in beauty, like the morn
That brightens in our Syrian skies;
Dark Passion glittered in his eye,
And Empire sparkled in his form!

'Once more, once more! Ah! sing that strain once more!'

The princess started and looked round. Before her stood Alroy. She rose, she would have retired; but, advancing, the conqueror stole her hand.

'Fair princess,' said Alroy, 'let it not be said that my presence banished at once beauty and music.'

'Sire, I doubt not that Honain awaits you. Let me summon him.'

'Lady, it is not with Honain that I would speak.'

He seated himself by her side. His countenance was pale, his heart trembled.

'This garden,' at length he observed in a low voice, 'this garden, a brief, brief space has glided away since first I wandered within its beauteous limits, and yet those days seem like the distant memory of another life.'

'It is another life,' said the princess. 'Ourselves, the world, all forms and usages, all feelings and all habits, verily they have changed, as if we had breathed within another sphere.'

''Tis a great change.'

'Since first you visited my bright kiosk. Pretty bauble! I pray it may be spared.'

'It is sacred, like yourself.'

'You are a courteous conqueror.'

'I am no conqueror, fair Schirene, but a slave more lowly than when I first bowed humbly in your presence.'

'And bore away a token not forgotten. Your rosary is here.'

'Let me claim it. It has been my consolation in much peril, beauteous lady. On the eve of battle I wound it round my heart.'

She held forth the rosary, and turned away her head. Her hand remained in his; he pressed it to his lips. His right arm retained her hand; he wound the other round her waist, as he fell upon his knee.

'O beautiful! O more than beautiful! for thou to me art like a dream unbroken,' exclaimed the young leader of Israel, 'let me, let me breathe my adoration. I offer thee not empire: I offer thee not wealth; I offer thee not all the boundless gratification of magnificent fancy, these may be thine, but all these thou hast proved; but, if the passionate affections of a spirit which never has yielded to the power of woman or the might of man, if the deep devotion of the soul of Alroy, be deemed an offering meet for the shrine of thy surpassing loveliness, I worship thee, Schirene, I worship thee, I worship thee!

'Since I first gazed upon thee, since thy beauty first rose upon my presence like a star bright with my destiny, in the still sanctuary of my secret love, thy idol has ever rested. Then, then, I was a thing whose very touch thy creed might count a contumely. I have avenged the insults of long centuries in the best blood of Asia; I have returned, in glory and in pride, to claim my ancient sceptre; but sweeter far than vengeance, sweeter far than the quick gathering of my sacred tribes, the rush of triumph and the blaze of empire, is this brief moment of adoring love, wherein I pour the passion of my life!

'O my soul, my life, my very being! thou art silent, but thy silence is sweeter than others' speech. Yield, yield thee, dear Schirene, yield to thy suppliant! Thy faith, thy father's faith, thy native customs, these, these shall be respected, beauteous lady! Pharaoh's daughter yielded her dusky beauty to my great ancestor. Thy face is like the bright inspiring day! Let it not be said that the daughter of the Nile shared Israel's crown, the daughter of the Tigris spurned our sceptre. I am not Solomon, but I am one that were Schirene the partner of my throne, would make his glowing annals read like a wearisome and misty tale to our surpassing lustre!'

He ceased, the princess turned her hitherto hidden countenance, and bowed it on his heart. 'O Alroy!' she exclaimed, 'I have no creed, no country, no life, but thee!'

## CHAPTER V.

'THE king is late to-day.'

'Is it true, Asriel, there is an express from Hamadan?'

'Of no moment, Ithamar. I had private letters from Abner. All is quiet.'

''Tis much past the hour. When do you depart, Scherirah?'

'The troops are ready. I wait orders. This morning's council will perchance decide.'

'This morning's council is devoted to the settlement of the civil affairs of the capital,' remarked Jabaster.

'Indeed!' said Asriel. 'Is your report prepared, Jabaster?'

''Tis here,' replied the high priest. 'The Hebrew legislator requires but little musing to shape his order. He has a model which time cannot destroy, nor thought improve.'

Ithamar and Asriel exchanged significant glances. Scherirah looked solemn. There was a pause, which was broken by Asriel.

''Tis a noble city, this Bagdad. I have not yet visited your quarters, Jabaster. You are well placed.'

'As it may be. I hope we shall not tarry here long. The great point is still not achieved.'

'How far is it to the holy city?' enquired Scherirah.

'A month's march,' replied Jabaster.

'And when you get there?' enquired Ithamar.

'You may fight with the Franks,' replied Asriel.

'Jabaster, how large is Jerusalem?' enquired Ithamar.

'Is it true, as I have sometimes heard, that it is not bigger than the serail here, gardens and all?'

'Its glory hath departed,' replied the high priest; 'the bricks have fallen, but we will rebuild with marble; and Sion, that is now without the Christian walls, shall yet sparkle, as in the olden time, with palaces and pavilions.'

A flourish of trumpets, the portals flew open, and Alroy entered, leaning on the arm of the envoy of Bagdad.

'Valiant leaders,' said Alroy to the astonished chieftains, 'in this noble stranger, you see one like yourselves entrusted with my unbounded confidence. Jabaster, behold thy brother!'

'Honain! art *thou* Honain?' exclaimed the pontiff starting from his seat. 'I have a thousand messengers after thee.' With a countenance alternately pallid with surprise and burning with affection, Jabaster embraced his brother, and, overpowered with emotion, hid his face on his shoulder.

'Sire,' at length exclaimed the high priest in a low and tremulous voice, 'I must pray your pardon that for an instant in this character I have indulged in any other thoughts than those that may concern your welfare. 'Tis past: and you, who know all, will forgive me.'

'All that respects Jabaster must concern my welfare. He is the pillar of my empire;' and holding forth his hand, Alroy placed the high priest on his right. 'Scherirah, you depart this eve.'

The rough captain bowed in silence.

'What is this?' continued Alroy, as Jabaster offered him a scroll. 'Ah! your report.' "Order of the Tribes," "Service of the Levites," "Princes of the People," "Elders of Israel!" The day may come when this may be effected. At present, Jabaster, we must be moderate, and content ourselves with arrangements which may ensure that order shall be maintained, property respected, and justice administered. Is it true that a gang has rifled a mosque?'

'Sire! of that I would speak. They are no plunderers, but men, perhaps too zealous, who have read and who have remembered that "Ye shall utterly destroy all the places wherein the nations which ye shall possess, served their gods upon the high mountains, and upon the hill, and under every green tree. And ye shall overthrow their altars, and "——'

'Jabaster, is this a synagogue? Come I to a council of valiant statesmen or dreaming Rabbis? For a thousand years we have been quoting the laws we dared not practise. Is it with such aid that we captured Nishabur and crossed the Tigris? Valiant, wise Jabaster, thou art worthy of better things, and capable of all. I entreat thee, urge such matters for the last time. Are these fellows in custody?'

'They were in custody. I have freed them.'

'Freed them! Hang them! Hang them on the most public grove. Is this the way to make the Moslem a duteous subject? Jabaster! Israel honours thee; and I, its chief, know that one more true, more valiant, or more learned, crowds not around our standard; but I see, the caverns of the Caucasus are not a school for empire.'

'Sire, I had humbly deemed the school for empire was the law of Moses.'

'Ay! adapted to these times.'

'Can aught divine be changed?'

'Am I as tall as Adam? If man, the crown, the rose of all this fair creation, the most divine of all divine inventions, if Time have altered even this choicest of all godlike works, why shall it spare a law made but to rule his conduct? Good Jabaster, we must establish the throne of Israel, that is my mission, and for the means, no matter how, or where. Asriel, what news of Medad?'

'All is quiet between the Tigris and Euphrates. It would be better to recall his division, which has been much harassed. I thought of relieving him by Abidan.'

'I think so, too. We may as well keep Abidan out of the city. If the truth were known, I'll wager some of his company plundered the mosque. We must issue a proclamation on that subject. My good Jabaster, we'll talk over these matters alone. At present I will leave you with your brother. Scherirah, sup with me to night; before you quit Asriel, come with me to my cabinet.'

## CHAPTER VI.

'I must see the king!'

'Holy priest, his highness has retired. It is impossible.'

'I must see the king. Worthy Pharez, I take all peril on myself.'

'Indeed his highness' orders are imperative. You cannot see him.'

'Knowest thou who I am?'

'One whom all pious Hebrews reverence.'

'I say I must see the king.'

'Indeed, indeed, holy Jabaster, it cannot be.'

'Shall Israel perish for a menial's place? Go to; I *will* see him.'

'Nay! if you *will*, I'll struggle for my duty.'

'Touch not the Lord's anointed. Dog, you shall suffer for this!'

So saying, Jabaster threw aside Pharez, and, with the attendant clinging to his robes, rushed into the royal chamber.

'What is all this?' exclaimed Alroy, starting from the divan. 'Jabaster! Pharez, withdraw! How now, is Bagdad in insurrection?'

'Worse, much worse, Israel soon will be.'

'Ay!'

'My fatal brother has told me all, nor would I sleep, until I lifted up my voice to save thee.'

'Am I in danger?'

'In the wilderness, when the broad desert quivered beneath thy trembling feet, and the dark heavens poured down their burning torrents, thou wert less so. In that hour of death, One guarded thee, who never forgets his fond and faithful offspring, and now, when He has brought thee out of the house of bondage; now, when thy fortunes, like a noble cedar, swell in the air and shadow all the land; thou, the very leader of His people, His chosen one, for whom He hath worked such marvels, thy heart is turned from thy fathers' God, and hankers after strange abominations.'

Through the broad arch that led into the gardens of the serail, the moonlight fell upon the tall figure and the upraised arm of the priest; Alroy stood with folded arms at some distance, watching Jabaster as he spoke, with a calm but searching glance. Suddenly he advanced with a quick step, and, placing his hand upon Jabaster's arm, said, in a low, enquiring tone, 'You are speaking of this marriage?'

'Of that which ruined Solomon.'

'Listen to me, Jabaster,' said Alroy, interrupting him, in a calm but peremptory tone. 'I cannot forget that I am speaking to my master, as well as to my friend. The Lord, who knoweth all things, hath deemed me worthy of His mission. My fitness for this high and holy office was not admitted without proof. A lineage, which none else could offer, mystic studies shared by few, a mind that dared encounter all things, and a frame that could endure most, these were my claims. But no more of this. I have passed the great ordeal; the Lord of Hosts hath found me not unworthy of His charge; I have established His ancient people; His altars blaze with sacrifices; His priests are honoured, bear witness thou, Jabaster, His omnipotent unity is declared. What wouldst thou more?'

'All!'

'Then Moses knew you well. It is a stiff-necked people.'

'Sire, bear with me. If I speak in heat, I speak in zeal. You ask me what I wish: my answer is, a national existence, which we have not. You ask me what I wish: my answer is, the Land of Promise. You ask me what I wish: my answer is, Jerusalem. You ask me what I wish: my answer is, the Temple, all we have forfeited, all we have yearned after, all for which we have fought, our beauteous country, our holy creed, our simple manners, and our ancient customs.'

'Manners change with time and circumstances; customs may be observed everywhere. The ephod on thy breast proves our faith; and, for a country, is the Tigris less than Siloah, or the Euphrates inferior to the Jordan?'

'Alas! alas! there was a glorious prime when Israel stood aloof from other nations, a fair and holy thing that God had hallowed. We were then a chosen family, a most peculiar people, set apart for God's entire enjoyment. All about us was solemn, deep, and holy. We shunned the stranger as an unclean thing that must defile our solitary sanctity, and, keeping to ourselves and to our God, our lives flowed on in one great solemn tide of deep religion, making the meanest of our multitude feel greater than the kings of other lands. It was a glorious time: I thought it had returned; but I awake from this, as other dreams.'

'We must leave off dreaming, good Jabaster, we must act. Were I, by any chance, to fall into one of those reveries, with which I have often lost the golden hours at Hamadan, or in our old cave, I should hear, some fine morning, his sultanship of Roum rattling at my gates.' Alroy smiled as he spoke; he would willingly have introduced a lighter tone into the dialogue, but the solemn countenance of the priest was not sympathetic with his levity.

'My heart is full, and yet I cannot speak: the memory of the past overpowers my thought. I had vainly deemed that my voice, inspired by the soul of truth, might yet preserve him; and now I stand here in his presence, silent and trembling, like a guilty thing. O, my prince! my pupil!' said the priest, advancing, falling on his knee, and seizing the robe of Alroy, 'by thy sacred lineage; by the sweet memory of thy ardent youth, and our united studies; by all thy zealous thoughts, and solemn musings, and glorious aspirations after fame; by all thy sufferings, and by all thy triumphs, and chiefly by the name of that great God, who hath elected thee his favoured child; by all the marvels of thy mighty mission, I do adjure thee! Arise, Alroy, arise and rouse thyself. The lure that snared thy fathers may trap thee, this Delilah may shear thy mystic locks. Spirits like thee act not by halves. Once fall out from the straight course before thee, and, though thou deemest 'tis but to saunter mid the summer trees, soon thou wilt find thyself in the dark depths of some infernal forest, where none may rescue thee!'

'What if I do inherit the eager blood of my great ancestor, at least I hold his sceptre. Shall aught of earthly power prevail against the supernatural sway of Heaven and Hades?'

'Sire, sire, the legend that came from Sinai is full of high instruction. But shape thy conduct by its oracles, and all were well. It says our people can be established only by him who rules them with the rod of Solomon. Sire, when the Lord offered his pleasure to that mighty king, thou knowest his deep discretion. Riches and length of days, empire and vengeance, these were not the choice of one to whom all accidents were proffered. The legend bears an inward spirit, as well as an outward meaning. The capture of the prize was a wise test of thy imperial fitness. Thou hast his sceptre, but, without his wisdom, 'tis but a staff of cedar.'

'Hah! Art thou there? I am glad to see Jabaster politic. Hear me, my friend. What my feelings be unto this royal lady, but little matters. Let them pass, and let us view this question by the light wherein you have placed it, the flame of policy and not of passion. I am no traitor to the God of Israel, in whose name I have conquered, and in whose name I shall rule; but thou art a learned doctor, thou canst inform us. I have heard no mandate to yield my glorious empire for my meanest province. I am Lord of Asia, so would I have my long posterity. Our people are but a remnant, a feeble fraction of the teeming millions that own my sway. What I hold I can defend; but my children may not inherit the spirit of their sire. The Moslemin will recognise their rule with readier hearts, when they remember that a daughter of their caliphs gave them life. You see I too am politic, my good Jabaster!'

'The policy of the son of Kareah[67]: 'twas fatal. He preferred Egypt to Judah, and he suffered. Sire, the Lord hath blessed Judah: it is His land. He would have it filled by His peculiar people, so that His worship might ever flourish. For this He has, by many curious rites and customs, marked us out from all other nations, so that we cannot, at the same time, mingle with them and yet be true to Him. We must exist alone. To preserve that loneliness, is the great end and essence of our law. What have we to do with Bagdad, or its people, where every instant we must witness some violation of our statutes? Can we pray with them? Can we eat with them? Alike in the highest duties, and the lowest occupations, of existence, we cannot mingle. From the altar of our God to our domestic boards, we are alike separated from them. Sire, you may be King of Bagdad, but you cannot, at the same time, be a Jew.'

'I am what I am. I worship the Lord of Hosts. Perhaps, in His mercy, He will accept the days of Nishabur and the Tigris, as a compensation for some slight relaxation in the ritual of the baker and the bath.'

'And mark my words: it was by the ritual of the baker and the bath that Alroy rose, and without it he will fall. The genius of the people, which he shared, raised him; and that genius has been formed by the law of Moses. Based on that law, he might indeed have handed down an empire to his long posterity; and now, though the tree of his fortunes seems springing up by the water-side, fed by a thousand springs, and its branches covered with dew, there is a gangrene in the sap, and to-morrow he may shrink like a shrivelled gourd. Alas! alas! for Israel! We have long fed on mallows; but to lose the vintage in the very day of fruition, 'tis very bitter. Ah! when I raised thy exhausted form in the cavern of Genthesma, and the star of David beamed brightly in the glowing heavens upon thy high fulfilment, who could have dreamed of a night like this? Farewell, sire.'

'Stop, Jabaster! earliest, dearest friend, pr'ythee, pr'ythee stop!'

The priest slowly turned, the prince hesitated.

'Part not in anger, good Jabaster.'

'In sorrow, sire, only in sorrow; but deep and terrible.'

'Israel is Lord of Asia, my Jabaster. Why should we fear?'

'Solomon built Tadmor in the wilderness, and his fleet brought gold from Ophir; and yet Alroy was born a slave.'

'But did not die one. The sultans of the world have fallen before me. I have no fear. Nay, do not go. At least you will give some credence to the stars, my learned Cabalist. See, my planet shines as brightly as my fortunes.' Alroy withdrew the curtain, and with Jabaster stepped out upon the terrace. A beautiful star glittered on high. As they gazed, its colour changed, and a blood-red meteor burst from its circle, and fell into space. The conqueror and the priest looked at each other at the same time. Their countenances were pale, enquiring, and agitated.

'Sire,' said Jabaster, 'march to Judah.'

'It portends war,' replied Alroy, endeavouring to recover himself. 'Perchance some troubles in Persia.'

'Troubles at home, no other. The danger is nigh. Look to thyself.'

A wild scream was heard in the gardens. It sounded thrice.

'What is this?' exclaimed Alroy, really agitated. 'Rouse the guard, Jabaster, search the gardens.'

''Tis useless and may do harm. It was a spirit that shrieked.'

'What said it?'

'MENE, MENE, TEKEL, UPHARSIN!'

## CHAPTER VII.

'THE old story, the priest against the king,' said Honain to Alroy, when at his morrow's interview, he had listened to the events of the preceding night. 'My pious brother wishes to lead you back to the Theocracy, and is fearful that, if he prays at Bagdad instead of Sion, he may chance to become only the head of an inferior sect, instead of revelling in the universal tithes of a whole nation. As for the meteor, Scherirah must have crossed river about the same time, and the Sultan of Roum may explain the bloody portent. For the shriek, as I really have no acquaintance with spirits, I must leave the miraculous communication to the favoured ears and initiated intelligences of your highness and my brother. It seems that it differed from "the Daughter of the Voice" in more respects than one, since it was not only extremely noisy, but, as it would appear, quite unintelligible except to the individual who had an interest in the interpretation, an ingenious one I confess. When I enter upon my functions as your highness's chamberlain, I will at least guarantee that your slumbers shall not be disturbed either by spirits or more unwelcome visitors.'

'Enter upon them at once, good Honain. How fares my Persian rose to-day, my sweet Schirene?'

'Feeding on your image in your absence. She spares no word to me, I do assure your Highness.'

'Nay, nay, we know you are a general favourite with the sex, Honain. I'faith I'm jealous.'

'I would your highness had cause,' said Honain, demurely.

## CHAPTER VIII.

THE approaching marriage between the King of the Hebrews and the Princess of Bagdad was published throughout Asia. Preparations were made on the plain of the Tigris for the great rejoicing. Whole forests were felled to provide materials for the buildings and fuel for the banqueting. All the governors of provinces and cities, all the chief officers and nobility of both nations, were specially invited, and daily arrived in state at Bagdad. Among them the Viceroy of the Medes and Persians, and his recent bride, the Princess Miriam, were conspicuous, followed by a train of nearly ten thousand persons.

A throne, ascended by one hundred steps covered with crimson cloth, and crowned by a golden canopy, was raised in the middle of the plain; on each side was a throne less elevated, but equally gorgeous. In the front of these thrones

an immense circus was described, formed by one hundred
chartaks or amphitheatres, ample room for the admittance
of the multitude being left between the buildings. These
chartaks were covered with bright brocades and showy
carpets; on each was hoisted a brilliant banner. In some of
them were bands of choice musicians, in others companies of
jugglers, buffoons, and storiers. Five chartaks on each side
of the thrones were allotted for the convenience of the court;
the rest were filled by the different trades of the city. In
one the fruiterers had formed a beautiful garden, glowing
with pomegranates, and gourds, and water-melons, oranges,
almonds, and pistachio-nuts; in another the butchers exhibited their meats carved in fanciful shapes, and the skins
of animals formed into ludicrous figures. Here assembled
the furriers, all dressed in masquerade, like leopards, lions,
tigers and foxes; and in another booth mustered the up-
holsterers, proud of a camel made of wood, and reeds, and
cord, and painted linen, a camel which walked about as if
alive, though ever and anon a curtain drawn aside discovered to the marvelling multitude the workman within,
performing in his own piece. Further on might be perceived the cotton manufacturers, whose chartak was full of
birds of all shapes and plumage, formed nevertheless of
their curious plant; and, in the centre rose a lofty minaret,
constructed of the same material, with the help of reeds,
although every one imagined it to be built with bricks and
mortar. It was covered with embroidered work, and on
the top was placed a stork, so cunningly devised that the
children pelted it with pistachio-nuts. The saddlers showed
their skill in two litters, open at top, each carried on a
dromedary, and in each a beautiful woman, who diverted
the spectators with light balls of gilt leather, throwing them
up both with their hands and feet. Nor were the mat-
makers backward in the proof of their dexterity, since,
instead of a common banner, they exhibited a large standard
of reeds worked with two lines of writing in Kufic, pro-
claiming the happy names of Alroy and Schirene. But
indeed in every chartak might be seen some wondrous

specimens of the wealth of Bagdad, and of the ingenuity of its unrivalled artisans.

Around this mighty circus, on every side for the space of many miles, the plain was studded with innumerable pavilions. At measured intervals were tables furnished with every species of provision, and attended by appointed servants; flagons of wine and jars of sherbets, mingled with infinite baskets of delicious fruits and trays of refreshing confectionery. Although open to all comers, so great and rapid was the supply, that these banqueting tables seemed ever laden; and that the joys of the people might be complete, they were allowed to pursue whatever pleasures they thought fit without any restraint, by proclamation, in these terms.

'THIS IS THE TIME OF FEASTING, PLEASURE, AND REJOICING. LET NO PERSON REPRIMAND OR COMPLAIN OF ANOTHER; LET NOT THE RICH INSULT THE POOR, OR THE STRONG THE WEAK: LET NO ONE ASK ANOTHER, "WHY HAVE YOU DONE THIS?"'

Millions of people were collected in this Paradise. They rejoiced, they feasted, they frolicked, they danced, they sang. They listened to the tales of the Arabian storier, at once enchanted and enchanting, or melted to the strain of the Persian poet, as he painted the moon-lit forehead of his heroine, and the wasting and shadowy form of his love-sick hero; they beheld with amazement the feats of the juggler of the Ganges, or giggled at the practised wit and the practical buffoonery of the Syrian mime. And the most delighted could still spare a fascinating glance to the inviting gestures and the voluptuous grace of the dancing girls of Egypt.[68] Everywhere reigned melody and merriment, rarity and beauty. For once mankind forgot their cares, and delivered themselves up to infinite enjoyment.

'I grow courteous,' said Kisloch the Kourd, assisting a party into one of the shows.

'And I humane,' said Calidas the Indian. 'Fellow, how dare you violate the proclamation, by thrashing that child?' He turned to one of the stewards of the table, who was belabouring the unfortunate driver of a camel which had stumbled and in its fall had shivered its burden, two panniers of porcelain.

'Mind your own business, fellow,' replied the steward, and be thankful that for once in your life you can dine.'

'Is this the way to speak to an officer?' said Calidas the Indian; 'I have half a mind to cut your tongue out.'

'Never mind, little fellow,' said the Guebre, 'here is a dirhem for you. Run away and be merry.'

'A miracle!' grinned the Negro; 'he giveth alms.'

'And you are witty,' rejoined the Guebre. ''Tis a wondrous day.'

'What shall we do?' said Kisloch.

'Let us dine,' proposed the Negro.

'Ay! under this plane-tree,' said Calidas. ''Tis pleasant to be alone. I hate everybody but ourselves.'

'Here stop, you rascal,' said the Guebre. 'What's your name?'

'I am a Hadgee,' said our old friend Abdallah, the servant of the charitable merchant Ali, and who was this day one of the officiating stewards.

'Are you a Jew, you scoundrel?' said the Guebre, 'that is the only thing worth being. Bring some wine, you accursed Giaour!'

'Instantly,' said Kisloch, 'and a pilau.'

'And a gazelle stuffed with almonds,' said Calidas.

'And some sugar-plums,' said the Negro.

'Quick, you infernal Gentile, or I'll send this javelin in your back,' hallooed the Guebre.

The servile Abdallah hastened away, and soon bustled back, bearing two flagons of wine, and followed by four servants, each with a tray covered with dainties.

'Where are you going, you accursed scoundrels?' grumbled Kisloch; 'wait upon the true believers.'

'We shall be more free alone,' whispered Calidas.

'Away, then, dogs,' growled Kisloch.

Abdallah and his attendants hurried off, but were soon summoned back.

M

'Why did you not bring Schiraz wine?' asked Calidas, with an eye of fire.

'The pilau is overdone,' thundered Kisloch.

'You have brought a lamb stuffed with pistachio-nuts, instead of a gazelle with almonds,' said the Guebre.

'Not half sugar-plums enough,' said the Negro.

'Everything is wrong,' said Kisloch. 'Go, and get us a Kabob.'

In time, however, even this unmanageable crew were satisfied; and, seated under their plane-tree, and stuffing themselves with all the dainties of the East, they became more amiable as their appetites decreased.

'A bumper, Calidas, and a song,' said Kisloch.

''Tis rare stuff,' said the Guebre; 'come, Cally, it should inspire you.'

'Here goes, then; mind the chorus.'

### THE SONG OF CALIDAS.

Drink, drink, deeply drink,
Never feel, and never think;
What's love? what's fame? a sigh, a smile.
Friendship? but a hollow wile.
If you've any thought or woe,
Drown them in the goblet's flow.
Yes! dash them in this brimming cup;
Dash them in, and drink them up.
Drink, drink, deeply drink,
Never feel, and never think.

'Hark, the trumpets! The King and Queen! The procession is coming. Let's away.'

'Again! they must be near. Hurry, hurry, for good places.'

'Break all the cups and dishes. Come along!'

The multitude from all quarters hurried to the great circus, amid the clash of ten thousand cymbals and the blast of innumerable trumpets. In the distance, issuing from the gates of Bagdad, might be discerned a brilliant crowd, the advance company of the bridal procession.

There came five hundred maidens crowned with flowers,

and beauteous as the buds that girt their hair. Their flowing robes were whiter than the swan, and each within her hand a palm-branch held.

Followed these a band of bright musicians, clothed in golden robes, and sounding silver trumpets.

Then five hundred youths, brilliant as stars, clad in jackets of white fox-skin, and alternately bearing baskets of fruit or flowers.

Followed these a band of bright musicians, clothed in silver robes, and sounding golden trumpets.

Six choice steeds, sumptuously caparisoned, each led by an Arab groom.[69]

The household of Medad, in robes of crimson, lined with sable.

The standard of Medad.

Medad, on a coal-black Arab, followed by three hundred officers of his division, all mounted on steeds of pure race.

Slaves, bearing the bridal present of Medad; six Damascus sabres of unrivalled temper.[70]

Twelve choice steeds, sumptuously caparisoned, each led by an Anatolian groom.

The household of Ithamar, in robes of violet, lined with ermine.

The standard of Ithamar.

Ithamar, on a snow-white Anatolian charger, followed by six hundred officers of his division, all mounted on steeds of pure race.

Slaves bearing the marriage present of Ithamar; a golden vase of rubies borne on a violet throne.

One hundred Negroes, their noses bored, and hung with rings of brilliants, playing upon wind instruments and kettle-drums.

The standard of the City of Bagdad.

The deputation from the citizens of Bagdad.

Two hundred mules, with caparisons of satin, embroidered with gold, and adorned with small golden bells. These bore the sumptuous wardrobe, presented by the city to their princess. Each mule was attended by a girl, dressed like a Peri, with starry wings, and a man, masked as a hideous Divo.

The standard of Egypt.

The deputation from the Hebrews of Egypt, mounted on dromedaries, with silver furniture.

Fifty slaves, bearing their present to the princess, with golden cords, a mighty bath of jasper, beatifully carved, the sarcophagus of some ancient temple, and purchased for an immense sum.

The standard of Syria.

The deputation from the Hebrews of the Holy Land, headed by Rabbi Zimri himself, each carrying in his hand his offering to the nuptial pair, a precious vase, containing earth from the Mount of Sion.

The standard of Hamadan.

The deputation from the citizens of Hamadan, headed by the venerable Bostenay himself, whose sumptuous charger was led by Caleb.

The present of the city of Hamadan to David Alroy, offered at his own suggestion; the cup in which the Prince of the Captivity carried his tribute, now borne full of sand.

Fifty choice steeds, sumptuously caparisoned, each led by a Median or Persian groom.

The household of Abner and Miriam, in number twelve hundred, clad in chain armour of ivory and gold.

The standard of the Medes and Persians.

Two white elephants, with golden litters, bearing the Viceroy and his Princess.

The offering of Abner to Alroy; twelve elephants of state, with furniture embroidered with jewels, each tended by an Indian clad in chain armour of ivory and gold.

The offering of Miriam to Schirene; fifty plants of roses from Rocnabad;[71] a white shawl of Cashmere fifty feet in length, which folded into the handle of a fan; fifty screens, each made of a feather of the roc;[72] and fifty vases of crystal full of exquisite perfumes, and each sealed with a talisman of precious stones.

' After these followed the eunuch guard.

Then came the band of the serail, consisting of three hundred dwarfs, hideous indeed to behold, but the most complete musicians in the world.

The steeds of Solomon, in number one hundred, each with a natural star upon its front, uncaparisoned, and led only by a bridle of diamonds.

The household of Alroy and Schirene. Foremost, the Lord Honain riding upon a chestnut charger, shod with silver; the dress of the rider, pink with silver stars. From his rosy turban depended a tremulous aigrette of brilliants,[72] blazing with a thousand shifting tints.

Two hundred pages followed him; and then servants of both sexes, gorgeously habited, amounting to nearly two thousand, carrying rich vases, magnificent caskets, and costly robes. The treasurer and two hundred of his underlings came next, showering golden dirhems on all sides.

The sceptre of Solomon borne by Asriel himself.

A magnificent and lofty car, formed of blue enamel with golden wheels, and axletrees of turquoises and brilliants, and drawn by twelve snow-white and sacred horses, four abreast; in the car Alroy and Schirene.

Five thousand of the sacred guard closed the procession.

Amid the exclamations of the people, this gorgeous procession crossed the plain, and moved around the mighty circus. The conqueror and his bride ascended their throne; its steps were covered by the youths and maidens. On the throne upon their right sat the venerable Bostenay; on the left, the gallant Viceroy and his Princess. The chartaks on each side were crowded with the court.

The deputations made their offerings, the chiefs and captains paid their homage, the trades of the city moved before the throne in order, and exhibited their various ingenuity. Thrice was the proclamation made, amid the sound of trumpets, and then began the games.

A thousand horsemen dashed into the arena and threw the jerreed. They galloped at full speed; they arrested their fiery charges in mid course, and flung their long javelins at the minute but sparkling target, the imitative

form of a rare and brilliant bird. The conquerors received
their prizes from the hand of the princess herself, bright
shawls, and jewelled daggers, and rosaries of gems. Sometimes the trumpets announced a prize from the vice-queen,
sometimes from the venerable Bostenay, sometimes from
the victorious generals, or the loyal deputations, sometimes
from the united trades, sometimes from the city of Bagdad,
sometimes from the city of Hamadan. The hours flow
away in gorgeous and ceaseless variety.

'I would we were alone, my own Schirene,' said Alroy
to his bride.

'I would so too; and yet I love to see all Asia prostrate
at the feet of Alroy.'

'Will the sun never set? Give me thy hand to play
with.'

'Hush! See Miriam smiles.'

'Lovest thou my sister, my own Schirene?'

'None dearer but thyself.'

'Talk not of my sister, but ourselves. Thinkest thou
the sun is nearer setting, love?'

'I cannot see; thine eyes they dazzle me, they are so
brilliant, sweet!'

'O! my soul, I could pour out my passion on thy breast.'

'Thou art very serious.'

'Love is ever so.'

'Nay, sweet! It makes me wild and fanciful. Now I
could do such things, but what I know not. I would we
had wings, and then we would fly away.'

'See, I must salute this victor in the games. Must I
unloose thy hand! Dear hand, farewell! Think of me
while I speak, my precious life. 'Tis done. Give back
thy hand, or else methinks I shall die. What's this?'

A horseman, in no holiday dress, but covered with dust,
rushed into the circus, bearing in his hand a tall lance, on
which was fixed a scroll. The marshals of the games
endeavoured to prevent his advance, but he would not be
stayed. His message was to the king alone. A rumour of
news from the army circulated throughout the crowd. And

news from the army it was. Another victory! Scherirah had defeated the Sultan of Roum, who was now a suppliant for peace and alliance. Sooth to say, the intelligence had arrived at dawn of day, but the courtly Honain had contrived that it should be communicated at a later and more effective moment.

There scarcely needed this additional excitement to this glorious day. But the people cheered, the golden dirhems were scattered with renewed profusion, and the intelligence was received by all parties as a solemn ratification by Jehovah, or by Allah, of the morning ceremony.

The sun set, the court rose, and returned in the same pomp to the serail. The twilight died away, a beacon fired on a distant eminence announced the entrance of Alroy and Schirene into the nuptial chamber, and suddenly, as by magic, the mighty city, every mosque, and minaret, and tower, and terrace, and the universal plain, and the numberless pavilions, and the immense circus, and the vast and winding river, blazed with light. From every spot a lamp, a torch, a lantern, tinted with every hue, burst forth; enormous cressets of silver radiancy beamed on the top of each chartak, and huge bonfires of ruddy flame started up along the whole horizon.

For seven days and seven nights this unparalleled scene of rejoicing, though ever various, never ceased. Long, long was remembered the bridal feast of the Hebrew prince and the caliph's daughter; long, long did the peasantry on the plains of Tigris sit down by the side of that starry river, and tell the wondrous tale to their marvelling posterity.

Now what a glorious man was David Alroy, lord of the mightiest empire in the world, and wedded to the most beautiful princess, surrounded by a prosperous and obedient people, guarded by invincible armies, one on whom Earth showered all its fortune, and Heaven all its favour; and all by the power of his own genius!

# PART IX.

## CHAPTER I.

'TWAS midnight, and the storm still raged; 'mid the roar of the thunder and the shrieks of the wind, the floods of forky lightning each instant revealed the broad and billowy breast of the troubled Tigris.

Jabaster stood gazing upon the wild scene from the gallery of his palace. His countenance was solemn, but disquieted.

'I would that he were here!' exclaimed the high priest. 'Yet why should I desire his presence, who heralds only gloom? Yet in his absence am I gay? I am nothing. This Bagdad weighs upon me like a cloak of lead: my spirit is dull and broken.'

'They say Alroy gives a grand banquet in the serail tonight, and toasts his harlot 'mid the thunderbolts. Is there no hand to write upon the wall? He is found wanting, he is weighed, and is indeed found wanting. The parting of his kingdom soon will come, and then, I could weep, oh! I could weep, and down these stern and seldom yielding cheeks pour the wild anguish of my desperate woe. So young, so great, so favoured! But one more step a God, and now a foul Belshazzar!

'Was it for this his gentle youth was passed in musing solitude and mystic studies? Was it for this the holy messenger summoned his most religious spirit? Was it for this he crossed the fiery desert, and communed with his fathers in their tombs? Is this the end of all his victories and all his vast achievements? To banquet with a wanton!

'A year ago, this very night, it was the eve of battle, I

stood within his tent to wait his final word. He mused awhile, and then he said, "Good night, Jabaster!" I believed myself the nearest to his heart, as he has ever been nearest to mine, but that's all over. He never says, "Good night, Jabaster," now. Why, what's all this? Methinks I am a child.

'The Lord's anointed is a prisoner now in the light grating of a bright kiosk, and never gazes on the world he conquered. Egypt and Syria, even farthest Ind, send forth their messengers to greet Alroy, the great, the proud, the invincible. And where is he? In a soft Paradise of girls and eunuchs, crowned with flowers, listening to melting lays, and the wild trilling of the amorous lute. He spares no hours to council; all is left to his prime favourites, of whom the leader is that juggling fiend I sometime called my brother.

'Why rest I here? Whither should I fly? Methinks my presence is still a link to decency. Should I tear off the ephod, I scarcely fancy 'twould blaze upon another's breast. He goes not to the sacrifice; they say he keeps no fast, observes no ritual, and that their festive fantasies will not be balked, even by the Sabbath. I have not seen him thrice since the marriage. Honain has told her I did oppose it, and she bears to me a hatred that only women feel. Our strong passions break into a thousand purposes: women have one. Their love is dangerous, but their hate is fatal.

'See! a boat bounding on the waters. On such a night, but one would dare to venture.'

Now visible, now in darkness, a single lantern at the prow, Jabaster watched with some anxiety the slight bark buffeting the waves. A flash of lightning illumined the whole river, and tipped with a spectral light even the distant piles of building. The boat and the toiling figure of the single rower were distinctly perceptible. Now all again was darkness; the wind suddenly subsided; in a few minutes the plash of the oars was audible, and the boat apparently stopped beneath the palace.

There was a knocking at the private portal.

'Who knocks?' enquired Jabaster.

'A friend to Israel.'

'Abidan, by his voice. Art thou alone?'

'The prophetess is with me; only she.'

'A moment. I'll open the gate. Draw the boat within the arch.'

'Jabaster descended from the gallery, and in a few moments returned with two visitors: the youthful prophetess Esther, and her companion, a man short in stature, but with a powerful and well-knit frame. His countenance was melancholy, and, with harshness in the lower part, not without a degree of pensive beauty in the broad clear brow and sunken eyes, unusual in Oriental visages.

'A rough night,' said Jabaster.

'To those who fear it,' replied Abidan. 'The sun has brought so little joy to me, I care not for the storm.'

'What news?'

'Woe! woe! woe!'

'Thy usual note, my sister. Will the day never come when we may change it?'

'Woe! woe! woe! unutterable woe!'

'Abidan, how fares it?'

'Very well.'

'Indeed!'

'As it may turn out.'

'You are brief.'

'Bitter.'

'Have you been to court, that you have learnt to be so wary in your words, my friend?'

'I know not what may happen. In time we may all become courtiers, though I fear, Jabaster, we have done too much to be rewarded. I gave him my blood, and you something more, and now we are at Bagdad. 'Tis a fine city. I wish to Heaven the shower of Sodom would rain upon its terraces.'

'I know thou hast something terrible to tell. I know it by that gloomy brow of thine, that lowers like the tempest. Speak out, man, I can bear the worst, for which I am prepared.'

'Take it, then. Alroy has proclaimed himself Caliph. Abner is made Sultan of Persia; Asriel, Ithamar, Medad, and the chief captains, Vizirs, Honain their chief. Four Moslem nobles are sworn into the council. The Princess goes to mosque in state next Friday; 'tis said thy pupil doth accompany her.'

'I'll not believe it! By the God of Sinai, I'll not believe it! Were my own eye the accursed witness of the deed, I'd not believe it. Go to mosque! They play with thee, my good Abidan, they play with thee.'

'As it may be. 'Tis a rumour, but rumours herald deeds. The rest of my intelligence is true. I had it from my kinsman, stout Zalmunna. He left the banquet.'

'Shall I go to him? Methinks one single word, To mosque! only a rumour and a false one. I'll never believe it; no, no, no, never, never! Is he not the Lord's anointed? The ineffable curse upon this daughter of the Moabite! No marvel that it thunders! By heavens, I'll go and beard him in his orgies!'

'You know your power better than Abidan. You bearded him before his marriage, yet——'

'He married. 'Tis true. Honain, their chief. And I kept his ring! Honain is my brother. Have I ne'er a dagger to cut the bond of brotherhood?'

'We have all daggers, Jabaster, if we knew but how to use them.'

''Tis strange, we met after twenty years of severance. You were not in the chamber, Abidan. 'Twas at council. We met after twenty years of severance. He is my brother. 'Tis strange, I say: I felt that man shrink from my embrace.'

'Honain is a philosopher, and believes in sympathy. 'Twould appear there was none between you. His system, then, absolves you from all ties.'

'You are sure the rest of the intelligence is true? I'll not believe the mosque, the rest is bad enough.'

'Zalmunna left the banquet. Hassan Subah's brother sat above him.'

'Subah's brother! 'Tis all over, then. Is he of the council?'

'Ay, and others.'

'Where now is Israel?'

'She should be in her tents.'

'Woe! woe! unutterable woe!' exclaimed the prophetess, who, standing motionless at the back of the chamber, seemed inattentive to their conversation.

'Jabaster paced the gallery with agitated steps. Suddenly he stopped, and, walking up to Abidan, seized his arm, and looked him sternly in the face. 'I know thy thoughts, Abidan,' exclaimed the priest; 'but it cannot be. I have dismissed, henceforth and for ever I have dismissed all feeling from my mind; now I have no brother, no friend, no pupil, and, I fear, no Saviour. Israel is all in all to me. I have no other life. 'Tis not compunction, then, that stays my arm. My heart's as hard as thine.'

'Why stays it, then?'

'Because with him we fall. He is the last of all his sacred line. There is no other hand to grasp our sceptre.'

'*Our* sceptre! what sceptre?'

'The sceptre of our kings.'

'Kings!'

'Ay, why dost thou look so dark?'

'How looked the prophet when the stiff-necked populace forsooth must have a king! Did he smile? Did he shout, and clap his hands, and cry, God save his Majesty! O, Jabaster! honoured, rare Jabaster! thou second Samuel of our lightheaded people! there was a time when Israel had no king except their God. Were we viler then? Did kings conquer Canaan? Who was Moses, who was Aaron, who was mighty Joshua? Was the sword of Gideon a kingly sword? Did the locks of Samson shade royal temples? Would a king have kept his awful covenant like solemn Jephtha? Royal words are light as air, when, to maintain them, you injure any other than a subject.

'Kings! why what's a king? Why should one man break the equal sanctity of our chosen race? Is their blood purer

than our own? We are all the seed of Abraham. Who was
Saul, and who was David? I never heard that they were
a different breed from our fathers. Grant them devout,
which they were not; and brave and wise, which other men
were; have their posterity a patent for all virtues? No,
Jabaster! thou ne'er didst err, but when thou placedst a
crown upon this haughty stripling. What he did, a thousand might have done. 'Twas thy mind inspired the deed.
And now he is a king; and now Jabaster, the very soul of
Israel, who should be our Judge and leader, Jabaster trem-
bles in disgrace, while our unhallowed Sanhedrim is filled
with Ammonites!'

'Abidan, thou hast touched me to the quick; thou hast
stirred up thoughts that ever and anon, like strong and fatal
vapours, have risen from the dark abyss of thought, and I
have quelled them.'

'Let them rise, I say; let them drown the beams of
that all-scorching sun we suffer under, that drinks all
vegetation up, and makes us languish with a dull exhaustion!'

'Joy! joy! unutterable joy!'

'Hark! the prophetess has changed her note; and yet
she hears us not. The spirit of the Lord is truly with her.
Come, Jabaster, I see thy heart is opening to thy people's
sufferings; thy people, my Jabaster, for art not thou our
Judge? at least, thou shalt be.'

'Can we call back the Theocracy? Is't possible?'

'But say the word, and it is done, Jabaster. Nay, stare
not. Dost thou think there are no true hearts in Israel?
Dost thou suppose thy children have beheld, without a
thought, the foul insults poured on thee; thee, their priest,
their adored high priest, one who recalls the best days of
the past, the days of their great Judges? But one word,
one single movement of that mitred head, and—— But I
speak unto a mind that feels more than I can express. Be
silent, tongue, thou art a babbling counsellor. Jabaster's
patriot soul needs not the idle schooling of a child. If he
be silent, 'tis that his wisdom deems that the hour is not

ripe; but, when her leader speaks, Israel will not be slack.'

'The Moslemin in council! We know what must come next. Our national existence is in its last agony. Methinks the time is very ripe, Abidan.'

'Why, so we think, great sir; and say the word, and twenty thousand spears will guard the Ark. I'll answer for my men. Stout Scherirah looks grimly on the Moabites. A word from thee, and the whole Syrian army will join our banner, the Lion of Judah, that shall be our flag. The tyrant and his satraps, let them die, and then the rest must join us. We'll proclaim the covenant, and, leaving Babylon to a bloody fate, march on to Sion!'

'Sion, his youthful dream, Sion!'

'You muse!'

'King or no king, he is the Lord's anointed. Shall this hand, that poured the oil on his hallowed head, wash out the balmy signet with his blood? Must I slay him? Shall this kid be seethed even in its mother's milk?'

'His voice is low, and yet his face is troubled. How now, sir?'

'What art thou? Ah! Abidan, trusty, stanch Abidan! You see, Abidan, I was thinking, my good Abidan, all this may be the frenzy of a revel. To-morrow's dawn may summon cooler counsels. The tattle of the table, it is sacred. Let us forget it; let us pass it over. The Lord may turn his heart. Who knows, who knows, Abidan!'

'Noble sir, a moment since your mind was like your faith, firm and resolved, and now——'

'School me not, school me not, good Abidan. There is that within my mind you cannot fathom; some secret sorrows which are all my own. Leave me, good friend, leave me awhile. When Israel calls me I shall not be wanting. Be sure of that, Abidan, be sure of that. Nay, do not go; the night is very rough, and the fair prophetess should not again stem the swelling river. I'll to my closet, and will soon return.'

Jabaster quitted the gallery, and entered a small apartment. Several large volumes, unclasped and open, were lying on various parts of the divan. Before them stood his brazen cabalistic table. He closed the chamber with a cautious air. He advanced into the centre of the apartment. He lifted up his hands to heaven, and clasped them with an expression almost of agony.

'Is it come to this?' he muttered in a tone of deep oppression. 'Is it come to this? What is't I have heard? what done? Down, tempting devil, down! O life! O glory! O my country, my chosen people, and my sacred creed! why do we live, why act? Why have we feeling for aught that's famous, or for aught that's holy? Let me die! let, let me die! The torture of existence is too great.'

He flung himself upon the couch; he buried his awful countenance in his robes. His mighty heart was convulsed with passion. There did he lie, that great and solemn man, prostrate and woe-begone.

## CHAPTER II.

'THE noisy banquet lingers in my ear; I love to be alone.'
'With me?'
'Thou art myself; I have no other life.'
'Sweet bird! It is now a caliph.'
'I am what thou willest, soul of my sweet existence! Pomp and dominion, fame and victory, seem now but flawed and dimly-shaded gems compared with thy bright smile!'
'My plaintive nightingale, shall we hunt to-day?'
'Alas! my rose, I would rather lie upon this lazy couch, and gaze upon thy beauty!'
'Or sail upon the cool and azure lake, in some bright barque, like to a sea-nymph's shell, and followed by the swans?'
'There is no lake so blue as thy deep eye; there is no swan so white as thy round arm!'
'Or shall we launch our falcons in the air, and bring the golden pheasant to our feet?'

'I am the golden pheasant at thy feet; why wouldst thou richer prey?'

'Rememberest thou thy earliest visit to this dear kiosk, my gentle mute? There thou stoodst with folded arms and looks demure as day, and ever and anon with those dark eyes stealing a glance which made my cheek quite pale. Methinks I see thee even yet, shy bird. Dost know, I was so foolish when it quitted me, dost know I cried?'

'Ah, no! thou didst not cry?'

'Indeed, I think I did.'

'Tell me again, my own Schirene, indeed didst cry?'

'Indeed I did, my soul!'

'I would those tears were in some crystal vase, I'd give a province for the costly urn.'

She threw her arms around his neck and covered his face with kisses.

Sunset sounded from the minarets. They arose and wandered together in the surrounding paradise. The sky was tinted with a pale violet flush, a single star floating by the side of the white moon, that beamed with a dim lustre, soft and shapely as a pearl.

'Beautiful!' exclaimed the pensive Schirene, as she gazed upon the star. O, my Alroy, why cannot we ever live alone, and ever in a Paradise?'

'I am wearied of empire,' replied Alroy with a smile, 'let us fly!'

'Is there no island, with all that can make life charming, and yet impervious to man? How little do we require! Ah! if these gardens, instead of being surrounded by hateful Bagdad, were only encompassed by some beautiful ocean!'

'My heart, we live in a paradise, and are seldom disturbed, thanks to Honain!'

'But the very consciousness that there are any other persons existing besides ourselves is to me painful. Every one who even thinks of you seems to rob me of a part of your being. Besides, I am weary of pomp and palaces. I should like to live in a sparry grot, and sleep upon a couch of sweet leaves!'

This interesting discussion was disturbed by a dwarf, who, in addition to being very small and very ugly, was dumb. He bowed before the Princess, and then had recourse to a great deal of pantomimic action, by which she discovered that it was dinner-time. No other person could have ventured to disturb the royal pair, but this little being was a privileged favourite.

So Alroy and Schirene entered the Serail. An immense cresset-lamp, fed with perfumed oil, threw a soft light round the sumptuous chamber. At the end stood a row of eunuchs in scarlet dresses, and each holding a tall silver staff. The Caliph and the Sultana threw themselves upon a couch covered with a hundred cushions; on one side stood a group consisting of the captain of the guard and other officers of the household, on the other, of beautiful female slaves magnificently attired.

The line of domestics at the end of the apartment opened, and a body of slaves advanced, carrying trays of ivory and gold, and ebony and silver, covered with the choicest dainties, curiously prepared. These were in turn offered to the Caliph and the Sultana by their surrounding attendants. The Princess accepted a spoon made of a single pearl, the long, thin golden handle of which was studded with rubies, and condescended to partake of some saffron soup, of which she was fond. Afterwards she regaled herself with the breast of a cygnet, stuffed with almonds, and stewed with violets and cream. Having now a little satisfied her appetite, and wishing to show a mark of her favour to a particular individual, she ordered the captain of the guard instantly to send him the whole of the next course [74] with her compliments. Her attention was then engaged with a dish of those delicate ortolans that feed upon the vine-leaves of Schiraz, and with which the Governor of Nishabur took especial care that she should be well provided. Tearing the delicate birds to pieces with her still more delicate fingers, she insisted upon feeding Alroy, who of course yielded to her solicitations. In the meantime, they refreshed themselves with their favourite sherbet of pomegranates, and the golden wine of Mount Lebanon.[75] The Caliph, who could eat no more ortolans, although fed by such delicate fingers, was at length obliged to call for 'rice,' which was synonymous to commanding the banquet to disappear. The attendants now brought to each basins of gold, and ewers of rock crystal filled with rose water, with towels of that rare Egyptian linen which can be made only of the cotton that grows upon the banks of the Nile. While they amused themselves with eating sugar-plums, and drinking coffee flavoured with cinnamon, the female slaves danced before them in the most graceful attitudes to the melody of invisible musicians.

'My enchanting Schirene,' said the Caliph, 'I have dined, thanks to your attention, very well. These slaves of yours dance admirably, and are exceedingly beautiful. Your music, too, is beyond all praise; but, for my own part, I would rather be quite alone, and listening to one of your songs.'

'I have written a new one to-day. You shall hear it.' So saying, she clapped her little white hands, and all the attendants immediately withdrew.

## CHAPTER III.

'THE stars are stealing forth, and so will I. Sorry sight! to view Jabaster, with a stealthy step, skulk like a thing dishonoured! Oh! may the purpose consecrate the deed! the die is cast.'

So saying, the High Priest, muffled up in his robe, emerged from his palace into the busy streets. It is at night that the vitality of Oriental life is most impressive. The narrow winding streets, crowded with a population breathing the now sufferable air, the illuminated coffee-houses, the groups of gay yet sober revellers, the music, and the dancing, and the animated recitals of the poet and the storier, all combine to invest the starry hours with a beguiling and even fascinating character of enjoyment and adventure.

It was the night after the visit of Abidan and the prophetess. Jabaster had agreed to meet Abidan in the square of the great mosque two hours after sunset, and thither he now repaired.

'I am somewhat before my time,' he said, as he entered the great square, over which the rising moon threw a full flood of light. A few dark shadows of human beings alone moved in the distance. The world was in the streets and coffee-houses. 'I am somewhat before my time,' said Jabaster. 'Conspirators are watchful. I am anxious for the meeting, and yet I dread it. Since he broke this business, I have never slept. My mind is a chaos. I will not think. If 'tis to be done, let it be done at once. I am more tempted to sheathe this dagger in Jabaster's breast than in Alroy's. If life or empire were the paltry stake, I would end a life that now can bring no joy, and yield authority that hath no charm; but Israel, Israel, thou for whom I have endured so much, let me forget Jabaster had a mother!

'But for this thought that links me with my God, and leads my temper to a higher state, how vain and sad, how wearisome and void, were this said world they think of! But for this thought, I could sit down and die. Yea! my great heart could crack, worn out, worn out; my mighty passions, with their fierce but flickering flame, sink down and die; and the strong brain that ever hath urged my course, and pricked me onward with perpetual thought, desert the rudder it so long hath held, like some baffled pilot in blank discomforture, in the far centre of an unknown sea.

'Study and toil, anxiety and sorrow, mighty action, perchance Time, and disappointment, which is worse than all, have done their work, and not in vain. I am no longer the same Jabaster that gazed upon the stars of Caucasus. Methinks even they look dimmer than of yore. The glory of my life is fading. My leaves are sear, tinged, but not tainted. I am still the same in one respect; I have not left my God, in deed or thought. Ah! who art thou?'

'A friend to Israel.'

'I am glad that Israel hath a friend. Noble Abidan, I have well considered all that hath passed between us. Sooth to say, you touched upon a string I've played before, but kept it for my loneliness; a jarring tune, indeed a jarring tune, but so it is, and being so, let me at once unto your friends, Abidan.'

'Noble Jabaster, thou art what I deemed thee.'

'Abidan, they say the consciousness of doing justly is the best basis of a happy mind.'

'Even so.'

'And thou believest it?'

'Without doubt.'

'We are doing very justly?'

''Tis a weak word for such a holy purpose.'

'I am most wretched!'

## CHAPTER IV.

The High Priest and his companion entered the house of Abidan. Jabaster addressed the already assembled guests.

'Brave Scherirah, it joys me to find thee here. In Israel's cause when was Scherirah wanting? Stout Zalmunna, we have not seen enough of each other: the blame is mine. Gentle prophetess, thy blessing!

'Good friends, why we meet here is known to all. Little did we dream of such a meeting when we crossed the Tigris. But that is nothing. We come to act, and not to argue. Our great minds, they are resolved: our solemn purpose requires no demonstration. If there be one among us who would have Israel a slave to Ishmael, who would lose all we have prayed for, all we have fought for, all we have won, and all for which we are prepared to die, if there be one among us who would have the ark polluted, and Jehovah's altar stained with a Gentile sacrifice, if there be one among

us who does not sigh for Sion, who would not yield his
breath to build the Temple and gain the heritage his fathers
lost, why, let him go! There is none such among us: then
stay, and free your country!'

'We are prepared, great Jabaster; we are prepared, all,
all!'

'I know it; you are like myself. Necessity hath taught
decision. Now for our plans. Speak, Zalmunna.'

'Noble Jabaster, I see much difficulty. Alroy no longer
quits his palace. Our entrance unwatched is, you well know,
impossible. What say you, Scherirah?'

'I doubt not of my men, but war against Alroy is, to say
nought of danger, of doubtful issue.'

'I am prepared to die, but not to fail,' said Abidan.
'We must be certain. Open war I fear. The mass of
the army will side with their leaders, and they are with
the tyrant. Let us do the deed, and they must join us.'

'Is it impossible to gain his presence to some sacrifice in
honour of some by-gone victory; what think ye?'

'I doubt much, Jabaster. At this moment he little
wishes to sanction our national ceremonies with his royal
person. The woman assuredly will stay him. And, even
if he come, success is difficult, and therefore doubtful.'

'Noble warriors, list to a woman's voice,' exclaimed the
prophetess, coming forward. "'Tis weak, but with such
instruments, even the aspirations of a child, the Lord will
commune with his chosen people. There is a secret way
by which I can gain the gardens of the palace. To-morrow
night, just as the moon is in her midnight bower, behold
the accursed pile shall blaze. Let Abidan's troop be all
prepared, and at the moment when the flames first ascend,
march to the Seraglio gate as if with aid. The affrighted
guard will offer no opposition. While the troops secure
the portals, you yourselves, Zalmunna, Abidan, and Jabaster, rush to the royal chamber and do the deed. In the
meantime, let brave Scherirah, with his whole division,
surround the palace, as if unconscious of the mighty
work. Then come you forward, show, if it need, with

tears, the fated body to the soldiery, and announce the Theocracy.'

'It is the Lord who speaks,' said Abidan, who was doubtless prepared for the proposition. 'He has delivered them into our hands.'

'A bold plan,' said Jabaster, musing, 'and yet I like it. 'Tis quick, and that is something. I think 'tis sure.'

'It cannot fail,' exclaimed Zalmunna, 'for if the flame ascend not, still we are but where we were.'

'I am for it,' said Scherirah.

'Well, then,' said Jabaster, 'so let it be. To-morrow's eve will see us here again prepared. Good night.'

'Good night, holy Priest. How seem the stars, Jabaster?'

'Very troubled; so have they been some days. What they portend I know not.'

'Health to Israel.'

'Let us hope so. Good night, sweet friends.'

'Good night, holy Jabaster. Thou art our corner-stone.'

'Israel hath no other hope but in Jabaster.'

'My Lord,' said Abidan, 'remain, I pray, one moment.'

'What is't? I fain would go.'

'Alroy must die, my Lord, but dost thou think a single death will seal the covenant?'

'The woman?'

'Ay! the woman! I was not thinking of the woman. Asrael, Ithamar, Medad?'

'Valiant soldiers! doubt not we shall find them useful instruments. I do not fear such loose companions. They follow their leaders, like other things born to obey. Having no head themselves, they must follow us who have.'

'I think so too. There is no other man who might be dangerous?'

Zalmunna and Scherirah cast their eyes upon the ground. There was a dead silence, broken by the prophetess.

'A judgment hath gone forth against Honain!'

'Nay! he is Lord Jabaster's brother,' said Abidan. 'It is enough to save a more inveterate foe to Israel, if such there be.'

'I have no brother, Sir. The man you speak of I will not slay, since there are others who may do that deed. And so again, good night.'

## CHAPTER V.

It was the dead of night, a single lamp burned in the chamber, which opened into an arched gallery that descended by a flight of steps into the gardens of the Serail.

A female figure ascended the flight with slow and cautious steps. She paused on the gallery, she looked around, one foot was in the chamber.

She entered. She entered a chamber of small dimensions, but richly adorned. In the farthest corner was a couch of ivory, hung with a gauzy curtain of silver tissue, which, without impeding respiration, protected the slumberer from the fell insects of an Oriental night. Leaning against an ottoman was a large brazen shield of ancient fashion, and near it some helmets and curious weapons.

'An irresistible impulse hath carried me into this chamber!' exclaimed the prophetess. 'The light haunted me like a spectre; and wheresoever I moved, it seemed to summon me.

'A couch and a slumberer!'

She approached the object, she softly withdrew the curtain. Pale and panting, she rushed back, yet with a light step. She beheld Alroy!

For a moment she leant against the wall, overpowered by her emotions. Again she advanced, and gazed on her unconscious victim.

'Can the guilty sleep like the innocent? Who would deem this gentle slumberer had betrayed the highest trust that ever Heaven vouchsafed to favoured man? He looks not like a tyrant and a traitor: calm his brow, and mild his placid breath! His long dark hair, dark as the raven's wing, hath broken from its fillet, and courses, like a wild and stormy night, over his pale and moon-lit brow. His cheek is delicate, and yet repose hath brought a flush; and on his lip there seems some word of love, that will not quit it. It is the same Alroy that blessed our vision when, like the fresh and glittering star of morn, he rose up in the desert, and bringing joy to others, brought to me only——

'Oh! hush my heart, and let thy secret lie hid in the charnel-house of crushed affections. Hard is the lot of woman: to love and to conceal is our sharp doom! O bitter life! O most unnatural lot! Man made society, and made us slaves. And so we droop and die, or else take refuge in idle fantasies, to which we bring the fervour that is meant for nobler ends.

'Beauteous hero! whether I bear thee most hatred or most love I cannot tell. Die thou must; yet I feel I should die with thee. Oh! that to-night could lead at the same time unto our marriage bed and funeral pyre. Must that white bosom bleed? and must those delicate limbs be hacked and handled by these bloody butchers? Is that justice? They lie, the traitors, when they call thee false to our God. Thou art thyself a god, and I could worship thee! See those beauteous lips; they move. Hark to the music!'

'Schirene, Schirene!'

'There wanted but that word to summon back my senses. Fool! whither is thy fancy wandering? I will not wait for tardy justice. I will do the deed myself. Shall I not kill my Sisera?' She seized a dagger from the ottoman, a rare and highly-tempered blade. Up she raised it in the air, and dashed it to his heart with superhuman force. It struck against the talisman which Jabaster had given to Alroy, and which, from a lingering superstition, he still wore; it struck, and shivered into a thousand pieces. The Caliph sprang from his couch; his eyes met the prophetess, standing over him in black despair, with the hilt of the dagger in her hand.

'What is all this? Schirene! Who art thou? Esther!' He jumped from the couch, called to Pharez, and seized her by both hands. 'Speak!' he continued. 'Art thou Esther? What dost thou here?'

She broke into a wild laugh; she wrestled with his grasp, and pulled him towards the gallery. He beheld the chief tower of the Serail in flames. Joining her hands together, grasping them both in one of his, and dragging her towards the ottoman, he seized a helmet and flung it upon the mighty shield. It sounded like a gong. Pharez started from his slumbers, and rushed into the chamber.

'Pharez! Treason! treason! Send instant orders that the palace gates be opened on no pretence whatever. Go, fly! See the captain himself. Summon the household. Order all to arms. Speed, for our lives!'

The whole palace was now roused. Alroy delivered Esther, exhausted, and apparently senseless, to a guard of eunuchs. Slaves and attendants poured in from all directions. Soon arrived Schirene, with dishevelled hair and hurried robes, attended by a hundred maidens, each bearing a torch.

'My soul, what ails thee?'

'Nothing, sweetest; all will soon be well,' replied Alroy, picking up, and examining the fragments of the shivered dagger, which he had just discovered.

'My life has been attempted; the palace is in flames; I suspect the city is in insurrection. Look to your mistress, maidens!' Schirene fell into their arms. 'I will soon be back.' So saying, he hurried to the grand court.

Several thousand persons, for the population of the Serail and its liberties was very considerable, were assembled in the grand court; eunuchs, women, pages, slaves, and servants, and a few soldiers; all in confusion and alarm, fire raging within, and mysterious and terrible outcries without. A cry of 'The Caliph! the Caliph!' announced the arrival of Alroy, and produced a degree of comparative silence.

'Where is the captain of the guard?' he exclaimed. 'That's well. Open the gates to none. Who will leap the wall, and bear a message to Asriel? You? That's well too. To-morrow you shall yourself command. Where's Mesrour?

Take the eunuch guard and the company of gardeners,[76] and suppress the flames at all cost. Pull down the intervening buildings. Abidan's troop arrived with succour, eh! I doubt it not. I expected them. Open to none. They force an entrance, eh! I thought so. So that javelin has killed a traitor. Feed me with arms. I'll keep the gate. Send again to Asriel. Where's Pharez?'

'By your side, my lord.'

'Run to the Queen, my faithful Pharez, and tell her that all's well. I wish it were! Didst ever hear a din so awful? Methinks all the tambours and cymbals of the city are in full chorus. Foul play, I guess. Oh! for Asriel! Has Pharez returned?'

'I am by your side, my lord.'

'How's the Queen?'

'She would gladly join your side.'

'No, no! Keep the gates there. Who says they are making fires before them? 'Tis true. We must sally, if the worst come to the worst, and die at least like soldiers. O Asriel! Asriel!'

'May it please your Highness, the troops are pouring in from all quarters.'

''Tis Asriel.'

'No, your Highness, 'tis not the guard. Methinks they are Scherirah's men.'

'Hum! What it all is, I know not; but very foul play, I do not doubt. Where's Honain?'

'With the Queen, Sire.'

''Tis well. What's that shout?'

'Here's the messenger from Asriel. Make way! way!'

'Well! how is't, Sir?'

'Please your Highness, I could not reach the guard.'

'Could not reach the guard! God of my fathers! who should let thee?'

'Sire, I was taken prisoner.'

'Prisoner! By the thunder of Sinai, are we at war? Who made thee prisoner?'

'Sire, they have proclaimed thy death.'

'Who?'

'The council of the Elders. So I heard. Abidan, Zalmunna——'

'Rebels and dogs! Who else?'

'The High Priest.'

'Hah! Is it there? Pharez, fetch me some drink. Is it true Scherirah has joined them?'

'His force surrounds the Serail. No aid can reach us without cutting through his ranks.'

'Oh! that I were there with my good guard! Are we to die here like rats, fairly murdered? Cowardly knaves! Hold out, hold out, my men! 'Tis sharp work, but some of us will smile at this hereafter. Who stands by Alroy to-night bravely and truly, shall have his heart's content to-morrow. Fear not: I was not born to die in a civic broil. I bear a charmed life. So to it.'

## CHAPTER VI.

'Go to the Caliph, good Honain, I pray thee, go. I can support myself, he needs thy counsel. Bid him not expose his precious life. The wicked men! Asriel must soon be here. What sayest thou?'

'There is no fear. Their plans are ill-devised. I have long expected this stormy night, and feel even now more anxious than alarmed.'

''Tis at me they aim; it is I whom they hate. The High Priest, too! Ay, ay! Thy proud brother, good Honain, I have ever felt he would not rest until he drove me from this throne, my right; or washed my hated name from out our annals in my life's blood. Wicked, wicked Jabaster! He frowned upon me from the first, Honain. Is he indeed thy brother?'

'I care not to remember. He aims at something further than thy life; but Time will teach us more than all our thoughts.'

## CHAPTER VII.

The fortifications of the Serail resisted all the efforts of the rebels. Scherirah remained in his quarters, with his troops under arms, and recalled the small force that he had originally sent out as much to watch the course of events as to assist Abidan. Asriel and Ithamar poured down their columns in the rear of that chieftain, and by dawn a division of the guard had crossed the river, the care of which had been entrusted to Scherirah, and had thrown themselves into the palace. Alroy sallied forth at the head of these fresh troops. His presence decided a result which was perhaps never doubtful. The division of Abidan fought with the desperation that became their fortunes. The carnage was dreadful, but their discomfiture complete. They no longer acted in masses, or with any general system. They thought only of self-preservation, or of selling their lives at the dearest cost. Some dispersed, some escaped. Others entrenched themselves in houses, others fortified the bazaar. All the horrors of war in the streets were now experienced. The houses were in flames, the thoroughfares flowed with blood.

At the head of a band of faithful followers, Abidan proved himself, by his courage and resources, worthy of success. At length, he was alone, or surrounded only by his enemies. With his back against a building in a narrow street, where the number of his opponents only embarrassed them, the three foremost of his foes fell before his irresistible scimetar. The barricadoed door yielded to the pressure of the multitude. Abidan rushed up the narrow stairs, and, gaining a landing-place, turned suddenly round, and cleaved the skull of his nearest pursuer. He hurled the mighty body at his followers, and, retarding their advance, himself dashed onward, and gained the terrace of the mansion. Three soldiers of the guard followed him as he bounded from terrace to terrace. One, armed with a javelin, hurled it at the chieftain. The weapon slightly wounded Abidan, who, drawing it from his arm, sent it back to the heart of its owner. The two other soldiers, armed only with swords, gained upon him. He arrived at the last terrace in the cluster of buildings. He stood at bay on the brink of the precipice. He regained his breath. They approached him. He dodged them in their course. Suddenly, with admirable skill, he flung his scimetar edgewise at the legs of his farthest foe, who stopped short, roaring with pain. The chieftain sprang at the foremost, and hurled him down into the street below, where he was dashed to atoms. A trap-door offered itself to the despairing eye of the rebel. He descended and found himself in a room filled with women. They screamed, he rushed through them, and descending a staircase, entered a chamber tenanted by a bed-ridden old man. The ancient invalid inquired the cause of the uproar, and died of fright before he could receive an answer, at the sight of the awful being before him, covered with streaming blood. Abidan secured the door, washed his blood-stained face, and disguising himself in the dusty robes of the deceased Armenian, sallied forth to watch the fray. The obscure street was silent. The chieftain proceeded unmolested. At the corner he found a soldier holding a charger for his captain. Abidan, unarmed, seized a poniard from the soldier's belt, stabbed him to the heart, and vaulting on the steed, galloped towards the river. No boat was to be found; he breasted the stream upon the stout courser. He reached the opposite bank. A company of camels were reposing by the side of a fountain. Alarm had dispersed their drivers. He mounted the fleetest in appearance; he dashed to the nearest gate of the city. The guard at the gate refused him a passage. He concealed his agitation. A marriage procession, returning from the country, arrived. He rushed into the centre of it, and overset the bride in her gilded waggon. In the midst of the confusion, the shrieks, the oaths, and the scuffle, he forced his way through the gate, scoured over the country, and never stopped until he had gained the desert.

## CHAPTER VIII.

THE uproar died away. The shouts of warriors, the shrieks of women, the wild clang of warfare, all were silent. The flames were extinguished, the carnage ceased. The insurrection was suppressed, and order restored. The city, all the houses of which were closed, was patrolled by the conquering troops, and by sunset the conqueror himself, in his hall of state, received the reports and the congratulations of his chieftains. The escape of Abidan seemed counterbalanced by the capture of Jabaster. After performing prodigies of valour, the High Priest had been overpowered, and was now a prisoner in the Serail. The conduct of Scherirah was not too curiously criticised; a commission was appointed to inquire into the mysterious affair, and Alroy retired to the bath [77] to refresh himself after the fatigues of the victory which he could not consider a triumph.

As he reposed upon his couch, melancholy and exhausted, Schirene was announced. The Princess threw herself upon his neck and covered him with embraces. His heart yielded to her fondness, his spirit became lighter, his depression melted away.

'My ruby!' said Schirene, and she spoke in a low smothered voice, her face hidden and nestled in his breast. 'My ruby! dost thou love me?'

He smiled in fondness as he pressed her to his heart.

'My ruby, thy pearl is so frightened, it dare not look upon thee. Wicked men! 'tis I whom they hate, 'tis I whom they would destroy.'

'There is no danger, sweet. 'Tis over now. Speak not, nay, do not think of it.'

'Ah! wicked men! There is no joy on earth while such things live. Slay Alroy, their mighty master, who, from vile slaves, hath made them princes! Ungrateful churls! I am so alarmed, I ne'er shall sleep again. What! slay my innocent bird, my pretty bird, my very heart! I'll not believe it. It is I whom they hate. I am sure they will kill me. You shall never leave me, no, no, no, no! You shall not leave me, love, never, never! Didst hear a noise? Methinks they are even here, ready to plunge their daggers in our hearts, our soft, soft hearts! I think you love me, child; indeed, I think you do!'

'Take courage, heart! There is no fear, my soul; I cannot love thee more, or else I would.'

'All joy is gone! I ne'er shall sleep again. O my soul! art thou indeed alive? Do I indeed embrace my own Alroy, or is it all a wild and troubled dream, and are my arms clasped round a shadowy ghost, myself a spectre in a sepulchre? Wicked, wicked men! Can it indeed be true? What, slay Alroy! my joy, my only life! Ah! woe is me; our bright felicity hath fled for ever!'

'Not so, sweet child; we are but as we were. A few quick hours, and all will be as bright as if no storm had crossed our sunny days.'

'Hast seen Asriel? He says such fearful things!'

'How now?'

'Ah me! I am desolate. I have no friend.'

'Schirene!'

'They will have my blood. I know they will have my blood.'

'Indeed, an idle fancy.'

'Idle! Ask Asriel, question Ithamar. Idle! 'tis written in their tablets, their bloody scroll of rapine and of murder. Thy death led only to mine, and, had they hoped my bird would but have yielded his gentle mate, they would have spared him. Ay! ay! 'tis I whom they hate, 'tis I whom they would destroy. This form, I fear it has lost its lustre, but still 'tis thine, and once thou saidst thou lovedst it; this form was to have been hacked and mangled; this ivory bosom was to have been ripped up and tortured, and this warm blood, that flows alone for thee, that fell Jabaster was to pour its tide     the altar of his ancient vengeance. He ever hated me!'

'Jabaster! Schirene! Where are we, and what are

we? Life, life, they lie, that call thee Nature! Nature never sent these gusts of agony. Oh! my heart will break. I drove him from my thought, and now she calls him up, and now must I remember he is my—prisoner! God of heaven, God of my fathers, is it come to this? Why did he not escape? Why must Abidan, a common cut-throat, save his graceless life, and this great soul, this stern and mighty being —— Ah me! I have lived long enough. Would they had not failed, would —— '

'Stop, stop, Alroy! I pray thee, love, be calm. I came to soothe thee, not to raise thy passions. I did not say Jabaster willed thy death, though Asriel says so; 'tis me he wars against; and if indeed Jabaster be a man so near thy heart, if he indeed be one so necessary to thy prosperity, and cannot live in decent order with thy slave that's here, I know my duty, Sir. I would not have thy fortunes marred to save my single heart, although I think 'twill break. I will go, I will die, and deem the hardest accident of life but sheer prosperity if it profit thee.'

'O Schirene! what wouldst thou? This, this is torture.'

'To see thee safe and happy; nothing more.'

'I am both, if thou art.'

'Care not for me, I am nothing.'

'Thou art all to me.'

'Calm thyself, my soul. It grieves me much that when I came to soothe I have only galled thee. All's well, all's well. Say that Jabaster lives. What then? He lives, and may he prove more duteous than before; that's all.'

'He lives, he is my prisoner, he awaits his doom. It must be given.'

'Yes, yes!'

'Shall we pardon?'

'My lord will do that which it pleases him.'

'Nay, nay, Schirene, I pray thee be more kind. I am most wretched. Speak, what wouldst thou?'

'If I must speak, I say at once his life.'

'Ah me!'

'If our past loves have any charm, if the hope of future joy, not less supreme, be that which binds thee to this shadowy world, as it does me, and does alone, I say his life, his very carnal life. He stands between us and our loves, Alroy, and ever has done. There is no happiness if Jabaster breathe; nor can I be the same Schirene to thee as I have been, if this proud rebel live to spy my conduct.'

'Banish him, banish him!'

'To herd with rebels. Is this thy policy?'

'O Schirene! I love not this man, although methinks I should: yet didst thou know but all!'

'I know too much, Alroy. From the first he has been to me a hateful thought. Come, come, sweet bird, a boon, a boon unto thy own Schirene, who was so frightened by these wicked men! I fear it has done more mischief than thou deemest. Ay! robbed us of our hopes. It may be so. A boon, a boon! It is not much I ask: a traitor's head. Come, give me thy signet ring. It will not; nay, then, I'll take it. What, resist! I know thou oft hast told me a kiss could vanquish all denial. There it is. Is't sweet? Shalt have another, and another too. I've got the ring! Farewell, my lovely bird, I'll soon return to pillow in thy nest.'

## CHAPTER IX.

'SHE has got the ring! What's this? what's this? Schirene! art gone? Nay, surely not. She jests. Jabaster! A traitor's head! What ho! there. Pharez, Pharez!'

'My lord.'

'Passed the Queen that way?'

'She did, my lord.'

'In tears?'

'Nay! very joyful!'

'Call Honain, quick as my thought. Honain! Honain!

He waits without. I have seen the best of life, that's very sure. My heart is cracking. She surely jests! Hah! Honain. Pardon these distracted looks. Fly to the Armoury! fly, fly!'

'For what, my lord?'

'Ay! for what, for what! My brain it wanders. Thy brother, thy great brother, the Queen, the Queen has stolen my signet ring, that is, I gave it her. Fly, fly! or in a word, Jabaster is no more. He is gone. Pharez! your arm; I swoon!'

## CHAPTER X.

'His Highness is sorely indisposed to-day.'

'They say he swooned this morn.'

'Ay, in the bath.'

'No, not in the bath. 'Twas when he heard of Jabaster's death.'

'How died he, Sir?'

'Self-strangled. His mighty heart could not endure disgrace, and thus he ended all his glorious deeds.'

'A great man!'

'We shall not soon see his match. The Queen had gained his pardon, and herself flew to the armoury to bear the news; alas! too late.'

'These are strange times. Jabaster dead!'

'A very great event.'

'Who will be High Priest?'

'I doubt if the appointment will be filled up.'

'Sup you with the Lord Ithamar to-night?'

'I do.'

'I also. We'll go together. The Queen had gained his pardon. Hum! 'tis strange.'

'Passing so. They say Abidan has escaped?'

'I hear it. Shall we meet Medad to-night?'

''Tis likely.'

# PART X.

## CHAPTER I.

'SHE comes not yet! her cheerful form, not yet it sparkles in our mournful sky. She comes not yet! the shadowy stars seem sad and lustreless without their Queen. She comes not yet!'

'WE ARE THE WATCHERS OF THE MOON,[8] AND LIVE IN LONE-LINESS TO HERALD LIGHT.'

'She comes not yet! her sacred form, not yet it summons to our holy feast. She comes not yet! our brethren far wait mute and motionless the saintly beam. She comes not yet!'

'WE ARE THE WATCHERS OF THE MOON, AND LIVE IN LONE-LINESS TO HERALD LIGHT.'

'She comes, she comes! her beauteous form sails with soft splendour in the glittering air. She comes, she comes! The beacons fire, and tell the nation that the month begins! She comes, she comes!'

'WE ARE THE WATCHERS OF THE MOON, TO TELL THE NATION THAT THE MONTH BEGINS.'

Instantly the holy watchers fired the beacons on the mountain top, and anon a thousand flames blazed round the land. From Caucasus to Lebanon, on every peak a crown of light.

## CHAPTER II.

'SIRE! a Tatar has arrived from Hamadan, who will see none but thyself. I have told him your Highness was engaged, and sent him to the Lord Honain; but all denial is lost upon him. And as I thought perhaps the Lady Miriam——'

'From Hamadan? You did well, Pharez. Admit him.'

The Tatar entered.

'Well, Sir; good news, I hope!'

'Sire, pardon me, the worst. I come from the Lord Abner, with orders to see the Caliph, and none else.'

'Well, Sir, you see the Caliph. Your mission? What of the Viceroy?'

'Sire, he bade me tell thee, that, the moment the beacon that announced the Feast of the New Moon was fired on Caucasus, the dreaded monarch of Karasmé, the great Alp Arslan, entered thy kingdom, and now overruns all Persia.'

'Hah! and Abner?'

'Is in the field, and prays for aid.'

'He shall have it. This is indeed great news! When left you Hamadan?'

'Night and day I have journeyed upon the swiftest dromedary. The third morn sees me at Bagdad.'

'You have done your duty. See this faithful courier be well tended, Pharez. Summon the Lord Honain.'

'Alp Arslan! Hah! a very famous warrior. The moment the beacon was fired. No sudden impulse then, but long matured. I like it not.'

'Sire,' said Pharez, re-entering, 'a Tatar has arrived from the frontiers of the province, who will see none but thyself. I have told him your Highness was deeply busied, and as methinks he brings but the same news, I——"

"'Tis very likely; yet never *think*, good Pharez. I'll see the man.'

The Tatar entered.

'Well, Sir, how now! from whom?'

'From Mozul. The Governor bade me see the Caliph and none else, and tell your Highness, that the moment the beacon that announced the Feast of the New Moon was fired on the mountains, the fell rebel Abidan raised the standard of Judah in the province, and proclaimed war against your Majesty.'

'In any force?'

'The royal power keeps within their walls.'

'Sufficient answer. Part of the same movement. We shall have some trouble. Hast summoned Honain?'

'I have, Sir.'

'Go, see this messenger be duly served, and, Pharez, come hither: let none converse with them. You understand?'

'Your Highness may assure yourself.'

'Abidan come to life. He shall not escape so well this time. I must see ˙Scherirah. I much suspect——what's this? More news!'

A third Tatar entered.

'May it please your Highness, this Tatar has arrived from the Syrian frontier.'

'Mischief in the wind, I doubt not. Speak out, knave!'

'Sire! pardon me; I bear but sad intelligence.'

'Out with the worst!'

'I come from the Lord Medad.'

'Well! has he rebelled? It seems a catching fever.'

'Ah! no, dread Sire, Lord Medad has no thought but for thy glory. Alas! alas! he has now to guard it against fearful odds. Lord Medad bade me see the Caliph and none else, and tell your Highness, that the moment the beacon which announced the Feast of the New Moon was fired on Lebanon, the Sultan of Roum and the old Arabian Caliph unfurled the standard of their Prophet, in great array, and are now marching towards Bagdad.'

'A clear conspiracy! Has Honain arrived? Summon a council of the Vizirs instantly. The world is up against me. Well! I'm sick of peace. They shall not find me napping!'

---

## CHAPTER III.

'You see, my lords,' said Alroy, ere the council broke up, 'we must attack them singly. There can be no doubt of that. If they join, we must combat at great odds. 'Tis in detail that we must rout them. I will myself to Persia. Ithamar must throw himself between the Sultan and Abidan, Medad fall back on Ithamar. Scherirah must guard the capital. Honain, you are Regent. And so farewell. I shall set off to-night. Courage, brave companions. 'Tis a storm, but many a cedar survives the thunderbolt.'

The council broke up.

'My own Scherirah!' said the Caliph, as they retired, 'stay awhile. I would speak with you alone. Honain,' continued Alroy, following the Grand Vizir out of the chamber, and leaving Scherirah alone, 'Honain, I have not yet interchanged a word with you in private. What think you of all this?'

'Sire, I am prepared for the worst, but hope the best.'

''Tis wise. If Abner could only keep that Karasmian in check! I am about to speak with Scherirah alone. I do suspect him much.'

'I'll answer for his treason.'

'Hah! I do suspect him. Therefore I give him no command. I would not have him too near his old companion, eh? We will garrison the city with his rebels.'

'Sire, these are not moments to be nice. Scherirah is a valiant captain, a very valiant captain, but lend me thy signet ring, I pray thee, Sire.'

Alroy turned pale.

'No, Sir, it has left me once, and never shall again. You have touched upon a string that makes me sad. There is a burden on my conscience, why, or what, I know not. I am innocent, you know I am innocent, Honain!'

'I'll answer for your Highness. He who has enough of the milk of human kindness to spare a thing like Scherirah, when he stands in his way, may well be credited for the nobler mercy that spared his better.'

'Ah me! there's madness in the thought. Why is he not here? Had I but followed; tush! tush! Go see the Queen, and tell her all that has happened. I'll to Scherirah.'

The Caliph returned.

'Thy pardon, brave Scherirah; in these moments my friends will pardon lapse of courtesy.'

'Your Highness is too considerate.'

'You see, Scherirah, how the wind blows, brave heart. There's much to do, no doubt. I am in sad want of some right trusty friend, on whose devoted bosom I can pillow all my necessities. I was thinking of sending you against this Arslan, but perhaps 'tis better that I should go myself. These are moments one should not seem to shrink, and yet we know not how affairs may run; no, we know not. The capital, the surrounding province: one disaster and these false Moslemin may rise against us. I should stay here, but if I leave Scherirah, I leave myself. I feel that deeply; 'tis a consolation. It may be that I must fall back upon the city. Be prepared, Scherirah. Let me fall back upon supporting friends. You have a great trust. Oh! use it wisely! Worthily I am sure you must do.'

'Your Highness may rest assured I have no other thought but for your weal and glory. Doubt not my devotion, Sire. I am not one of those mealy-mouthed youths, full of their own deeds and lip-worship, Sire, but I have a life devoted to your service, and ready at all times to peril all things.'

'I know that, Scherirah, I know it; I feel it deeply. What think you of these movements?'

'They are not ill combined, and yet I doubt not your Majesty will prove your fortunes most triumphant.'

'Think you the soldiery are in good cue?'

'I'll answer for my own. They are rough fellows, like myself, a little too blunt, perhaps, your Highness. We are not holiday guards, but we know our duty, and we will do it.'

'That's well, that's all I want. I shall review the troops before I go. Let a donative be distributed among them; and, by the bye, I have always forgotten it, your legion should be called the Legion of Syria. We owe our fairest province to their arms.'

'I shall convey to them your Highness' wish. Were it possible, 'twould add to their devotion.'

'I do not wish it. They are my very children. Sup at the Serail to-night, Scherirah. We shall be very private. Yet let us drink together ere we part. We are old friends, you know. Hast not forgotten our ruined city?'

## CHAPTER IV.

ALROY entered the apartment of Schirene. 'My soul! thou knowest all?'

She sprang forward and threw her arms around his neck.

'Fear not, my life, we'll not disgrace our Queen. 'Twill be quick work. Two-thirds of them have been beaten before, and for the new champion, our laurels must not fade, and his blood shall nourish fresh ones.'

'Dearest, dearest Alroy, go not thyself, I pray thee. May not Asriel conquer?'

'I hope so, in my company. For a time we part, a short one. 'Tis our first parting: may it be our last!'

'Oh! no, no, no : oh! say not we must part.'

'The troops are under arms; to-morrow's dawn will hear my trumpet.'

'I will not quit thee, no! I will not quit thee. What business has Schirene without Alroy? Hast thou not often told me I am thy inspiration? In the hour of danger shall I be wanting? Never! I will not quit thee; no, I will not quit thee.'

'Thou art ever present in my thoughts, my soul. In the battle I shall think of her for whom alone I conquer.'

'Nay, nay, I'll go, indeed I must, Alroy. I'll be no hindrance, trust me, sweet boy, I will not. I'll have no train, no, not a single maid. Credit me, I know how a true soldier's wife should bear herself. I'll watch thee sleeping, and I'll tend thee wounded, and when thou goest forth to combat I'll gird thy sabre round thy martial side, and whisper triumph with victorious kisses.'

'My own Schirene, there's victory in thine eyes. We'll beat them, girl.'

'Abidan, doubly false Abidan! would he were doubly hanged! Ere she died, the fatal prophetess foretold this time, and gloated on his future treachery.'

'Think not of him.'

'And the Karasmian; think you he is very strong?'

'Enough, love, for our glory. He is a potent warrior: I trust that Abner will not rob us of our intended victory.'

'So you triumph, I care not by whose sword. Dost go indeed to-morrow?'

'At break of dawn. I pray thee stay, my sweet!'

'Never! I will not quit thee. I am quite prepared. At break of dawn? 'Tis near on midnight now. I'll lay me down upon this couch awhile, and travel in my litter. Art sure Alp Arslan is himself in the field?'

'Quite sure, my sweet.'

'Confusion on his crown! We'll conquer. Goes Asriel with us?'

'Ay!'

'That's well; at break of dawn. I'm somewhat drowsy. Methinks I'll sleep awhile.'

'Do, my best heart; I'll to my cabinet, and at break of dawn I'll wake thee with a kiss.'

## CHAPTER V.

THE Caliph repaired to his cabinet, where his secretaries were occupied in writing. As he paced the chamber, he dictated to them the necessary instructions.

'Who is the officer on guard?'

'Benaiah, Sire.'

'I remember him. He saved me a broken skull upon the Tigris. This is for him. The Queen accompanies us. She is his charge. These papers for the Vizir. Let the troops be under arms by daybreak. This order of the day for the Lord Asriel. Send this instantly to Hamadan. Is the Tatar despatched to Medad? 'Tis well. You have done your duty. Now to rest. Pharez?'

'My lord.'

'I shall not sleep to-night. Give me my drink. Go rest, good boy. I have no wants. Good night.'

'Good night, my gracious lord!'

'Let me ponder! I am alone. I am calm, and yet my spirit is not quick. I am not what I was. Four-and-twenty hours ago who would have dreamed of this? All at stake again! Once more in the field, and struggling at once for empire and existence! I do lack the mighty spirit of my former days. I am not what I was. I have little faith. All about me seems changed, and dull, and grown mechanical. Where are those flashing eyes and conquering visages that clustered round me on the battle eve, round me, the Lord's anointed? I see none such. They are changed, as I am. Why! this Abidan was a host, and now he fights against me. She spoke of the prophetess; I remember that woman was the stirring trumpet of our ranks, and now where is she? The victim of my justice! And where is he, the mightier far, the friend, the counsellor, the constant guide, the master of my boyhood; the firm, the fond, the faithful guardian of all my bright career; whose days and nights were one unbroken study to make me glorious? Alas! I feel more like a doomed and desperate renegade than a young hero on the eve of battle, flushed with the memory of unbroken triumphs!

'Hah! what awful form art thou that risest from the dusky earth before me? Thou shouldst be one I dare not name, yet will: the likeness of Jabaster. Away! why frownest thou upon me? I did not slay thee. Do I live, or dream, or what? I see him, ay! I see thee. I fear thee not, I fear nothing. I am Alroy.

'Speak, oh speak! I do conjure thee, mighty spectre, speak. By all the memory of the past, although 'tis madness, I do conjure thee, let me hear again the accents of my boyhood.'

'ALROY, ALROY, ALROY!'

'I listen, as to the last trump.'

'MEET ME ON THE PLAIN OF NEHAUEND.'

''Tis gone! As it spoke it vanished. It was Jabaster! God of my fathers, it was Jabaster! Life is growing too wild. My courage is broken! I could lie down and die. It was Jabaster! The voice sounds in my ear like distant thunder: "*Meet me on the plain of Nehauend.*" I'll not fail thee, noble ghost, although I meet my doom. Jabaster! Have I seen Jabaster! Indeed! indeed! Methinks I'm mad. Hah! What's that?'

An awful clap of thunder broke over the palace, followed by a strange clashing sound that seemed to come from one of the chambers. The walls of the Serail rocked.

'An earthquake!' exclaimed Alroy. 'Would that the earth would open and swallow all! Hah! Pharez, has it roused thee, too? Pharez, we live in strange times.'

'Your Highness is very pale.'

'And so art thou, lad! Wouldst have me merry? Pale! we may well be pale, didst thou know all. Hah! that awful sound again! I cannot bear it, Pharez, I cannot bear it. I have borne many things, but this I cannot.'

'My lord, 'tis in the Armoury.'

'Run, see. No, I'll not be alone. Where's Benaiah? Let him go. Stay with me, Pharez, stay with me. I pray thee stay, my child.'

Pharez led the Caliph to a couch, on which Alroy lay pale and trembling, In a few minutes he inquired whether Benaiah had returned.

'Even now he comes, Sire.'

'Well, how is it?'

'Sire! a most awful incident. As the thunder broke over the palace, the sacred standard fell from its resting-place, and has shivered into a thousand pieces. Strange to say, the sceptre of Solomon can neither be found nor traced.'

'Say nothing of the past as ye love me, lads. Let none enter the Armoury. Leave me, Benaiah, leave me, Pharez.'

They retired. Alroy watched their departure with a glance of inexpressible anguish. The moment that they had disappeared, he flew to the couch, and throwing himself upon his knees, and, covering his face with his hands, burst into passionate tears, and exclaimed, 'O! my God, I have deserted thee, and now thou hast deserted me!'

## CHAPTER VI.

SLEEP crept over the senses of the exhausted and desperate Caliph. He threw himself upon the divan, and was soon buried in profound repose. He might have slept an hour; he awoke suddenly. From the cabinet in which he slept, you entered a vast hall, through a lofty and spacious arch, generally covered with drapery, which was now withdrawn. To the astonishment of Alroy, this presence-chamber appeared at this moment to blaze with light. He rose from his couch, he advanced; he perceived, with feelings of curiosity and fear, that the hall was filled with beings, terrible indeed to behold, but to his sight more terrible than strange. In the colossal and mysterious forms that lined the walls of the mighty chamber, and each of which held in its extended arm a streaming torch, he recognised the awful Afrites. At the end of the hall, upon a sumptuous throne, surrounded by priests and courtiers, there was seated a monarch, on whom Alroy had before gazed, Solomon the Great! Alroy beheld him in state and semblance the same Solomon, whose sceptre the Prince of the Captivity had seized in the royal tombs of Judah.

The strange assembly seemed perfectly unconscious of the presence of the child of Earth, who, with a desperate courage, leant against a column of the arch, and watched, with wonder, their mute and motionless society. Nothing was said, nothing done. No one moved, no one, even by gesture, seemed sensible of the presence of any other apparition save himself.

Suddenly there advanced from the bottom of the hall, near unto Alroy, a procession. Pages and dancing girls, with eyes of fire and voluptuous gestures, warriors with mighty arms, and venerable forms with ample robes and flowing beards. And, as they passed, even with all the activity of their gestures, they made no sound; neither did the musicians, whereof there was a great band playing upon harps and psalteries, and timbrels and cornets, break, in the slightest degree, the almighty silence.

This great crowd poured on in beautiful order, the procession never terminating, yet passing thrice round the hall, bowing to him that was upon the throne, and ranging themselves in ranks before the Afrites.

And there came in twelve forms, bearing a great seal: the stone green, and the engraven characters of living flame, and the characters were those on the talisman of Jabaster, which Alroy still wore next to his heart. And the twelve forms placed the great seal before Solomon, and humbled themselves, and the King bowed. At the same moment Alroy was sensible of a pang next to his heart. He instantly put his hand to the suffering spot, and lo! the talisman crumbled into dust.

The procession ceased; a single form advanced. Recent experience alone prevented Alroy from sinking before the spectre of Jabaster. Such was the single form. It advanced, bearing the sceptre. It advanced, it knelt before the throne, it offered the sceptre to the crowned and solemn vision. And the form of Solomon extended its arm, and took the sceptre, and instantly the mighty assembly vanished!

Alroy advanced immediately into the chamber, but all was dark and silent. A trumpet sounded. He recognised the note of his own soldiery. He groped his way to a curtain, and, pulling it aside, beheld the first streak of dawn.

## CHAPTER VII.

Once more upon his charger, once more surrounded by his legions, once more his senses dazzled and inflamed by the waving banners and the inspiring trumpets, once more conscious of the power still at his command, and the mighty stake for which he was about to play, Alroy in a great degree recovered his usual spirit and self-possession. His energy returned with his excited pulse, and the vastness of the impending danger seemed only to stimulate the fertility of his genius.

He pushed on by forced marches towards Media, at the head of fifty thousand men. At the end of the second day's march, fresh couriers arrived from Abner, informing him that, unable to resist the valiant and almost innumerable host of the King of Karasmé, he had entirely evacuated Persia, and had concentrated his forces in Louristan. Alroy, in consequence of this information, despatched orders to Scherirah, to join him with his division instantly, and leave the capital to its fate.

They passed again the mountains of Kerrund, and joined Abner and the army of Media, thirty thousand strong, on the river Abzah. Here Alroy rested one night, to refresh his men, and on the ensuing morn pushed on to the Persian frontier, unexpectedly attacked the advanced posts of Alp Arslan, and beat them back with great loss into the province. But the force of the King of Karasmé was so considerable, that the Caliph did not venture on a general engagement, and therefore he fell back, and formed in battle array upon the neighbouring plain of Nehauend, the theatre of one of his earliest and most brilliant victories, where he awaited the hourly-expected arrival of Scherirah.

The King of Karasmé, who was desirous of bringing affairs to an issue, and felt confident in his superior force, instantly advanced. In two or three days at farthest, it was evident that a battle must be fought that would decide the fate of the East.

On the morn ensuing their arrival at Nehauend, while the Caliph was out hunting, attended only by a few officers, he was suddenly attacked by an ambushed band of Karasmians. Alroy and his companions defended themselves with such desperation that they at length succeeded in beating off their assailants, although triple their number. The leader of the Karasmians, as he retreated, hurled a dart at the Caliph, which must have been fatal, had not a young officer of the guard interposed his own breast, and received the deadly wound. The party, in confusion, returned with all speed to the camp, Alroy himself bearing the expiring victim of desperate loyalty and military enthusiasm.

The bleeding officer was borne to the royal pavilion, and placed upon the imperial couch. The most skilful leech was summoned; he examined the wound, but shook his head. The dying warrior was himself sensible of his desperate condition. His agony could only be alleviated by withdrawing the javelin, which would occasion his immediate decease. He desired to be left alone with his Sovereign.

'Sire!' said the officer, 'I must die; and I die without a pang. To die in your service, I have ever considered the most glorious end. Destiny has awarded it to me; and if I have not met my fate upon the field of battle, it is some consolation that my death has preserved the most valuable of lives. Sire! I have a sister.'

'Waste not thy strength, dear friend, in naming her. Rest assured I shall ever deem thy relatives my own.'

'I doubt it not. Would I had a thousand lives for such a master! I have a burden on my conscience, Sire, nor can I die in peace unless I speak of it.'

'Speak, speak freely. If thou hast injured any one, and the power or wealth of Alroy can redeem thy oppressed spirit, he will not spare, he will not spare, be assured of that.'

'Noble, noble master, I must be brief; for, although, while this javelin rests within my body, I yet may live, the agony is great. Sire, the deed of which I speak doth concern thee.'

'Ay!'

'I was on guard the day Jabaster died.'

'Powers of heaven! I am all ear. Speak on, speak on!'

'He died self-strangled, so they say?'

'So they ever told me.'

'Thou art innocent, thou art innocent! I thank my God, my King is innocent!'

'Rest assured of that, as there is hope in Israel. Tell me all.'

'The Queen came with the signet ring. To such authority I yielded way. She entered, and after her, the Lord Honain. I heard high words! I heard Jabaster's voice. He struggled, yes! he struggled; but his mighty form, wounded and fettered, could not long resist. Foul play, foul play, Sire! What could I do against such adversaries? They left the chamber with a stealthy step. Her eyes met mine. I never could forget that fell and glittering visage.'

'Thou ne'er hast spoken of this awful end?'

'To none but thee. And why I speak it now I cannot tell, save that it seems some inspiration urges me; and methinks they who did this may do even feller works, if such there be.'

'Thou hast robbed me of all peace and hope of peace; and yet I thank thee. Now I know the worth of life. I have never loved to think of that sad day; and yet, though I have sometimes dreamed of villainous work, the worst were innocence to thy dread tale.'

''Tis told; and now I pray thee secure thy secret, by drawing from my agonised frame this javelin.'

'Trusty heart, 'tis a sad office.'

'I die with joy if thou performest it.'

''Tis done.'

'God save Alroy.'

## CHAPTER VIII.

WHILE Alroy, plunged in thought, stood over the body of the officer, there arose a flourish of triumphant music, and a eunuch, entering the pavilion, announced the arrival of Schirene from Kerrund. Almost immediately afterwards, the Princess, descending from her litter, entered the tent; Alroy tore off his robe, and threw it over the corpse.

'My own,' exclaimed the Princess, as she ran up to the Caliph. 'I have heard all. Be not alarmed for me. I dare look upon a corpse. You know I am a soldier's bride. I am used to blood.'

'Alas!'

'Why so pale? Thou dost not kiss me! Has this unhinged thee so? 'Tis a sad deed; and yet to-morrow's dawn may light up thousands to as grim a fate. Why? thou tremblest! Alas! kind soul! The single death of this fond, faithful heart, hath quite upset my love. Yet art thou used to battle. Why! this is foolishness. Art not glad to see me? What, not one smile! And I have come to fight for thee! I will be kissed!'

She flung herself upon his neck. Alroy faintly returned her embrace, and bore her to a couch. He clapped his hands, and two soldiers entered and bore away the corpse.

'The pavilion, Schirene, is now fitter for thy presence. Rest thyself; I shall soon return.' Thus speaking, he quitted her.

He quitted her; but her humbled look of sorrowful mortification pierced to his heart. He thought of all her love and all her loveliness, he called to mind all the marvellous story of their united fortunes. He felt that for her and her alone he cared to live, that without her quick sympathy, even success seemed unendurable. His judgment fluctuated in an eddy of passion and reason. Passion conquered. He dismissed from his intelligence all cognizance of good and evil; he determined, under all circumstances, to cling ever to her; he tore from his mind all memory of the late disclosure. He returned to the pavilion with a countenance beaming with affection; he found her weeping, he folded her in his arms, he kissed her with a thousand kisses, and whispered between each kiss his ardent love.

## CHAPTER IX.

'Twas midnight. Schirene reposed in the arms of Alroy. The Caliph, who was restless and anxious for the arrival of Scherirah, was scarcely slumbering, when the sound of a voice thoroughly aroused him. He looked around; he beheld the spectre of Jabaster. His hair stood on end, his limbs seemed to loosen, a cold dew crept over his frame, as he gazed upon the awful form within a yard of his couch. Unconsciously he disembarrassed his arms of their fair burden, and, rising on the couch, leant forward.

'Alroy, Alroy, Alroy!'

'I am here.'

'To-morrow Israel is avenged!'

'Who is that?' exclaimed the Princess, wakening.

In a frenzy of fear, Alroy, quite forgetting the spectre, turned and pressed his hand over her eyes. When he again looked round, the apparition was invisible

'What wouldst thou, Alroy?'

'Nothing, sweet! A soldier's wife must bear strange sights, yet I would save you some. One of my men, forgetful you were here, burst into my tent in such a guise as scarce would suit a female eye. I must away, my child. I'll call thy slaves. One kiss! Farewell! but for a time.'

## CHAPTER X.

'"To-morrow Israel will be avenged." What! in Karasmian blood? I have no faith. No matter. All is now beyond my influence. A rushing destiny carries me onward. I cannot stem the course, nor guide the vessel. How now! Who is the officer on guard?'

'Benomi, Sire, thy servant.'

'Send to the Viceroy. Bid him meet me here. Who is this?'

'A courier from the Lord Scherirah, Sire, but just arrived. He passed last night the Kerrund mountains, Sire, and will be with you by the break of day.'

'Good news. Go fetch Abner. Haste! He'll find me here anon. I'll visit the camp awhile. Well, my brave fellows, you have hither come to conquer again with Alroy. You have fought before, I warrant, on the plain of Nehauend. 'Tis a rich soil, and shall be richer with Karasmian gore.'

'God save your Majesty! Our lives are thine.'

'Please you, my little ruler,' said a single soldier, addressing Alroy; 'pardon my bluntness, but I knew you before you were a Caliph.'

'Stout heart, I like thy freedom. Pr'ythee say on.'

'I was a-saying, I hope you will lead us in the charge to-morrow. Some say you will not.'

'They say falsely.'

'I thought so. I'll ever answer for my little ruler, but then the Queen?'

'Is a true soldier's wife, and lives in the camp.'

'That's brave! There, I told you so, comrades; you would not believe me, but I knew our little ruler before you did. I lived near the gate at Hamadan, please your Highness: old Shelomi's son.'

'Give me thy hand; a real friend. What is't ye eat here, boys? Let me taste your mess. I'faith I would my cook could dress me such a pilau! 'Tis admirable!'

The soldiers gathered round their chieftain with eyes beaming with adoration. 'Twas a fine picture, the hero in the centre, the various groups around, some conversing with him, some cooking, some making coffee, all offering him by word or deed some testimonial of their devotion.

and blending with that devotion the most perfect frankness.

'We shall beat them, lads!'

'There is on fear with you, you always beat.'

'I do my best, and so do you. A good general without good troops is little worth.'

'I'faith that's true. One must have good troops. What think you of Alp Arslan?'

'I think he may give us as much trouble as all our other enemies together, and that's not much.'

'Brave, bravo! God save Alroy!'

Benomi approached, and announced that the Viceroy was in attendance.

'I must quit you, my children,' said Alroy. 'We'll sup once more together when we have conquered.'

'God save you, Sire; and we will confound your enemies.'

'Good night, my lads. Ere the dawn break we may have hot work.'

'We are ready, we are ready. God save Alroy.'

'They are in good cue, and yet 'twas a different spirit that inspired our early days. That I strongly feel. These are men true to a leader who has never failed them, and confident in a cause that leads to plunder. They are but splendid mercenaries. No more. Oh! where are now the fighting men of Judah! Where are the men who, when they drew their scimetars, joined in a conquering psalm of holy triumph! Last eve of battle you would have thought the field a mighty synagogue. Priests and altars, flaming sacrifices, and smoking censers, groups of fiery zealots hanging with frenzy on prophetic lips, and sealing with their blood and holiest vows a solemn covenant to conquer Canaan. All is changed, as I am. How now, Abner? You are well muffled!'

'Is it true Scherirah is at hand?'

'I doubt not all is right. Would that the dawn would break!'

'The enemy is advancing. Some of their columns are

in sight. My scouts have dodged them. They intend doubtless to form upon the plain.'

'They are in sight, eh! Then we will attack them at once ere they are formed. Rare, rare! We'll beat them yet. Courage, dear brother. Scherirah will be here at dawn in good time, very good time: very, very good time.'

'I like the thought.'

'The men are in good heart. At break of dawn, charge with thirty thousand cavalry upon their forming ranks. I'll take the right, Asriel the left. It shall be a family affair, dear Abner. How is Miriam?'

'I heard this morn, quite well. She sends you her love and prayers. The Queen is here?'

'She came this eve. Quite well.'

'She must excuse all courtesy.'

'Say nothing. She is a soldier's wife. She loves thee well, dear Abner.'

'I know that. I hope my sword may guard her children's throne.'

'Well, give thy orders. Instant battle, eh?'

'Indeed I think so.'

'I'll send couriers to hurry Scherirah. All looks well. Reserve the guard.'

'Ay, ay! Farewell, dear Sire. When we meet again, I trust your enemies may be your slaves!'

## CHAPTER XI.

At the first streak of dawn the Hebrew cavalry, with the exception of the guard, charged the advancing columns of the Karasmians with irresistible force, and cut them in pieces. Alp Arslan rallied his troops, and at length succeeded in forming his main body in good order. Alroy and Asriel led on their divisions, and the battle now became general. It raged for several hours, and was on both sides well maintained. The slaughter of the Karasmians was great, but their stern character and superior numbers counterbalanced for a time all the impetuosity of the Hebrews and all the energy of their leaders. This day Alroy threw into the shade all his former exploits. Twelve times he charged at the head of the Sacred Guard, and more than once penetrated to the very pavilion of Alp Arslan.

In vain he endeavoured singly, and hand to hand, to meet that famous chieftain. Both monarchs fought in the ranks, and yet Fate decided that their scimetars should never cross. Four hours before noon, it was evident to Alroy, that, unless Scherirah arrived, he could not prevail against the vast superiority of numbers. He was obliged early to call his reserve into the field, and although the number of the slain on the side of Arslan exceeded any in the former victories of the Hebrews, still the Karasmians maintained an immense front, which was constantly supplied by fresh troops. Confident in his numbers, and aware of the weakness of his antagonists, Arslan contented himself with acting on the defensive, and wearying his assailants by resisting their terrible and repeated charge.

For a moment, Alroy at the head of the Sacred Guard had withdrawn from the combat. Abner and Asriel still maintained the fight, and the Caliph was at the same time preparing for new efforts, and watching with anxiety for the arrival of Scherirah. In the fifth hour, from an eminence he marked with exultation the advancing banners of his expected succours. Confident now that the day was won, he announced the exhilarating intelligence to his soldiers; and, while they were excited by the animating tidings, led them once more to the charge. It was irresistible; Scherirah seemed to have arrived only for the pursuit, only in time to complete the victory. What then was the horror, the consternation of Alroy, when Benaiah, dashing up to him, informed him that the long-expected succours consisted of the united forces of Scherirah and Abidan, and had attacked him in the rear. Human genius could afford no resource. The exhausted Hebrews, whose energies had been tasked to the utmost, were surrounded. The Karasmians made a general and simultaneous advance.

In a few minutes the Hebrew army was thrown into confusion. The stoutest warriors threw away their swords in despair. Every one thought only of self-preservation. Even Abner fled towards Hamadan. Asriel was slain. Alroy, finding it was all over, rushed to his pavilion at the head of about three hundred of the guards, seized the fainting Schirene, threw her before him on his saddle, and cutting his way through all obstacles, dashed into the desert.

For eight-and-forty hours they never stopped. Their band was soon reduced one-third. On the morning of the third day they dismounted and refreshed themselves at a well. Half only regained their saddles. Schirene never spoke. On they rushed again, each hour losing some exhausted co-mate. At length, on the fifth day, about eighty strong, they arrived at a grove of palm-trees. Here they dismounted. And Alroy took Schirene in his arms, and the shade seemed to revive her. She opened her eyes, and pressed his hand and smiled. He gathered her some dates, and she drank some water.

'Our toils will soon be over, sweetest,' he whispered to her; 'I have lost everything but thee.'

Again they mounted, and, proceeding at a less rapid pace, they arrived towards evening at the ruined city, whither Alroy all this time had been directing his course. Dashing down the great street, they at length entered the old amphitheatre. They dismounted. Alroy made a couch with their united cloaks for Schirene. Some collected fuel, great store of which was found, and kindled large fires. Others, while it was yet light, chased the gazelles, and were sufficiently fortunate to provide their banquet, or fetched water from the well known to their leader. In an hour's time, clustering round their fires in groups, and sharing their rude fare, you might have deemed them, instead of the discomfited and luxurious guards of a mighty monarch, the accustomed tenants of this wild abode.

'Come, my lads,' said Alroy, as he rubbed his hands over the ascending flame, 'at any rate this is better than the desert!'

## CHAPTER XII.

AFTER all his exertions, Alroy fell into profound and dreamless sleep. When he awoke, the sun had been long up. Schirene was still slumbering. He embraced her, and she opened her eyes and smiled.

'You are now a bandit's bride,' he said. 'How like you our new life?'

'Well! with thee.'

'Rest here, my sweetest: I must rouse our men, and see how fortune speeds.' So saying, and tripping lightly over many a sleeping form, he touched Benaiah.

'So! my brave captain of the guard, still napping! Come! stir, stir.'

Benaiah jumped up with a cheerful face. 'I am ever ready, Sire.'

'I know it; but remember I am no more a king, only a co-mate. Away with me, and let us form some order.'

The companions quitted the amphitheatre and reconnoitred the adjoining buildings. They found many stores, the remains of old days, mats, tents, and fuel, drinking-bowls, and other homely furniture. They fixed upon a building for their stable, and others for the accommodation of their band. They summoned their companions to the open place, the scene of Hassan Subah's fate, where Alroy addressed them and explained to them his plans. They were divided into companies; each man had his allotted duty. Some were placed on guard at different parts; some were sent out to the chase, or to collect dates from the Oasis; others led the horses to the contiguous pasture, or remained to attend to their domestic arrangements. The amphitheatre was cleared out. A rude but convenient pavilion was formed for Schirene. They covered its ground with mats, and each emulated the other in his endeavours to study her accommodation. Her kind words and inspiring smiles animated at the same time their zeal and their invention.

They soon became accustomed to their rough but adventurous life. Its novelty pleased them, and the perpetual excitement of urgent necessity left them no time to mourn over their terrible vicissitudes. While Alroy lived, hope indeed never deserted their sanguine bosoms. And such was the influence of his genius, that the most desponding felt that to be discomfited with him was preferable to conquest with another. They were a faithful and devoted band, and merry faces were not wanting when at night they assembled in the amphitheatre for their common meal.

No sooner had Alroy completed his arrangements than he sent forth spies in all directions to procure intelligence, and especially to communicate, if possible, with Ithamar and Medad, provided that they still survived and maintained themselves in any force.

A fortnight passed away without the approach of any stranger; at the end of which, there arrived four personages at their haunt, not very welcome to their chief, who, however, concealed his chagrin at their appearance. These were Kisloch the Kourd, and Calidas the Indian, and their inseparable companions, the Guebre and the Negro.

## CHAPTER XIII.

'NOBLE Captain,' said Kisloch, 'we trust that you will permit us to enlist in the band. This is not the first time we have served under your orders in this spot. Old comates i'faith, who have seen the best and the worst. We suspected where you might be found, although, thanks to the ever felicitous invention of man, it is generally received that you died in battle. I hope your Majesty is well,' added Kisloch, bowing to Schirene.

'You are welcome, friends,' replied Alroy; 'I know your worth. You have seen, as you say, the best and the worst, and will, I trust, see better. Died in battle, eh! that's good.'

' 'Tis so received,' said Calidas.

'And what news of our friends?'

'Not over good, but strange.'

'How so?'

'Hamadan is taken.'

'I am prepared; tell me all.'

'Old Bostenay and the Lady Miriam are borne prisoners to Bagdad.'

'Prisoners?'

'But so: all will be well with them, I trow. The Lord Honain is in high favour with the conqueror, and will doubtless protect them.'

'Honain in favour?'

'Even so. He made terms for the city, and right good ones.'

'Hah! he was ever dexterous. Well! if he save my sister, I care not for his favour.'

'There is no doubt. All may yet be well, Sir.'

'Let us act, not hope. Where's Abner?'

'Dead.'

'How?'

'In battle.'

'Art sure?'

'I saw him fall, and fought beside him.'

'A soldier's death is all our fortune now. I am glad he was not captured. Where's Medad, Ithamar?'

'Fled into Egypt.'

'We have no force whatever, then?'

'None but your guards here.'

'They are strong enough to plunder a caravan. Honain, you say, in favour?'

'Very high. He'll make good terms for us.'

'This is strange news.'

'Very, but true.'

'Well! you are welcome! Share our fare; 'tis rough, and somewhat scanty; but we have feasted, and may feast again. Fled into Egypt, eh?'

'Ay! Sir.'

'Schirene, shouldst like to see the Nile?'

'I have heard of crocodiles.'

## CHAPTER XIV.

If the presence of Kisloch and his companions were not very pleasing to Alroy, with the rest of the band they soon became great favourites. Their local knowledge, and their experience of desert life, made them valuable allies, and their boisterous jocularity and unceasing merriment were not unwelcome in the present monotonous existence of the fugitives. As for Alroy himself, he meditated an escape to Egypt. He determined to seize the first opportunity of procuring some camels, and then, dispersing his band, with the exception of Benaiah and a few faithful retainers, he trusted that, disguised as merchants, they might succeed in crossing Syria, and entering Africa by Palestine. With these plans and prospects, he became each day more cheerful and more sanguine as to the future. He had in his possession some valuable jewels, which he calculated upon disposing of at Cairo for a sum sufficient for all his purposes; and having exhausted all the passions of life while yet a youth, he looked forward to the tranquil termination of his existence in some poetic solitude with his beautiful companion.

One evening, as they returned from the Oasis, Alroy guiding the camel that bore Schirene, and ever and anon looking up in her inspiring face, her sanguine spirit would have indulged in a delightful future.

'Thus shall we pass the desert, sweet,' said Schirene. 'Can this be toil?'

'There is no toil with love,' replied Alroy.

'And we were made for love, and not for empire,' rejoined Schirene.

'The past is a dream,' said Alroy. 'So sages teach us; but, until we act, their wisdom is but wind. I feel it now. Have we ever lived in aught but deserts, and fed on aught but dates? Methinks 'tis very natural. But that I am tempted by the security of distant lands, I could remain here a free and happy outlaw. Time, custom, and necessity form our natures. When I first met Scherirah in these ruins, I shrank with horror from degraded man; and now I sigh to be his heir. We must not think!'

'No love, we'll only hope,' replied Schirene; and they passed through the gates.

The night was beautiful, the air was still warm and sweet. Schirene gazed upon the luminous heavens. 'We thought not of these skies when we were at Bagdad,' she exclaimed; 'and yet, my life, what was the brightness of our palaces compared to these? All is left to us that man should covet, freedom, beauty, and youth. I do believe, ere long, Alroy, we shall look back upon the wondrous past as on another and a lower world. Would that this were Egypt! 'Tis my only wish.'

'And it shall soon be gratified. All will soon be arranged. A few brief days, and then Schirene will mount her camel for a longer ride than just to gather dates. You'll make a sorry traveller, I fear!'

'Not I; I'll tire you all.'

They reached the circus, and seated themselves round the blazing fire. Seldom had Alroy, since his fall, appeared more cheerful. Schirene sang an Arab air to the band, who joined in joyous chorus. It was late ere they sought repose; and they retired to their rest, sanguine and contented.

A few hours afterwards, at the break of dawn, Alroy was roused from his slumbers by a rude pressure on his breast. He started; a ferocious soldier was kneeling over him; he would have spurned him; he found his hand manacled. He would have risen; his feet were bound. He looked round for Schirene, and called her name; he was answered only by a shriek. The amphitheatre was filled with Karasmian troops. His own men were surprised and overpowered. Kisloch and the Guebre had been on guard. He was raised from the ground, and flung upon a camel, which was instantly trotted out of the circus. On every side he beheld a wild scene of disorder and dismay. He was speechless from passion and despair. The camel was dragged into the desert. A body of cavalry instantly surrounded it, and they set off at a rapid pace. The whole seemed the work of an instant.

How many days had passed Alroy knew not. He had taken no account of time. Night and day were to him the same. He was in a stupor. But the sweetness of the air and the greenness of the earth at length partially roused his attention. He was just conscious that they had quitted the desert. Before him was a noble river; he beheld the Euphrates from the very spot he had first viewed it in his pilgrimage. The strong association of ideas called back his memory. A tear stole down his cheek; the bitter drop stole to his parched lips; he asked the nearest horseman for water. The guard gave him a wetted sponge, with which he contrived with difficulty to wipe his lips, and then he let it fall to the ground. The Karasmian struck him.

They arrived at the river. The prisoner was taken from the camel and placed in a covered boat. After some hours they stopped and disembarked at a small village. Alroy was placed upon an ass with his back to its head. His clothes were soiled and tattered. The children pelted him with mud. An old woman, with a fanatic curse, placed a crown of paper on his brow. With difficulty his brutal guards prevented their victim from being torn to pieces. And in such fashion, towards noon of the fourteenth day, David Alroy again entered Bagdad.

## CHAPTER XV.

THE intelligence of the capture of Alroy spread through the agitated city. The Moolahs bustled about as if they had received a fresh demonstration of the authenticity of the prophetic mission. All the Dervishes began begging. The men discussed affairs in the coffee-houses, and the women chatted at the fountains.[79]

'They may say what they like, but I wish him well,'

said a fair Arab, as she arranged her veil. 'He may be an impostor, but he was a very handsome one.'

'All the women are for him, that's the truth,' responded a companion; 'but then we can do him no good.'

'We can tear their eyes out,' said a third.

'And what do you think of Alp Arslan, truly?' inquired a fourth.

'I wish he were a pitcher, and then I could break his neck,' said a fifth.

'Only think of the Princess!' said a sixth.

'Well! she has had a glorious time of it,' said a seventh.

'Nothing was too good for her,' said an eighth.

'I like true love,' said a ninth.

'Well! I hope he will be too much for them all yet,' said a tenth.

'I should not wonder,' said an eleventh.

'He can't,' said a twelfth, 'he has lost his sceptre.'

'You don't say so?' said a thirteenth.

'It is too true,' said a fourteenth.

'Do you think he was a wizard?' said a fifteenth. 'I vow if there be not a fellow looking at us behind those trees.'

'Impudent scoundrel!' said a sixteenth. 'I wish it were Alroy. Let us all scream, and put down our veils.'

And the group ran away.

---

## CHAPTER XVI.

Two stout soldiers were playing chess [80] in a coffee-house.

'May I slay my mother,' said one, 'but I cannot make a move. I fought under him at Nehauend; and though I took the amnesty, I have half a mind now to seize my sword and stab the first Turk that enters.'

'"Twere but sheer justice,' said his companion. 'By my

father's blessing, he was the man for a charge. They may say what they like, but compared with him, Alp Arslan is a white-livered Giaour.'

'Here is confusion to him and to thy last move. There's the dirhem, I can play no more. May I slay my mother, though, but I did not think he would let himself be taken.'

'By the blessing of my father, nor I; but then he was asleep.'

'That makes a difference. He was betrayed.'

'All brave men are. They say Kisloch and his set pocket their fifty thousand by the job.'

'May each dirhem prove a plague-spot!'

'Amen! Dost remember Abner?'

'May I slay my mother if I ever forget him. He spoke to his men like so many lambs. What has become of the Lady Miriam?'

'She is here.'

'That will cut Alroy.'

'He was ever fond of her. Dost remember she gained Adoram's life?'

'Oh! she could do anything, next to the Queen.'

'Before her, I say, before her. He has refused the Queen, he never refused the Lady Miriam.'

'Because she asked less.'

'Dost know it seemed to me that things never went on so well after Jabaster's death?'

'So say I. There was a something, eh?'

'A sort of a peculiar, as it were, kind of something, eh?'

'You have well described it. Every man felt the same. I have often mentioned it to my comrades. Say what you like, said I, but slay my mother, if ever since the old man strangled himself, things did not seem, as it were, in their natural propinquity. 'Twas the phrase I used.'

'A choice one. Unless there is a natural propinquity, the best-arranged matters will fall out. However, the ass sees farther than his rider, and so it was with Alroy, the best commander I ever served under, all the same.'

'Let us go forth and see how affairs run.'

'Ay, do. If we hear any one abuse Alroy, we'll cleave his skull.'

'That will we. There are a good many of our stout fellows about; we might do something yet.'

'Who knows?'

## CHAPTER XVII.

A SUBTERRANEAN DUNGEON of the citadel of Bagdad held in its gloomy limits the late lord of Asia. The captive did not sigh, or weep, or wail. He did not speak. He did not even think. For several days he remained in a state of stupor. On the morning of the fourth day, he almost unconsciously partook of the wretched provision which his gaolers brought him. Their torches, round which the bats whirled and flapped their wings, and twinkled their small eyes, threw a ghastly glare over the nearer walls of the dungeon, the extremity of which defied the vision of the prisoner; and, when the gaolers retired, Alroy was in complete darkness.

The image of the past came back to him. He tried in vain to penetrate the surrounding gloom. His hands were manacled, his legs also were loaded with chains. The notion that his life might perhaps have been cruelly spared in order that he might linger on in this horrible state of conscious annihilation filled him with frenzy. He would have dashed his fetters against his brow, but the chain restrained him. He flung himself upon the damp and rugged ground. His fall disturbed a thousand obscene things. He heard the quick glide of a serpent, the creeping retreat of the clustering scorpions, and the swift escape of the dashing rats. His mighty calamities seemed slight when compared with these petty miseries. His great soul could not support him under these noisome and degrading incidents. He sprang, in disgust, upon his feet, and stood fearful of moving, lest every step should introduce him to some new abomination. At length, exhausted nature was unable any longer to sustain him. He groped his way to the rude seat, cut in the rocky wall, which was his only accommodation. He put forth his hand. It touched the slimy fur of some wild animal, that instantly sprang away, its fiery eyes sparkling in the dark. Alroy recoiled with a sensation of woe-begone dismay. His shaken nerves could not sustain him under this base danger, and these foul and novel trials. He could not refrain from an exclamation of despair; and, when he remembered that he was now far beyond the reach of all human solace and sympathy, even all human aid, for a moment his mind seemed to desert him; and he wrung his hands in forlorn and almost idiotic woe.

An awful thing it is, the failure of the energies of a master-mind. He who places implicit confidence in his genius will find himself some day utterly defeated and deserted. 'Tis bitter! Every paltry hind seems but to breathe to mock you. Slow, indeed, is such a mind to credit that the never-failing resource can at least be wanting. But so it is. Like a dried-up fountain, the perennial flow and bright fertility have ceased, and ceased for ever. Then comes the madness of retrospection.

Draw a curtain! draw a curtain! and fling it over this agonising anatomy.

The days of childhood, his sweet sister's voice and smiling love, their innocent pastimes, and the kind solicitude of faithful servants, all the soft detail of mild domestic life: these were the sights and memories that flitted in wild play before the burning vision of Alroy, and rose upon his tortured mind. Empire and glory, his sacred nation, his imperial bride; these, these were nothing. Their worth had vanished with the creative soul that called them into action. The pure sympathies of nature alone remained, and all his thought and grief, all his intelligence, all his emotion, were centred in his sister.

It was the seventh morning. A guard entered at an unaccustomed hour, and, sticking a torch into a niche in the wall, announced that a person was without who had permission to speak to the prisoner. They were the first human accents that had met the ear of Alroy during his captivity, which seemed to him an age, a long dark period, that cancelled all things. He shuddered at the harsh tones. He tried to answer, but his unaccustomed lips refused their office. He raised his heavy arms, and endeavoured to signify his consciousness of what had been uttered. Yet, indeed, he had not listened to the message without emotion. He looked forward to the grate with strange curiosity; and, as he looked, he trembled. The visitor entered, muffled in a dark caftan. The guard disappeared; and the caftan falling to the ground, revealed Honain.

'My beloved Alroy,' said the brother of Jabaster; and he advanced, and pressed him to his bosom. Had it been Miriam, Alroy might have at once expired; but the presence of this worldly man called back his worldliness. The revulsion of his feelings was wonderful. Pride, perhaps even hope, came to his aid; all the associations seemed to counsel exertion; for a moment he seemed the same Alroy.

'I rejoice to find at least thee safe, Honain.'

'I also, if my security may lead to thine.'

'Still whispering hope!'

'Despair is the conclusion of fools.'

'O Honain! 'tis a great trial. I can play my part, and yet methinks 'twere better we had not again met. How is Schirene?'

'Thinking of thee.'

''Tis something that she can think. My mind has gone. Where's Miriam?'

'Free.'

'That's something. Thou hast done that. Good, good Honain, be kind to that sweet child, if only for my sake. Thou art all she has left.'

'She hath thee.'

'Her desolation.'

'Live and be her refuge.'

'How's that? These walls! Escape? No, no; it is impossible.'

'I do not deem it so.'

'Indeed! I'll do anything. Speak! Can we bribe? can we cleave their skulls? can we——'

'Calm thyself, my friend. There is no need of bribes, no need of bloodshed. We must make terms.'

'Terms! We might have made them on the plains of Nehauend. Terms! Terms with a captive victim?'

'Why victim?'

'Is Arslan then so generous?'

'He is a beast, more savage than the boar that grinds its tusks within his country's forests.'

'Why speakest thou then of hope?'

'I spoke of certainty. I did not mention hope.'

'Dear Honain, my brain is weak; but I can bear strange things, or else I should not be here. I feel thy thoughtful friendship; but indeed there need no winding words to tell my fate. Pr'ythee speak out.'

'In a word, thy life is safe.'

'What! spared?'

'If it please thee.'

'Please me? Life is sweet. I feel its sweetness. I want but little. Freedom and solitude are all I ask. My life spared! I'll not believe it. Thou hast done this deed, thou mighty man, that masterest all souls. Thou hast not forgotten me; thou hast not forgotten the days gone by, thou hast not forgotten thine own Alroy! Who calls thee worldly is a slanderer. O Honain! thou art too faithful!'

'I have no thought but for thy service, Prince.'

'Call me not Prince, call me thine own Alroy. My life spared! 'Tis wonderful! When may I go? Let no one see me. Manage that, Honain. Thou canst manage all things. I am for Egypt. Thou hast been to Egypt, hast thou not, Honain?'

'A very wondrous land, 'twill please thee much.'

'When may I go? Tell me when I may go. When may I quit this dark and noisome cell? 'Tis worse than all their tortures, dear Honain. Air and light, and I really think

my spirit never would break, but this horrible dungeon——
I scarce can look upon thy face, sweet friend. 'Tis serious.'

'Wouldst thou have me gay?'

'Yes! if we are free.'

'Alroy! thou art a great spirit, the greatest that I e'er knew, have ever read of. I never knew thy like, and never shall.'

'Tush, tush, sweet friend, I am a broken reed, but still I am free. This is no time for courtly phrases. Let's go, and go at once.'

'A moment, dear Alroy. I am no flatterer. What I said came from my heart, and doth concern us much and instantly. I was saying thou hast no common mind, Alroy; indeed thou hast a mind unlike all others. Listen, my Prince. Thou hast read mankind deeply and truly. Few have seen more than thyself, and none have so rare a spring of that intuitive knowledge of thy race, which is a gem to which experience is but a jeweller, and without which no action can befriend us.'

'Well, well!'

'A moment's calmness. Thou hast entered Bagdad in triumph, and thou hast entered the same city with every contumely which the base spirit of our race could cast upon its victim. 'Twas a great lesson.'

'I feel it so.'

'And teaches us how vile and valueless is the opinion of our fellow-men.'

'Alas! 'tis true.'

'I am glad to see thee in this wholesome temper. 'Tis full of wisdom.'

'The miserable are often wise.'

'But to believe is nothing unless we act. Speculation should only sharpen practice. The time hath come to prove thy lusty faith in this philosophy. I told thee we could make terms. I have made them. To-morrow it was doomed Alroy should die—and what a death! A death of infinite torture! Hast ever seen a man impaled?'[81]

'Hah!'

'To view it is alone a doom.'

'God of Heaven!'

'It is so horrible, that 'tis ever marked, that when this direful ceremony occurs, the average deaths in cities greatly increase. 'Tis from the turning of the blood in the spectators, who yet from some ungovernable madness cannot refrain from hurrying to the scene. I speak with some authority. I speak as a physician.'

'Speak no more, I cannot endure it.'

'To-morrow this doom awaited thee. As for Schirene——'

'Not for her, oh! surely not for her?'

'No, they were merciful. She is a Caliph's daughter. 'Tis not forgotten. The axe would close her life. Her fair neck would give slight trouble to the headsman's art. But for thy sister, but for Miriam, she is a witch, a Jewish witch! They would have burnt her alive!'

'I'll not believe it, no, no, I'll not believe it: damnable, bloody demons! When I had power I spared all, all but—— ah, me! ah, me! why did I live?'

'Thou dost forget thyself; I speak of that which was to have been, not of that which is to be. I have stepped in and communed with the conqueror. I have made terms.'

'What are they, what can they be?'

'Easy. To a philosopher like Alroy an idle ceremony.'

'Be brief, be brief.'

'Thou seest thy career is a great scandal to the Moslemin. I mark their weakness, and I have worked upon it. Thy mere defeat or death will not blot out the stain upon their standard and their faith. The public mind is wild with fantasies since Alroy rose. Men's opinions flit to and fro with that fearful change that bodes no stable settlement of states. None know what to cling to, or where to place their trust. Creeds are doubted, authority disputed. They would gladly account for thy success by other than human means, yet must deny thy mission. There also is the fame of a fair and mighty Princess, a daughter of their Caliphs, which they would gladly clear. I mark all this, observe and work upon it. So, could we devise some means by which thy lingering followers could be for ever silenced, this great scandal fairly erased, and the public frame brought to a sounder and more tranquil pulse, why, they would concede much, much, very much.'

'Thy meaning, not thy means, are evident.'

'They are in thy power.'

'In mine? 'Tis a deep riddle. Pr'ythee solve it.'

'Thou wilt be summoned at to-morrow's noon before this Arslan. There, in the presence of the assembled people who are now with him as much as they were with thee, thou wilt be accused of magic, and of intercourse with the infernal powers. Plead guilty.'

'Well! is there more?'

'Some trifle. They will then examine thee about the Princess. It is not difficult to confess that Alroy won the Caliph's daughter by an irresistible spell, and now 'tis broken.'

'So, so. Is that all?'

'The chief. Thou canst then address some phrases to the Hebrew prisoners, denying thy Divine mission, and so forth, to settle the public mind, observe, upon this point for ever.'

'Ay, ay, and then——?'

'No more, except for form. (Upon the completion of the conditions, mind, you will be conveyed to what land you please, with such amount of treasure as you choose.) There is no more, except, I say, for form, I would, if I were you ('twill be expected), I would just publicly affect to renounce our faith, and bow before their Prophet.'

'Hah! Art thou there? Is this thy freedom? Get thee behind me, tempter! Never, never, never! Not a jot, not a jot: I'll not yield a jot. Were my doom one everlasting torture, I'd spurn thy terms! Is this thy high contempt of our poor kind, to outrage my God! to prove myself the vilest of the vile, and baser than the basest? Rare philosophy! O Honain! would we had never met!'

'Or never parted. True. Had my word been taken, Alroy would ne'er have been betrayed.'

'No more; I pray thee, sir, no more. Leave me.'

'Were this a palace, I would. Harsh words are softened by a friendly ear, when spoken in affliction.'

'Say what they will, I am the Lord's anointed. As such I should have lived, as such at least I'll die.'

'And Miriam?'

'The Lord will not desert her: she ne'er deserted Him.'

'Schirene?'

'Schirene! why! for her sake alone I will die a hero. Shall it be said she loved a craven slave, a base impostor, a vile renegade, a villanous dealer in drugs and charms? Oh! no, no, no! if only for her sake, her sweet, sweet sake, my end shall be like my great life. As the sun I rose, like him I set. Still the world is warm with my bright fame, and my last hour shall not disgrace my noon, stormy indeed, but glorious!'

Honain took the torch from the niche, and advanced to the grate. It was not fastened: he drew it gently open, and led forward a veiled and female figure. The veiled and female figure threw herself at the feet of Alroy, who seemed lost to what was passing. A soft lip pressed his hand. He started, his chains clanked.

'Alroy!' softly murmured the kneeling female.

'What voice is that?' wildly exclaimed the Prince of the Captivity. 'It falls upon my ear like long-forgotten music. I'll not believe it. No! I'll not believe it. Art thou Schirene?'

'I am that wretched thing they called thy bride.'

'Oh! this indeed is torture! What impalement can equal this sharp moment? Look not on me, let not our eyes meet! They have met before, like to the confluence of two shining rivers blending in one great stream of rushing light. Bear off that torch, sir. Let impenetrable darkness cover our darker fortunes.'

'Alroy.'

'She speaks again. Is she mad, as I am, that thus she plays with agony?'

'Sire,' said Honain advancing, and laying his hand gently

on the arm of the captive, 'I pray thee moderate this passion. Thou hast some faithful friends here, who would fain commune in calmness for thy lasting welfare.'

'Welfare! He mocks me.'

'I beseech thee, Sire, be calm. If, indeed, I speak unto that great Alroy whom all men fear and still may fear, I pray remember, 'tis not in palaces or in the battle-field alone that the heroic soul can conquer and command. Scenes like these are the great proof of a superior soul. While we live, our body is a temple where our genius pours forth its godlike inspiration, and while the altar is not overthrown, the deity may still work marvels. Then rouse thyself, great Sire; bethink thee that, a Caliph or a captive, there is no man within this breathing world like to Alroy. Shall such a being fall without a struggle, like some poor felon, who has nought to trust to but the dull shuffling accident of Chance? I, too, am a prophet, and I feel thou still wilt conquer.'

'Give me my sceptre then, give me the sceptre! I speak to the wrong brother! It was not thou, it was not thou that gavest it me.'

'Gain it once more. The Lord deserted David for a time; still he pardoned him, and still he died a king.'

'A woman worked his fall.'

'But thee a woman raises. This great Princess, has she not suffered too? Yet her spirit is still unbroken. List to her counsel: it is deep and fond.'

'So was our love.'

'And is, my Alroy!' exclaimed the Princess. 'Be calm, I pray thee! For my sake be calm; I am calm for thine. Thou hast listened to all Honain has told thee, that wise man, my Alroy, who never erred. 'Tis but a word he counsels, an empty word, a most unmeaning form. But speak it, and thou art free, and Alroy and Schirene may blend again their glorious careers and lives of sweet fruition. Dost thou not remember when, walking in the garden of our joy, and palled with empire, how often hast thou sighed for some sweet isle unknown to man, where thou mightst pass thy days with no companion but my faithful self, and no adventures but our constant loves? O! my beloved, that life may still be thine! And dost thou falter? Dost call thyself forlorn with such fidelity, and deem thyself a wretch, when Paradise with all its beauteous gates but wooes thy entrance? Oh! no, no, no, no! thou hast forgot Schirene: I fear me much, thy over-fond Schirene, who doats upon thy image in thy chains more than she did when those sweet hands of thine were bound with gems and played with her bright locks!'

'She speaks of another world. I do remember something. Who has sent this music to a dungeon? My spirit softens with her melting words. My eyes are moist. I weep! 'Tis pleasant. Sorrow is joy compared with my despair. I never thought to shed a tear again. My brain is cooler.'

'Weep, weep, I pray thee weep; but let me kiss away thy tears, my soul! Didst think thy Schirene had deserted thee? Ah! that was it that made my bird so sad. It shall be free, and fly in a sweet sky, and feed on flowers with its faithful mate. Ah me! I am once more happy with my boy. There was no misery but thy absence, sweet! Methinks this dungeon is our bright kiosk! Is that the sunbeam, or thy smile, my love, that makes the walls so joyful?'

'Did I smile? I'll not believe it.'

'Indeed you did. Ah! see he smiles again. Why this is freedom! There is no such thing as sorrow. 'Tis a lie to frighten fools!'

'Why, Honain, what's this? 'Twould seem I am really joyful. There's inspiration in her very breath. I am another being. Nay! waste not kisses on those ugly fetters.'

'Methinks they are gold.'

They were silent. Schirene drew Alroy to his rough seat, and gently placing herself on his knees, threw her arms round his neck, and buried her face in his breast. After a few minutes she raised her head, and whispered in his ear in irresistible accents of sweet exultation, 'We shall be free to-morrow!'

'To-morrow! is the trial so near?' exclaimed the captive, with an agitated voice and changing countenance. 'To-morrow!' He threw Schirene aside somewhat hastily, and sprang from his seat. 'To-morrow! would it were over! To-morrow! Methinks there is within that single word the fate of ages! Shall it be said to-morrow that Alroy—— Hah! what art thou that risest now before me? Dread, mighty spirit, thou hast come in time to save me from perdition. Take me to thy bosom, 'tis not stabbed. They did not stab thee. Thou seest me here communing with thy murderers. What then? I am innocent. Ask them, dread ghost, and call upon their fiendish souls to say I am pure. They would make me dark as themselves, but shall not.'

'Honain, Honain!' exclaimed the Princess in a terrible whisper as she flew to the Physician. 'He is wild again. Calm him, calm him. Mark! how he stands with his extended arms, and fixed vacant eyes, muttering most awful words! My spirit fails me. It is too fearful.'

The Physician advanced and stood by the side of Alroy, but in vain attempted to catch his attention. He ventured to touch his arm. The Prince started, turned round, and recognising him, exclaimed in a shrieking voice, 'Off, fratricide!'

Honain recoiled, pale and quivering. Schirene sprang to his arm. 'What said he, Honain? Thou dost not speak. I never saw thee pale before. Art thou, too, mad?'

'Would I were!'

'All men are growing wild. I am sure he said something. I pray thee tell me what was it?'

'Ask him.'

'I dare not. Tell me, tell me, Honain!'

'That I dare not.'

'Was it a word?'

'Ay! a word to wake the dead. Let us begone.'

'Without our end? Coward! I'll speak to him. My own Alroy,' sweetly whispered the Princess, as she advanced before him.

'What, has the fox left the tigress! Is't so, eh? Are

there no judgments? Are the innocent only haunted? I am innocent! I did not strangle thee! He said rightly, "Beware, beware! they who did this may do even feller deeds." And here they are quick at their damned work. Thy body suffered, great Jabaster, but me they would strangle body and soul!'

The Princess shrieked, and fell into the arms of the advancing Honain, who bore her out of the dungeon.

## CHAPTER XVIII.

AFTER the fall of Hamadan, Bostenay and Miriam had been carried prisoners to Bagdad. Through the interference of Honain, their imprisonment had been exempted from the usual hardships, but they were still confined to their chambers in the citadel. Hitherto all the endeavours of Miriam to visit her brother had been fruitless. Honain was the only person to whom she could apply for assistance, and he, in answer to her importunities, only regretted his want of power to aid her. In vain had she attempted, by the offer of some remaining jewels, to secure the co-operation of her guards, with whom her loveliness and the softness of her manners had already ingratiated her. She had not succeeded even in communicating with Alroy. But after the unsuccessful mission of Honain to the dungeon, the late Vizier visited the sister of the captive, and, breaking to her with delicate skill the intelligence of the impending catastrophe, he announced that he had at length succeeded in obtaining for her the desired permission to visit her brother; and, while she shuddered at the proximity of an event for which she had long attempted to prepare herself, Honain, with some modifications, whispered the means by which he flattered himself that it might yet be averted. Miriam listened to him in silence, nor could he, with all his consummate art, succeed in extracting from her the slightest indication of her own opinion as to their expediency. They parted, Honain as sanguine as the wicked ever are.

As Miriam dreaded, both for herself and for Alroy, the shock of an unexpected meeting, she availed herself of the influence of Honain to send Caleb to her brother, to prepare him for her presence, and to consult him as to the desirable moment. Caleb found his late master lying exhausted on the floor of his dungeon. At first he would not speak or even raise his head, nor did he for a long time apparently recognise the faithful retainer of his uncle. But at length he grew milder, and when he fully comprehended who the messenger was, and the object of the mission, he at first seemed altogether disinclined to see his sister, but in the end postponed their meeting for the present, and, pleading great exhaustion, fixed for that sad interview the first hour of dawn.

The venerable Bostenay had scarcely ever spoken since the fall of his nephew; indeed it was but too evident that his faculties, even if they had not entirely deserted him, were at least greatly impaired. He never quitted his couch; he took no notice of what occurred. He evinced no curiosity, scarcely any feeling. If indeed he occasionally did mutter an observation, it was generally of an irritable character, nor truly did he appear satisfied if anyone approached him, save Miriam, from whom alone he would accept the scanty viands which he ever appeared disinclined to touch. But his devoted niece, amid all her harrowing affliction, could ever spare to the protector of her youth a placid countenance, a watchful eye, a gentle voice, and a ready hand. Her religion and her virtue, the strength of her faith, and the inspiration of her innocence, supported this pure and hapless lady amid all her undeserved and unparalleled sorrows.

It was long past midnight; the young widow of Abner reposed upon a couch in a soft slumber. The amiable Beruna and the beautiful Bathsheba, the blinds withdrawn, watched the progress of the night.

'Shall I wake her?' said the beautiful Bathsheba. 'Methinks the stars are paler! She bade me rouse her long before the dawn.'

'Her sleep is too benign! Let us not wake her,' replied the amiable Beruna. 'We rouse her only to sorrow.'

'May her dreams at least be happy;' rejoined the beautiful Bathsheba. 'She sleeps tranquilly, as a flower.'

'The veil has fallen from her head,' said the amiable Beruna. 'I will replace it lightly on her brow. Is that well, my Bathsheba?'

'It is well, sweet Beruna. Her face shrouded by the shawl is like a pearl in its shell. See! she moves!'

'Bathsheba!'

'I am here, sweet lady.'

'Is it near dawn?'

'Not yet, sweet lady; it is yet night. It is long past the noon of night, sweet lady; methinks I scent the rising breath of morn; but still 'tis night, and the young moon shines like a sickle in the heavenly field, amid the starry harvest.'

'Beruna, gentle girl, give me thy arm. I'll rise.'

The maidens advanced, and gently raising their mistress, supported her to the window.

'Since our calamities,' said Miriam, 'I have never enjoyed such tranquil slumber. My dreams were slight, but soothing. I saw him, but he smiled. Have I slept long, sweet girls? Ye are very watchful.'

'Dear lady, let me bring thy shawl. The air is fresh——'

'But sweet; I thank thee, no. My brow is not so cool as to need a covering. 'Tis a fair night!'

Miriam gazed upon the wide prospect of the moonlit capital. The elevated position of the citadel afforded an extensive view of the mighty groups of buildings, each in itself a city, broken only by some vast and hooded cupola, the tall, slender, white minarets of the mosques, or the black and spiral form of some lonely cypress, and through which the rushing Tigris, flooded with light, sent forth its broad and brilliant torrent. All was silent; not a single boat floated on the fleet river, not a solitary voice broke the stillness of slumbering millions. She gazed, and, as she gazed, she could not refrain from contrasting the present scene, which seemed the sepulchre of all the passions of our race, with the unrivalled excitement of that stirring spectacle which Bagdad exhibited on the celebration of the marriage of Alroy. How different then, too, was her position from her present, and how happy! The only sister of a devoted brother, the lord and conqueror of Asia, the bride of his most victorious captain, one worthy of all her virtues, and whose youthful valour had encircled her brow with a diadem. For Miriam, exalted station had brought neither cares nor crimes. It had, as it were, only rendered her charity universal, and her benevolence omnipotent. She could not accuse herself, this blessed woman: she could not accuse herself, even in this searching hour of self-knowledge: she could not accuse herself, with all her meekness, and modesty, and humility, of having for a moment forgotten her dependence on her God, or her duty to her neighbour.

But when her thoughts recurred to that being from whom they were indeed scarcely ever absent; and when she remembered him, and all his life, and all the thousand incidents of his youth, mysteries to the world, and known only to her, but which were indeed the prescience of his fame, and thought of all his surpassing qualities and all his sweet affection, his unrivalled glory and his impending fate, the tears, in silent agony, forced their way down her pale and pensive cheek. She bowed her head upon Bathsheba's shoulder, and sweet Beruna pressed her quivering hand.

The moon set, the stars grew white and ghastly, and vanished one by one. Over the distant plain of the Tigris, the scene of the marriage pomp, the dark purple horizon shivered into a rich streak of white and orange. The solemn strain of the Muezzin sounded from the minarets. Some one knocked at the door. It was Caleb.

'I am ready,' said Miriam; and for a moment she covered her face with her right hand. 'Think of me, sweet maidens; pray for me!'

## CHAPTER XIX.

LEANING on Caleb, and lighted by a gaoler, bearing torches, Miriam descended the damp and broken stairs that led to the dungeon. She faltered as she arrived at the grate. She stopped, and leant against the cold and gloomy wall. The gaoler and Caleb preceded her. She heard the voice of Alroy. It was firm and sweet. Its accents reassured her. Caleb came forth with a torch, and held it to her foot; and, as he bent down, he said, 'My lord bade me beg you to be of good heart, for he is.'

The gaoler, having stuck his torch in the niche, withdrew. Miriam desired Caleb to stay without. Then, summoning up all her energies, she entered the dreadful abode. Alroy was standing to receive her. The light fell full upon his countenance. It smiled. Miriam could no longer restrain herself. She ran forward, and pressed him to her heart.

'O, my best, my long beloved,' whispered Alroy; 'such a meeting indeed leads captivity captive!'

But the sister could not speak. She leant her head upon his shoulder, and closed her eyes, that she might not weep.

'Courage, dear heart; courage, courage!' whispered the captive. 'Indeed I am happy!'

'My brother, my brother!'

'Had we met yesterday, you would have found me perhaps a little vexed. But to-day I am myself again. Since I crossed the Tigris, I know not that I have felt such self-content. I have had sweet dreams, dear Miriam, full of solace. And, more than dreams, the Lord has pardoned me, I truly think.'

'O, my brother! your words are full of comfort; for, indeed, I too have dreamed, and dreamed of consolation. My spirit, since our fall, has never been more tranquil.'

'Indeed I am happy.'

'Say so again, my David; let me hear again these words of solace!'

'Indeed, 'tis very true, my faithful friend. It is not spoken in kind mockery to make you joyous. For know, last eve, whether the Lord repented of his wrath, or whether some dreadful trials, of which I will not speak, and wish not to remember, had made atonement for my manifold sins. but so it was, that, about the time my angel Miriam sent her soothing message, a feeling of repose came over me, such as I long have coveted. Anon, I fell into a slumber, deep and sweet, and, instead of those wild and whirling images that of late have darted from my brain when it should rest, glimpses of empire and conspiracy, snatches of fierce wars and mocking loves, I stood beside our native fountain's brink, and gathered flowers with my earliest friend. As I placed the fragrant captives in your flowing locks, there came Jabaster, that great, injured man, no longer stern and awful, but with benignant looks, and full of love. And he said, "David, the Lord hath marked thy faithfulness, in spite of the darkness of thy dungeon." So he vanished. He spoke, my sister, of some strange temptations by heavenly aid withstood. No more of that. I awoke. And lo! I heard my name still called. Full of my morning dream, I thought it was you, and I answered, "Dear sister, art thou here?" But no one answered; and then, reflecting, my memory recognised those thrilling tones that summoned Alroy in Jabaster's cave.'

'The Daughter of the Voice?'

'Even that sacred messenger. I am full of faith. The Lord hath pardoned me. Be sure of that.'

'I cannot doubt it, David. You have done great things for Israel; no one in these latter days has risen like you. If you have fallen, you were young, and strangely tempted.'

'Yet Israel, Israel! Did I not feel a worthier leader will yet arise, my heart would crack. I have betrayed my country!'

'Oh no, no, no! You have shown what we can do and shall do. Your memory alone is inspiration. A great career, although baulked of its end, is still a landmark of human energy. Failure, when sublime, is not without its purpose. Great deeds are great legacies, and work with wondrous usury. By what Man has done, we learn what Man can do; and gauge the power and prospects of our race.'

'Alas! there is no one to guard my name. 'Twill be reviled; or worse, 'twill be forgotten.'

'Never! the memory of great actions never dies. The sun of glory, though awhile obscured, will shine at last. And so, sweet brother, perchance some poet, in some distant age, within whose veins our sacred blood may flow, his fancy fired with the national theme, may strike his harp to Alroy's wild career, and consecrate a name too long forgotten?'

'May love make thee a prophetess!' exclaimed Alroy, as he bent down his head and embraced her. 'Do not tarry,' he whispered. ''Tis better that we should part in this firm mood.'

She sprang from him, she clasped her hands. 'We will not part,' she exclaimed with energy;· 'I will die with thee.'

'Blessed girl, be calm! Do not unman me.'

·I am calm. See! I do not weep. Not a tear, not a tear. They are all in my heart.'

'Go, go, my Miriam, angel of light. Tarry no longer; I pray thee go. I would not think of the past. Let all my mind be centred in the present. Thy presence calls back our bygone days, and softens me too much. My duty to my uncle. Go, dear one, go!'

'And leave thee, leave thee to—— Oh! my David, thou hast seen, thou hast heard——Honain?'

'No more; let not that accursed name profane those holy lips. Raise not the demon in me.'

'I am silent. Yet 'tis madness! O! my brother, thou hast a fearful trial.'

'The God of Israel is my refuge. He saved our fathers in the fiery furnace. He will save me.'

'I am full of faith. I pray thee let me stay.'

'I would be silent; I would be alone. I cannot speak,

Miriam. I ask one favour, the last and dearest, from her who has never had a thought but for my wishes; blessed being, leave me.'

'I go. O Alroy, farewell! Let me kiss you. Again, once more! Let me kneel and bless you. Brother, beloved brother, great and glorious brother, I am worthy of you: I will not weep. I am prouder in this dread moment of your love than all your foes can be of their hard triumph!'

## CHAPTER XX.

BERUNA and Bathsheba received their mistress when she returned to her chamber. They marked her desolate air. She was silent, pale, and cold. They bore her to her couch, whereon she sat with a most listless and unmeaning look; her quivering lips parted, her eyes fixed upon the ground in vacant abstraction, and her arms languidly folded before her. Beruna stole behind her, and supported her back with pillows, and Bathsheba, unnoticed, wiped the slight foam from her mouth. Thus Miriam remained for several hours, her faithful maidens in vain watching for any indication of her self-consciousness.

Suddenly a trumpet sounded.

'What is that?' exclaimed Miriam, in a shrill voice, and looking up with a distracted glance.

Neither of them answered, since they were aware that it betokened the going forth of Alroy to his trial.

Miriam remained in the same posture, and with the same expression of wild inquiry. Another trumpet sounded, and after that a shout of the people. Then she raised up her arms to heaven, and bowed her head, and died.

## CHAPTER XXI.

'Has the second trumpet sounded?'

'To be sure: run, run for a good place. Where is Abdallah?'

'Selling sherbet in the square. We shall find him. Has Alroy come forth?'

'Yes! he goes the other way. We shall be too late. Only think of Abdallah selling sherbet!'

'Father, let me go?'

'You will be in the way; you are too young: you will see nothing. Little boys should stay at home.'

'No, they should not. I will go. You can put me on your shoulders.'

'Where is Ibrahim? Where is Ali? We must all keep together. We shall have to fight for it. I wish Abdallah were here. Only think of his selling sherbet!'

'Keep straight forward. That is right. It is no use going that way. The Bazaar is shut. There is Fakreddin, there is Osman Effendi. He has got a new page.'

'So he has, I declare; and a very pretty boy too.'

'Father, will they impale Alroy alive?'

'I am sure I do not know. Never ask questions, my dear. Little boys never should.'

'Yes, they should. I hope they will impale him alive. I shall be so disappointed if they do not.'

'Keep to the left. Dash through the Butchers' Bazaar: that is open. All right, all right. Did you push me, sir?'

'Suppose I did push you, sir, what then, sir?'

'Come along, don't quarrel. That is a Karasmian. They think they are to do what they like. We are five to one to be sure, but still there is nothing like peace and quiet. I wish Abdallah were here with his stout shoulders. Only think of his selling sherbet!'

## CHAPTER XXII.

The Square of the Grand Mosque, the same spot where Jabaster met Abidan by appointment, was the destined scene of the pretended trial of Alroy. Thither by break of day the sight-loving thousands of the capital had repaired. In the centre of the square, a large circle was described by a crimson cord, and guarded by Karasmian soldiers. Around this the swelling multitude pressed like the gathering waves of ocean, but, whenever the tide set in with too great an impulse, the savage Karasmians appeased the ungovernable element by raising their battle-axes, and brutally breaking the crowns and belabouring the shoulders of their nearest victims. As the morning advanced, the terraces of the surrounding houses, covered with awnings, were crowded with spectators. All Bagdad was astir. Since the marriage of Alroy, there had never been such a merry morn as the day of his impalement.

At one end of the circle was erected a magnificent throne. Half way between the throne and the other end of the circle, but further back, stood a company of Negro eunuchs, hideous to behold, who, clothed in white, and armed with various instruments of torture, surrounded the enormous stakes, tall, thin, and sharp, that were prepared for the final ceremony.

The flourish of trumpets, the clash of cymbals, and the wild beat of the tambour, announced the arrival of Alp Arslan from the Serail. An avenue to the circle had been preserved through the multitude. The royal procession might be traced as it wound through the populace, by the sparkling and undulating line of plumes of honour, and the dazzling forms of the waving streamers, on which were inscribed the names of Allah and the Prophet. Suddenly, amid the bursts of music, and the shouts of the spectators, many of whom on the terraces humbled themselves on their knees, Alp Arslan mounted the throne, around which ranged themselves his chief captains, and a deputation of the Moollahs, and Imams, and Cadis, and other principal personages of the city.

The King of Karasmé was tall in stature, and somewhat meagre in form. He was fair, or rather sandy-coloured, with a red beard, and blue eyes, and a flat nose. The moment he was seated, a trumpet was heard in the distance from an opposite quarter, and it was soon understood throughout the assembly that the great captive was about to appear.

A band of Karasmian guards first entered the circle, and ranged themselves round the cord, with their backs to the spectators. After them came fifty of the principal Hebrew prisoners, with their hands bound behind them, but evidently more for form than security. To these succeeded a small covered waggon drawn by mules, and surrounded by guards, from which was led forth, his legs relieved from their manacles, but his hands still in heavy chains, David Alroy!

A universal buzz of blended sympathy, and wonder, and fear, and triumph arose, throughout the whole assembly. Each man involuntarily stirred. The vast populace moved to and fro in agitation. His garments soiled and tattered, his head bare, and his long locks drawn off his forehead, pale and thin, but still unsubdued, the late conqueror and Caliph of Bagdad threw around a calm and imperial glance upon those who were but recently his slaves.

The trumpets again sounded, order was called, and a crier announced that his Highness Alp Arslan, the mighty Sovereign of Karasmé, their Lord, Protector, and King, and avenger of Allah and the Prophet, against all rebellious and evil-minded Jews and Giaours, was about to speak. There was a deep and universal silence, and then sounded a voice high as the eagle's in a storm.

'David Alroy!' said his conqueror, 'you are brought hither this day neither for trial nor for judgment. Captured in arms against your rightful sovereign, you are of course prepared, like other rebels, for your doom.

Such a crime alone deserves the most avenging punishments. What then do you merit, who are loaded with a thousand infamies, who have blasphemed Allah and the Prophet, and, by the practice of magic arts and the aid of the infernal powers, have broken the peace of kingdoms, occasioned infinite bloodshed, outraged all law, religion, and decency, misled the minds of your deluded votaries, and especially by a direct compact with Eblis, by horrible spells and infamous incantations, captivated the senses of an illustrious Princess, heretofore famous for the practice of every virtue, and a descendant of the Prophet himself.

'Behold these stakes of palm-wood, sharper than a lance! The most terrible retribution that human ingenuity has devised for the guilty awaits you. But your crimes baffle all human vengeance. Look forward for your satisfactory reward to those infernal powers by whose dark co-operation you have occasioned such disasters. Your punishment is public, that all men may know that the guilty never escape, and that, if your heart be visited by the slightest degree of compunction for your numerous victims, you may this day, by the frank confession of the irresistible means by which you seduced them, exonerate your victims from the painful and ignominious end with which, through your influence, they are now threatened. Mark, O assembled people, the infinite mercy of the Vicegerent of Allah! He allows the wretched man to confess his infamy, and to save, by his confession, his unfortunate victims. I have said it. Glory to Allah!'

And the people shouted, 'He has said it, he has said it! Glory to Allah! He is great, he is great! and Mahomet is his prophet!'

'Am I to speak?' inquired Alroy, when the tumult had subsided. The melody of his voice commanded universal attention.

Alp Arslan nodded his head in approbation.

'King of Karasmé! I stand here accused of many crimes. Now hear my answers. 'Tis said I am a rebel. My answer is, I am a Prince as thou art, of a sacred race, and far more ancient. I owe fealty to no one but to my God, and if I have broken that I am yet to learn that Alp Arslan is the avenger of His power. As for thy God and Prophet, I know not them, though they acknowledge mine. 'Tis well understood in every polity, my people stand apart from other nations, and ever will, in spite of suffering. So much for blasphemy; I am true to a deep faith of ancient days, which even the sacred writings of thy race still reverence. For the arts magical I practised, and the communion with infernal powers 'tis said I held, know, King, I raised the standard of my faith by the direct commandment of my God, the great Creator of the universe. What need of magic, then? What need of paltering with petty fiends, when backed by His omnipotence? My magic was His inspiration. Need I prove why, with such aid, my people crowded round me? The time will come when from out our ancient seed, a worthier chief will rise, not to be quelled even by thee, Sire.

'For that unhappy Princess of whom something was said (with no great mercy, as it seemed to me), that lady is my wife, my willing wife; the daughter of a Caliph, still my wife, although your stakes may make her soon a widow. I stand not here to account for female fancies. Believe me, Sire, she gave her beauty to my raptured arms with no persuasions but such as became a soldier and a king. It may seem strange to thee upon thy throne, that the flower of Asia should be plucked by one so vile as I am. Remember, the accidents of Fortune are most strange. I was not always what I am. We have met before. There was a day, and that too not long since, when, but for the treachery of some knaves I mark here, Fortune seemed half inclined to reverse our fates. Had I conquered, I trust I should have shown more mercy.'

The King of Karasmé was the most passionate of men. He had made a speech according to the advice and instructions of his councillors, who had assured him that the tone he adopted would induce Alroy to confess all that he required, and especially to vindicate the reputation of the

Princess Schirene, who had already contrived to persuade
Alp Arslan that she was the most injured of her sex. The
King of Karasmé stamped thrice on the platform of his
throne, and exclaimed with great fire, 'By my beard, ye
have deceived me! The dog has confessed nothing!'

All the councillors and chief captains, and the Moollahs,
and the Imams, and the Cadis, and the principal personages
of the city were in consternation. They immediately consulted together, and, after much disputation, agreed that,
before they proceeded to extremities, it was expedient to
prove what the prisoner would not confess. A venerable
Scheik, clothed in flowing robes of green, with a long
white beard, and a turban like the tower of Babel, then
rose. His sacred reputation procured silence while he
himself delivered a long prayer, supplicating Allah and the
Prophet to confound all blaspheming Jews and Giaours,
and to pour forth words of truth from the mouths of
religious men. And then the venerable Scheik summoned
all witnesses against David Alroy. Immediately advanced
Kisloch the Kourd, who, being placed in an eminent position, the Cadi of Bagdad drew forth a scroll from his velvet
bag, and read to him a deposition, wherein the worthy
Kisloch stated that he first became acquainted with the
prisoner, David Alroy, in some ruins in the desert, the
haunt of banditti, of whom Alroy was the chief; that he,
Kisloch, was a reputable merchant, and that his caravan
had been plundered by these robbers, and he himself captured; that, on the second night of his imprisonment,
Alroy appeared to him in the likeness of a lion, and on the
third, of a bull with fiery eyes; that he was in the habit of
constantly transforming himself; that he frequently raised
spirits; that, at length, on one terrible night, Eblis himself
came in great procession, and presented Alroy with the
sceptre of Solomon Ben Daoud; and that the next day
Alroy raised his standard, and soon after massacred Hassan
Subah and his Seljuks, by the visible aid of many terrible
demons.

Calidas the Indian, the Guebre, and the Negro, and a

few congenial spirits, were not eclipsed in the satisfactory character of their evidence by the luminous testimony of Kisloch the Kourd. The irresistible career of the Hebrew conqueror was undeniably accounted for, and the honour of Moslem arms, and the purity of Moslem faith, were established in their pristine glory and all their unsullied reputation. David Alroy was proved to be a child of Eblis, a sorcerer, and a dealer in charms and magical poisons. The people listened with horror and with indignation. They would have burst through the guards and torn him in pieces, had not they been afraid of the Karasmian battleaxes. So they consoled themselves with the prospect of his approaching tortures.

The Cadi of Bagdad bowed himself before the King of Karasmé, and whispered at a respectful distance in the royal ear. The trumpets sounded, the criers enjoined silence, and the royal lips again moved.

'Hear, O ye people, and be wise. The chief Cadi is about to read the deposition of the royal Princess Schirene, chief victim of the sorcerer.'

And the deposition was read, which stated that David Alroy possessed, and wore next to his heart, a talisman, given him by Eblis, the virtue of which was so great that, if once it were pressed to the heart of any woman, she was no longer mistress of her will. Such had been the unhappy fate of the daughter of the Commander of the Faithful.

'Is it so written?' inquired the captive.

'It is so written,' replied the Cadi, 'and bears the imperial signature of the Princess.'

'It is a forgery.'

The King of Karasmé started from his throne, and in his rage nearly descended its steps. His face was like scarlet, his beard was like a flame. A favourite minister ventured gently to restrain the royal robe.

'Kill the dog on the spot,' muttered the King of Karasmé.

'The Princess is herself here,' said the Cadi, 'to bear

witness to the spells of which she was a victim, but from which, by the power of Allah and the Prophet, she is now released.'

Alroy started!

'Advance, royal Princess,' said the Cadi, 'and, if the deposition thou hast heard be indeed true, condescend to hold up the imperial hand that adorned it with thy signature.'

A band of eunuchs near the throne gave way; a female figure veiled to her feet appeared. She held up her hand amid the breathless agitation of the whole assembly; the ranks of the eunuchs again closed; a shriek was heard, and the veiled figure disappeared.

'I am ready for thy tortures, King,' said Alroy, in a tone of deep depression. His firmness appeared to have deserted him. His eyes were cast upon the ground. Apparently he was buried in profound thought, or had delivered himself up to despair.

'Prepare the stakes,' said Alp Arslan.

An involuntary, but universal, shudder might be distinguished through the whole assembly.

A slave advanced and offered Alroy a scroll. He recognised the Nubian who belonged to Honain. His former minister informed him that he was at hand, that the terms he offered in the dungeon might even yet be granted; that if Alroy would, as he doubted not, as he entreated him, accept them, he was to place the scroll in his bosom, but that if he were still inexorable, still madly determined on a horrible and ignominious end, he was to tear the scroll and throw it in to the arena. Instantly Alroy took the scroll, and with great energy tore it into a thousand pieces. A puff of wind carried the fragments far and wide. The mob fought for these last memorials of David Alroy, and this little incident occasioned a great confusion.

In the meantime the negroes prepared the instruments of torture and of death.

'The obstinacy of this Jewish dog makes me mad,' said

the King of Karasmé to his courtiers. 'I will hold some parley with him before he dies.' The favourite minister entreated his sovereign to be content; but the royal beard grew so red, and the royal eyes flashed forth such terrible sparks of fire, that even the favourite minister at length gave way.

The trumpet sounded, the criers called silence, and the voice of Alp Arslan was again heard.

'Thou dog, dost see what is preparing for thee? Dost know what awaits thee in the halls of thy master Eblis? Can a Jew be influenced even by false pride? Is not life sweet? Is it not better to be my slipper-bearer than to be impaled?'

'Magnanimous Alp Arslan,' replied Alroy in a tone of undisguised contempt; 'thinkest thou that any torture can be equal to the recollection that I have been conquered by thee?'

'By my beard, he mocks me!' exclaimed the Karasmian monarch, 'he defies me! Touch not my robe. I will parley with him. Ye see no farther than a hooded hawk, ye sons of a blind mother. This is a sorcerer; he hath yet some master spell; he will yet save himself. He will fly into the air, or sink into the earth. He laughs at our tortures.' The King of Karasmé precipitately descended the steps of his throne, followed by his favourite minister, and his councillors, and chief captains, and the Cadis, and the Moollahs, and the Imams, and the principal personages of the city.

'Sorcerer!' exclaimed Alp Arslan, 'insolent sorcerer! base son of a base mother! dog of dogs! dost thou defy us? Does thy master Eblis whisper hope? Dost thou laugh at our punishments? Wilt thou fly into the air? wilt thou sink into the earth? eh, eh? Is it so, is it so?' The breathless monarch ceased, from the exhaustion of passion. He tore his beard out by the roots, he stamped with uncontrollable rage.

'Thou art wiser than thy councillors, royal Arslan; I do defy thee. My master, although not Eblis, has not deserted me. I laugh at thy punishments. Thy tortures I despise. I shall both sink into the earth and mount into the air. Art thou answered?'

'By my beard,' exclaimed the enraged Arslan, 'I am answered. Let Eblis save thee if he can;' and the King of Karasmé, the most famous master of the sabre in Asia, drew his blade like lightning from its sheath, and took off the head of Alroy at a stroke. It fell, and, as it fell, a smile of triumphant derision seemed to play upon the dying features of the hero, and to ask of his enemies, 'Where now are all your tortures?'[52]

# NOTES TO ALROY.

NOTE 1, page 3.—*We shall yet see an ass mount a ladder.*
Hebrew proverb.

NOTE 2, page 10.—*Our walls are hung with flowers you love.*

It is the custom of the Hebrews in many of their festivals, especially in the feast of the Tabernacle, to hang the walls of their chambers with garlands of flowers.

NOTE 3, page 11.—*The traditionary tomb of Esther and Mordecai.*

'I accompanied the priest through the town over much ruin and rubbish to an enclosed piece of ground, rather more elevated than any in its immediate vicinity. In the centre was the Jewish tomb—a square building of brick, of a mosque-like form, with a rather elongated dome at the top. The door is in the ancient sepulchral fashion of the country, very small, consisting of a single stone of great thickness, and turning on its own pivots from one side. Its key is always in possession of the eldest of the Jews resident at Hamadan. Within the tomb are two sarcophagi, made of a very dark wood, carved with great intricacy of pattern and richness of twisted ornament, with a line of inscription in Hebrew,' &c.—*Sir R. K. Porter's Travels in Persia*, vol. ii. p. 107.

NOTE 4, page 13.—*A marble fountain, the richly-carved cupola supported by twisted columns.*

The vast magnificence and elaborate fancy of the tombs and fountains is a remarkable feature of Oriental architecture. The Eastern nations devote to these structures the richest and the most durable materials. While the palaces of Asiatic monarchs are in general built only of wood, painted in fresco, the rarest marbles are dedicated to the sepulchre and the spring, which are often richly gilt, and adorned even with precious stones.

NOTE 5, page 14.—*The chorus of our maidens.*

It is still the custom for the women in the East to repair at sunset in company to the fountain for their supply of water. In Egypt, you may observe at twilight the women descending the banks of the Nile in procession from every town and village. Their graceful drapery, their long veils not concealing their flashing eyes, and the classical forms of their vases, render this a most picturesque and agreeable spectacle.

### Note 6, page 20.

I describe the salty deserts of Persia, a locality which my tale required; but I have ventured to introduce here, and in the subsequent pages, the principal characteristics of the great Arabian deserts: the mirage, the simoom, the gazelle, the oasis.

### Note 7, page 23.—*Jackals and marten-cat.*

At nightfall, especially in Asia Minor, the lonely horseman will often meet the jackals on their evening prowl. Their moaning is often heard during the night. I remember, when becalmed off Troy, the most singular screams were heard at intervals throughout the night, from a forest on the opposite shore, which a Greek sailor assured me proceeded from a marten-cat, which had probably found the carcass of some horse.

### Note 8, page 25.

*Elburz*, or *Elborus*, the highest range of the Caucasus.

### Note 9, page 26.—*A circular and brazen table, sculptured with strange characters and mysterious figures; near it was a couch, on which lay several volumes.*

A cabalistic table, perhaps a zodiac. The books were doubtless *Sepher Happeliah*, the Book of Wonders; *Sepher Hakkaneh*, the Book of the Pen; and *Sepher Habbahir*, the Book of Light. This last unfolds the most sublime mysteries.

### Note 10, page 27.—*Answered the Cabalist.*

'Simeon ben Jochai, who flourished in the second century, and was a disciple of Akibha, is called by the Jews the Prince of the Cabalists. After the suppression of the sedition in which his master had been so unsuccessful, he concealed himself in a cave, where, according to the Jewish historians, he received revelations, which he afterwards delivered to his disciples, and which they carefully preserved in the book called *Sohar*. His master, Akibha, who lived soon after the destruction of Jerusalem, was the author of the famous book *Jezirah*, quoted by the Jews as of Divine authority. When Akibha was far advanced in life, appeared the famous impostor Barchochebas, who, under the character of the Messiah, promised to deliver his countrymen from the power of the Emperor Adrian. Akibha espoused his cause, and afforded him the protection and support of his name, and an army of two hundred thousand men repaired to his standard. The Romans at first slighted the insurrection; but when they found the insurgents spread slaughter and rapine wherever they came, they sent out a military force against them. At first, the issue of the contest was doubtful. The Messiah himself was not taken until the end of four years.'—*Enfield, Philosophy of the Jews*, vol. ii.

'Two methods of instruction were in use among the Jews; the one public, or *exoteric*; the other secret, or *esoteric*. The exoteric doctrine was that which was openly taught the people from the law of Moses and the traditions of the fathers. The esoteric was that which treated of the mysteries of the Divine nature, and other sublime subjects, and was known by the name of the Cabala. The latter was, after the manner of the Pythagorean and Egyptian mysteries, taught only to certain persons, who were bound, under the most solemn anathema, not to divulge it. Concerning the miraculous origin and preservation of the Cabala, the Jews relate many marvellous tales. They derive these mysteries from Adam, and assert that, while the first man was in Paradise, the angel Rasiel brought him a book from heaven, which contained the doctrines of heavenly wisdom, and that, when Adam received this book, angels came down to him to learn its contents, but that he refused to admit them to the knowledge of sacred things entrusted to him alone; that, after the Fall, this book was taken back into heaven; that, after many prayers and tears, God restored it to Adam, from whom it passed to Seth. In the degenerate age before the flood this book was lost, and the mysteries it contained almost forgotten; but they were restored by special revelation to Abraham, who committed them to writing in the book *Jezirah*.'—*Vide Enfield*, vol. ii. p. 219.

'The Hebrew word *Cabala*,' says Dom Calmet, 'signifies tradition, and the Rabbins, who are named Cabalists, apply themselves principally to the combination of certain words, numbers, and letters, by the means of which they boasted they could reveal the future, and penetrate the sense of the most difficult passages of Scripture. This science does not appear to have any fixed principles, but depends upon certain ancient traditions, whence its name *Cabala*. The Cabalists have a great number of names which they style sacred, by means of which they raise spirits, and affect to obtain supernatural intelligence.'—See *Calmet, art. Cabala*.

'We spake before,' says Lightfoot, 'of the commonness of Magick among them, one singular means whereby they kept their own in delusion, and whereby they affronted ours. The general expectation of the nation of Messias coming when he did, had this double and contrary effect, that it forwarded those that belonged to God to believe and receive the Gospel; and those that did not, it gave encouragement to some to take upon them they were Christ or some great prophet, and to others it gave some persuasion to be deluded by them. These deceivers dealt most of them with Magick, and that cheat ended not when Jerusalem ended, though one would have thought that had been a fair term of not further expecting Messias; but, since the people were willing to be deceived by such expectation, there rose up deluders still that were willing to deceive them.'—*Lightfoot*, vol. ii. p. 371.

For many curious details of the Cabalistic Magic, *Vide Basnage*, vol. v. p. 384, &c.

NOTE 11, page 28.—*Read the stars no longer.*

'The modern Jews,' says Basnage, 'have a great idea of the influence of the stars.' Vol. iv. p. 454. But astrology was most prevalent among the Babylonian Rabbins, of whom Jabaster was one. Living in the ancient land of the Chaldeans, these sacred sages imbibed a taste for the mystic lore of their predecessors. The stars moved, and formed letters and lines, when consulted by any of the highly-initiated of the Cabalists. This they styled the Celestial Alphabet.

NOTE 12, page 32.—*The Daughter of the Voice.*

'Both the Talmudick and the latter Rabbins,' says Lightfoot, 'make frequent mention of *Bath Kol*, or *Filia Vocis*, or an echoing voice which served under the second temple for their utmost refuge of revelation. For when Urim and Thummim, the oracle, was ceased, and prophecy was decayed and gone, they had, as they say, certain strange and extraordinary voices upon certain extraordinary occasions, which were their warnings and advertisements in some special matters. Infinite instances of this might be adduced, if they might be believed. Now here it may be questioned why they called it *Bath Kol, the daughter of a voice*, and not a voice itself? If the strictness of the Hebrew word *Bath* be to be stood upon, which always it is not, it may be answered, that it is called the *Daughter of a Voice* in relation to the oracles of Urim and Thummim. For whereas that was a voice given from off the mercy-seat, within the vail, and this, upon the decay of that oracle, came as it were in its place, it might not unfitly or improperly be called a *daughter*, or successor of that voice.'—*Lightfoot*, vol. i. pp. 485, 486.

Consult also the learned Doctor, vol. ii. pp. 128, 129 : 'It was used for a testimony from heaven, but was indeed performed by magic art.'

NOTE 13, page 37.—*The walls and turrets of an extensive city.*

In Persia, and the countries of the Tigris and Euphrates, the traveller sometimes arrives at deserted cities of great magnificence and antiquity. Such, for instance, is the city of Anneh. I suppose Alroy to have entered one of the deserted capitals of the Seleucidæ. They are in general the haunt of bandits.

NOTE 14, page 41.—*Punctured his arm.*

From a story told by an Arab.

NOTE 15, page 44.—*The pilgrim could no longer sustain himself.*
An endeavour to paint the simoom.

NOTE 16, page 45.—*By the holy stone.*

The Caaba.—The Caaba is the same to the Mahomedan as the Holy Sepulchre to the Christian. It is the most unseemly, but the most sacred, part of the mosque at Mecca, and is a small, square stone building.

NOTE 17, page 47.—*I am a Hakim;*

*i.e. Physician*, an almost sacred character in the East. As all Englishmen travel with medicine-chests, the Turks are not to be wondered at for considering us physicians.

NOTE 18, page 49.—*Threw their wanton jerreeds in the air.*

The Persians are more famous for throwing the jerreed than any other nation. A Persian gentleman, while riding quietly by your side, will suddenly dash off at full gallop, then suddenly check his horse, and take a long aim with his lance with admirable precision. I should doubt, however, whether he could hurl a lance a greater distance or with greater force and effect than a Nubian, who will fix a mark at sixty yards with his javelin.

NOTE 19, page 49.—*Some pounded coffee.*

The origin of the use of coffee is obscure; but there is great reason to believe that it had not been introduced in the time of Alroy. When we consider that the life of an Oriental at the present day mainly consists in drinking coffee and smoking tobacco, we cannot refrain from asking ourselves, 'What did he do before either of these comparatively modern inventions was discovered?' For a long time, I was inclined to suspect that tobacco might have been in use in Asia before it was introduced into Europe; but a passage in old Sandys, in which he mentions the wretched tobacco smoked in Turkey, and accounts for it by that country being supplied with 'the dregs of our markets,' demonstrates that, in his time, there was no native growth in Asia. Yet the choicest tobaccoes are now grown on the coast of Syria, the real Levant. But did the Asiatics smoke any other plant or substance before tobacco? In Syria, at the present day, they smoke a plant called *timbac;* the Chinese smoke opium; the artificial preparations for the hookah are known to all Indians. I believe, however, that these are all refinements, and for this reason, that in the classic writers, who were as well acquainted with the Oriental nations as ourselves, we find no allusion to the practice of smoking. The anachronism of the pipe I have not therefore ventured to commit, and that of coffee will, I trust, be pardoned.

NOTE 20, page 49.—*Wilder gestures of the dancing girls.*

These dancing girls abound throughout Asia. The most famous are the Almeh of Egypt, and the Nautch of India. These last are a caste, the first only a profession.

NOTE 21, page 54.—*For thee the bastinado.*

The bastinado is the common punishment of the East, and an effective and dreaded one. It is administered on the soles of the feet, the instrument a long cane or palm-branch. Public executions are very rare.

NOTE 22, page 62.—*A door of tortoiseshell and mother-o'-pearl.*

This elegant mode of inlay is common in Oriental palaces, and may be observed also in Alhambra, at Granada.

NOTE 23, page 62.—*A vaulted, circular, and highly embossed roof, of purple, scarlet, and gold.*

In the very first style of Saracenic architecture. See the Hall of the Ambassadors in Alhambra, and many other chambers in that exquisite creation.

NOTE 24, p. 63.—*Nubian eunuchs dressed in rich habits of scarlet and gold.*

Thus the guard of Nubian Eunuchs of the present Pacha of Egypt, Mehemet Ali, or rather Caliph, a title which he wishes to assume. They ride upon white horses.

NOTE 25, page 63.—*A quadrangular court of roses.*

So in Alhambra, 'THE COURT OF MYRTLES,' leading to the Court of Columns, wherein is the famous Fountain of Lions.

NOTE 26, page 63.—*An Abyssinian giant.*

A giant is still a common appendage to an Oriental court even at the present day. See a very amusing story in the picturesque 'Persian Sketches' of that famous elchee, Sir John Malcolm.

NOTE 27, page 64.—*Surrounded by figures of every rare quadruped.*

'The hall of audience,' says Gibbon, from Cardonne, speaking of the magnificence of the Saracens of Cordova, ' was encrusted with gold and pearls, and a great basin in the centre was surrounded with the curious and costly figures of birds and quadrupeds.'—*Decline and Fall*, vol. x. p. 39.

NOTE 28, page 64.—*A tree of gold and silver.*

'Among the other spectacles of rare and stupendous luxury was a tree of gold and silver, spreading into eighteen large branches, on which, and on the lesser boughs, sat a variety of birds made of the same precious metals, as well as the leaves of the tree. While the machinery effected spontaneous motions, the several birds warbled their natural harmony.'— *Gibbon*, vol. x. p. 38, from Abulfeda, describing the court of the Caliphs of Bagdad in the decline of their power.

NOTE 29, page 65.—*Four hundred men led as many white bloodhounds, with collars of gold and rubies.*

I have somewhere read of an Indian or Persian monarch whose coursing was conducted in this gorgeous style: if I remember right, it was Mahmoud the Gaznevide.

NOTE 30, page 65.—*A steed marked on its forehead with a star.*

The sacred steed of Solomon.

NOTE 31, page 66.—*Instead of water, each basin was replenished with the purest quicksilver.*

' In a lofty pavilion of the gardens, one of those basins and fountains so delightful in a sultry climate, was replenished, not with water, but with the purest quicksilver.'—*Gibbon*, vol. x. from Cardonne.

NOTE 32, page 66.—*Playing with a rosary of pearls and emeralds.*

Moslems of rank are never without the rosary, sometimes of amber and rare woods, sometimes of jewels. The most esteemed is of that peculiar substance called Mecca wood.

NOTE 33, page 66.—*The diamond hilt of a small poniard.*
The insignia of a royal female.

NOTE 34, page 70.—*You have been at Paris.*

Paris was known to the Orientals at this time as a city of considerable luxury and importance. The Embassy from Haroun Alraschid to Charlemagne, at an earlier date, is of course recollected.

NOTE 35, page 76.—*At length beheld the lost capital of his fathers.*

The finest view of Jerusalem is from the Mount of Olives. It is little altered since the period when David Alroy is supposed to have gazed upon it, but it is enriched by the splendid Mosque of Omar, built by the Moslem conquerors on the supposed site of the temple, and which, with its gardens, and arcades, and courts, and fountains, may fairly be described as the most imposing of Moslem fanes. I endeavoured to enter it at the hazard of my life. I was detected, and surrounded by a crowd of turbaned fanatics, and escaped with difficulty; but I saw enough to feel that minute inspection would not belie the general character I formed of it from the Mount of Olives. I caught a glorious glimpse of splendid courts, and light airy gates of Saracenic triumph, flights of noble steps, long arcades, and interior gardens, where silver fountains spouted their tall streams amid the taller cypresses.

NOTE 36, page 76.—*Entered Jerusalem by the gate of Sion.*

The gate of Sion still remains, and from it you descend into the valley of Siloah.

NOTE 37, page 79.—*King Pirgandicus.*

According to a Talmudical story, however, of which I find a note, this monarch was not a Hebrew but a Gentile, and a very wicked one. He once invited eleven famous doctors of the holy nation to supper. They were received in the most magnificent style, and were then invited, under pain of death, either to eat pork, to accept a pagan mistress, or to drink wine consecrated to idols. After long consultation, the doctors, in great tribulation, agreed to save their heads by accepting the last alternative, since the two first were forbidden by the law of Moses, and the last only by the Rabbins. The King assented, the doctors drank the impure wine, and, as it was exceedingly good, drank freely. The wine, as will sometimes happen, created a terrible appetite; the table was covered with dishes, and the doctors, heated by the grape, were not sufficiently careful of what they partook. In short, the wicked King Pirgandicus contrived that they should sup off pork, and being carried from the table quite tipsy, each of the eleven had the mortification of finding himself next morning in the arms of a pagan mistress.

In the course of the year all the eleven died sudden deaths, and this visitation occurred to them, not because they had violated the law of Moses, but because they believed that the precepts of the Rabbins could be outraged with more impunity than the Word of God.

NOTE 38, page 79.—*And conquered Julius Cæsar.*
This classic hero often figures in the erratic pages of the Talmud.

NOTE 39, page 79.—*The Tombs of the Kings.*

The present pilgrim to Jerusalem will have less trouble than Alroy in discovering the Tombs of the Kings, though he probably would not as easily obtain the sceptre of Solomon. The tombs that bear this title are of the time of the Asmonean princes, and of a more ambitious character than any other of the remains. An open court, about fifty feet in breadth, and extremely deep, is excavated out of the rock. One side is formed by a portico, the frieze of which is sculptured in a good Syro-Greek style. There is no grand portal; you crawl into the tombs by a small opening on one of the sides. There are a few small chambers with niches, recesses, and sarcophagi. some sculptured in the same flowing style as the frieze. This is the most important monument at Jerusalem; and Dr. Clarke, who has lavished wonder and admiration on the tombs of Zachariah and Absalom, has declared the Tombs of the Kings to be one of the marvellous productions of antiquity.

NOTE 40.—Page 80.

'*Rabbi Hillel* was one of the eminentest that ever was among the Jewish Doctors, both for birth, learning, rule, and children. He was of the seed of David by his mother's side, being of the posterity of Shephatiah, the son of Abital, David's wife. He was brought up in Babel, from whence he came up to Jerusalem at forty years old, and there studied the law forty years more under Shemaiah and Abtalion, and after them he was President of the Sanhedrim forty years more. The beginning of his Presidency is generally concluded upon to have been just one hundred years before the Temple was destroyed; by which account he began eight-and-twenty years before our Saviour was born, and died when he was about twelve years old. He is renowned for his fourscore scholars."—*Lightfoot*, vol. ii. p. 2008.

The great rival of Hillel was Shammai. Their controversies, and the fierceness of their partisans, are a principal feature of Rabbinical history. They were the same as the Scotists and Thomists. At last the Bath Kol interfered, and decided for Hillel, but in a spirit of conciliatory dexterity. The Bath Kol came forth and spake thus: 'The words both of the one party and the other are the words of the living God, but the certain decision of the matter is according to the decrees of the school of Hillel. And henceforth, whoever shall transgress the decrees of the school of Hillel is punishable with death.'

NOTE 41, page 82.—*A number of small, square, low chambers.*

These excavated cemeteries, which abound in Palestine and Egypt, were often converted into places of worship by the Jews and early Christians. Sandys thus describes the Synagogue at Jerusalem in his time.

NOTE 42, page 83.—*Their heads mystically covered.*

The Hebrews cover their heads during their prayers with a sacred shawl.

NOTE 43, page 83.—*Expounded the law to the congregation of the peop'e.*

The custom, I believe, even to the present day, among the Hebrews, a remnant of their old academies, once so famous.

NOTE 44, page 84.—*The Valley of Jehoshaphat and the Tomb of Absalom.*

In the Vale of Jehoshaphat, among many other tombs, are two of considerable size, and which, although of a corrupt Grecian architecture, are dignified by the titles of the tombs of Zachariah and Absalom.

NOTE 45, page 86.—*The scanty rill of Siloah.*

The sublime Siloah is now a muddy rill; you descend by steps to the fountain which is its source, and which is covered with an arch. Here the blind man received his sight; and, singular enough, to this very day the healing reputation of its waters prevails, and summons to its brink all those neighbouring Arabs who suffer from the ophthalmic affections not uncommon in this part of the world.

NOTE 46, page 86.—*Several isolated tombs of considerable size.*

There are no remains of ancient Jerusalem, or the ancient Jews. Some tombs there are which may be ascribed to the Asmonean princes; but all the monuments of David, Solomon, and their long posterity, have utterly disappeared.

NOTE 47, page 87.—*Are cut strange characters and unearthly forms.*

As at Benihassan, and many other of the sculptured catacombs of Egypt.

NOTE 48, page 88.—*A crowd of bats rushed forward and extinguished his torch.*

In entering the Temple of Dendera, our torches were extinguished by a crowd of bats.

NOTE 49, page 88.—*The gallery was of great extent, with a gradual declination.*

So in the great Egyptian tombs.

NOTE 50, page 89.—*The Afrite, for it was one of those dread beings.*

Beings of a monstrous form, the most terrible of all the orders of the Dives.

NOTE 51, page 89.—*An avenue of colossal lions of red granite.*

An avenue of Sphinxes more than a mile in length connected the quarters of Luxoor and Carnak in Egyptian Thebes. Its fragments remain. Many other avenues of Sphinxes and lion-headed Kings may be observed in various parts of Upper Egypt.

NOTE 52, page 91.—*A stupendous portal, cut out of the solid rock, four hundred feet in height, and supported by clusters of colossal Caryatides.*

See the great rock temple of Ipsambul in Lower Nubia. The sitting colossi are nearly seventy feet in height. But there is a Torso of a statue of Rameses the Second at Thebes, vulgarly called the great Memnon, which measures upwards of sixty feet round the shoulders.

NOTE 53, page 92.—*Fifty steps of ivory, and each step guarded by golden lions.*

See 1st Kings, chap. x. 18–20.

NOTE 54, page 101.—*Crossed the desert on a fleet dromedary.*

The difference between a camel and a dromedary is the difference between a hack and a thorough-bred horse. There is no other.

NOTE 55, page 102.—*That celestial alphabet known to the true Cabalist.*
See Note 11.

NOTE 56, page 112.—*The last of the Seljuks had expired.*

The Orientals are famous for their massacres: that of the Mamlouks by the present Pacha of Egypt, and of the Janissaries of the Sultan, are notorious. But one of the most terrible, and effected under the most difficult and dangerous circumstances, was the massacre of the Albanian Beys by the Grand Vizir, in the autumn of 1830. I was in Albania at the time.

NOTE 57, page 115.—*The minarets were illumined.*

So, I remember, at Constantinople, at the commencement of 1831, at the departure of the Mecca caravan, and also at the annual feast of Ramadan.

NOTE 58, page 117.—*One asking alms with a wire run through his cheek.*

Not uncommon. These Dervishes frequent the bazaars.

NOTE 59, page 121.—*One hundred thousand warriors were now assembled.*

In countries where the whole population are armed, a vast military force is soon assembled. Barchochebas was speedily at the head of two hundred thousand fighting men, and held the Romans long in check under one of their most powerful emperors.

NOTE 60, page 121.—*Some high-capped Tatar with despatches.*

I have availed myself of a familiar character in Oriental life, but the use of a Tatar as a courier in the time of Alroy is, I fear, an anachronism.

NOTE 61, page 122.—*Each day some warlike Atabek, at the head of his armed train, poured into the capital of the Caliphs.*

I was at Yanina, the capital of Albania, when the Grand Vizir summoned the chieftains of the country, and was struck by their magnificent arrays each day pouring into the city.

NOTE 62, page 129.—*It is the Sabbath eve.*

'They began their Sabbath from sunset, and the same time of day they ended it.'—*Talm. Hierosolym. in Sheveith*, fol. 33, col. 1.

The eve of the Sabbath, or the day before, was called the day of the preparation for the Sabbath.—*Luke* xxiii. 54.

'And from the time of the evening sacrifice and forward, they began to fit themselves for the Sabbath, and to cease from their works, so as not to go to the barber, not to sit in judgment, &c.; nay, thenceforward they would not set things on working, which, being set a-work, would complete their business of themselves, unless it would be completed before the Sabbath came—*as wool was not put to dye, unless it could take colour while it was yet day*,' &c.—*Talm. in Sab.*, par. 1; *Lightfoot*, vol. i. p. 218.

'Towards sunsetting, when the Sabbath was now approaching, they lighted up the Sabbath lamp. Men and women were bound to have a lamp lighted up in their houses on the Sabbath, though they were never so poor—nay, though they were forced to go a-begging for oil for this purpose; and the lighting up of this lamp was a part of making the Sabbath a delight; and women were especially commanded to look to this business.'—*Maimonides in Sab.*, par. 36.

NOTE 63, page 132.—*The presence of the robes of honour.*

These are ever carried in procession, and their number denotes the rank and quality of the chief, or of the individual to whom they are offered.

NOTE 64, page 134.—*Pressed it to his lips, and placed it in his vest.*

The elegant mode in which the Orientals receive presents.

NOTE 65, page 138.—*A cap of transparent pink porcelain, studded with pearls.*

Thus a great Turk, who afforded me hospitality, was accustomed to drink his coffee.

NOTE 66, page 142.—*Slippers powdered with pearls.*

The slippers in the East form a very fanciful portion of the costume. It is not uncommon to see them thus adorned and beautifully embroidered. In precious embroidery and enamelling, the Turkish artists are unrivalled.

NOTE 67, page 155.—*The policy of the son of Kareah.*

*Vide* Jeremiah, chap. xlii.

NOTE 68, page 160.—*The inviting gestures and the voluptuous grace of the dancing girls of Egypt.*

A sculptor might find fine studies in the Egyptian Almeh.

NOTE 69, page 163.—*Six choice steeds sumptuously caparisoned.*

Led horses always precede a great man. I think there were usually twelve before the Sultan when he went to Mosque, which he did in public every Friday.

NOTE 70, page 163.—*Six Damascus sabres of unrivalled temper.*

But sabres are not to be found at Damascus, any more than cheeses at Stilton, or oranges at Malta. The art of watering the blade is, however, practised, I believe, in Persia. A fine Damascus blade will fetch fifty or even one hundred guineas English.

NOTE 71, page 164.—*Roses from Rocnabad.*

A river in Persia famous for its bowery banks of roses.

NOTE 72, page 164.—*Screens made of the feather of a roc.*

The screens and fans in the East, made of the plumage of rare birds, with jewelled handles, are very gorgeous.

NOTE 73, page 165.—*A tremulous aigrette of brilliants.*

Worn only by persons of the highest rank. The Sultan presented Lord Nelson after the Battle of the Nile with an aigrette of diamonds.

NOTE 74, page 177.—*To send him the whole of the next course.*

These compliments from the tables of the great are not uncommon in the East. When at the head-quarters of the Grand Vizir at Yanina, his Highness sent to myself and my travelling companions, a course from his table, singers and dancing girls.

NOTE 75, page 178.—*The golden wine of Mount Lebanon.*

A most delicious wine, from its colour, brilliancy, and rare flavour, justly meriting this title, is made on Lebanon; but it will not, unfortunately, bear exportation, and even materially suffers in the voyage from the coast to Alexandria.

NOTE 76, page 186.—*And the company of gardeners.*

These gardeners of the Serail form a very efficient body of police.

NOTE 77, page 190.—*Alroy retired to the bath.*

The bath is a principal scene of Oriental life. Here the Asiatics pass a great portion of their day. The bath consists of a long suite of chambers of various temperatures, in which the different processes of the elaborate ceremony are performed.

NOTE 78, page 195.—*We are the watchers of the moon.*

The Feast of the New Moon is one of the most important festivals of the Hebrews. 'Our year,' says the learned author of the 'Rites and Ceremonies,' 'is divided into twelve lunar months, some of which consist of twenty-nine, others of thirty days, which difference is occasioned by the various appearance of the new moon, in point of time: for if it appeared on the 30th day, the 29th was the last day of the precedent month; but if it did not appear till the 31st day, the 30th was the last day, and the 31st the first of the subsequent month; and that was an intercalary moon, of all which take the following account.

'Our nation heretofore, not only observing the rules of some fixed calculation, also celebrated the feast of the New Moon, according to the phasis or first appearance of the moon, which was done in compliance with God's command, as our received traditions inform us.

'Hence it came to pass that the first appearance was not to be determined only by rules of art, but also by the testimony of such persons as deposed before the Sanhedrim, or Great Senate, that they had seen the New Moon. So a committee of three were appointed from among the said Sanhedrim to receive the deposition of the parties aforesaid, who, after having calculated what time the moon might possibly appear, dispatched some persons *into high and mountainous places, to observe and give their evidence accordingly, concerning the first appearance of the moon.*

' As soon as the new moon was either consecrated or appointed to be observed, notice was given by the Sanhedrim to the rest of the nation what day had been fixed for the New Moon, or first day of the month, because that was to be the rule and measure according to which they were obliged to keep their feasts and fasts in every month respectively.

' This notice was given to them in time of peace, *by firing of beacons, set up for that purpose,* which was looked upon as the readiest way of communication, but, in time of war, when all places were full of enemies, who made use of beacons to amuse our nation with, it was thought fit to discontinue it.'

NOTE 79, page 221.—*The women chatted at the fountain.*

The bath and the fountain are the favourite scenes of feminine conversation.

NOTE 80, page 222.—*Playing chess.*

On the walls of the palace of Amenoph the Second, called Medeenot Abuh, at Egyptian Thebes, the King is represented playing chess with the Queen. This monarch reigned long before the Trojan war.

NOTE 81, page 228.—*Impaled.*

A friend of mine witnessed this horrible punishment in Upper Egypt. The victim was a man who had secretly murdered nine persons. He held an official post, and invited travellers and pilgrims to his house, whom he regularly disposed of and plundered. I regret that I have mislaid his MS. account of the ceremony.

NOTE 82, page 252.

In the *Germen Davidis of Ganz*, translated into Latin by Vorstius, Lug. 1654, is an extract from a Hebrew MS. containing an account of Alroy. I subjoin a passage respecting his death for the learned reader.

' *Scribit R. Maimonides, Sultanum interrogasse illum, num esset Messias, et dixisse, Sum, et quæsivisse ab illo regem, quodnam signum habes? Et respondisse, ut præcideret caput, et se in vitam reversurum. Tunc regem jussisse ut caput ejus amputarent, et obiisse; sed hoc illi dixisse, ne gravibus tormentis ipsum enecaret.*'

' Septem annis ante decretum hoc, de quo supra locuti sumus, habuerunt Israelitæ vehementes angustias propter virum Belial, qui seipsum fecit Messiam; et rex atque principes valde accensi sunt excandescentiâ contra Judæos, ut dicerent, eos quærere interitum regni sui Messiæ petitione. Maledicti hujus nomen vocatum fuit David El-David, aut Alroy, ex urbe Omadia; et erat ibi cœtus magnus, circiter mille familias divites, refertas, honestas et felices continens. Atque Ecclesia hæc erat principium cœtuum habitantium circa fluvium Sabbathion, atque erant plus quam centum Ecclesiæ. Erat hic initium regionis Mediæ, atque lingua eorum erat idioma Thargum: inde autem usque ad regionem Golan est iter 50 dierum, et sunt sub imperio Regis Persiæ, cui dant quotannis tributum a 15 annis et ultra aureum unum. Vir autem hic David El-David studuit coram principe captivitatis Chasdai et coram excellente Scholarcha in urbe Bagdad, qui eximius erat sapiens in Thalmude et omnibus scientiis exoticis, atque in omnibus libris divinatorum, magorum et Chaldæorum. Hic vero David El-David ex audacia et arrogantia cordis sui elevavit manum contra regem, et collegit Judæos habitantes in monte Chophtan, et seduxit eos, ut exirent in prælium cum omnibus gentibus. Ostendit iis signa; sed ignorabant quanam virtute: erant enim homines, qui asserebant istud per modum magiæ et præstigiationis fieri; alii dicebant, potentiam ejus magnam esse propter manum Dei. Qui consortium ejus veniebant, vocabant eum Messiam, eumque laudabant et extollebant.

\* \* \* \* \*

"In regno Persiæ alio quodam tempore surrexit vir quidam Judæus, et seipsum fecit Messiam, atque valde prospere egit; et numerosus ex Israele ad illum confluxit populus. Cùm viro audiret rex omnem ejus potentiam, atque propositum ejus esse descendere in prælium cum ipso, misit ad Judæos congregatos in regione sua, iisque dixit: Nisi egerint cum hocce viro, ut e medio tollatur, certo sciant, se eos omnes gladio interempturum, et uno die infantes ac fœminas deleturum. Tunc congregatus est totus populus Israelis simul, atque contendit ad virum illum, cociditque coram illo in terram: vehementer supplicatus est, clamavit atque ploravit, ut reverteretur a via sua: et cur seipsum et omnes afflictos conjiceret in periculum: jam enim regem jurasse se immissurum eis gladium, et quomodo posset intueri afflictionem omnium cœtuum Persiæ. Respondit: *Veni servatum vos, et non vultis. Quem metuistis? Quisnam coram me consistet? Et quid aget rex Persiæ, ut non reformidet me, et gladium meum?* Interrogarunt eum, quodnam signum haberet quod esset Messias: Respondit, QUIA FELICITER REM GERERET, NEQUE MESSIAM OPUS HABERE ALIO SIGNO. Responderunt multos similiter egisse, neque prosperâ usos fuisse fortunâ; tunc rejecit eos a facie sua cum superba indignatione.'

# IXION IN HEAVEN.

# ADVERTISEMENT.

'Ixion, King of Thessaly, famous for its horses, married Dia, daughter of Deioneus, who, in consequence of his son-in-law's non-fulfilment of his engagements, stole away some of the monarch's steeds. Ixion concealed his resentment under the mask of friendship. He invited his father-in-law to a feast at Larissa, the capital of his kingdom; and when Deioneus arrived according to his appointment, he threw him into a pit which he had previously filled with burning coals. This treachery so irritated the neighbouring princes, that all of them refused to perform the usual ceremony, by which a man was then purified of murder, and Ixion was shunned and despised by all mankind. Jupiter had compassion upon him, carried him to heaven, and introduced him to the Father of the Gods. Such a favour, which ought to have awakened gratitude in Ixion, only served to inflame his bad passions; he became enamoured of Juno, and attempted to seduce her. Juno was willing to gratify the passion of Ixion, though, according to others,' &c.—*Classical Dictionary*, art. 'Ixion.'

# IXION IN HEAVEN.

## PART I.

### I.

The thunder groaned, the wind howled, the rain fell in hissing torrents, impenetrable darkness covered the earth.

A blue and forky flash darted a momentary light over the landscape. A Doric temple rose in the centre of a small and verdant plain, surrounded on all sides by green and hanging woods.

'Jove is my only friend,' exclaimed a wanderer, as he muffled himself up in his mantle; 'and were it not for the porch of his temple, this night, methinks, would complete the work of my loving wife and my dutiful subjects.'

The thunder died away, the wind sank into silence, the rain ceased, and the parting clouds exhibited the glittering crescent of the young moon. A sonorous and majestic voice sounded from the skies:—

'Who art thou that hast no other friend than Jove?'

'One whom all mankind unite in calling a wretch.'

'Art thou a philosopher?'

'If philosophy be endurance. But for the rest, I was sometime a king, and am now a scatterling.'

'How do they call thee?'

'Ixion of Thessaly.'

'Ixion of Thessaly! I thought he was a happy man. I heard that he was just married.'

'Father of Gods and men! for I deem thee such, Thessaly

is not Olympus. Conjugal felicity is only the portion of the Immortals!'

'Hem! What! was Dia jealous, which is common; or false, which is commoner; or both, which is commonest?'

'It may be neither. We quarrelled about nothing. Where there is little sympathy, or too much, the splitting of a straw is plot enough for a domestic tragedy. I was careless, her friends stigmatised me as callous; she cold, her friends styled her magnanimous. Public opinion was all on her side, merely because I did not choose that the world should interfere between me and my wife. Dia took the world's advice upon every point, and the world decided that she always acted rightly. However, life is life, either in a palace or a cave. I am glad you ordered it to leave off thundering.'

'A cool dog this. And Dia left thee?'

'No; I left her.'

'What, craven?'

'Not exactly. The truth is——'tis a long story. I was over head and ears in debt.'

'Ah! that accounts for everything. Nothing so harassing as a want of money! But what lucky fellows you Mortals are with your *post-obits!* We Immortals are deprived of this resource. I was obliged to get up a rebellion against my father, because he kept me so short, and could not die.'

'You could have married for money. I did.'

'I had no opportunity, there was so little female society in those days. When I came out, there were no heiresses except the Parcæ, confirmed old maids; and no very rich dowager, except my grandmother, old Terra.'

'Just the thing; the older the better. However, I married Dia, the daughter of Deioneus, with a prodigious portion; but after the ceremony the old gentleman would not fulfil his part of the contract without my giving up my stud. Can you conceive anything more unreasonable? I smothered my resentment at the time; for the truth is, my tradesmen all renewed my credit on the strength of the match, and so we went on very well for a year; but at last they began to smell a rat, and grew importunate. I entreated Dia to interfere; but she was a paragon of daughters, and always took the side of her father. If she had only been dutiful to her husband, she would have been a perfect woman. At last I invited Deioneus to the Larissa races, with the intention of conciliating him. The unprincipled old man bought the horse that I had backed, and by which I intended to have redeemed my fortunes, and withdrew it. My book was ruined. I dissembled my rage. I dug a pit in our garden, and filled it with burning coals. As my father-in-law and myself were taking a stroll after dinner, the worthy Deioneus fell in, merely by accident. Dia proclaimed me the murderer of her father, and, as a satisfaction to her wounded feelings, earnestly requested her subjects to decapitate her husband. She certainly was the best of daughters. There was no withstanding public opinion, an infuriated rabble, and a magnanimous wife at the same time. They surrounded my palace: I cut my way through the greasy-capped multitude, sword in hand, and gained a neighbouring Court, where I solicited my brother princes to purify me from the supposed murder. If I had only murdered a subject, they would have supported me against the people; but Deioneus being a crowned head, like themselves, they declared they would not countenance so immoral a being as his son-in-law. And so, at length, after much wandering, and shunned by all my species, I am here, Jove, in much higher society than I ever expected to mingle.'

'Well, thou art a frank dog, and in a sufficiently severe scrape. The Gods must have pity on those for whom men have none. It is evident that Earth is too hot for thee at present, so I think thou hadst better come and stay a few weeks with us in Heaven.'

'Take my thanks for hecatombs, great Jove. Thou art, indeed, a God!'

'I hardly know whether our life will suit you. We dine at sunset; for Apollo is so much engaged that he cannot join us sooner, and no dinner goes off well without him. In the morning you are your own master, and must find amusement where you can. Diana will show you some tolerable sport. Do you shoot?'

'No arrow surer. Fear not for me, Ægiochus: I am always at home. But how am I to get to you?'

'I will send Mercury; he is the best travelling companion in the world. What ho! my Eagle!'

The clouds joined, and darkness again fell over the earth.

## II.

'So! tread softly. Don't be nervous. Are you sick?'

'A little nausea; 'tis nothing.'

'The novelty of the motion. The best thing is a beefsteak. We will stop at Taurus and take one.'

'You have been a great traveller, Mercury?'

'I have seen the world.'

'Ah! a wondrous spectacle. I long to travel.'

'The same thing over and over again. Little novelty and much change. I am wearied with exertion, and if I could get a pension would retire.'

'And yet travel brings wisdom.'

'It cures us of care. Seeing much we feel little, and learn how very petty are all those great affairs which cost us such anxiety.'

'I feel that already myself. Floating in this blue æther, what the devil is my wife to me, and her dirty earth! My persecuting enemies seem so many pismires; and as for my debts, which have occasioned me so many brooding moments, honour and infamy, credit and beggary, seem to me alike ridiculous.'

'Your mind is opening, Ixion. You will soon be a man of the world. To the left, and keep clear of that star.'

'Who lives there?'

'The Fates know, not I. Some low people who are trying to shine into notice. 'Tis a parvenu planet, and only sprung into space within this century. We do not visit them.'

'Poor devils! I feel hungry.'

'All right. We shall get into Heaven by the first dinner bolt. You cannot arrive at a strange house at a better moment. We shall just have time to dress. I would not spoil my appetite by luncheon. Jupiter keeps a capital cook.'

'I have heard of Nectar and Ambrosia.'

'Poh! nobody touches them. They are regular old-fashioned celestial food, and merely put upon the side-table. Nothing goes down in Heaven now but infernal cookery. We took our *chef* from Proserpine.'

'Were you ever in Hell?'

'Several times. 'Tis the fashion now among the Olympians to pass the winter there.'

'Is this the season in Heaven?'

'Yes; you are lucky. Olympus is quite full.'

'It was kind of Jupiter to invite me.'

'Ay! he has his good points. And, no doubt, he has taken a liking to you, which is all very well. But be upon your guard. He has no heart, and is as capricious as he is tyrannical.'

'Gods cannot be more unkind to me than men have been.'

'All those who have suffered think they have seen the worst. A great mistake. However, you are now in the high road to preferment, so we will not be dull. There are some good fellows enough amongst us. You will like old Neptune.'

'Is he there now?'

'Yes, he generally passes his summer with us. There is little stirring in the ocean at that season.'

'I am anxious to see Mars.'

'Oh! a brute, more a bully than a hero. Not at all in the best set. These mustachioed gentry are by no means the rage at present in Olympus. The women are all literary now, and Minerva has quite eclipsed Venus. Apollo is our hero. You must read his last work.'

'I hate reading.'

'So do I. I have no time, and seldom do anything in

T

that way but glance at a newspaper. Study and action will not combine.'

'I suppose I shall find the Goddesses very proud?'

'You will find them as you find women below, of different dispositions with the same object. Venus is a flirt; Minerva a prude, who fancies she has a correct taste and a strong mind; and Juno a politician. As for the rest, faint heart never won fair lady, take a friendly hint, and do not be alarmed.'

'I fear nothing. My mind mounts with my fortunes. We are above the clouds. They form beneath us a vast and snowy region, dim and irregular, as I have sometimes seen them clustering upon the horizon's ridge at sunset, like a raging sea stilled by some sudden supernatural frost and frozen into form! How bright the air above us, and how delicate its fragrant breath! I scarcely breathe, and yet my pulses beat like my first youth. I hardly feel my being. A splendour falls upon your presence. You seem, indeed, a God! Am I so glorious? This, this is Heaven!'

### III.

The travellers landed on a vast flight of sparkling steps of lapis-lazuli. Ascending, they entered beautiful gardens; winding walks that yielded to the feet, and accelerated your passage by their rebounding pressure; fragrant shrubs covered with dazzling flowers, the fleeting tints of which changed every moment; groups of tall trees, with strange birds of brilliant and variegated plumage, singing and reposing in their sheeny foliage, and fountains of perfumes.

Before them rose an illimitable and golden palace, with high spreading domes of pearl, and long windows of crystal. Around the huge portal of ruby was ranged a company of winged genii, who smiled on Mercury as he passed them with his charge.

'The father of Gods and men is dressing,' said the son of Maia. 'I shall attend his toilet and inform him of your arrival. These are your rooms. Dinner will be ready in half an hour. I will call for you as I go down. You can be formally presented in the evening. At that time, inspired by liqueurs and his matchless band of wind instruments, you will agree with the world that Ægiochus is the most finished God in existence.'

## IV.

' Now, Ixion, are you ready ? '
' Even so. What says Jove ? '
' He smiled, but said nothing. He was trying on a new robe. By this time he is seated. Hark! the thunder. Come on!'

They entered a cupolaed hall. Seats of ivory and gold were ranged round a circular table of cedar, inlaid with the campaigns against the Titans, in silver exquisitely worked, a nuptial present of Vulcan. The service of gold plate threw all the ideas of the King of Thessaly as to royal magnificence into the darkest shade. The enormous plateau represented the constellations. Ixion viewed the father of Gods and men with great interest, who, however, did not notice him. He acknowledged the majesty of that countenance whose nod shook Olympus. Majestically robust and luxuriantly lusty, his tapering waist was evidently immortal, for it defied Time, and his splendid auburn curls, parted on his forehead with celestial precision, descended over cheeks glowing with the purple radiancy of perpetual manhood.

The haughty Juno was seated on his left hand and Ceres on his right. For the rest of the company there was Neptune, Latona, Minerva, and Apollo, and when Mercury and Ixion had taken their places, one seat was still vacant.

' Where is Diana ? ' inquired Jupiter, with a frown.
' My sister is hunting,' said Apollo.
' She is always too late for dinner,' said Jupiter. ' No habit is less Goddess-like.'
' Godlike pursuits cannot be expected to induce Goddess-like manners,' said Juno, with a sneer.
' I have no doubt Diana will be here directly,' said Latona, mildly.

Jupiter seemed pacified, and at that instant the absent guest returned.

'Good sport, Di?' inquired Neptune.

'Very fair, uncle. Mamma,' continued the sister of Apollo, addressing herself to Juno, whom she ever thus styled when she wished to conciliate her, 'I have brought you a new peacock.'

Juno was fond of pets, and was conciliated by the present.

'Bacchus made a great noise about this wine, Mercury,' said Jupiter, 'but I think with little cause. What think you?'

'It pleases me, but I am fatigued, and then all wine is agreeable."

'You have had a long journey,' replied the Thunderer. 'Ixion, I am glad to see you in Heaven.'

'Your Majesty arrived to-day?' inquired Minerva, to whom the King of Thessaly sat next.

'Within this hour.'

'You must leave off talking of Time now,' said Minerva, with a severe smile. 'Pray is there anything new in Greece?'

'I have not been at all in society lately.'

'No new edition of Homer? I admire him exceedingly.'

'All about Greece interests me,' said Apollo, who, although handsome, was a somewhat melancholy lack-a-daisical looking personage, with his shirt collar thrown open, and his long curls theatrically arranged. 'All about Greece interests me. I always consider Greece my peculiar property. My best poems were written at Delphi. I travelled in Greece when I was young. I envy mankind.'

'Indeed!' said Ixion.

'Yes: they at least can look forward to a termination of the ennui of existence, but for us Celestials there is no prospect. Say what they like, Immortality is a bore.'

'You eat nothing, Apollo,' said Ceres.

'Nor drink,' said Neptune.

'To eat, to drink, what is it but to live; and what is life

but death, if death be that which all men deem it, a thing insufferable, and to be shunned. I refresh myself now only with soda-water and biscuits. Ganymede, bring some.'

Now, although the *cuisine* of Olympus was considered perfect, the forlorn poet had unfortunately fixed upon the only two articles which were not comprised in its cellar or larder. In Heaven, there was neither soda-water nor biscuits. A great confusion consequently ensued; but at length the bard, whose love of fame was only equalled by his horror of getting fat, consoled himself with a swan stuffed with truffles, and a bottle of strong Tenedos wine.

'What do you think of Homer?' inquired Minerva of Apollo. 'Is he not delightful?'

'If you think so.'

'Nay, I am desirous of your opinion.'

'Then you should not have given me yours, for your taste is too fine for me to dare to differ with it.'

'I have suspected, for some time, that you are rather a heretic.'

'Why, the truth is,' replied Apollo, playing with his rings, 'I do not think much of Homer. Homer was not esteemed in his own age, and our contemporaries are generally our best judges. The fact is, there are very few people who are qualified to decide upon matters of taste. A certain set, for certain reasons, resolve to cry up a certain writer, and the great mass soon join in. All is cant. And the present admiration of Homer is not less so. They say I have borrowed a great deal from him. The truth is, I never read Homer since I was a child, and I thought of him then what I think of him now, a writer of some wild irregular power, totally deficient in taste. Depend upon it, our contemporaries are our best judges, and his contemporaries decided that Homer was nothing. A great poet cannot be kept down. Look at my case. Marsyas said of my first volume that it was pretty good poetry for a God, and in answer I wrote a satire, and flayed Marsyas alive. But what is poetry, and what is criticism, and what is life? Air. And what is Air? Do you know? I don't. All is mystery, and all is gloom, and ever and anon from out the clouds a star breaks forth, and glitters, and that star is Poetry.'

'Splendid!' exclaimed Minerva.

'I do not exactly understand you,' said Neptune.

'Have you heard from Proserpine, lately?' inquired Jupiter of Ceres.

'Yesterday,' said the domestic mother. 'They talk of soon joining us. But Pluto is at present so busy, owing to the amazing quantity of wars going on now, that I am almost afraid he will scarcely be able to accompany her.'

Juno exchanged a telegraphic nod with Ceres. The Goddesses rose, and retired.

'Come, old boy,' said Jupiter to Ixion, instantly throwing off all his chivalric majesty, 'I drink your welcome in a magnum of Maraschino. Damn your poetry, Apollo, and Mercury give us one of your good stories.'

### V.

'Well! what do you think of him?' asked Juno.

'He appears to have a fine mind,' said Minerva.

'Poh! he has very fine eyes,' said Juno.

'He seems a very nice, quiet young gentleman,' said Ceres.

'I have no doubt he is very amiable,' said Latona.

'He must have felt very strange,' said Diana.

### VI.

Hercules arrived with his bride Hebe; soon after the Graces dropped in, the most delightful personages in the world for a *soirée*, so useful and ready for anything. Afterwards came a few of the Muses, Thalia, Melpomene, and Terpsichore, famous for a charade or a proverb. Jupiter liked to be amused in the evening. Bacchus also came, but finding that the Gods had not yet left their wine, retired to pay them a previous visit.

## VII.

Ganymede announced coffee in the saloon of Juno. Jupiter was in superb good humour. He was amused by his mortal guest. He had condescended to tell one of his best stories in his best style, about Leda, not too scandalous, but gay.

'Those were bright days,' said Neptune.

'We can remember,' said the Thunderer, with a twinkling eye. 'These youths have fallen upon duller times. There are no fine women now. Ixion, I drink to the health of your wife.'

'With all my heart, and may we never be nearer than we are at present.'

'Good! i'faith; Apollo, your arm. Now for the ladies. La, la, la, la! la, la, la, la!'

## VIII.

The Thunderer entered the saloon of Juno with that bow which no God could rival; all rose, and the King of Heaven seated himself between Ceres and Latona. The melancholy Apollo stood apart, and was soon carried off by Minerva to an assembly at the house of Mnemosyne. Mercury chatted with the Graces, and Bacchus with Diana. The three Muses favoured the company with singing, and the Queen of Heaven approached Ixion.

'Does your Majesty dance?' she haughtily inquired.

'On earth; I have few accomplishments even there, and none in Heaven.'

'You have led a strange life! I have heard of your adventures.'

'A king who has lost his crown may generally gain at least experience.'

'Your courage is firm.'

'I have felt too much to care for much. Yesterday I was a vagabond exposed to every pitiless storm, and now I am the guest of Jove. While there is life there is hope, and he who laughs at Destiny will gain Fortune. I would go through the past again to enjoy the present, and feel that, after all, I am my wife's debtor, since, through her conduct, I can gaze upon you.'

'No great spectacle. If that be all, I wish you better fortune.'

'I desire no greater.'

'You are moderate.'

'I am perhaps more unreasonable than you imagine.'

'Indeed!'

Their eyes met; the dark orbs of the Thessalian did not quail before the flashing vision of the Goddess. Juno grew pale. Juno turned away.

## PART II.

'Others say it was only a cloud.'

### I.

MERCURY and Ganymede were each lolling on an opposite couch in the antechamber of Olympus.

'It is wonderful,' said the son of Maia, yawning.

'It is incredible,' rejoined the cup-bearer of Jove, stretching his legs.

'A miserable mortal!' exclaimed the God, elevating his eyebrows.

'A vile Thessalian!' said the beautiful Phrygian, shrugging his shoulders.

'Not three days back an outcast among his own wretched species!'

'And now commanding everybody in Heaven.'

'He shall not command me, though,' said Mercury.

'Will he not?' replied Ganymede. 'Why, what do you think? only last night; hark! here he comes.'

The companions jumped up from their couches; a light laugh was heard. The cedar portal was flung open, and Ixion lounged in, habited in a loose morning robe, and kicking before him one of his slippers.

'Ah!' exclaimed the King of Thessaly, 'the very fellows I wanted to see! Ganymede, bring me some nectar; and, Mercury, run and tell Jove that I shall not dine at home to-day.'

The messenger and the page exchanged looks of indignant consternation.

'Well! what are you waiting for?' continued Ixion, looking round from the mirror in which he was arranging his locks. The messenger and the page disappeared.

'So! this is Heaven,' exclaimed the husband of Dia, flinging himself upon one of the couches; 'and a very pleasant place too. These worthy Immortals required their minds to be opened, and I trust I have effectually performed the necessary operation. They wanted to keep me down with their dull old-fashioned celestial airs, but I fancy I have given them change for their talent. To make your way in Heaven you must command. These exclusives sink under the audacious invention of an aspiring mind. Jove himself is really a fine old fellow, with some notions too. I am a prime favourite, and no one is greater authority with Ægiochus on all subjects, from the character of the fair sex or the pedigree of a courser, down to the cut of a robe or the flavour of a dish. Thanks, Ganymede,' continued the Thessalian, as he took the goblet from his returning attendant.

'I drink to your *bonnes fortunes*. Splendid! This nectar makes me feel quite immortal. By-the-bye, I hear sweet sounds. Who is in the Hall of Music?'

'The Goddesses, royal sir, practise a new air of Euterpe, the words by Apollo. 'Tis pretty, and will doubtless be very popular, for it is all about moonlight and the misery of existence.'

'I warrant it.'

'You have a taste for poetry yourself?' inquired Ganymede.

'Not the least,' replied Ixion.

'Apollo,' continued the heavenly page, 'is a great genius, though Marsyas said that he never would be a poet because he was a god, and had no heart. But do you think, sir, that a poet does indeed need a heart?'

'I really cannot say. I know my wife always said I had a bad heart and worse head; but what she meant, upon my honour I never could understand.'

'Minerva will ask you to write in her album.'

'Will she indeed! I am sorry to hear it, for I can scarcely scrawl my signature. I should think that Jove himself cared little for all this nonsense.'

'Jove loves an epigram. He does not esteem Apollo's works at all. Jove is of the classical school, and admires satire, provided there be no allusions to gods and kings.'

'Of course; I quite agree with him. I remember we had a confounded poet at Larissa who proved my family lived before the deluge, and asked me for a pension. I refused him, and then he wrote an epigram asserting that I sprang from the veritable stones thrown by Deucalion and Pyrrha at the re-peopling of the earth, and retained all the properties of my ancestors.'

'Ha, ha! Hark! there's a thunderbolt! I must run to Jove.'

'And I will look in on the musicians. This way, I think?'

'Up the ruby staircase, turn to your right, down the amethyst gallery. Farewell!'

'Good bye; a lively lad that!'

II.

The King of Thessaly entered the Hall of Music with its golden walls and crystal dome. The Queen of Heaven was reclining in an easy chair, cutting out peacocks in small sheets of note paper. Minerva was making a pencil observation on a manuscript copy of the song: Apollo listened with deference to her laudatory criticisms. Another divine dame, standing by the side of Euterpe, who was seated by the harp, looked up as Ixion entered. The wild liquid glance of her soft but radiant countenance denoted the famed Goddess of Beauty.

Juno just acknowledged the entrance of Ixion by a slight and haughty inclination of the head, and then resumed her employment. Minerva asked him his opinion of her amendment, of which he greatly approved. Apollo greeted him with a melancholy smile, and congratulated him on being mortal. Venus complimented him on his visit to Olympus, and expressed the pleasure that she experienced in making his acquaintance.

'What do you think of Heaven?' inquired Venus, in a soft still voice, and with a smile like summer lightning.

'I never found it so enchanting as at this moment,' replied Ixion.

'A little dull? For myself, I pass my time chiefly at Cnidos: you must come and visit me there. 'Tis the most charming place in the world. 'Tis said, you know, that our onions are like other people's roses. We will take care of you, if your wife come.'

'No fear of that. She always remains at home and piques herself on her domestic virtues, which means pickling, and quarrelling with her husband.'

'Ah! I see you are a droll. Very good indeed. Well, for my part, I like a watering-place existence. Cnidos, Paphos, Cythera; you will usually find me at one of these places. I like the easy distraction of a career without any visible result. At these fascinating spots your gloomy race, to whom, by-the-bye, I am exceedingly partial, appear emancipated from the wearing fetters of their regular, dull, orderly, methodical, moral, political, toiling existence. I pride myself upon being the Goddess of Watering-places. You really must pay me a visit at Cnidos.'

'Such an invitation requires no repetition. And Cnidos is your favourite spot?'

'Why, it was so; but of late it has become so inundated with invalid Asiatics and valetudinarian Persians, that the simultaneous influx of the handsome heroes who swarm in from the islands to look after their daughters, scarcely compensates for the annoying presence of their yellow faces and shaking limbs. No, I think, on the whole, Paphos is my favourite.'

'I have heard of its magnificent luxury.'

'Oh! 'tis lovely! Quite my idea of country life. Not a single tree! When Cyprus is very hot, you run to Paphos for a sea-breeze, and are sure to meet every one whose presence is in the least desirable. All the bores remain behind, as if by instinct.'

'I remember when we married, we talked of passing the honeymoon at Cythera, but Dia would have her waiting-maid and a bandbox stuffed between us in the chariot, so I got sulky after the first stage, and returned by myself.'

'You were quite right. I hate bandboxes: they are always in the way. You would have liked Cythera if you had been in the least in love. High rocks and green knolls, bowery woods, winding walks, and delicious sunsets. I have not been there much of late,' continued the Goddess, looking somewhat sad and serious, 'since: but I will not talk sentiment to Ixion.'

'Do you think, then, I am insensible?'

'Yes.'

'Perhaps you are right. We mortals grow callous.'

'So I have heard. How very odd!' So saying, the Goddess glided away and saluted Mars, who at that moment entered the hall. Ixion was presented to the military hero, who looked fierce and bowed stiffly. The King of Thessaly turned upon his heel. Minerva opened her album, and invited him to inscribe a stanza.

'Goddess of Wisdom,' replied the King, 'unless you inspire me, the virgin page must remain pure as thyself. I can scarcely sign a decree.'

'Is it Ixion of Thessaly who says this; one who has seen so much, and, if I am not mistaken, has felt and thought so much? I can easily conceive why such a mind may desire to veil its movements from the common herd, but pray concede to Minerva the gratifying compliment of assuring her that she is the exception for whom this rule has been established.'

'I seem to listen to the inspired music of an oracle. Give me a pen.'

'Here is one, plucked from a sacred owl.'

'So! I write. There! Will it do?'

Minerva read the inscription:—

I HAVE SEEN THE WORLD, AND MORE THAN THE WORLD: I HAVE STUDIED THE HEART OF MAN, AND NOW I CONSORT WITH IMMORTALS. THE FRUIT OF MY TREE OF KNOWLEDGE IS PLUCKED, AND IT IS THIS, '𝔄𝔡𝔳𝔢𝔫𝔱𝔲𝔯𝔢𝔰 𝔞𝔯𝔢 𝔱𝔬 𝔱𝔥𝔢 𝔄𝔡𝔳𝔢𝔫𝔱𝔲𝔯𝔬𝔲𝔰.'

*Written in the Album of Minerva, by*
𝔍𝔵𝔦𝔬𝔫 𝔦𝔫 𝔥𝔢𝔞𝔳𝔢𝔫.

'''Tis brief,' said the Goddess, with a musing air, 'but full of meaning. You have a daring soul and pregnant mind.'

'I have dared much: what I may produce we have yet to see.'

'I must to Jove,' said Minerva, '.to council. We shall meet again. Farewell, Ixion.'

'Farewell, Glaucopis.'

The King of Thessaly stood away from the remaining guests, and leant with folded arms and pensive brow against a wreathed column. Mars listened to Venus with an air of deep devotion. Euterpe played an inspiring accompaniment to their conversation. The Queen of Heaven seemed engrossed in the creation of her paper peacocks.

Ixion advanced and seated himself on a couch near Juno. His manner was divested of that reckless bearing and careless coolness by which it was in general distinguished. He was, perhaps, even a little embarrassed. His ready tongue deserted him. At length he spoke.

'Has your Majesty ever heard of the peacock of the Queen of Mesopotamia?'

'No,' replied Juno, with stately reserve; and then she added with an air of indifferent curiosity, 'Is it in any way remarkable?'

'Its breast is of silver, its wings of gold, its eyes of carbuncle, its claws of amethyst.'

'And its tail?' eagerly inquired Juno.

'That is a secret,' replied Ixion. 'The tail is the most wonderful part of all.'

'Oh! tell me, pray tell me!'

'I forgot.'

'No, no, no; it is impossible!' exclaimed the animated Juno. 'Provoking mortal!' continued the Goddess. 'Let me entreat you; tell me immediately.'

'There is a reason which prevents me.'

'What can it be? How very odd! What reason can it possibly be? Now tell me; as a particular, a personal favour, I request you, do tell me.'

'What! The tail or the reason? The tail is wonderful, but the reason is much more so. I can only tell one. Now choose.'

'What provoking things these human beings are! The tail is wonderful, but the reason is much more so. Well then, the reason; no, the tail. Stop, now, as a particular favour, pray tell me both. What can the tail be made of and what can the reason be? I am literally dying of curiosity.'

'Your Majesty has cut out that peacock wrong,' remarked Ixion. 'It is more like one of Minerva's owls.'

'Who cares about paper peacocks, when the Queen of Mesopotamia has got such a miracle!' exclaimed Juno; and she tore the labours of the morning to pieces, and threw away the fragments with vexation. 'Now tell me instantly; if you have the slightest regard for me, tell me instantly. What was the tail made of?'

'And you do not wish to hear the reason?'

'That afterwards. Now! I am all ears.' At this moment Ganymede entered, and whispered the Goddess, who rose in evident vexation, and retired to the presence of Jove.

### III.

The King of Thessaly quitted the Hall of Music. Moody, yet not uninfluenced by a degree of wild excitement, he wandered forth into the gardens of Olympus. He came to a beautiful green retreat surrounded by enormous cedars, so vast that it seemed they must have been coeval with the creation; so fresh and brilliant, you would have deemed them wet with the dew of their first spring. The turf, softer than down, and exhaling, as you pressed it, an exquisite perfume, invited him to recline himself upon this natural couch. He threw himself upon the aromatic herbage, and leaning on his arm, fell into a deep reverie.

Hours flew away; the sunshiny glades that opened in the distance had softened into shade.

'Ixion, how do you do?' inquired a voice, wild, sweet, and thrilling as a bird. The King of Thessaly started and looked up with the distracted air of a man roused from a dream, or from complacent meditation over some strange, sweet secret. His cheek was flushed, his dark eyes flashed fire; his brow trembled, his dishevelled hair played in the fitful breeze. The King of Thessaly looked up, and beheld a most beautiful youth.

Apparently, he had attained about the age of puberty. His stature, however, was rather tall for his age, but exquisitely moulded and proportioned. Very fair, his somewhat round cheeks were tinted with a rich but delicate glow, like the rose of twilight, and lighted by dimples that twinkled like stars. His large and deep-blue eyes sparkled with exultation, and an air of ill-suppressed mockery quivered round his pouting lips. His light auburn hair, braided off his white forehead, clustered in massy curls on each side of his face, and fell in sunny torrents down his neck. And from the back of the beautiful youth there fluttered forth two wings, the tremulous plumage of which seemed to have been bathed in a sunset: so various, so radiant, and so novel were its shifting and wondrous tints; purple, and crimson, and gold; streaks of azure, dashes of orange and glossy black; now a single feather, whiter than light, and sparkling like the frost, stars of emerald and carbuncle, and then the prismatic blaze of an enormous brilliant! A quiver hung at the side of the beautiful youth, and he leant upon a bow.

'Oh! god, for god thou must be!' at length exclaimed Ixion. 'Do I behold the bright divinity of Love?'

'I am indeed Cupid,' replied the youth; 'and am curious to know what Ixion is thinking about.'

'Thought is often bolder than speech.'

'Oracular, though a mortal! You need not be afraid to trust me. My aid I am sure you must need. Whoever was found in a reverie on the green turf, under the shade of spreading trees, without requiring the assistance of Cupid? Come! be frank, who is the heroine? Some love-sick nymph deserted on the far earth; or worse, some treacherous mistress, whose frailty is more easily forgotten than her charms? 'Tis a miserable situation, no doubt. It cannot be your wife?'

'Assuredly not,' replied Ixion, with energy.

'Another man's?'

'No.'

'What! an obdurate maiden?'

Ixion shook his head.

'It must be a widow, then,' continued Cupid. 'Who ever heard before of such a piece of work about a widow!'

'Have pity upon me, dread Cupid!' exclaimed the King of Thessaly, rising suddenly from the ground, and falling on his knee before the God. 'Thou art the universal friend of man, and all nations alike throw their incense on thy altars. Thy divine discrimination has not deceived thee. I *am* in love; desperately, madly, fatally enamoured. The object of my passion is neither my own wife nor another man's. In spite of all they have said and sworn, I am a moral member of society. She is neither a maid nor a widow. She is——'

'What? what?' exclaimed the impatient deity.

'A Goddess!' replied the King.

'Wheugh!' whistled Cupid. 'What! has my mischievous mother been indulging you with an innocent flirtation?'

'Yes; but it produced no effect upon me.'

'You have a stout heart, then. Perhaps you have been reading poetry with Minerva, and are caught in one of her Platonic man-traps.'

'She set one, but I broke away.'

'You have a stout leg, then. But where are you, where are you? Is it Hebe? It can hardly be Diana, she is so cold. Is it a Muse, or is it one of the Graces?'

Ixion again shook his head.

'Come, my dear fellow,' said Cupid, quite in a confidential tone, 'you have told enough to make further reserve mere affectation. Ease your heart at once, and if I can assist you, depend upon my exertions.'

'Beneficent God!' exclaimed Ixion, 'if I ever return to

Larissa, the brightest temple in Greece shall hail thee for its inspiring deity. I address thee with all the confiding frankness of a devoted votary. Know, then, the heroine of my reverie was no less a personage than the Queen of Heaven herself!'

'Juno! by all that is sacred!' shouted Cupid.

'I am here,' responded a voice of majestic melody. The stately form of the Queen of Heaven advanced from a neighbouring bower. Ixion stood with his eyes fixed upon the ground, with a throbbing heart and burning cheeks. Juno stood motionless, pale, and astounded. The God of Love burst into excessive laughter.

'A pretty pair,' he exclaimed, fluttering between both, and laughing in their faces. 'Truly a pretty pair. Well! I see I am in your way. Good bye!' And so saying, the God pulled a couple of arrows from his quiver, and with the rapidity of lightning shot one in the respective breasts of the Queen of Heaven and the King of Thessaly.

### IV.

The amethystine twilight of Olympus died away. The stars blazed with tints of every hue. Ixion and Juno returned to the palace. She leant upon his arm; her eyes were fixed upon the ground; they were in sight of the gorgeous pile, and yet she had not spoken. Ixion, too, was silent, and gazed with abstraction upon the glowing sky.

Suddenly, when within a hundred yards of the portal, Juno stopped, and looking up into the face of Ixion with an irresistible smile, she said, 'I am sure you cannot now refuse to tell me what the Queen of Mesopotamia's peacock's tail was made of!'

'It is impossible now,' said Ixion. 'Know, then, beautiful Goddess, that the tail of the Queen of Mesopotamia's peacock was made of some plumage she had stolen from the wings of Cupid.'

'And what was the reason that prevented you from telling me before?'

'Because, beautiful Juno, I am the most discreet of men, and respect the secret of a lady, however trifling.'

'I am glad to hear that,' replied Juno, and they re-entered the palace.

## V.

Mercury met Juno and Ixion in the gallery leading to the grand banqueting hall.

'I was looking for you,' said the God, shaking his head. 'Jove is in a sublime rage. Dinner has been ready this hour.'

The King of Thessaly and the Queen of Heaven exchanged a glance and entered the saloon. Jove looked up with a brow of thunder, but did not condescend to send forth a single flash of anger. Jove looked up and Jove looked down. All Olympus trembled as the father of Gods and men resumed his soup. The rest of the guests seemed nervous and reserved, except Cupid, who said immediately to Juno, 'Your Majesty has been detained?'

'I fell asleep in a bower reading Apollo's last poem,' replied Juno. 'I am lucky, however, in finding a companion in my negligence. Ixion, where have you been?'

'Take a glass of nectar, Juno,' said Cupid, with eyes twinkling with mischief; 'and perhaps Ixion will join us.'

This was the most solemn banquet ever celebrated in Olympus. Every one seemed out of humour or out of spirits. Jupiter spoke only in monosyllables of suppressed rage, that sounded like distant thunder.

Apollo whispered to Minerva. Mercury never opened his lips, but occasionally exchanged significant glances with Ganymede. Mars compensated, by his attentions to Venus, for his want of conversation. Cupid employed himself in asking disagreeable questions. At length the Goddesses retired. Mercury exerted himself to amuse Jove, but the Thunderer scarcely deigned to smile at his best stories. Mars picked his teeth, Apollo played with his rings, Ixion was buried in a profound reverie.

## VI.

It was a great relief to all when Ganymede summoned them to the presence of their late companions.

'I have written a comment upon your inscription,' said Minerva to Ixion, 'and am anxious for your opinion of it.'

'I am a wretched critic,' said the King, breaking away from her. Juno smiled upon him in the distance.

'Ixion,' said Venus, as he passed by, 'come and talk to me.'

The bold Thessalian blushed, he stammered out an unmeaning excuse, he quitted the astonished but good-natured Goddess, and seated himself by Juno, and as he seated himself his moody brow seemed suddenly illumined with brilliant light.

'Is it so?' said Venus.

'Hem!' said Minerva.

'Ha, ha!' said Cupid.

Jupiter played piquette with Mercury.

'Everything goes wrong to-day,' said the King of Heaven; 'cards wretched, and kept waiting for dinner, and by—— a mortal!'

'Your Majesty must not be surprised,' said the good-natured Mereury, with whom Ixion was no favourite. 'Your Majesty must not be very much surprised at the conduct of this creature. Considering what he is, and where he is, I am only astonished that his head is not more turned than it appears to be. A man, a thing made of mud, and in Heaven! Only think, sire! Is it not enough to inflame the brain of any child of clay? To be sure, keeping your Majesty from dinner is little short of celestial high treason. I hardly expected that, indeed. To order me about, to treat Ganymede as his own lacquey, and, in short, to command the whole household; all this might be expected from such a person in such a situation, but I confess I did think he had some little respect left for your Majesty.'

'And he does order you about, eh?' inquired Jove. 'I have the spades.'

'Oh! 'tis quite ludicrous,' responded the son of Maia. 'Your Majesty would not expect from me the offices that this upstart daily requires.'

'Eternal destiny! is't possible? That is my trick. And Ganymede, too?'

'Oh! quite shocking, I assure you, sire,' said the beautiful cupbearer, leaning over the chair of Jove with all the easy insolence of a privileged favourite. 'Really sire, if Ixion is to go on in the way he does, either he or I must quit.'

'Is it possible?' exclaimed Jupiter. 'But I can believe anything of a man who keeps me waiting for dinner. Two and three make five.'

'It is Juno that encourages him so,' said Ganymede.

'Does she encourage him?' inquired Jove.

'Everybody notices it,' protested Ganymede.

'It is indeed a little noticed,' observed Mercury.

'What business has such a fellow to speak to Juno?' exclaimed Jove. 'A mere mortal, a mere miserable mortal! You have the point. How I have been deceived in this fellow! Who ever could have supposed that, after all my generosity to him, he would ever have kept me waiting for dinner?'

'He was walking with Juno,' said Ganymede. 'It was all a sham about their having met by accident. Cupid saw them.'

'Ha!' said Jupiter, turning pale; 'you don't say so! Repiqued, as I am a God. That is mine. Where is the Queen?'

'Talking to Ixion, sire,' said Mercury. 'Oh, I beg your pardon, sire; I did not know you meant the queen of diamonds.'

'Never mind. I am repiqued, and I have been kept waiting for dinner. Accursed be this day! Is Ixion really talking to Juno? We will not endure this.'

## VII.

'Where is Juno?' demanded Jupiter.

'I am sure I cannot say,' said Venus, with a smile.

'I am sure I do not know,' said Minerva, with a sneer

'Where is Ixion?' said Cupid, laughing outright.

'Mercury, Ganymede, find the Queen of Heaven instantly,' thundered the father of Gods and men.

The celestial messenger and the heavenly page flew away out of different doors. There was a terrible, an immortal silence. Sublime rage lowered on the brow of Jove like a storm upon the mountain-top. Minerva seated herself at the card-table and played at Patience. Venus and Cupid tittered in the background. Shortly returned the envoys, Mercury looking solemn, Ganymede malignant.

'Well?' inquired Jove; and all Olympus trembled at the monosyllable.

Mercury shook his head.

'Her Majesty has been walking on the terrace with the King of Thessaly,' replied Ganymede.

'Where is she now, sir?' demanded Jupiter.

Mercury shrugged his shoulders.

'Her Majesty is resting herself in the pavilion of Cupid, with the King of Thessaly,' replied Ganymede.

'Confusion!' exclaimed the father of Gods and men; and he rose and seized a candle from the table, scattering the cards in all directions. Every one present, Minerva and Venus, and Mars and Apollo, and Mercury and Ganymede, and the Muses, and the Graces, and all the winged Genii— each seized a candle; rifling the chandeliers, each followed Jove.

'This way,' said Mercury.

'This way,' said Ganymede.

'This way, this way!' echoed the celestial crowd.

'Mischief!' cried Cupid; 'I must save my victims.'

They were all upon the terrace. The father of Gods and men, though both in a passion and a hurry, moved with dignity. It was, as customary in Heaven, a clear and starry night; but this eve Diana was indisposed, or otherwise engaged, and there was no moonlight. They were in sight of the pavilion.

'What are you?' inquired Cupid of one of the Genii, who accidentally extinguished his candle.

'I am a Cloud,' answered the winged Genius.

'A Cloud! Just the thing. Now do me a shrewd turn, and Cupid is ever your debtor. Fly, fly, pretty Cloud, and encompass yon pavilion with your form. Away! ask no questions; swift as my word.'

'I declare there is a fog,' said Venus.

'An evening mist in Heaven!' said Minerva.

'Where is Nox?' said Jove. 'Everything goes wrong. Who ever heard of a mist in Heaven?'

'My candle is out,' said Apollo.

'And mine, too,' said Mars.

'And mine, and mine, and mine,' said Mercury and Ganymede, and the Muses and the Graces.

'All the candles are out!' said Cupid; 'a regular fog. I cannot even see the pavilion: it must be hereabouts, though,' said the God to himself. 'So, so; I should be at home in my own pavilion, and am tolerably accustomed to stealing about in the dark. There is a step; and here, surely, is the lock. The door opens, but the Cloud enters before me. Juno, Juno,' whispered the God of Love, 'we are all here. Be contented to escape, like many other innocent dames, with your reputation only under a cloud: it will soon disperse; and lo! the heaven is clearing.'

'It must have been the heat of our flambeaux,' said Venus; 'for see, the mist is vanished; here is the pavilion.'

Ganymede ran forward, and dashed open the door. Ixion was alone.

'Seize him!' said Jove.

'Juno is not here,' said Mercury, with an air of blended congratulation and disappointment.

'Never mind,' said Jove; 'seize him! He kept me waiting for dinner.'

'Is this your hospitality, Ægiochus?' exclaimed Ixion,

in a tone of bullying innocence. 'I shall defend myself.'

'Seize him, seize him!' exclaimed Jupiter. 'What! do you all falter? Are you afraid of a mortal?'

'And a Thessalian?' added Ganymede.

No one advanced.

'Send for Hercules,' said Jove.

'I will fetch him in an instant,' said Ganymede.

'I protest,' said the King of Thessaly, 'against this violation of the most sacred rights.'

'The marriage tie?' said Mercury.

'The dinner-hour?' said Jove.

'It is no use talking sentiment to Ixion,' said Venus; 'all mortals are callous.'

'Adventures are to the adventurous,' said Minerva.

'Here is Hercules! here is Hercules!'

'Seize him!' said Jove; 'seize that man.'

In vain the mortal struggled with the irresistible demigod.

'Shall I fetch your thunderbolt, Jove?' inquired Ganymede.

'Anything short of eternal punishment is unworthy of a God,' answered Jupiter, with great dignity. 'Apollo, bring me a wheel of your chariot.'

'What shall I do to-morrow morning?' inquired the God of Light.

'Order an eclipse,' replied Jove. 'Bind the insolent wretch to the wheel; hurl him to Hades; its motion shall be perpetual.'

'What am I to bind him with?' inquired Hercules.

'The girdle of Venus,' replied the Thunderer.

'What is all this?' inquired Juno, advancing, pale and agitated.

'Come along; you shall see,' answered Jupiter. 'Follow me, follow me.'

They all followed the leader, all the Gods, all the Genii; in the midst, the brawny husband of Hebe bearing Ixion aloft, bound to the fatal wheel. They reached the terrace;

they descended the sparkling steps of lapis-lazuli. Hercules held his burthen on high, ready, at a nod, to plunge the hapless but presumptuous mortal through space into Hades. The heavenly group surrounded him, and peeped over the starry abyss. It was a fine moral, and demonstrated the usual infelicity that attends unequal connections.

'Celestial despot!' said Ixion.

In a moment all sounds were hushed, as they listened to the last words of the unrivalled victim. Juno, in despair, leant upon the respective arms of Venus and Minerva.

'Celestial despot!' said Ixion, 'I defy the immortal ingenuity of thy cruelty. My memory must be as eternal as thy torture: that will support me.'

# THE INFERNAL MARRIAGE.

Proserpine was the daughter of Jupiter and Ceres. Pluto, the God of Hell, became enamoured of her. His addresses were favoured by her father, but opposed by Ceres. Under these circumstances, he surprised her on the plains of Enna, and carried her off in his chariot.

# THE INFERNAL MARRIAGE.

## PART I.

### 1.

It was clearly a runaway match—never indeed was such a sublime elopement. The four horses were coal-black, with blood-red manes and tails; and they were shod with rubies. They were harnessed to a basaltic car by a single rein of flame. Waving his double-pronged trident in the air, the God struck the blue breast of Cyane, and the waters instantly parted. In rushed the wild chariot, the pale and insensible Proserpine clinging to the breast of her grim lover.

Through the depths of the hitherto unfathomed lake the infernal steeds held their breathless course. The car jolted against its bed. 'Save me!' exclaimed the future Queen of Hades, and she clung with renewed energy to the bosom of the dark bridegroom. The earth opened; they entered the kingdom of the Gnomes. Here Pluto was popular. The lurid populace gave him a loud shout. The chariot whirled along through shadowy cities and by dim highways, swarming with a busy race of shades.

'Ye flowery meads of Enna!' exclaimed the terrified Proserpine, 'shall I never view you again? What an execrable climate!'

'Here, however, in-door nature is charming,' responded Pluto. ''Tis a great nation of manufacturers. You are better, I hope, my Proserpine. The passage of the water is never very agreable, especially to ladies.'

'And which is our next stage?' inquired Proserpine.

'The centre of Earth,' replied Pluto. 'Travelling is so much improved that at this rate we shall reach Hades before night.'

'Alas!' exclaimed Proserpine, 'is not this night?'

'You are not unhappy, my Proserpine?'

'Beloved of my heart, I have given up everything for you! I do not repent, but I am thinking of my mother.'

'Time will pacify the Lady Ceres. What is done cannot be undone. In the winter, when a residence among us is even desirable, I should not be surprised were she to pay us a visit.'

'Her prejudices are so strong,' murmured the bride. 'O! my Pluto, I hope your family will be kind to me.'

'Who could be unkind to Proserpine? Ours is a very domestic circle. I can assure you that everything is so well ordered among us that I have no recollection of a domestic broil.'

'But marriage is such a revolution in a bachelor's establishment,' replied Proserpine, despondingly. 'To tell the truth, too, I am half frightened at the thought of the Furies. I have heard that their tempers are so violent.'

'They mean well; their feelings are strong, but their hearts are in the right place. I flatter myself you will like my nieces, the Parcæ. They are accomplished, and favourites among the men.'

'Indeed!'

'Oh! quite irresistible.'

'My heart misgives me. I wish you had at least paid them the compliment of apprising them of our marriage.'

'Cheer up. For myself, I have none but pleasant anticipations. I long to be at home once more by my own fireside, and patting my faithful Cerberus.'

'I think I shall like Cerberus; I am fond of dogs.'

'I am sure you will. He is the most faithful creature in the world.'

'Is he very fierce?'

'Not if he takes a fancy to you; and who can help taking a fancy to Proserpine?'

'Ah! my Pluto, you are in love.'

## II.

'Is this Hades?' inquired Proserpine.

An avenue of colossal bulls, sculptured in basalt and breathing living flame, led to gates of brass, adorned with friezes of rubies, representing the wars and discomfiture of the Titans. A crimson cloud concealed the height of the immense portal, and on either side hovered o'er the extending walls of the city; a watch-tower or a battlement occasionally flashing forth, and forcing their forms through the lurid obscurity.

'Queen of Hades! welcome to your capital!' exclaimed Pluto.

The monarch rose in his car and whirled a javelin at the gates. There was an awful clang, and then a still more terrible growl.

'My faithful Cerberus!' exclaimed the King.

The portals flew open, and revealed the gigantic form of the celebrated watch-dog of Hell. It completely filled their wide expanse. Who but Pluto could have viewed without horror that enormous body covered with shaggy spikes, those frightful paws clothed with claws of steel, that tail like a boa constrictor, those fiery eyes that blazed like the blood-red lamps in a pharos, and those three forky tongues, round each of which were entwined a vigorous family of green rattlesnakes!

'Ah! Cerby! Cerby!' exclaimed Pluto; 'my fond and faithful Cerby!'

Proserpine screamed as the animal gambolled up to the side of the chariot and held out its paw to its master. Then, licking the royal palm with its three tongues at once, it renewed its station with a wag of its tail which raised such a cloud of dust that for a few minutes nothing was perceptible.

'The monster!' exclaimed Proserpine.

'My love,' exclaimed Pluto, with astonishment.

'The hideous brute!'

'My dear!' exclaimed Pluto.

'He shall never touch me.'

'Proserpine!'

'Don't touch me with that hand. You never shall touch me, if you allow that disgusting animal to lick your hand.'

'I beg to inform you that there are few beings of any kind for whom I have a greater esteem than that faithful and affectionate beast.'

'Oh! if you like Cerberus better than me, I have no more to say,' exclaimed the bride, bridling up with indignation.

'My Proserpine is perverse,' replied Pluto; 'her memory has scarcely done me justice.'

'I am sure you said you liked Cerberus better than anything in the world,' continued the Goddess, with a voice trembling with passion.

'I said no such thing,' replied Pluto, somewhat sternly.

'I see how it is,' replied Proserpine, with a sob; 'you are tired of me.'

'My beloved!'

'I never expected this.'

'My child!'

'Was it for this I left my mother?'

'Powers of Hades! How you can say such things!'

'Broke her heart?'

'Proserpine! Proserpine!'

'Gave up daylight?'

'For the sake of Heaven, then, calm yourself!'

'Sacrificed everything?'

'My love! my life! my angel! what is all this?'

'And then to be abused for the sake of a dog!'

'By all the shades of Hell, but this is enough to provoke even immortals. What have I done, said, or thought, to justify such treatment?'

'Oh! me!'

'Proserpine!'

'Heigho!'

'Proserpine! Proserpine!'

'So soon is the veil withdrawn!'

'Dearest, you must be unwell. This journey has been too much for you.'

'On our very bridal day to be so treated!'

'Soul of my existence, don't make me mad. I love you, I adore you; I have no hope, no wish, no thought but you. I swear it; I swear it by my sceptre and my throne. Speak, speak to your Pluto: tell him all your wish, all your desire. What would you have me do?'

'Shoot that horrid beast.'

'Ah! me!'

'What, you will not! I thought how it would be. I am Proserpine, your beloved, adored Proserpine. You have no wish, no hope, no thought but for me! I have only to speak, and what I desire will be instantly done! And I do speak, I tell you my wish, I express to you my desire, and I am instantly refused! And what have I requested? Is it such a mighty favour? Is it anything unreasonable? Is there, indeed, in my entreaty anything so vastly out of the way? The death of a dog, a disgusting animal, which has already shaken my nerves to pieces; and if ever (here she hid her face in his breast), if ever that event should occur which both must desire, my Pluto, I am sure the very sight of that horrible beast will, I dare not say what it will do.'

Pluto looked puzzled.

'Indeed, my Proserpine, it is not in my power to grant your request; for Cerberus is immortal, like ourselves.'

'Me! miserable!'

'Some arrangement, however, may be made to keep him out of your sight and hearing. I can banish him.'

'Can you, indeed? Oh! banish him, my Pluto! pray banish him! I never shall be happy until Cerberus is banished.'

'I will do anything you desire; but I confess to you I have some misgivings. He is an invaluable watch-dog; and I fear, without his superintendence, the guardians of the gate will scarcely do their duty.'

'Oh! yes: I am sure they will, my Pluto! I will ask

them to, I will ask them myself, I will request them, as a particular and personal favour to myself, to be very careful indeed. And if they do their duty, and I am sure they will, they shall be styled, as a reward, "Proserpine's Own Guards."'

'A reward, indeed!' said the enamoured monarch, as, with a sigh, he signed the order for the banishment of Cerberus in the form of his promotion to the office of Master of the royal and imperial blood-hounds.

### III.

The burning waves of Phlegethon assumed a lighter hue. It was morning. It was the morning after the arrival of Pluto and his unexpected bride. In one of the principal rooms of the palace three beautiful females, clothed in cerulean robes spangled with stars, and their heads adorned with golden crowns, were at work together. One held a distaff, from which the second spun; and the third wielded an enormous pair of adamantine shears, with which she perpetually severed the labours of her sisters. Tall were they in stature and beautiful in form. Very fair; an expression of haughty serenity pervaded their majestic countenances. Their three companions, however, though apparently of the same sex, were of a different character. If women can ever be ugly, certainly these three ladies might put in a valid claim to that epithet. Their complexions were dark and withered, and their eyes, though bright, were bloodshot. Scantily clothed in black garments, not unstained with gore, their wan and offensive forms were but slightly veiled. Their hands were talons; their feet cloven; and serpents were wreathed round their brows instead of hair. Their restless and agitated carriage afforded also not less striking contrast to the polished and aristocratic demeanour of their companions. They paced the chamber with hurried and unequal steps, and wild and uncouth gestures; waving, with a reckless ferocity, burning torches and whips of scorpions. It is hardly necessary to add that these were the Furies, and that the conversation which I am about to report was carried on with the Fates.

'A thousand serpents!' shrieked Tisiphone. 'I will never believe it.'

'Racks and flames!' squeaked Megæra. 'It is impossible.'

'Eternal torture!' moaned Alecto. ''Tis a lie.'

'Not Jupiter himself should convince us!' the Furies joined in infernal chorus.

''Tis nevertheless true,' calmly observed the beautiful Clotho.

'You will soon have the honour of being presented to her,' added the serene Lachesis.

'And whatever we may feel,' observed the considerate Atropos, 'I think, my dear girls, you had better restrain yourselves.'

'And what sort of thing is she?' inquired Tisiphone, with a shriek.

'I have heard that she is lovely,' answered Clotho. 'Indeed, it is impossible to account for the affair in any other way.'

''Tis neither possible to account for nor to justify it,' squeaked Megæra.

'Is there, indeed, a Queen in Hell?' moaned Alecto.

'We shall hold no more drawing-rooms,' said Lachesis.

'We will never attend hers,' said the Furies.

'You must,' replied the Fates.

'I have no doubt she will give herself airs,' shrieked Tisiphone.

'We must remember where she has been brought up, and be considerate,' replied Lachesis.

'I dare say you three will get on very well with her,' squeaked Megæra. 'You always get on well with people.'

'We must remember how very strange things here must appear to her,' observed Atropos.

'No one can deny that there are some very disagreeable sights,' said Clotho.

'There is something in that,' replied Tisiphone, looking

in the glass, and arranging her serpents; 'and for my part, poor girl, I almost pity her, when I think she will have to visit the Harpies.'

## IV.

At this moment four little pages entered the room, who, without exception, were the most hideous dwarfs that ever attended upon a monarch. They were clothed only in parti-coloured tunics, and their breasts and legs were quite bare. From the countenance of the first you would have supposed he was in a convulsion; his hands were clenched and his hair stood on end: this was Terror! The protruded veins of the second seemed ready to burst, and his rubicund visage decidedly proved that he had blood in his head: this was Rage! The third was of an ashen colour throughout: this was Paleness! And the fourth, with a countenance not without traces of beauty, was even more disgusting than his companions from the quantity of horrible flies, centipedes, snails, and other noisome, slimy, and indescribable monstrosities that were crawling all about his body and feeding on his decaying features. The name of this fourth page was Death!

'The King and Queen!' announced the Pages.

Pluto, during the night, had prepared Proserpine for the worst, and had endeavoured to persuade her that his love would ever compensate for all annoyances. She was in excellent spirits and in very good humour; therefore, though she could with difficulty stifle a scream when she recognised the Furies, she received the congratulations of the Parcæ with much cordiality.

'I have the pleasure, Proserpine, of presenting you to my family,' said Pluto.

'Who, I am sure, hope to make Hades agreeable to your Majesty,' rejoined Clotho. The Furies uttered a suppressed sound between a murmur and a growl.

'I have ordered the chariot,' said Pluto. 'I propose to take the Queen a ride, and show her some of our lions.'

'She will, I am sure, be delighted,' said Lachesis.

'I long to see Ixion,' said Proserpine.

'The wretch!' shrieked Tisiphone.

'I cannot help thinking that he has been very unfairly treated,' said Proserpine.

'What!' squeaked Megæra. 'The ravisher!'

'Ay! it is all very well,' replied Proserpine; 'but, for my part, if we knew the truth of that affair ——'

'Is it possible that your Majesty can speak in such a tone of levity of such an offender?' shrieked Tisiphone.

'Is it possible?' moaned Alecto.

'Ah! you have heard only one side of the question; but for my part, knowing as much of Juno as I do ——'

'The Queen of Heaven!' observed Atropos, with an intimidating glance.

'The Queen of Fiddlestick!' said Proserpine; 'as great a flirt as ever existed, with all her prudish looks.'

The Fates and the Furies exchanged glances of astonishment and horror.

'For my part,' continued Proserpine, 'I make it a rule to support the weaker side, and nothing will ever persuade me that Ixion is not a victim, and a pitiable one.'

'Well! men generally have the best of it in these affairs,' said Lachesis, with a forced smile.

'Juno ought to be ashamed of herself,' said Proserpine. 'Had I been in her situation, they should have tied me to a wheel first. At any rate, they ought to have punished him in Heaven. I have no idea of those people sending every *mauvais sujet* to Hell.'

'But what shall we do?' inquired Pluto, who wished to turn the conversation.

'Shall we turn out a sinner and hunt him for her Majesty's diversion?' suggested Tisiphone, flanking her serpents.

'Nothing of the kind will ever divert me,' said Proserpine; 'for I have no hesitation in saying that I do not at all approve of these eternal punishments, or, indeed, of any punishment whatever.'

'The heretic!' whispered Tisiphone to Megæra. Alecto moaned.

'It might be more interesting to her Majesty,' said Atropos, ' to witness some of those extraordinary instances of predestined misery with which Hades abounds. Shall we visit Œdipus ? '

'Poor fellow !' exclaimed Proserpine. 'For myself, I willingly confess that Torture disgusts and Destiny puzzles me.'

The Fates and the Furies all alike started.

'I do not understand this riddle of Destiny,' continued the young Queen. 'If you, Parcæ, have predestined that a man should commit a crime, it appears to me very unjust that you should afterwards call upon the Furies to punish him for its commission.'

'But man is a free agent,' observed Lachesis, in as mild a tone as she could command.

'Then what becomes of Destiny ? ' replied Proserpine.

'Destiny is eternal and irresistible,' replied Clotho. ' All is ordained ; but man is, nevertheless, master of his own actions.'

'I do not understand that,' said Proserpine.

'It is not meant to be understood,' said Atropos ; 'but you must nevertheless believe it.'

'I make it a rule only to believe what I understand,' replied Proserpine.

'It appears,' said Lachesis, with a blended glance of contempt and vengeance, 'that your Majesty, though a Goddess, is an Atheist.'

'As for that, anybody may call me just what they please, provided they do nothing else. So long as I am not tied to a wheel or whipped with scorpions for speaking my mind, I shall be as tolerant of the speech and acts of others as I expect them to be tolerant of mine. Come, Pluto, I am sure that the chariot must be ready ! '

So saying, her Majesty took the arm of her spouse, and with a haughty curtsey left the apartment.

'Did you ever !' shrieked Tisiphone, as the door closed.

' No ! never !' squeaked Megæra.

'Never ! never !' moaned Alecto.

'She must understand what she believes, must she?' said Lachesis, scarcely less irritated.

'I never heard such nonsense,' said Clotho.

'What next!' said Atropos.

'Disgusted with Torture!' exclaimed the Furies.

'Puzzled with Destiny!' said the Fates.

### v.

It was the third morning after the Infernal Marriage; the slumbering Proserpine reposed in the arms of the snoring Pluto. There was a loud knocking at the chamber-door. Pluto jumped up in the middle of a dream.

'My life, what is the matter?' exclaimed Proserpine.

The knocking was repeated and increased. There was also a loud shout of 'treason, murder, and fire!'

'What is the matter?' exclaimed the God, jumping out of bed and seizing his trident. 'Who is there?'

'Your pages, your faithful pages! Treason! treason! For the sake of Hell, open the door. Murder, fire, treason!'

'Enter!' said Pluto, as the door was unlocked.

And Terror and Rage entered.

'You frightful things, get out of the room!' cried Proserpine.

'A moment, my angel!' said Pluto, 'a single moment. Be not alarmed, my best love; I pray you be not alarmed. Well, imps, why am I disturbed?'

'Oh!' said Terror. Rage could not speak, but gnashed his teeth and stamped his feet.

'O-o-o-h!' repeated Terror.

'Speak, cursed imps!' cried the enraged Pluto; and he raised his arm.

'A man! a man!' cried Terror. 'Treason, treason! a man! a man!'

'What man?' said Pluto, in a rage.

'A man, a live man, has entered Hell!'

'You don't say so?' said Proserpine; 'a man, a live man. Let me see him immediately.'

'Where is he?' said Pluto; 'what is he doing?'

'He is here, there, and everywhere! asking for your wife, and singing like anything.'

'Proserpine!' said Pluto, reproachfully; but, to do the God justice, he was more astounded than jealous.

'I am sure I shall be delighted to see him; it is so long since I have seen a live man,' said Proserpine. 'Who can he be? A man, and a live man! How delightful! It must be a messenger from my mother.'

'But how came he here?'

'Ah! how came he here?' echoed Terror.

'No time must be lost!' exclaimed Pluto, scrambling on his robe. 'Seize him, and bring him into the council chamber. My charming Proserpine, excuse me for a moment.'

'Not at all; I will accompany you.'

'But, my love, my sweetest, my own, this is business; these are affairs of state. The council chamber is not a place for you.'

'And why not?' said Proserpine. 'I have no idea of ever leaving you for a moment. Why not for me as well as for the Fates and the Furies? Am I not Queen? I have no idea of such nonsense!'

'My love!' said the deprecating husband.

'You don't go without me,' said the imperious wife, seizing his robe.

'I must,' said Pluto.

'Then you shall never return,' said Proserpine.

'Enchantress! be reasonable.'

'I never was, and I never will be,' replied the Goddess.

'Treason! treason!' screamed Terror.

'My love, I must go!'

'Pluto,' said Proserpine, 'understand me once for all, I will not be contradicted.'

Rage stamped his foot.

'Proserpine, understand me once for all, it is impossible,' said the God, frowning.

'My Pluto!' said the Queen. 'Is it my Pluto who speaks thus sternly to me? Is it he who, but an hour ago, a short hour ago, died upon my bosom in transports and stifled me with kisses! Unhappy woman! wretched, miserable Proserpine! Oh! my mother! my kind, my affectionate mother! Have I disobeyed you for this! For this have I deserted you! For this have I broken your beloved heart!' She buried her face in the crimson counterpane, and bedewed its gorgeous embroidery with her fast-flowing tears.

'Treason!' shouted Terror.

'Ha! ha! ha!' exclaimed the hysterical Proserpine.

'What am I to do?' cried Pluto. 'Proserpine, my adored, my beloved, my enchanting Proserpine, compose yourself; for my sake, compose yourself. I love you! I adore you! You know it! oh! indeed you know it!'

The hysterics increased.

'Treason! treason!' shouted Terror.

'Hold your infernal tongue,' said Pluto. 'What do I care for treason when the Queen is in this state?' He knelt by the bedside, and tried to stop her mouth with kisses, and ever and anon whispered his passion. 'My Proserpine, I beseech you to be calm; I will do anything you like. Come, come, then, to the council!'

The hysterics ceased; the Queen clasped him in her arms and rewarded him with a thousand embraces. Then, jumping up, she bathed her swollen eyes with a beautiful cosmetic that she and her maidens had distilled from the flowers of Enna; and, wrapping herself up in her shawl, descended with his Majesty, who was quite as much puzzled about the cause of this disturbance as when he was first roused.

VI.

Crossing an immense covered bridge, the origin of the Bridge of Sighs at Venice, over the royal gardens, which consisted entirely of cypress, the royal pair, preceded by the pages in waiting, entered the council chamber. The council was already assembled. On either side of a throne of sulphur, from which issued the four infernal rivers of

Lethe, Phlegethon, Cocytus, and Acheron, were ranged the Eumenides and the Parcæ. Lachesis and her sisters turned up their noses when they observed Proserpine; but the Eumenides could not stifle their fury, in spite of the hints of their more subdued but not less malignant companions.

'What is all this?' inquired Pluto.

'The constitution is in danger,' said the Parcæ in chorus.

'Both in church and state,' added the Furies. ''Tis a case of treason and blasphemy;' and they waved their torches and shook their whips with delighted anticipation of their use.

'Detail the circumstances,' said Pluto, waving his hand majestically to Lachesis, in whose good sense he had great confidence.

'A man, a living man, has entered your kingdom, unknown and unnoticed,' said Lachesis.

'By my sceptre, is it true?' said the astonished King. 'Is he seized?'

'The extraordinary mortal baffles our efforts,' said Lachesis. 'He bears with him a lyre, the charmed gift of Apollo, and so seducing are his strains that in vain our guards advance to arrest his course; they immediately begin dancing, and he easily eludes their efforts. The general confusion is indescribable. All business is at a standstill: Ixion rests upon his wheel; old Sisyphus sits down on his mountain, and his stone has fallen with a terrible plash into Acheron. In short, unless we are energetic, we are on the eve of a revolution.'

'His purpose?'

'He seeks yourself and—her Majesty,' added Lachesis, with a sneer.

'Immediately announce that we will receive him.'

The unexpected guest was not slow in acknowledging the royal summons. A hasty treaty was drawn up; he was to enter the palace unmolested, on condition that he ceased playing his lyre. The Fates and the Furies exchanged significant glances as his approach was announced.

The man, the live man, who had committed the unprecedented crime of entering Hell without a licence, and the previous deposit of his soul as security for the good behaviour of his body, stood before the surprised and indignant Court of Hades. Tall and graceful in stature, and crowned with laurels, Proserpine was glad to observe that the man, who was evidently famous, was also good-looking.

'Thy purpose, mortal?' inquired Pluto, with awful majesty.

'Mercy!' answered the stranger in a voice of exquisite melody, and sufficiently embarrassed to render him interesting.

'What is mercy?' inquired the Fates and the Furies.

'Speak, stranger, without fear,' said Proserpine. 'Thy name?'

'Is Orpheus; but a few days back the too happy husband of the enchanting Eurydice. Alas! dread King, and thou too, beautiful and benignant partner of his throne, I won her by my lyre, and by my lyre I would redeem her. Know, then, that in the very glow of our gratified passion a serpent crept under the flowers on which we reposed, and by a fatal sting summoned my adored to the shades. Why did it not also summon me? I will not say why should I not have been the victim in her stead; for I feel too keenly that the doom of Eurydice would not have been less forlorn, had she been the wretched being who had been spared to life. O King! they whispered on earth that thou too hadst yielded thy heart to the charms of love. Pluto, they whispered, is no longer stern: Pluto also feels the all-subduing influence of beauty. Dread monarch, by the self-same passion that rages in our breasts alike, I implore thy mercy. Thou hast risen from the couch of love, the arm of thy adored has pressed upon thy heart, her honied lips have clung with rapture to thine still echo in thy ears all the enchanting phrases of her idolatry. Then, by the memory of these, by all the higher and ineffable joys to which these lead, King of Hades, spare me, oh! spare me, Eurydice!'

Proserpine threw her arms round the neck of her husband, and, hiding her face in his breast, wept.

'Rash mortal, you demand that which is not in the power of Pluto to concede,' said Lachesis.

'I have heard much of treason since my entrance into Hades,' replied Orpheus, 'and this sounds like it.'

'Mortal!' exclaimed Clotho, with contempt.

'Nor is it in your power to return, sir,' said Tisiphone, shaking her whip.

'We have accounts to settle with you,' said Megæra.

'Spare her, spare her,' murmured Proserpine to her lover.

'King of Hades!' said Lachesis, with much dignity, 'I hold a responsible office in your realm, and I claim the constitutional privilege of your attention. I protest against the undue influence of the Queen. She is a power unknown in our constitution, and an irresponsible agent that I will not recognise. Let her go back to the drawing-room, where all will bow to her.'

'Hag!' exclaimed Proserpine. 'King of Hades, I, too, can appeal to you. Have I accepted your crown to be insulted by your subjects?'

'A subject, may it please your Majesty, who has duties as strictly defined by our infernal constitution as those of your royal spouse; duties, too, which, let me tell you, Madam, I and *my order* are resolved to perform.'

'Gods of Olympus!' cried Proserpine. 'Is this to be a Queen?'

'Before we proceed further in this discussion,' said Lachesis, 'I must move an inquiry into the conduct of his Excellency the Governor of the Gates. I move, then, that Cerberus be summoned.'

Pluto started, and the blood rose to his dark cheek. 'I have not yet had an opportunity of mentioning,' said his Majesty, in a low tone, and with an air of considerable confusion, 'that I have thought fit, as a reward for his past services, to promote Cerberus to the office of the Master of the Hounds. He therefore is no longer responsible.'

'O—h!' shrieked the Furies, as they elevated their hideous eyes.

'The constitution has invested your Majesty with a power in the appointment of your Officers of State which your Majesty has undoubtedly a right to exercise,' said Lachesis. 'What degree of discretion it anticipated in the exercise, it is now unnecessary, and would be extremely disagreeable, to discuss. I shall not venture to inquire by what new influence your Majesty has been guided in the present instance. The consequence of your Majesty's conduct is obvious, in the very difficult situation in which your realm is now placed. For myself and my colleagues, I have only to observe that we decline, under this crisis, any further responsibility; and the distaff and the shears are at your Majesty's service the moment your Majesty may find convenient successors to the present holders. As a last favour, in addition to the many we are proud to remember we have received from your Majesty, we entreat that we may be relieved from their burthen as quickly as possible.' (Loud cheers from the Eumenides.)

'We had better recall Cerberus,' said Pluto, alarmed, 'and send this mortal about his business.'

'Not without Eurydice. Oh! not without Eurydice,' said the Queen.

'Silence, Proserpine,' said Pluto.

'May it please your Majesty,' said Lachesis, 'I am doubtful whether we have the power of expelling anyone from Hades. It is not less the law that a mortal cannot remain here; and it is too notorious for me to mention the fact that none here have the power of inflicting death.'

'Of what use are all your laws,' exclaimed Proserpine, 'if they are only to perplex us? As there are no statutes to guide us, it is obvious that the King's will is supreme. Let Orpheus depart, then, with his bride.'

'The latter suggestion is clearly illegal,' said Lachesis.

'Lachesis, and ye, her sisters,' said Proserpine, 'forget, I beseech you, any warm words that may have passed between us, and, as a personal favour to one who would willingly be your friend, release Eurydice. What! you shake your heads! Nay; of what importance can be a single miserable shade, and one, too, summoned so cruelly before her time, in these thickly-peopled regions?'

''Tis the principle,' said Lachesis; ''tis the principle. Concession is ever fatal, however slight. Grant this demand; others, and greater, will quickly follow. Mercy becomes a precedent, and the realm is ruined.'

'Ruined!' echoed the Furies.

'And I say *preserved!*' exclaimed Proserpine with energy. 'The State is in confusion, and you yourselves confess that you know not how to remedy it. Unable to suggest a course, follow mine. I am the advocate of Mercy; I am the advocate of Concession; and, as you despise all higher impulses, I meet you on your own grounds. I am their advocate for the sake of policy, of expediency.'

'Never!' said the Fates.

'Never!' shrieked the Furies.

'What, then, will you do with Orpheus?'

The Parcæ shook their heads; even the Eumenides were silent.

'Then you are unable to carry on the King's government; for Orpheus must be disposed of; all agree to that. Pluto, reject these counsellors, at once insulting and incapable. Give me the distaff and the fatal shears. At once form a new Cabinet; and let the release of Orpheus and Eurydice be the basis of their policy.' She threw her arms round his neck and whispered in his ear.

Pluto was perplexed; his confidence in the Parcæ was shaken. A difficulty had occurred with which they could not cope. It was true the difficulty had been occasioned by a departure from their own exclusive and restrictive policy. It was clear that the gates of Hell ought never to have been opened to the stranger; but opened they had been. Forced to decide, he decided on the side of *expediency*, and signed a decree for the departure of Orpheus and Eurydice. The Parcæ immediately resigned their posts, and the Furies walked off in a huff. Thus, on the third day of the Infernal Marriage, Pluto found that he had quarrelled with all his family, and that his ancient administration was broken up. The King was without a friend, and Hell was without a Government!

# PART II.

### I.

LET us change the scene from Hades to Olympus.

A chariot drawn by dragons hovered over that superb palace whose sparkling steps of lapis-lazuli were once pressed by the daring foot of Ixion. It descended into the beautiful gardens, and Ceres, stepping out, sought the presence of Jove.

'Father of Gods and men,' said the majestic mother of Proserpine, 'listen to a distracted parent! All my hopes were centred in my daughter, the daughter of whom you have deprived me. Is it for this that I endured the pangs of childbirth? Is it for this that I suckled her on this miserable bosom? Is it for this that I tended her girlish innocence, watched with vigilant fondness the development of her youthful mind, and cultured with a thousand graces and accomplishments her gifted and unrivalled promise? to lose her for ever!'

'Beloved Bona Dea,' replied Jove, 'calm yourself!'

'Jupiter, you forget that I am a mother.'

'It is the recollection of that happy circumstance that alone should make you satisfied.'

'Do you mock me? Where is my daughter?'

'In the very situation you should desire. In her destiny all is fulfilled which the most affectionate mother could hope. What was the object of all your care and all her accomplishments? a good *partie*; and she has made one.'

'To reign in Hell!'

'"Better to reign in Hell than serve in Heaven." What! would you have had her a cup-bearer, like Hebe, or a messenger, like Hermes? Was the daughter of Jove and Ceres to be destined to a mere place in our household! Lady! she is the object of envy to half the Goddesses. Bating our own bed, which she could not share, what lot more distinguished than hers? Recollect that Goddesses, who desire a becoming match, have a very limited circle to elect from. Even Venus was obliged to put up with Vulcan. It will not do to be too nice. Thank your stars that she is not an old maid like Minerva.'

'But Mars? he loved her."

'A young officer only with his half-pay, however good his connections, is surely not a proper mate for our daughter.'

'Apollo?'

'I have no opinion of a literary son-in-law. These scribblers are at present the fashion, and are very well to ask to dinner; but I confess a more intimate connection with them is not at all to my taste.'

'I meet Apollo everywhere.'

'The truth is, he is courted because every one is afraid of him. He is the editor of a daily journal, and under the pretence of throwing light upon every subject, brings a great many disagreeable things into notice, which is excessively inconvenient. Nobody likes to be paragraphed; and for my part I should only be too happy to extinguish the Sun and every other newspaper were it only in my power.'

'But Pluto is so old, and so ugly, and, all agree, so ill-tempered.'

'He has a splendid income, a magnificent estate; his settlements are worthy of his means. This ought to satisfy a mother; and his political influence is necessary to me, and this satisfies a father.'

'But the heart——'

'As for that, she fancies she loves him; and whether she do or not, these feelings, we know, never last. Rest assured, my dear Ceres, that our girl has made a brilliant match, in spite of the gloomy atmosphere in which she has to reside.'

'It must end in misery. I know Proserpine. I confess it with tears, she is a spoiled child.'

'This may occasion Pluto many uneasy moments; but that is nothing to you or me. Between ourselves, I shall not be at all surprised if she plague his life out.'

'But how can she consort with the Fates? How is it possible for her to associate with the Furies? She, who is used to the gayest and most amiable society in the world? Indeed, indeed, 'tis an ill-assorted union!'

'They are united, however; and, take my word for it, my dear madam, that you had better leave Pluto alone. The interference of a mother-in-law is proverbially never very felicitous.'

II.

In the meantime affairs went on swimmingly in Tartarus. The obstinate Fates and the sulky Furies were unwittingly the cause of universal satisfaction. Everyone enjoyed himself, and enjoyment when it is unexpected is doubly satisfactory. Tantalus, Sisyphus, and Ixion, for the first time during their punishment, had an opportunity for a little conversation.

'Long live our reforming Queen,' said the ex-king of Lydia. 'You cannot conceive, my dear companions, anything more delightful than this long-coveted draught of cold water; its flavour far surpasses the memory of my choicest wines. And as for this delicious fruit, one must live in a hot climate, like our present one, sufficiently to appreciate its refreshing gust. I would, my dear friends, you could only share my banquet.'

'Your Majesty is very kind,' replied Sisyphus, 'but it seems to me that nothing in the world will ever induce me again to move. One must have toiled for ages to comprehend the rapturous sense of repose that now pervades my exhausted frame. Is it possible that that damned stone can really have disappeared?'

'You say truly,' said Ixion, 'the couches of Olympus cannot compare with this resting wheel.'

'Noble Sisyphus,' rejoined Tantalus, 'we are both of us acquainted with the cause of our companion's presence in these infernal regions, since his daring exploit has had the good fortune of being celebrated by one of the fashionable authors of this part of the world.'

'I have never had time to read his work,' interrupted Ixion. 'What sort of a fellow is he?'

'One of the most conceited dogs that I ever met with,' replied the King. 'He thinks he is a great genius, and perhaps he has some little talent for the extravagant.'

'Are there any critics in Hell?'

'Myriads. They abound about the marshes of Cocytus, where they croak furiously. They are all to a man against our author.'

'That speaks more to his credit than his own self-opinion,' rejoined Ixion.

'*A nous moutons!*' exclaimed Tantalus; 'I was about to observe that I am curious to learn for what reason our friend Sisyphus was doomed to his late terrible exertions.'

'For the simplest in the world,' replied the object of the inquiry; 'because I was not a hypocrite. No one ever led a pleasanter life than myself, and no one was more popular in society. I was considered, as they phrased it, the most long-headed prince of my time, and was in truth a finished man of the world. I had not an acquaintance whom I had not taken in, and gods and men alike favoured me. In an unlucky moment, however, I offended the infernal deities, and it was then suddenly discovered that I was the most abandoned character of my age. You know the rest.'

'You seem,' exclaimed Tantalus, 'to be relating my own history; for I myself led a reckless career with impunity, until some of the Gods did me the honour of dining with me, and were dissatisfied with the repast. I am convinced myself that, provided a man frequent the temples, and observe with strictness the sacred festivals, such is the force of public opinion, that there is no crime which he may not commit without hazard.'

'Long live hypocrisy!' exclaimed Ixion. 'It is not my forte. But if I began life anew, I would be more observant in my sacrifices.'

'Who could have anticipated this wonderful revolution!' exclaimed Sisyphus, stretching himself. 'I wonder what will occur next! Perhaps we shall be all released.'

'You say truly,' said Ixion. 'I am grateful to our reforming Queen; but I have no idea of stopping here. This cursed wheel indeed no longer whirls; but I confess my expectations will be much disappointed if I cannot free myself from these adamantine bonds that fix me to its orb.'

'And one cannot drink water for ever,' said Tantalus.

'D—n all half measures,' said Ixion. 'We must proceed in this system of amelioration.'

'Without doubt,' responded his companion.

'The Queen must have a party,' continued the audacious lover of Juno. 'The Fates and the Furies never can be conciliated. It is evident to me that she must fall unless she unbinds these chains of mine.'

'And grants me full liberty of egress and regress,' exclaimed Sisyphus.

'And me a bottle of the finest golden wine of Lydia,' said Tantalus.

### III.

The infernal honeymoon was over. A cloud appeared in the hitherto serene heaven of the royal lovers. Proserpine became unwell. A mysterious languor pervaded her frame; her accustomed hilarity deserted her. She gave up her daily rides; she never quitted the palace, scarcely her chamber. All day long she remained lying on a sofa, and whenever Pluto endeavoured to console her she went into hysterics. His Majesty was quite miserable, and the Fates and the Furies began to hold up their heads. The two court physicians could throw no light upon the complaint, which baffled all their remedies. These, indeed, were not numerous, for the two physicians possessed each only one idea. With one every complaint was nervous; the other traced everything to the liver. The name of the first was Dr. Blue-Devil; and of the other Dr. Blue-Pill. They were most eminent men.

Her Majesty getting worse every day, Pluto, in despair,

determined to send for Æsculapius. It was a long way to send for a physician; but then he was the most fashionable one in the world. He cared not how far he travelled to visit a patient, because he was paid by the mile; and it was calculated that his fee for quitting earth, and attending the Queen of Hell, would allow him to leave off business.

What a wise physician was Æsculapius! Physic was his abhorrence. He never was known, in the whole course of his practice, ever to have prescribed a single drug. He was a handsome man, with a flowing beard curiously perfumed, and a robe of the choicest purple. He twirled a cane of agate, round which was twined a serpent of precious stones, the gift of Juno, and he rode in a chariot drawn by horses of the Sun. When he visited Proserpine, he neither examined her tongue nor felt her pulse, but gave her an account of a fancy ball which he had attended the last evening he passed on *terra firma*. His details were so interesting that the Queen soon felt better. The next day he renewed his visit, and gave her an account of a new singer that had appeared at Ephesus. The effect of this recital was so satisfactory, that a bulletin in the evening announced that the Queen was convalescent. The third day Æsculapius took his departure, having previously enjoined change of scene for her Majesty, and a visit to the Elysian Fields!

IV.

'Heh, heh!' shrieked Tisiphone.
'Hah, hah!' squeaked Megæra.
'Hoh, hoh!' moaned Alecto.
'Now or never,' said the infernal sisters. 'There is a decided reaction. The moment she embarks, unquestionably we will flare up.' So they ran off to the Fates.

'We must be prudent,' said Clotho.
'Our time is not come,' remarked Lachesis.
'I wish the reaction was more decided,' said Atropos; 'but it is a great thing that they are going to be parted, for the King must remain.'

The opposition party, although aiming at the same result, was therefore evidently divided as to the means by which it was to be obtained. The sanguine Furies were for fighting it out at once, and talked bravely of the strong conservative spirit only dormant in Tartarus. Even the Radicals themselves are dissatisfied: Tantalus is no longer contented with water, or Ixion with repose. But the circumspect Fates felt that a false step at present could never be regained. They talked, therefore, of watching events. Both divisions, however, agreed that the royal embarkation was to be the signal for renewed intrigues and renovated exertions.

V.

When Proserpine was assured that she must be parted for a time from Pluto, she was inconsolable. They passed the night in sorrowful embraces. She vowed that she could not live a day without him, and that she certainly should die before she reached the first post. The mighty heart of the King of Hades was torn to pieces with contending emotions. In the agony of his overwhelming passion the security of his realm seemed of secondary importance compared with the happiness of his wife. Fear and hatred of the Parcæ and the Eumenides equalled, however, in the breast of Proserpine, her affection for her husband. The consciousness that his absence would be a signal for a revolution, and that the crown of Tartarus might be lost to her expected offspring, animated her with a spirit of heroism. She reconciled herself to the terrible separation, on condition that Pluto wrote to her every day.

'Adieu! my best, my only beloved!' ejaculated the unhappy Queen; 'do not forget me for a moment; and let nothing in the world induce you to speak to any of those horrid people. I know them; I know exactly what they will be at: the moment I am gone they will commence their intrigues for the restoration of the reign of doom and torture. Do not listen to them, my Pluto. Sooner than have recourse to them, seek assistance from their former victims.'

'Calm yourself, my Proserpine. Anticipate no evil. I shall be firm; do not doubt me. I will cling with tenacity to that *juste milieu* under which we have hitherto so eminently prospered. Neither the Parcæ and the Eumenides, nor Ixion and his friends, shall advance a point. I will keep each faction in awe by the bugbear of the other's supremacy. Trust me, I am a profound politician.'

### VI.

It was determined that the progress of Proserpine to the Elysian Fields should be celebrated with a pomp and magnificence becoming her exalted station. The day of her departure was proclaimed as a high festival in Hell. Tiresias, absent on a secret mission, had been summoned back by Pluto, and appointed to attend her Majesty during her journey and her visit, for Pluto had the greatest confidence in his discretion. Besides, as her Majesty had not at present the advantage of any female society, it was necessary that she should be amused; and Tiresias, though old, ugly, and blind, was a wit as well as a philosopher, the most distinguished diplomatist of his age, and considered the best company in Hades.

An immense crowd was assembled round the gates of the palace on the morn of the royal departure. With what anxious curiosity did they watch those huge brazen portals! Every precaution was taken for the accommodation of the public. The streets were lined with troops of extraordinary stature, whose nodding plumes prevented the multitude from catching a glimpse of anything that passed, and who cracked the sculls of the populace with their scimitars if they attempted in the slightest degree to break the line. Moreover, there were seats erected which any one might occupy at a reasonable rate; but the lord steward, who had the disposal of the tickets, purchased them all for himself, and then resold them to his fellow-subjects at an enormous price.

At length the hinges of the gigantic portals gave an

ominous creak, and, amid the huzzas of men and the shrieks of women, the procession commenced.

First came the infernal band. It consisted of five hundred performers, mounted on different animals. Never was such a melodious blast. Fifty trumpeters, mounted on zebras of all possible stripes and tints, and working away at huge ramshorns with their cheeks like pumpkins. Then there were bassoons mounted on bears, clarionets on camelopards, oboes on unicorns, and troops of musicians on elephants, playing on real serpents, whose prismatic bodies indulged in the most extraordinary convolutions imaginable, and whose arrowy tongues glittered with superb agitation at the exquisite sounds which they unintentionally delivered. Animals there were, too, now unknown and forgotten; but I must not forget the fellow who beat the kettledrums, mounted on an enormous mammoth, and the din of whose reverberating blows would have deadened the thunder of Olympus.

This enchanting harmony preceded the regiment of Proserpine's own guards, glowing in adamantine armour and mounted on coal-black steeds. Their helmets were quite awful, and surmounted by plumes plucked from the wings of the Harpies, which were alone enough to terrify an earthly host. It was droll to observe this troop of gigantic heroes commanded by infants, who, however, were arrayed in a similar costume, though, of course, on a smaller scale. But such was the admirable discipline of the infernal forces, that, though lions to their enemies, they were lambs to their friends; and on the present occasion their colonel was carried in a cradle.

After these came twelve most worshipful baboons, in most venerable wigs. They were clothed with scarlet robes lined with ermine, and ornamented with gold chains, and mounted on the most obstinate and inflexible mules in Tartarus. These were the judges. Each was provided with a pannier of choice cobnuts, which he cracked with great gravity, throwing the shells to the multitude, an infernal ceremony, there held emblematic of their profession.

The Lord Chancellor came next in a grand car. Although his wig was even longer than those of his fellow functionaries, his manners and the rest of his costume afforded a strange contrast to them. Apparently never was such a droll, lively fellow. His dress was something between that of Harlequin and Scaramouch. He amused himself by keeping in the air four brazen balls at the same time, swallowing daggers, spitting fire, turning sugar into salt, and eating yards of pink ribbon, which, after being well digested, re-appeared through his nose. It is unnecessary to add, after this, that he was the most popular Lord Chancellor that had ever held the seals, and was received with loud and enthusiastic cheers, which apparently repaid him for all his exertions. Notwithstanding his numerous and curious occupations, I should not omit to add that his Lordship, nevertheless, found time to lead by the nose a most meek and milk-white jackass that immediately followed him, and which, in spite of the remarkable length of its ears, seemed the object of great veneration. There was evidently some mystery about this animal difficult to penetrate. Among other characteristics, it was said, at different seasons, to be distinguished by different titles; for sometimes it was styled 'The Public,' at others 'Opinion,' and occasionally was saluted as the 'King's Conscience.'

Now came a numerous company of Priests, in flowing and funereal robes, bearing banners, inscribed with the various titles of their Queen; on some was inscribed Hecate, on others Juno Inferna, on others Theogamia, Libera on some, on others Cotytto. Those that bore banners were crowned with wreaths of narcissus, and mounted on bulls blacker than night, and of a severe and melancholy aspect. Others walked by their side, bearing branches of cypress.

And here I must stop to notice a droll characteristic of the priestly economy of Hades. To be a good pedestrian was considered an essential virtue of an infernal clergyman; but to be mounted on a black bull was the highest distinction of the craft. It followed, therefore, that, originally, promotion to such a seat was the natural reward of any priest who had distinguished himself in the humbler career of a good walker; but in process of time, as even infernal as well as human institutions are alike liable to corruption, the black bulls became too often occupied by the halt and the crippled, the feeble and the paralytic, who used their influence at Court to become thus exempted from the performance of the severer duties of which they were incapable. This violation of the priestly constitution excited at first great murmurs among the abler but less influential brethren. But the murmurs of the weak prove only the tyranny of the strong; and so completely in the course of time do institutions depart from their original character, that the imbecile riders of the black bulls now avowedly defended their position on the very grounds which originally should have unseated them, and openly maintained that it was very evident that the stout were intended to walk, and the feeble to be carried.

The priests were followed by fifty dark chariots, drawn by blue satyrs. Herein was the wardrobe of the Queen, and her Majesty's cooks.

Tiresias came next, in a basalt chariot, yoked to royal steeds. He was attended by Manto, who shared his confidence, and who, some said, was his daughter, and others his niece. Venerable seer! Who could behold that flowing beard, and the thin grey hairs of that lofty and wrinkled brow, without being filled with sensations of awe and affection? A smile of bland benignity played upon his passionless and reverend countenance. Fortunate the monarch who is blessed with such a counsellor! Who could have supposed that all this time Tiresias was concocting an epigram on Pluto!

The Queen! The Queen!

Upon a superb throne, placed upon an immense car, and drawn by twelve coal-black steeds, four abreast, reposed the royal daughter of Ceres. Her rich dark hair was braided off her high pale forehead, and fell in voluptuous clusters over her back. A tiara sculptured out of a single brilliant, and which darted a flash like lightning on the surrounding multitude, was placed somewhat negligently on the right side of her head; but no jewels broke the entrancing swell of her swan-like neck, or were dimmed by the lustre of her ravishing arms. How fair was the Queen of Hell! How thrilling the solemn lustre of her violet eye! A robe, purple as the last hour of twilight, encompassed her transcendent form, studded with golden stars!

## VII.

Through the dim hot streets of Tartarus moved the royal procession, until it reached the first winding of the river Styx. Here an immense assemblage of yachts and barges, dressed out with the infernal colours, denoted the appointed spot of the royal embarkation. Tiresias dismounting from his chariot, and leaning on Manto, now approached her Majesty, and requesting her royal commands, recommended her to lose no time in getting on board.

'When your Majesty is once on the Styx,' observed the wily seer, 'it may be somewhat difficult to recall you to Hades; but I know very little of Clotho, may it please your Majesty, if she have not already commenced her intrigues in Tartarus.'

'You alarm me!' said Proserpine.

'It was not my intention. Caution is not fear.'

'But do you think that Pluto——'

'May it please your Majesty, I make it a rule never to think. I know too much.'

'Let us embark immediately!'

'Certainly; I would recommend your Majesty to get off at once. Myself and Manto will accompany you, and the cooks. If an order arrive to stay our departure, we can then send back the priests.'

'You counsel well, Tiresias. I wish you had not been absent on my arrival. Affairs might have gone better.'

'Not at all. Had I been in Hell, your enemies would

have been more wary. Your Majesty's excellent spirit carried you through triumphantly; but it will not do so twice. You turned them out, and I must keep them out.'

'So be it, my dear friend.' Thus saying, the Queen descended her throne, and leaving the rest of her retinue to follow with all possible despatch, embarked on board the infernal yacht, with Tiresias, Manto, the chief cook, and some chosen attendants, and bid adieu for the first time, not without agitation, to the gloomy banks of Tartarus.

## VIII.

The breeze was favourable, and, animated by the exhortations of Tiresias, the crew exerted themselves to the utmost. The barque swiftly scudded over the dark waters. The river was of great breadth, and in this dim region the crew were soon out of sight of land.

'You have been in Elysium?' inquired Proserpine of Tiresias.

'I have been everywhere,' replied the seer, 'and though I am blind have managed to see a great deal more than my fellows.'

'I have often heard of you,' said the Queen, 'and I confess that yours is a career which has much interested me. What vicissitudes in affairs have you not witnessed! And yet you have somehow or other contrived to make your way through all the storms in which others have sunk, and are now, as you always have been, in an exalted position. What can be your magic? I would that you would initiate me. I know that you are a prophet, and that even the Gods consult you.'

'Your Majesty is complimentary. I certainly have had a great deal of experience. My life has no doubt been a long one, but I have made it longer by never losing a moment. I was born, too, at a great crisis in affairs. Everything that took place before the Trojan war passes for nothing in the annals of wisdom. That was a great revolution in all affairs human and divine, and from that event we must now date all our knowledge. Before the Trojan war we used to talk of the rebellion of the Titans, but that business now is an old almanac. As for my powers of prophecy, believe me, that those who understand the past are very well qualified to predict the future. For my success in life, it may be principally ascribed to the observance of a simple rule—I never trust anyone, either God or man. I make an exception in favour of the Goddesses, and especially of your Majesty,' added Tiresias, who piqued himself on his gallantry.

While they were thus conversing, the Queen directed the attention of Manto to a mountainous elevation which now began to rise in the distance, and which, from the rapidity of the tide and the freshness of the breeze, they approached at a swift rate.

'Behold the Stygian mountains,' replied Manto. 'Through their centre runs the passage of Night which leads to the regions of Twilight.'

'We have, then, far to travel?'

'Assuredly it is no easy task to escape from the gloom of Tartarus to the sunbeams of Elysium,' remarked Tiresias; 'but the pleasant is generally difficult; let us be grateful that in our instance it is not, as usual, forbidden.'

'You say truly; I am sorry to confess how very often it appears to me that sin is enjoyment. But see! how awful are these perpendicular heights, piercing the descending vapours, with their peaks clothed with dark pines! We seem land-locked.'

But the experienced master of the infernal yacht knew well how to steer his charge through the intricate windings of the river, which here, though deep and navigable, became as wild and narrow as a mountain stream; and, as the tide no longer served them, and the wind, from their involved course, was as often against them as in their favour, the crew were obliged to have recourse to their oars, and rowed along until they arrived at the mouth of an enormous cavern, from which the rapid stream apparently issued.

'I am frightened out of my wits,' exclaimed Proserpine. 'Surely this cannot be our course?'

'I hold, from your Majesty's exclamation,' said Tiresias, 'that we have arrived at the passage of Night. When we have proceeded some hundred yards, we shall reach the adamantine portals. I pray your Majesty be not alarmed. I alone have the signet which can force these mystic gates to open. I must be stirring myself. What, ho! Manto.'

'Here am I, father. Hast thou the seal?'

'In my breast. I would not trust it to my secretaries. They have my portfolios full of secret despatches, written on purpose to deceive them; for I know that they are spies in the pay of Minerva; but your Majesty perceives, with a little prudence, that even a traitor may be turned to account.'

Thus saying, Tiresias, leaning on Manto, hobbled to the poop of the vessel, and exclaiming aloud, 'Behold the mighty seal of Dis, whereon is inscribed the word the Titans fear,' the gates immediately flew open, revealing the gigantic form of the Titan Porphyrion, whose head touched the vault of the mighty cavern, although he was up to his waist in the waters of the river.

'Come, my noble Porphyrion,' said Tiresias, 'bestir thyself, I beseech thee. I have brought thee a Queen. Guide her Majesty, I entreat thee, with safety through this awful passage of Night.'

'What a horrible creature,' whispered Proserpine. 'I wonder you address him with such courtesy.'

'I am always courteous,' replied Tiresias. 'How know I that the Titans may not yet regain their lost heritage? They are terrible fellows; and ugly or not, I have no doubt that even your Majesty would not find them so ill-favoured were they seated in the halls of Olympus.'

'There is something in that,' replied Proserpine. 'I almost wish I were once more in Tartarus.'

The Titan Porphyrion in the meantime had fastened a chain-cable to the vessel, which he placed over his shoulder, and turning his back to the crew, then wading through the waters, he dragged on the vessel in its course. The cavern widened, the waters spread. To the joy of Proserpine, apparently, she once more beheld the moon and stars.

'Bright crescent of Diana!' exclaimed the enraptured Queen, 'and ye too, sweet stars, that I have so often watched on the Sicilian plains; do I, then, indeed again behold you? or is it only some exquisite vision that entrances my being? for, indeed, I do not feel the freshness of that breeze that was wont to renovate my languid frame; nor does the odorous scent of flowers wafted from the shores delight my jaded senses. What is it? Is it life or death; earth, indeed, or hell?'

''Tis nothing,' said Tiresias, 'but a great toy. You must know that Saturn—until at length, wearied by his ruinous experiments, the Gods expelled him his empire—was a great dabbler in systems. He was always for making moons brighter than Dian, and lighting the stars by gas; but his systems never worked. The tides rebelled against their mistress, and the stars went out with a horrible stench. This is one of his creations, the most ingenious, though a failure. Jove made it a present to Pluto, who is quite proud of having a sun and stars of his own, and reckons it among the choice treasures of his kingdoms.'

'Poor Saturn! I pity him; he meant well.'

'Very true. He is the paviour of the high-street of Hades. But we cannot afford kings, and especially Gods, to be philosophers. The certainty of misrule is better than the chance of good government; uncertainty makes people restless.'

'I feel very restless myself; I wish we were in Elysium!'

'The river again narrows!' exclaimed Manto. 'There is no other portal to pass. The Saturnian moon and stars grow fainter, there is a grey tint expanding in the distance; 'tis the realm of Twilight; your Majesty will soon disembark.'

## PART III.

### I.

*Containing an account of Tiresias at his Rubber.*

TRAVELLERS who have left their homes generally grow mournful as the evening draws on; nor is there, perhaps, any time at which the pensive influence of twilight is more predominant than on the eve that follows a separation from those we love. Imagine, then, the feelings of the Queen of Hell, as her barque entered the very region of that mystic light, and the shadowy shores of the realm of Twilight opened before her. Her thoughts reverted to Pluto; and she mused over all his fondness, all his adoration, and all his indulgence, and the infinite solicitude of his affectionate heart, until the tears trickled down her beautiful cheeks, and she marvelled she ever could have quitted the arms of her lover.

'Your Majesty,' observed Manto, who had been whispering to Tiresias, 'feels, perhaps, a little wearied?'

'By no means, my kind Manto,' replied Proserpine, starting from her reverie. 'But the truth is, my spirits are unequal; and though I really cannot well fix upon the cause of their present depression, I am apparently not free from the contagion of the surrounding gloom.'

'It is the evening air,' said Tiresias. 'Your Majesty had perhaps better re-enter the pavilion of the yacht. As for myself, I never venture about after sunset. One grows romantic. Night was evidently made for in-door nature. I propose a rubber.'

To this popular suggestion Proserpine was pleased to accede, and herself and Tiresias, Manto and the captain of the yacht, were soon engaged at the proposed amusement.

Tiresias loved a rubber. It was true he was blind, but then, being a prophet, that did not signify. Tiresias, I say, loved a rubber, and was a first-rate player, though, perhaps, given a little too much to *finesse*. Indeed, he so much enjoyed taking in his fellow-creatures, that he sometimes could not resist deceiving his own partner. Whist is a game which requires no ordinary combination of qualities; at the same time, memory and invention, a daring fancy, and a cool head. To a mind like that of Tiresias, a pack of cards was full of human nature. A rubber was a microcosm; and he ruffed his adversary's king, or brought in a long suit of his own with as much dexterity and as much enjoyment as, in the real business of existence, he dethroned a monarch, or introduced a dynasty.

'Will your Majesty be pleased to draw your card?' requested the sage. 'If I might venture to offer your Majesty a hint, I would dare to recommend your Majesty not to play before your turn. My friends are fond of ascribing my success in my various missions to the possession of peculiar qualities. No such thing: I owe everything to the simple habit of always waiting till it is my turn to speak. And believe me, that he who plays before his turn at whist, commits as great a blunder as he who speaks before his turn during a negotiation.'

'The trick, and two by honours,' said Proserpine. 'Pray, my dear Tiresias, you who are such a fine player, how came you to trump my best card?'

'Because I wanted the lead. And those who want to lead, please your Majesty, must never hesitate about sacrificing their friends.'

'I believe you speak truly. I was right in playing that thirteenth card?'

'Quite so. Above all things, I love a thirteenth card. I send it forth, like a mock project in a revolution, to try the strength of parties.'

'You should not have forced me, Lady Manto,' said the Captain of the yacht, in a grumbling tone, to his partner.

z

'By weakening me, you prevented me bringing in my spades. We might have made the game.'

'You should not have been forced,' said Tiresias. 'If she made a mistake, who was unacquainted with your plans, what a terrible blunder you committed to share her error without her ignorance!'

'What, then, was I to lose a trick?'

'Next to knowing when to seize an opportunity,' replied Tiresias, 'the most important thing in life is to know when to forego an advantage.'

'I have cut you an honour, sir,' said Manto.

'Which reminds me,' replied Tiresias, 'that, in the last hand, your Majesty unfortunately forgot to lead through your adversary's ace. I have often observed that nothing ever perplexes an adversary so much as an appeal to his honour.'

'I will not forget to follow your advice,' said the Captain of the yacht, playing accordingly.

'By which you have lost the game,' quietly remarked Tiresias. 'There are exceptions to all rules, but it seldom answers to follow the advice of an opponent.'

Confusion!' exclaimed the Captain of the yacht.

'Four by honours, and the trick, I declare,' said Proserpine. 'I was so glad to see you turn up the queen, Tiresias.'

'I also, Madam. Without doubt there are few cards better than her royal consort, or, still more, the imperial ace. Nevertheless, I must confess, I am perfectly satisfied whenever I remember that I have the Queen on my side.'

Proserpine bowed.

## II.

*Containing a Visit from a liberal Queen to a dethroned Monarch; and a Conversation between them respecting the 'Spirit of the Age.'*

'I have a good mind to do it, Tiresias,' said Queen Proserpine, as that worthy sage paid his compliments to her at her toilet, at an hour which should have been noon.

'It would be a great compliment,' said Tiresias.

'And it is not much out of our way?'

'By no means,' replied the secr. ''Tis an agreeable half-way house. He lives in good style.'

'And whence can a dethroned monarch gain a revenue?' inquired the Queen.

'Your Majesty, I see, is not at all learned in politics. A sovereign never knows what an easy income is till he has abdicated. He generally commences squabbling with his subjects about the supplies; he is then expelled, and voted, as compensation, an amount about double the sum which was the cause of the original quarrel.'

'What do you think, Manto?' said Proserpine, as that lady entered the cabin; 'we propose paying a visit to Saturn. He has fixed his residence, you know, in these regions of twilight.'

'I love a junket,' replied Manto, 'above all things. And, indeed, I was half frightened out of my wits at the bare idea of toiling over this desert. All is prepared, please your Majesty, for our landing. Your Majesty's litter is quite ready.'

''Tis well,' said Proserpine; and leaning on the arm of Manto, the Queen came upon deck, and surveyed the surrounding country, a vast grey flat, with a cloudless sky of the same tint: in the distance some lowering shadows, which seemed like clouds but were in fact mountains.

'Some half-dozen hours,' said Tiresias, 'will bring us to the palace of Saturn. We shall arrive for dinner; the right hour. Let me recommend your Majesty to order the curtains of your litter to be drawn, and, if possible, to resume your dreams.'

'They were not pleasant,' said Proserpine, 'I dreamt of my mother and the Parcæ. Manto, methinks I'll read. Hast thou some book?'

'Here is a poem, Madam, but I fear it may induce those very slumbers you dread.'

'How call you it?'

'"The Pleasures of Oblivion." The poet apparently is fond of his subject.'

'And is, I have no doubt, equal to it. Hast any prose?'

'An historical novel or so.'

'Oh! if you mean those things as full of costume as a fancy ball, and almost as devoid of sense, I'll have none of them. Close the curtains; even visions of the Furies are preferable to these insipidities.'

The halt of the litter roused the Queen from her slumbers. 'We have arrived,' said Manto, as she assisted in withdrawing the curtains.

The train had halted before a vast propylon of rose-coloured granite. The gate was nearly two hundred feet in height, and the sides of the propylon, which rose like huge moles, were sculptured with colossal figures of a threatening aspect. Passing through the propylon, the Queen of Hell and her attendants entered an avenue in length about three-quarters of a mile, formed of colossal figures of the same character and substance, alternately raising in their arms javelins or battle-axes, as if about to strike. At the end of this heroic avenue appeared the palace of Saturn. Ascending a hundred steps of black marble, you stood before a portico supported by twenty columns of the same material and shading a single portal of bronze. Apparently the palace formed an immense quadrangle; a vast tower rising from each corner, and springing from the centre a huge and hooded dome. A crowd of attendants, in grey and sad-coloured raiment, issued from the portal of the palace at the approach of Proserpine, who remarked with strange surprise their singular countenances and demeanour; for rare in this silent assemblage was any visage resembling aught she had seen, human or divine. Some bore the heads of bats; of owls and beetles others; some fluttered moth-like wings, while the shoulders of other bipeds were surmounted, in spite of their human organisation, with the heads of rats and weasels, of marten-cats and of foxes. But they were all remarkably civil; and Proserpine, who was now used to wonders, did not shriek at all, and scarcely shuddered.

The Queen of Hell was ushered through a superb hall, and down a splendid gallery, to a suite of apartments where a body of damsels of a most distinguished appearance

awaited her. Their heads resembled those of the most
eagerly-sought, highly-prized, and oftenest-stolen lap-dogs.
Upon the shoulders of one was the visage of the smallest
and most thorough-bred little Blenheim in the world.
Upon her front was a white star, her nose was nearly flat,
and her ears were tied under her chin, with the most jaunty
air imaginable. She was an evident flirt; and a solemn
prude of a spaniel, with a black and tan countenance, who
seemed a sort of duenna, evidently watched her with no
little distrust. The admirers of blonde beauties would,
however, have fallen in love with a poodle, with the finest
head of hair imaginable, and most voluptuous shoulders.
This brilliant band began barking in the most insinuating
tone on the appearance of the Queen; and Manto, who was
almost as dexterous a linguist as Tiresias himself, informed
her Majesty that these were the ladies of her bedchamber;
upon which Proserpine, who, it will be remembered, had no
passion for dogs, ordered them immediately out of her
room.

'What a droll place!' exclaimed the Queen. 'Do you
know we are later than I imagined? A hasty toilet to-day;
I long to see Saturn. It is droll, I am hungry. My purple
velvet, I think; it may be considered a compliment. No
diamonds, only jet; a pearl or two, perhaps. Didst ever see
the King? They say he is gentlemanlike, though a bigot.
No! no rouge to-day; this paleness is quite *apropos*. Were
I as radiant as usual, I should be taken for Aurora.'

So leaning on Manto, and preceded by the ladies of her
bed-chamber, whom, notwithstanding their repulse, she
found in due attendance in the antechamber, Proserpine
again continued her progress down the gallery, until they
stopped at a door, which opening, she was ushered into the
grand circular saloon, crowned by the dome, whose exterior
the Queen had already observed. The interior of this
apartment was entirely of black and grey marble, with the
exception of the dome itself, which was of ebony, richly
carved, and supported by more than a hundred columns.
There depended from the centre of the arch a single chan-

delier of frosted silver, which was itself as big as an ordinary chamber, but of the most elegant form, and delicate and fantastic workmanship. As the Queen entered the saloon, a personage of venerable appearance, dressed in a suit of black velvet, and leaning on an ivory cane, advanced to salute her. There was no mistaking this personage; his manners were at once so courteous and so dignified. He was clearly their host; and Proserpine, who was quite charmed with his grey locks and his black velvet cap, his truly paternal air, and the beneficence of his unstudied smile, could scarcely refrain from bending her knee, and pressing her lips to his extended hand.

'I am proud that your Majesty has remembered me in my retirement,' said Saturn, as he led Proserpine to a seat.

Their mutual compliments were soon disturbed by the announcement of dinner, and Saturn offering his arm to the Queen with an air of politeness which belonged to the old school, but which the ladies admire in old men, handed Proserpine to the banqueting-room. They were followed by some of the principal personages of her Majesty's suite, and a couple of young Titans, who enjoyed the posts of Aides-de-Camp to the ex-King, and whose duties consisted of carving at dinner.

It was a most agreeable dinner, and Proserpine was delighted with Saturn, who, of course, sat by her side, and paid her every possible attention. Saturn, whose manners, as has been observed, were of the old school, loved a good story, and told several. His anecdotes, especially of society previous to the Trojan war, were highly interesting. There ran through all his behaviour, too, a tone of high breeding and of consideration for others which was really charming; and Proserpine, who had expected to find in her host a gloomy bigot, was quite surprised at the truly liberal spirit with which he seemed to consider affairs in general. Indeed this unexpected tone made so great an impression upon her, that finding a good opportunity after dinner, when they were sipping their coffee apart from the rest of the company, she could not refrain from entering into some conversation with the ex-King upon the subject, and the conversation ran thus:

'Do you know,' said Proserpine, 'that much as I have been pleased and surprised during my visit to the realms of twilight, nothing has pleased, and I am sure nothing has surprised me more, than to observe the remarkably liberal spirit in which your Majesty views the affairs of the day.'

'You give me a title, beautiful Proserpine, to which I have no claim,' replied Saturn. 'You forget that I am now only Count Hesperus; I am no longer a king, and believe me, I am very glad of it.'

'What a pity, my dear sir, that you would not condescend to conform to the Spirit of the age. For myself, I am quite a reformer.'

'So I have understood, beautiful Proserpine, which I confess has a little surprised me; for to tell you the truth, I do not consider that reform is exactly *our* trade.'

'Affairs cannot go on as they used,' observed Proserpine, oracularly; 'we must bow to the Spirit of the age.'

'And what is that?' inquired Saturn.

'I do not exactly know,' replied Proserpine, 'but one hears of it everywhere.'

'I also heard of it a great deal,' replied Saturn, 'and was also recommended to conform to it. Before doing so, however, I thought it as well to ascertain its nature, and something also of its strength.'

'It is terribly strong,' observed Proserpine.

'But you think it will be stronger?' inquired the ex-King.

'Certainly; every day it is more powerful.'

'Then if, on consideration, we were to deem resistance to it advisable, it is surely better to commence the contest at once than to postpone the struggle.'

'It is useless to talk of resisting; one must conform.'

'I certainly should consider resistance useless,' replied Saturn, 'for I tried it and failed; but at least one has a chance of success; and yet, having resisted this spirit and failed, I should not consider myself in a worse plight than you would voluntarily place yourself in by conforming to it.'

'You speak riddles,' said Proserpine.

'To be plain, then,' replied Saturn, 'I think you may as well at once give up your throne, as conform to this spirit.'

'And why so?' inquired Proserpine very ingenuously.'

'Because,' replied Saturn, shrugging up his shoulders, 'I look upon the Spirit of the age as a spirit hostile to Kings and Gods.'

III.

*Containing the Titans; or a View of a subverted Faction.*

The next morning Saturn himself attended his beautiful guest over his residence, which Proserpine greatly admired. ''Tis the work of the Titans,' replied the ex-King. 'There never was a party so fond of building palaces.'

'To speak the truth,' said Proserpine, 'I am a little disappointed that I have not had an opportunity, during my visit, of becoming acquainted with some of the chiefs of that celebrated party; for, although a Liberal, I am a female one, and I like to know every sort of person who is distinguished.'

'The fact is,' replied her host, 'that the party has never recovered from the thunderbolt of that scheming knave Jupiter, and do not bear their defeat so philosophically as years, perhaps, permit me to do. If we have been vanquished by the Spirit of the age,' continued Saturn, 'you must confess that, in our case, the conqueror did not assume a material form very remarkable for its dignity. Had Creation resolved itself into its original elements, had Chaos come again, or even old Cœlus, the indignity might have been endured; but to be baffled by an Olympian *juste milieu*, and to find, after all the clamour, that nothing has been changed save the places, is, you will own, somewhat mortifying.'

'But how do you reconcile,' inquired the ingenuous Proserpine, 'the success of Jupiter with the character which you ascribed last night to the Spirit of the age?'

'Why, in truth,' said Saturn, 'had I not entirely freed myself from all party feeling, I might adduce the success of my perfidious and worthless relative as very good demonstration that the Spirit of the age is nothing better than an *ignis fatuus*. Nevertheless, we must discriminate. Even the success of Jupiter, although he now conducts himself in direct opposition to the emancipating principles he at first professed, is no less good evidence of their force; for by his professions he rose. And, for my part, I consider it a great homage to public opinion to find every scoundrel now-a-days professing himself a Liberal.'

'You are candid,' said Proserpine. 'I should like very much to see the Titans.'

'My friends are at least consistent,' observed Saturn; 'though certainly at present I can say little more for them. Between the despair of one section of the party, and the over-sanguine expectations of the other, they are at present quite inactive, or move only to ensure fresh rebuffs.'

'You see little of them, then?'

'They keep to themselves: they generally frequent a lonely vale in the neighbourhood.'

'I should so like to see them!' exclaimed Proserpine.

'Say nothing to Tiresias,' said old Saturn, who was half in love with his fair friend, 'and we will steal upon them unperceived.' So saying, the God struck the earth with his cane, and there instantly sprang forth a convenient car, built of curiously carved cedar, and borne by four enormous tawny-coloured owls. Seating himself by the side of the delighted Proserpine, Saturn commanded the owls to bear them to the Valley of Lamentations.

'Twas an easy fly: the chariot soon descended upon the crest of a hill: and Saturn and Proserpine, leaving the car, commenced, by a winding path, the slight ascent of a superior elevation. Having arrived there, they looked down upon a valley, apparently land-locked by black and barren mountains of the most strange, although picturesque forms.

In the centre of the valley was a black pool or tarn, bordered with dark purple flags of an immense size, twining and twisting among which might be observed the glancing and gliding folds of several white serpents; while crocodiles and alligators, and other horrible forms, poked their foul snouts with evident delight in a vast mass of black slime, which had, at various times, exuded from the lake. A single tree only was to be observed in this desolate place, an enormous and blasted cedar, with scarcely a patch of verdure, but extending its black and barren branches nearly across the valley. Seated on a loosened crag, but leaning against the trunk of the cedar, with his arms folded, his mighty eyes fixed on the ground, and his legs crossed with that air of complete repose which indicates that their owner is in no hurry again to move them, was

> 'A form, some granite god we deemed,
> Or king of palmy Nile, colossal shapes
> Such as Syene's rosy quarries yield
> To Memphian art; Horus, Osiris called,
> Or Amenoph, who, on the Theban plain,
> With magic melody the sun salutes;
> Or he, far mightier, to whose conquering car
> Monarchs were yoked, Rameses: by the Greeks
> Sesostris styled. And yet no sculptor's art
> Moulded this shape, for form it seemed of flesh,
> Yet motionless; its dim unlustrous orbs
> Gazing in stilly vacancy, its cheek
> Grey as its hairs, which, thin as they might seem,
> No breath disturbed; a solemn countenance,
> Not sorrowful, though full of woe sublime,
> As if despair were now a distant dream
> Too dim for memory.'

' 'Tis their great leader,' said Saturn, as he pointed out the Titan to Proserpine, ' the giant Enceladus. He got us into all our scrapes, but I must do him the justice to add, that he is the only one who can ever get us out of them. They say he has no heart; but I think his hook nose is rather fine.'

'Superb!' said Proserpine. 'And who is that radiant and golden-haired youth who is seated at his feet?'

' 'Tis no less a personage than Hyperion himself,' replied

Saturn, 'the favourite counsellor of Enceladus. He is a fine orator, and makes up by his round sentences and choice phrases for the rhetorical deficiencies of his chief, who, to speak the truth, is somewhat curt and husky. They have enough now to do to manage their comrades and keep a semblance of discipline in their routed ranks. Mark that ferocious Briareus there scowling in a corner! Didst ever see such a moustache! He glances, methinks, with an evil eye on the mighty Enceladus; and, let me tell you, Briareus has a great following among them; so they say of him you know, that he hath fifty heads and a hundred arms. See! how they gather around him.'

'Who speaks now to Briareus?'

'The young and valiant Mimas. Be assured he is counselling war. We shall have a debate now.'

'Yon venerable personage, who is seated by the margin of the pool, and weeping with the crocodiles——'

'Is old Oceanus.'

'He is apparently much affected by his overthrow.'

'It is his wont to weep. He used to cry when he fought, and yet he was a powerful warrior.'

'Hark!' said Proserpine.

The awful voice of Briareus broke the silence. What a terrible personage was Briareus! His wild locks hung loose about his shoulders, and blended with his unshorn beard.

'Titans!' shouted the voice which made many a heart tremble, and the breathless Proserpine clasp the arm of Saturn. 'Titans! Is that spirit dead that once heaped Ossa upon Pelion? Is it forgotten, even by ourselves, that a younger born revels in our heritage? Are these forms that surround me, indeed, the shapes at whose dread sight the base Olympians fled to their fitting earth? Warriors, whose weapons were the rocks, whose firebrands were the burning woods, is the day forgotten when Jove himself turned craven, and skulked in Egypt? At least my memory is keen enough to support my courage, and whatever the dread Enceladus may counsel, my voice is still for war!'

There ensued, after this harangue of Briareus, a profound and thrilling silence, which was, however, broken in due time by the great leader of the Titans himself.

'You mouth it well, Briareus,' replied Enceladus calmly. 'And if great words would re-seat us in Olympus, doubtless, with your potent aid, we might succeed. It never should be forgotten, however, that had we combined at first, in the spirit now recommended, the Olympians would never have triumphed; and least of all our party should Briareus and his friends forget the reasons of our disunion.'

'I take thy sneer, Enceladus,' said the young and chivalric Mimas, 'and throw it in thy teeth. This learn, then, from Briareus and his friends, that if we were lukewarm in the hour of peril, the fault lies not to our account, but with those who had previously so conducted themselves, that, when the danger arrived, it was impossible for us to distinguish between our friends and our foes. Enceladus apparently forgets that had the Olympians never been permitted to enter Heaven, it would have been unnecessary ever to have combined against their machinations.'

'Recrimination is useless,' said a Titan, interposing. 'I was one of those who supported Enceladus in the admission of the Olympians above, and I regret it. But at the time, like others, I believed it to be the only mode of silencing the agitation of Jupiter.'

'I separated from Enceladus on that question,' said a huge Titan, lying his length on the ground and leaning one arm on a granite crag; 'but I am willing to forget all our differences and support him with all my heart and strength in another effort to restore our glorious constitution.'

'Titans,' said Enceladus, 'who is there among you who has found me a laggard in the day of battle? When the Olympians, as Briareus thinks it necessary to remind you, fled, I was your leader. Remember, however, then, that there were no thunderbolts. As for myself, I candidly confess to you, that, since the invention of these weapons by Jove, I do not see how war can be carried on by us any longer with effect."

'By the memory of old Cœlus and these fast-flowing tears,' murmured the venerable Oceanus, patting at the same time a crocodile on the back, 'I call you all to witness that I have no interest to deceive you. Nevertheless, we should not forget that, in this affair of the thunderbolts, it is the universal opinion that there is a very considerable re-action. I have myself, only within these few days, received authentic information that several have fallen of late without any visible ill effects; and I am credibly assured that, during the late storm in Thessaly, a thunderbolt was precipitated into the centre of a vineyard, without affecting the flavour of a single grape.'

Here several of the Titans, who had gathered round Enceladus, shook their heads and shrugged their shoulders, and a long and desultory conversation ensued upon the copious and very controversial subject of Re-action. In the meantime Rhœtus, a young Titan, whispered to one of his companions, that for his part he was convinced that the only way to beat the Olympians was to turn them into ridicule; and that he would accordingly commence at once with the pasquinade on the private life of Jupiter, and some peculiarly delicate criticisms on the characters of the Goddesses.

## PART IV.

#### I.

*Containing the first View of Elysium.*

THE toilsome desert was at length passed, and the royal cavalcade ascended the last chasm of mountains that divided Elysium, or the Regions of Bliss, from the Realm of Twilight. As she quitted those dim and dreary plains, the spirit of Proserpine grew lighter, and she indulged in silent but agreeable anticipations of the scene which she was now approaching. On reaching, however, the summit of the mountainous chain, and proceeding a short distance over the rugged table-land into which it now declined, her Majesty was rather alarmed at perceiving that her progress was impeded by a shower of flame that extended, on either side, as far as the eye could reach. Her alarm, however, was of short continuance; for, on the production of his talisman by Tiresias, the shower of flame instantly changed into silvery drops of rose-water and other delicious perfumes. Amid joyous peals of laughter, and some slight playful screams on the part of the ladies, the cavalcade ventured through the ordeal. Now the effect of this magical bath was quite marvellous. A burthen seemed suddenly to have been removed from the spirits of the whole party; their very existence seemed renewed; the blood danced about their veins in the liveliest manner imaginable; and a wild but pleasing titillation ran like lightning through their nerves. Their countenances sparkled with excitement; and they all talked at the same time. Proserpine was so occupied with her own sensations, that she did not immediately remark the extraordinary change that had occurred in the appearance of the country immediately on passing this magical barrier. She perceived that their course now led over the most elastic and carefully-shaven turf; groups of beautiful shrubs occasionally appeared, and she discovered with delight that their flowers constantly opened, and sent forth from their bells diminutive birds of radiant plumage. Above them, too, the clouds vanished, and her head was canopied by a sky, unlike, indeed, all things and tints of earth, but which reminded her, in some degree, of the splendour of Olympus.

Proserpine, restless with delight, quitted her litter, and followed by Manto, ran forward to catch the first view of Elysium.

'I am quite out of breath,' said her Majesty, 'and really must sit down on this bank of violets. Was ever anything in the world so delightful! Why, Olympus is nothing to it! And after Tartarus, too, and that poor unhappy Saturn, and his Titans and his twilight, it really is too much for me. How I do long for the view! and yet, somehow or other, my heart beats so I cannot walk.'

'Will your Majesty re-ascend your litter?' suggested Manto.

'Oh, no! that is worse than anything. They are a mile behind; they are so slow. Why, Manto! what is this?'

A beautiful white dove hovered in the air over the head of Proserpine and her attendant, and then dropping an olive branch into the lap of the Queen, flapped its wings and whirled away. But what an olive branch! the stem was of agate; each leaf was an emerald; and on the largest, in letters of brilliants, was this inscription:

*The Elysians to their beautiful Queen.*

'Oh, is it not superb?' exclaimed Proserpine. 'What charming people, and what excellent subjects! What loyalty and what taste!'

So saying, the enraptured Proserpine rose from the bank of violets, and had scarcely run forwards fifty yards when she suddenly stopped, and started with an exclamation of wonder. The table-land had ceased. She stood upon a precipice of white marble, in many parts clothed with thick bowers of myrtle; before her extended the wide-spreading plains of Elysium. They were bounded upon all sides by gentle elevations entirely covered with flowers, and occasionally shooting forward into the champaign country; behind these appeared a range of mountains clothed with bright green forests, and still loftier heights behind them, exhibiting, indeed, only bare and sharply-pointed peaks glittering with prismatic light. The undulating plain was studded in all directions with pavilions and pleasure-houses, and groves and gardens glowing with the choicest and most charming fruit; and a broad blue river wound through it, covered with brilliant boats, the waters flashing with phosphoric light as they were cut by the swift and gliding keels. And in the centre of the plain rose a city, a mighty group of all that was beautiful in form and costly in materials, bridges and palaces and triumphal gates of cedar and of marble, columns and minarets of gold, and cupolas and domes of ivory; and over and anon appeared delicious gardens, raised on the terraces of the houses; and groups of palm trees with their tall, thin stems, and quivering and languid crests, rose amid the splendid masonry. A sweet soft breeze touched the cheek of the entranced Proserpine, and a single star of silver light glittered in the rosy sky.

'''Tis my favourite hour,' exclaimed Proserpine. 'Thus have I gazed upon Hesperus in the meads of Enna! What a scene! How fortunate that we should have arrived at sunset!'

'Ah, Madam!' observed Manto, 'in Elysium the sky is ever thus. For the Elysians, the sun seems always to have just set!'

'Fortunate people!' replied Proserpine. 'In them, immortality and enjoyment seem indeed blended together. A strange feeling, half of languor, half of voluptuousness, steals over my senses! It seems that I at length behold the region of my girlish dreams. Such once I fancied Olympus. Ah! why does not my Pluto live in Elysium?'

II.

*Containing some account of the Manners of the Elysians, and of the Palace of Proserpine, and her strange Dream.*

THE Elysians consisted of a few thousand beatified mortals, the only occupation of whose existence was enjoyment; the rest of the population comprised some millions of Gnomes and Sylphs, who did nothing but work, and ensured by their labour the felicity of the superior class. Every Elysian, male or female, possessed a magnificent palace in the city, and an elegant pavilion on the plain; these, with a due proportion of chariots, horses, and slaves, constituted a proper establishment. The Sylphs and the Gnomes were either scattered about the country, which they cultivated, or lived in the city, where they kept shops, and where they emulated each other in displaying the most ingenious articles of luxury and convenience for the enjoyment and accommodation of the Elysians. The townspeople, indeed, rather affected to look down upon the more simple-minded agriculturists; but if these occasionally felt a little mortification in consequence, they might have been consoled, had they been aware that their brethren and sisters who were in the service of the Elysians avenged their insults, for these latter were the finest Gnomes and Sylphs imaginable, and scarcely deigned to notice any one who was in trade. Whether there were any coin or other circulating medium current in Elysium is a point respecting which I must confess I have not sufficient information to decide; but if so, it certainly would appear that all money transactions were confined to the Gnomes and the Sylphs, for the Elysians certainly never paid for anything. Perhaps this exemption might have been among their peculiar privileges, and was a substitute for what we call credit, a convenience of which the ancients appear to have had a limited conception. The invention, by Jupiter, of an aristocratic immortality, as a reward for a well-spent life on earth, appears to have been an ingenious idea. It really is a reward, very stimulative of good conduct before we shuffle off the mortal coil, and remarkably contrasts with the democracy of the damned. The Elysians, with a splendid climate, a teeming soil, and a nation made on purpose to wait upon them, of course enjoyed themselves very much. The arts flourished, the theatres paid, and they had a much finer opera than at Ephesus or at Halicarnassus. Their cookery was so refined, that one of the least sentimental ceremonies in the world was not only deprived of all its grossness, but was actually converted into an elegant amusement, and so famous that their artists were even required at Olympus. If their dinners were admirable, which is rare, their assemblies were amusing, which is still more uncommon. All the arts of society were carried to perfection in Elysium; a dull thing was never said, and an awkward thing never done. The Elysians, indeed, being highly refined and gifted, for they comprised in their order the very cream of terrestrial society, were naturally a liberal-minded race of nobles, and capable of appreciating every kind of excellence. If a Gnome or a Sylph, therefore, in any way distinguished themselves; if they sang very well, or acted very well, or if they were at all eminent for any of the other arts of amusement, ay! indeed if the poor devils could do nothing better than write a poem or a novel, they were sure to be noticed by the Elysians, who always bowed to them as they passed by, and sometimes indeed even admitted them into their circles.

Scarcely had the train of Proserpine rejoined her on the brink of the precipice, than they heard the flourish of trumpets near at hand, soon followed by a complete harmony of many instruments. A chorus of sweet voices was next distinguished, growing each instant more loud and clear; and in a few minutes, issuing from a neighbouring grove, came forth a band of heroes and beautiful women, dressed in dazzling raiment, to greet the Queen. A troop of chariots of light and airy workmanship followed, and a crowd of Gnomes and Sylphs singing and playing on various instruments, and dancing with gestures of grace and delicacy. Congratulating the Queen on her arrival in Elysium, and requesting the honour of being permitted to attend her to her palace, they ushered Proserpine and her companions to the chariots, and soon, winding down a gradual declivity, they entered the plain.

If a bird's-eye view of the capital had enchanted Proserpine, the agreeable impression was not diminished, as is generally the case, by her entrance into the city. Never were so much splendour and neatness before combined. Passing through a magnificent arch, Proserpine entered a street of vast and beautiful proportions, lined on each side with palaces of various architecture, painted admirably in fresco, and richly gilt. The road was formed of pounded marbles of various colours, laid down in fanciful patterns, and forming an unrivalled mosaic; it was bounded on each side by a broad causeway of jasper, of a remarkably bright green, clouded with milk-white streaks. This street led to a sumptuous square, forming alone the palace destined for Proserpine. Its several fronts were supported and adorned by ten thousand columns, imitating the palm and the lotus; nor is it possible to conceive anything more light and graceful than the general effect of this stupendous building. Each front was crowned with an immense dome of alabaster, so transparent, that when the palace was illuminated the rosy heaven grew pale, and an effect similar to moonlight was diffused over the canopy of Elysium. And in the centre of the square a Leviathan, carved in white coral, and apparently flouncing in a huge basin of rock crystal, spouted forth from his gills a fountain twelve hundred feet in height; from one gill ascended a stream of delicious wine, which might be tempered, if necessary, by the iced water that issued from the other.

At the approach of the Queen, the gigantic gates of the palace, framed of carved cedar, flew open with a thrilling burst of music, and Proserpine found herself in a hall wherein several hundred persons, who formed her household, knelt in stillness before her. Wearied with her long journey, and all the excitement of the day, Proserpine signified to one of the Elysians in attendance her desire for refreshment and repose. Immediately the household rose, and gracefully bowing retired in silence, while four ladies of the bed-chamber, very different from the dogfaced damsels of the realm of Twilight, advanced with a gracious smile, and each pressing a white hand to her heart, invited her Majesty to accompany them. Twelve beautiful pages in fanciful costume, and each bearing a torch of cinnamon, preceded them, and Proserpine ascended a staircase of turquoise and silver. As she passed along, she caught glimpses of costly galleries, and suites of gorgeous chambers, but she was almost too fatigued to distinguish anything. A confused vision of long lines of white columns, roofs of carved cedar, or ceilings glowing with forms of exquisite beauty, walls covered with lifelike tapestry, or reflecting in their mighty mirrors her own hurrying figure, and her picturesque attendants, alone remained. She rejoiced when she at length arrived in a small chamber, in which preparations evidently denoted that it was intended she should rest. It was a pretty little saloon, brilliantly illuminated, and hung with tapestry depicting a party of nymphs and shepherds feasting in an Arcadian scene. In the middle of the chamber a banquet was prepared, and as Proserpine seated herself, and partook of some of the delicacies which a page immediately presented to her, there arose, from invisible musicians, a joyous and festive strain, which accompanied her throughout her repast. When her Majesty had sufficiently refreshed herself, and as the banquet was removing, the music assumed a softer and more subduing, occasionally even a solemn tone; the tapestry, slowly shifting, at length represented the same characters sunk in repose; the attendants all this time gradually extinguishing the lights, and stealing on tiptoe from the chamber. So that, at last, the music, each moment growing fainter, entirely ceased; the figures on the tapestry were scarcely perceptible by the dim lustre of a single remaining lamp; and the slumbering Proserpine fell back upon her couch.

But the Queen of Hell was not destined to undisturbed repose. A dream descended on her brain, and the dream was terrible and strange. She beheld herself a child, playing, as was her wont, in the gardens of Enna, twining garlands of roses, and chasing butterflies. Suddenly, from a bosky thicket of myrtle, slowly issued forth an immense serpent, dark as night, but with eyes of the most brilliant tint, and approached the daughter of Ceres. The innocent child, ignorant of evil, beheld the monster without alarm. Not only did she neither fly nor shriek, but she even welcomed and caressed the frightful stranger, patted its voluminous back, and admired its sparkling vision. The serpent, fascinated instead of fascinating, licked her feet with his arrowy tongue, and glided about for her diversion in a thousand shapes. Emboldened by its gentleness, the little Proserpine at length even mounted on its back, and rode in triumph among her bowers. Every day the dark serpent issued from the thicket, and every day he found a welcome playmate. Now it came to pass that one day the serpent, growing more bold, induced the young Proserpine to extend her ride beyond the limits of Enna. Night came on, and as it was too late to return, the serpent carried her to a large cave, where it made for her a couch of leaves, and while she slept the affectionate monster kept guard for her protection at the mouth of the cavern. For some reason or other which was not apparent, for in dreams there are always some effects without causes, Proserpine never returned to Enna, but remained and resided with cheerfulness in this cavern. Each morning the serpent went forth alone to seek food for its charge, and regularly returned with a bough in its mouth laden with delicious fruits. One day, during the absence of her guardian, a desire seized Proserpine to quit the cavern, and accordingly she went forth. The fresh air and fragrance of the earth were delightful to her, and she roamed about, unconscious of time, and thoughtless of her return. And as she sauntered along, singing to herself, a beautiful white dove, even the same dove that had welcomed her in the morning on the heights of Elysium, flew before her with its wings glancing in the sunshine. It seemed that the bird wished to attract the attention of the child, so long and so closely did it hover about her; now resting on a branch, as if inviting capture, and then skimming away only to return more swiftly; and occasionally, when for a moment unnoticed, even slightly flapping the rambler with its plume. At length the child was taken with a fancy to catch the bird. But no sooner had she evinced this desire, than the bird, once apparently so anxious to be noticed, seemed resolved to lead her a weary chace; and hours flew away ere Proserpine, panting and exhausted, had captured the beautiful rover and pressed it to her bosom.

It was, indeed, a most beautiful bird, and its possession repaid her for all her exertions. But lo! as she stood, in a wild sylvan scene caressing it, smoothing its soft plumage, and pressing its head to her cheek, she beheld in the distance approaching her the serpent, and she beheld her old friend with alarm. Apparently her misgiving was not without cause. She observed in an instant that the appearance and demeanour of the serpent were greatly changed. It approached her swift as an arrow, its body rolling in the most agitated contortions, its jaws were distended as if to devour her, its eyes flashed fire, its tongue was a forked flame, and its hiss was like a stormy wind. Proserpine shrieked, and the Queen of Hell awoke from her dream.

### III.

*Containing some account of the wonderful Morality of the Elysians. Of Helen and Dido. General Society and Coteries. Characters of Achilles, Amphion, Patroclus and Memnon.*

The next morning the Elysian world called to pay their respects to Proserpine. Her Majesty, indeed, held a drawing-room, which was fully and brilliantly attended. Her beauty and her graciousness were universally pronounced enchanting. From this moment the career of Proserpine was a series of magnificent entertainments. The principal Elysians vied with each other in the splendour and variety of the amusements, which they offered to the notice of their Queen. Operas, plays, balls, and banquets followed in dazzling succession. Proserpine, who was almost inexperienced in society, was quite fascinated. She regretted the years she had wasted in her Sicilian solitude; she marvelled that she ever could have looked forward with delight to a dull annual visit to Olympus; she almost regretted that, for the sake of an establishment, she could have been induced to cast her lot in the regal gloom of Tartarus. Elysium exactly suited her. The beauty of the climate and the country, the total absence of care, the constant presence of amusement, the luxury, gaiety, and refined enjoyment perfectly accorded with her amiable disposition, her lively fancy and her joyous temper. She drank deep and eagerly of the cup of pleasure. She entered into all the gay pursuits of her subjects; she even invented new combinations of diversion. Under her inspiring rule every one confessed that Elysium became every day more Elysian.

The manners of her companions greatly pleased her. She loved those faces always wreathed with smiles, yet never bursting into laughter. She was charmed at the amiable tone in which they addressed each other. Never apparently were people at the same time so agreeable, so obliging, and so polished. For in all they said and did might be detected that peculiar air of high-breeding which pervades the whole conduct of existence with a certain indefinable spirit of calmness, so that your nerves are never shaken by too intense an emotion, which eventually produces a painful reaction. Whatever they did, the Elysians were careful never to be vehement; a grand passion, indeed, was unknown in these happy regions; love assumed the milder form of flirtation; and as for enmity, you were never abused except behind your back, or it exuded itself in an epigram, or, at the worst, a caricature scribbled upon a fan.

There is one characteristic of the Elysians which, in justice to them, I ought not to have omitted. They were eminently a moral people. If a lady committed herself, she was lost for ever, and packed off immediately to the realm of Twilight. Indeed, they were so particular, that the moment one of the softer sex gave the slightest symptoms of preference to a fortunate admirer, the Elysian world immediately began to look unutterable things, shrug its moral shoulders, and elevate its charitable eye-brows. But if the preference, by any unlucky chance, assumed the nobler aspect of devotion, and the unhappy fair one gave any indication of really possessing a heart, rest assured she was already half way on the road to perdition. Then commenced one of the most curious processes imaginable, peculiar I apprehend to Elysium, but which I record that the society of less fortunate lands may avail itself of the advantage, and adopt the regulation in its moral police. Immediately that it was clearly ascertained that two persons of different sexes took an irrational interest in each other's society, all the world instantly went about, actuated by a purely charitable sentiment, telling the most extraordinary falsehoods concerning them that they could devise. Thus it was the fashion to call at one house and announce that you had detected the unhappy pair in a private box at the theatre, and immediately to pay your respects at another mansion and declare that you had observed them on the very same day, and at the very same hour, in a boat on the river. At the next visit, the gentleman had been discovered driving her in his cab; and in the course of the morning the scene of indiscretion was the Park, where they had been watched walking by moonlight, muffled up in sables and cashmeres.

This curious process of diffusing information was known in Elysium under the title of '*being talked about*;' and although the stories thus disseminated were universally understood to be fictions, the Elysians ascribed great virtue to the proceeding, maintaining that many an indiscreet fair one had been providentially alarmed by thus becoming the subject of universal conversation; that thus many a reputation had been saved by this charitable slander. There were some malignant philosophers, indeed, doubtless from that silly love of paradox in all ages too prevalent, who pretended that all this Elysian morality was one great delusion, and that this scrupulous anxiety about the conduct of others arose from a principle, not of *Purity*, but of *Corruption*. The woman who is 'talked about,' these sages would affirm, is generally virtuous, and she is only abused because she devotes to one the charms which all wish to enjoy.

Thus Dido, who is really one of the finest creatures that ever existed, and who with a majestic beauty combines an heroic soul, has made her way with difficulty to the Elysian circle, to which her charms and rank entitle her; while Helen, who, from her very *début*, has been surrounded by fifty lovers, and whose intrigues have ever been notorious, is the very queen of fashion; and all this merely because she has favoured fifty instead of one, and in the midst of all her scrapes has contrived to retain the countenance of her husband.

Apropos of Dido, the Queen of Carthage was the person in all Elysium for whom Proserpine took the greatest liking. Exceedingly beautiful, with the most generous temper and the softest heart in the world, and blessed by nature with a graceful simplicity of manner, which fashion had never sullied, it really was impossible to gaze upon the extraordinary brilliancy of her radiant countenance, to watch the symmetry of her superb figure, and to listen to the artless yet lively observations uttered by a voice musical as a bell, without being fairly bewitched.

When we first enter society, we are everywhere; yet there are few, I imagine, who, after a season, do not subside into a coterie. When the glare of saloons has ceased to dazzle, and we are wearied with the heartless notice of a crowd, we require refinement and sympathy. We find them, and we sink into a clique. And after all, can the river of life flow on more agreeably than in a sweet course of pleasure with those we love? To wander in the green shade of secret woods and whisper our affection; to float on the sunny waters of some gentle stream, and listen to a serenade; to canter with a light-hearted cavalcade over breezy downs, or cool our panting chargers in the summer stillness of winding and woody lanes; to banquet with the beautiful and the witty; to send care to the devil, and indulge the whim of the moment; the priest, the warrior, and the statesman may frown and struggle as they like; but this is existence, and this, this is Elysium!

So Proserpine deemed when, wearied with the monotony of the great world, she sought refuge in the society of Dido and Atalanta, Achilles, Amphion, and Patroclus or Memnon. When Æneas found that Dido had become fashionable, he made overtures for a reconciliation, but Dido treated him with calm contempt. The pious Æneas, indeed, was the aversion of Proserpine. He was the head of the Elysian saints, was president of a society to induce the Gnomes only to drink water, and was so horrified at the general conduct of the Elysians, that he questioned the decrees of Minos and Rhadamanthus, who had permitted them to enter the happy region so easily. The pious Æneas was of opinon that everybody ought to have been damned except himself. Proserpine gave him no encouragement. Achilles was the finest gentleman in Elysium. No one dressed or rode like him. He was very handsome, very witty, very unaffected, and had an excellent heart. Achilles was the leader of the Elysian youth, who were indeed devoted to him: Proserpine took care, therefore, that he should dangle in her train. Amphion had a charming voice for a supper after the opera. He was a handsome little fellow, but not to be depended upon. He broke a heart, or a dinner engagement, with the same reckless sentimentality; for he was one of those who always weep when they betray you, and whom you are sure never to see again immediately that they have vowed eternal friendship. Patroclus was a copy of Achilles without his talents and vivacity, but elegant and quiet. Of all these, Memnon was perhaps the favourite of Proserpine; nor must he be forgotten; amiable, gay, brilliant, the child of whim and impulse, in love with every woman he met for four-and-twenty hours, and always marvelling at his own delusion!

# POPANILLA.

# ADVERTISEMENT.

This narrative of an imaginary voyage was first published in 1827.

*Captain Popanilla a brilliant satire on the manners and customs of the times, scene of the adventures the Isle of Fantaisie (Ireland) Vraibleusia (England) the capital of which is the city of Hubbub (London) a —*

# POPANILLA.

## CHAPTER I.

There is an island in the Indian Ocean, so unfortunate as not yet to have been visited either by Discovery Ships or Missionary Societies. It is a place where all those things are constantly found which men most desire to see, and with the sight of which they are seldom favoured. It abounds in flowers, and fruit, and sunshine. Lofty mountains, covered with green and mighty forests, except where the red rocks catch the fierce beams of the blazing sun, bowery valleys, broad lakes, gigantic trees, and gushing rivers bursting from rocky gorges, are crowned with a purple and ever cloudless sky. Summer, in its most unctuous state and most mellow majesty, is here perpetual. So intense and overpowering, in the daytime, is the rich union of heat and perfume, that living animal or creature is never visible; and were you and I to pluck, before sunset, the huge fruit from yonder teeming tree, we might fancy ourselves for the moment the future sinners of another Eden. Yet a solitude it is not.

The island is surrounded by a calm and blue lagoon, formed by a ridge of coral rocks, which break the swell of the ocean, and prevent the noxious spray from banishing the rich shrubs which grow even to the water's edge. It is a few minutes before sunset, that the first intimation of animal existence in this seeming solitude is given, by the appearance of mermaids; who, floating on the rosy sea, congregate about these rocks. They sound a loud but melodious chorus from their sea-shells, and a faint and distant chorus soon answers from the island. The mermaidens immediately repeat their salutations, and are greeted with a nearer and a louder answer. As the red and rayless sun drops into the glowing waters, the choruses simultaneously join; and rushing from the woods, and down the mountain steeps to the nearest shore, crowds of human beings, at the same moment, appear and collect.

The inhabitants of this island, in form and face, do not misbecome the clime and the country. With the vivacity of a Faun, the men combine the strength of a Hercules and the beauty of an Adonis; and, as their more interesting companions flash upon his presence, the least classical of poets might be excused for imagining that, like their blessed Goddess, the women had magically sprung from the brilliant foam of that ocean which is gradually subsiding before them.

But sunset in this land is not the signal merely for the evidence of human existence. At the moment that the Islanders, crowned with flowers, and waving goblets and garlands, burst from their retreats, upon each mountain peak a lion starts forward, stretches his proud tail, and, bellowing to the sun, scours back exulting to his forest; immense bodies, which before would have been mistaken for the trunks of trees, now move into life, and serpents, untwining their green and glittering folds, and slowly bending their crested heads around, seem proudly conscious of a voluptuous existence; troops of monkeys leap from tree to tree; panthers start forward, and alarmed, not alarming, instantly vanish; a herd of milk-white elephants tramples over the back-ground of the scene; and instead of gloomy owls and noxious beetles, to hail the long-enduring twilight, from the bell of every opening flower beautiful birds, radiant with every rainbow tint, rush with a long and living melody into the cool air.

The twilight in this island is not that transient moment of unearthly bliss, which, in our less favoured regions, always leaves us so thoughtful and so sad; on the contrary, it lasts many hours, and consequently the Islanders are neither moody nor sorrowful. As they sleep during the day, four or five hours of 'tipsy dance and revelry' are exercise and not fatigue. At length, even in this delightful region, the rosy tint fades into purple, and the purple into blue; the white moon gleams, and at length glitters; and the invisible stars first creep into light, and then blaze into radiancy. But no hateful dews discolour their loveliness! and so clear is the air, that instead of the false appearance of a studded vault, the celestial bodies may be seen floating in œther, at various distances and of various tints. Ere the showery fire-flies have ceased to shine, and the blue lights to play about the tremulous horizon, amid the voices of a thousand birds, the dancers solace themselves with the rarest fruits, the most delicate fish, and the most delicious wines; but flesh they love not. They are an innocent and a happy, though a voluptuous and ignorant race. They have no manufactures, no commerce, no agriculture, and no printing-presses; but for their slight clothing they wear the bright skins of serpents; for corn, Nature gives them the bread-fruit; and for intellectual amusement, they have a pregnant fancy and a ready wit; tell inexhaustible stories, and always laugh at each other's jokes. A natural instinct gave them the art of making wine; and it was the same benevolent Nature that blessed them also with the knowledge of the art of making love. But time flies even here. The lovely companions have danced, and sung, and banqueted, and laughed; what further bliss remains for man? They rise, and in pairs wander about the island, and then to their bowers; their life ends with the Night they love so well; and ere Day, the everlasting conqueror, wave his flaming standard in the luminous East, solitude and silence will again reign in the ISLE OF FANTAISIE.

## CHAPTER II.

The last and loudest chorus had died away, and the Islanders were pouring forth their libation to their great enemy the Sun, when suddenly a vast obscurity spread over the glowing West. They looked at each other, and turned pale, and the wine from their trembling goblets fell useless on the shore. The women were too frightened to scream, and, for the first time in the Isle of Fantaisie, silence existed after sunset. They were encouraged when they observed that the darkness ceased at that point in the heavens which overlooked their coral rocks; and perceiving that their hitherto unsullied sky was pure, even at this moment of otherwise universal gloom, the men regained their colour, touched the goblets with their lips, further to reanimate themselves, and the women, now less discomposed, uttered loud shrieks.

Suddenly the wind roared with unaccustomed rage, the sea rose into large billows, and a ship was seen tossing in the offing. The Islanders, whose experience of navigation extended only to a slight paddling in their lagoon, in the half of a hollow trunk of a tree, for the purpose of fishing, mistook the tight little frigate for a great fish; and being now aware of the cause of this disturbance, and at the same time feeling confident that the monster could never make way through the shallow waters to the island, they recovered their courage, and gazed upon the labouring leviathan with the same interested nonchalance with which students at a modern lecture observe an expounding philosopher.

'What a shadow he casts over the sky!' said the King, a young man, whose divine right was never questioned by his female subjects. 'What a commotion in the waters, and what a wind he snorts forth! It certainly must be the largest fish that exists. I remember my father telling me that a monstrous fish once got entangled among our rocks, and this part of the island really smelt for a month;

I cannot help fancying that there is a rather odd smell now; pah!'

A favourite Queen flew to the suffering monarch, and pressing her aromatic lips upon his offended nostrils, his Majesty recovered.

The unhappy crew of the frigate, who, with the aid of their telescopes, had detected the crowds upon the shore, now fired their signal guns of distress, which came sullenly booming through the wind.

'Oh! the great fish is speaking!' was the universal exclamation.

'I begin to get frightened,' said the favourite Queen. 'I am sure the monster is coming here!' So saying, her Majesty grasped up a handful of pearls from the shore, to defend herself.

As screaming was now the fashion, all the women of course screamed; and animated by the example of their sovereign, and armed with the marine gems, the Amazons assumed an imposing attitude.

Just at the moment that they had worked up their enthusiasm to the highest pitch, and were actually desirous of dying for their country, the ship sunk.

## CHAPTER III.

IT is the flush of noon; and, strange to say, a human figure is seen wandering on the shore of the Isle of Fantaisie.

'One of the crew of the wrecked frigate, of course? What an' escape! Fortunate creature! interesting man! Probably the indefatigable Captain Parry; possibly the undaunted Captain Franklin; perhaps the adventurous Captain Lyon!'

No! sweet blue-eyed girl! my plots are not of that extremely guessable nature so admired by your adorable sex. Indeed, this book is so constructed that if you were even, according to custom, to commence its perusal by

B B

reading the last page, you would not gain the slightest assistance in finding out ' how the story ends.'

The wanderer belongs to no frigate-building nation. He is a true Fantaisian; who having, in his fright, during yesterday's storm, lost the lock of hair which, in a moment of glorious favour, he had ravished from his fair mistress's brow, is now, after a sleepless night, tracing every remembered haunt of yesterday, with the fond hope of regaining his most precious treasure. Ye Gentlemen of England, who live at home at ease, know full well the anxiety and exertion, the days of management, and the nights of meditation which the rape of a lock requires, and you can consequently sympathize with the agitated feelings of the handsome and the hapless Popanilla.

The favourite of all the women, the envy of all the men, Popanilla passed a pleasant life. No one was a better judge of wine, no one had a better taste for fruit, no one danced with more elegant vivacity, and no one whispered compliments in a more meaning tone. His stories ever had a point, his repartees were never ill-natured. What a pity that such an amiable fellow should have got into such a scrape!

In spite of his grief, however, Popanilla soon found that the ardency of his passion evaporated under a smoking sun; and, exhausted, he was about to return home from his fruitless search, when his attention was attracted by a singular appearance. He observed before him, on the shore, a square and hitherto unseen form. He watched it for some minutes, but it was motionless. He drew nearer, and observed it with intense attention; but, if it were a being, it certainly was fast asleep. He approached close to its side, but it neither moved nor breathed. He applied his nose to the mysterious body, and the elegant Fantaisian drew back immediately from a most villanous smell of pitch. Not to excite too much, in this calm age, the reader's curiosity, let him know at once that this strange substance was a sea-chest. Upon it was marked, in large black letters, S. D. K. No. 1.

For the first time in his life Popanilla experienced a feeling of overwhelming curiosity. His fatigue, his loss, the scorching hour, and the possible danger were all forgotten in an indefinite feeling that the body possessed contents more interesting than its unpromising exterior, and in a resolute determination that the development of the mystery should be reserved only for himself.

Although he felt assured that he must be unseen, he could not refrain from throwing a rapid glance of anxiety around him. It was a moment of perfect stillness: the island slept in sunshine, and even the waves had ceased to break over the opposing rocks. A thousand strange and singular thoughts rushed into his mind, but his first purpose was ever uppermost; and at length, unfolding his girdle of skin, he tied the tough cincture round the chest, and, exerting all his powers, dragged his mysterious waif into the nearest wood.

But during this operation the top fell off, and revealed the neatest collection of little packages that ever pleased the eye of the admirer of spruce arrangement. Popanilla took up packets upon all possible subjects; smelt them, but they were not savory; he was sorely puzzled. At last, he lighted on a slender volume bound in brown calf, which, with the confined but sensual notions of a savage, he mistook for gingerbread, at least. It was 'The Universal Linguist, by Mr. Hamilton; or, the Art of Dreaming in Languages.'

No sooner had Popanilla passed that well-formed nose, which had been so often admired by the lady whose lock of hair he had unfortunately lost, a few times over a few pages of the Hamiltonian System than he sank upon his bed of flowers, and, in spite of his curiosity, was instantly overcome by a profound slumber. But his slumber, though deep, was not peaceful, and he was the actor in an agitating drama.

He found himself alone in a gay and glorious garden. In the centre of it grew a pomegranate tree of prodigious size; its top was lost in the sky, and its innumerable branches sprang out in all directions, covered with large fruit of a rich golden hue. Beautiful birds were perched upon all parts of the tree, and chanted with perpetual melody the beauties of their bower. Tempted by the delicious sight, Popanilla stretched forward his ready hand to pluck; but no sooner had he grasped the fruit than the music immediately ceased, the birds rushed away, the sky darkened, the tree fell under the wind, the garden vanished, and Popanilla found himself in the midst of a raging sea, buffeting the waves.

He would certainly have been drowned had he not been immediately swallowed up by the huge monster which had not only been the occasion of the storm of yesterday, but, ah! most unhappy business! been the occasion also of his losing that lock of hair.

Ere he could congratulate himself on his escape he found fresh cause for anxiety, for he perceived that he was no longer alone. No friends were near him; but, on the contrary, he was surrounded by strangers of a far different aspect. They were men certainly; that is to say, they had legs and arms, and heads, and bodies as himself; but instead of that bloom of youth, that regularity of feature, that amiable joyousness of countenance, which he had ever been accustomed to meet and to love in his former companions, he recoiled in horror from the swarthy complexions, the sad visages, and the haggard features of his present ones. They spoke to him in a harsh and guttural accent. He would have fled from their advances; but then he was in the belly of a whale! When he had become a little used to their tones he was gratified by finding that their attentions were far from hostile; and, after having received from them a few compliments, he began to think that they were not quite so ugly. He discovered that the object of their inquiries was the fatal pomegranate which still remained in his hand. They admired its beauty, and told him that they greatly esteemed an individual who possessed such a mass of precious ore. Popanilla begged to undeceive them, and courteously presented the fruit. No sooner, however, had he parted with this apple of discord, than the countenances of his companions changed. Immediately discovering its real nature, they loudly accused Popanilla of having deceived them; he remonstrated, and they recriminated; and the great fish, irritated by their clamour, lashed its huge tail, and with one efficacious vomit spouted the innocent Popanilla high in the air. He fell with such a dash into the waves that he was awakened by the sound of his own fall.

The dreamer awoke amidst real chattering, and scuffling, and clamour. A troop of green monkeys had been aroused by his unusual occupation, and had taken the opportunity of his slumber to become acquainted with some of the first principles of science. What progress they had made it is difficult to ascertain; because, each one throwing a tract at Popanilla's head, they immediately disappeared. It is said, however, that some monkeys have been since seen skipping about the island, with their tails cut off; and that they have even succeeded in passing themselves off for human beings among those people who do not read novels, and are consequently unacquainted with mankind.

The morning's adventure immediately rushed into Popanilla's mind, and he proceeded forthwith to examine the contents of his chest; but with advantages which had not been yet enjoyed by those who had previously peeped into it. The monkeys had not been composed to sleep by the 'Universal Linguist' of Mr. Hamilton. As for Popanilla, he took up a treatise on hydrostatics, and read it straight through on the spot. For the rest of the day he was hydrostatically mad; nor could the commonest incident connected with the action or conveyance of water take place without his speculating on its cause and consequence.

So enraptured was Popanilla with his new accomplishments and acquirements that by degrees he avoided attendance on the usual evening assemblages, and devoted himself solely to the acquirement of useful knowledge. After a short time his absence was remarked; but the greatest and the most gifted has only to leave his coterie, called the world, for a few days, to be fully convinced of what slight importance he really is. And so Popanilla, the delight of society and the especial favourite of the women, was in a very short time not even inquired after. At first, of course, they supposed that he was in love, or that he had a slight cold, or that he was writing his memoirs; and as these suppositions, in due course, take their place in the annals of society as circumstantial histories, in about a week one knew the lady, another had heard him sneeze, and a third had seen the manuscript. At the end of another week Popanilla was forgotten.

## CHAPTER IV.

SIX months had elapsed since the first chest of the cargo of Useful Knowledge destined for the fortunate Maldives had been digested by the recluse Popanilla; for a recluse he had now become. Great students are rather dull companions. Our Fantaisian friend, during his first studies, was as moody, absent, and querulous as are most men of genius during that mystical period of life. He was consequently avoided by the men and quizzed by the women, and consoled himself for the neglect of the first and the taunts of the second by the indefinite sensation that he should, some day or other, turn out that little being called a great man. As for his mistress, she considered herself insulted by being addressed by a man who had lost her lock of hair. When the chest was exhausted Popanilla was seized with a profound melancholy. Nothing depresses a man's spirits more completely than a self-conviction of self-conceit; and Popanilla, who had been accustomed to consider himself and his companions as the most elegant portion of the visible creation, now discovered, with dismay, that he and his fellow-islanders were nothing more than a horde of useless savages.

This mortification, however, was soon succeeded by a proud consciousness that he, at any rate, was now civilised;

and that proud consciousness by a fond hope that in a short
time he might become a civiliser. Like all projectors, he
was not of a sanguine temperament; but he did trust that
in the course of another season the Isle of Fantaisie might
take its station among the nations. He was determined,
however, not to be too rapid. It cannot be expected that
ancient prejudices can in a moment be eradicated, and new
modes of conduct instantaneously substituted and established. Popanilla, like a wise man, determined to conciliate.
His views were to be as liberal, as his principles were enlightened. Men should be forced to do nothing. Bigotry,
and intolerance, and persecution were the objects of his
decided disapprobation; resembling, in this particular, all
the great and good men who have ever existed, who have
invariably maintained this opinion so long as they have
been in the minority.

Popanilla appeared once more in the world.

'Dear me! is that you, Pop?' exclaimed the ladies.
'What have you been doing with yourself all this time?
Travelling, I suppose. Every one travels now. Really you
travelled men get quite bores. And where did you get that
coat, if it be a coat?'

Such was the style in which the Fantaisian females
saluted the long absent Popanilla; and really, when a man
shuts himself up from the world for a considerable time,
and fancies that in condescending to re-enter it he has
surely the right to expect the homage due to a superior
being, these salutations are awkward. The ladies of England peculiarly excel in this species of annihilation; and
while they continue to drown puppies, as they daily do, in
a sea of sarcasm, I think no true Englishman will hesitate
one moment in giving them the preference for tact and
manner over all the vivacious French, all the self-possessing
Italian, and all the tolerant German women. This is a claptrap, and I have no doubt will sell the book.

Popanilla, however, had not re-entered society with the
intention of subsiding into a nonentity; and he therefore
took the opportunity, a few minutes after sunset, just as

his companions were falling into the dance, to beg the favour of being allowed to address his sovereign only for one single moment.

'Sire!' said he, in that mild tone of subdued superciliousness with which we should always address kings, and which, while it vindicates our dignity, satisfactorily proves that we are above the vulgar passion of envy, 'Sire!' but let us not encourage that fatal faculty of oratory so dangerous to free states, and therefore let us give only the 'substance of Popanilla's speech.'* He commenced his address in a manner somewhat resembling the initial observations of those pleasing pamphlets which are the fashion of the present hour; and which, being intended to diffuse information among those who have not enjoyed the opportunity and advantages of study, and are consequently of a gay and cheerful disposition, treat of light subjects in a light and polished style. Popanilla, therefore, spoke of man in a savage state, the origin of society, and the elements of the social compact, in sentences which would not have disgraced the mellifluous pen of Bentham. From these he naturally digressed into an agreeable disquisition on the Anglo-Saxons; and, after a little badinage on the Bill of Rights, flew off to an airy *aperçu* of the French Revolution. When he had arrived at the Isle of Fantaisie he begged to inform his Majesty that man was born for something else besides enjoying himself. It was, doubtless, extremely pleasant to dance and sing, to crown themselves with chaplets, and to drink wine; but he was 'free to confess' that he did not imagine that the most barefaced hireling of corruption could for a moment presume to maintain that there was any utility in pleasure. If there were no utility in pleasure, it was quite clear that pleasure could profit no one. If, therefore, it were unprofitable, it was injurious; because that which does not produce a profit is equivalent to a loss;

---

* *Substance of a speech*, in Parliamentary language, means a printed edition of an harangue which contains all that was uttered in the House, and about as much again.

therefore pleasure is a losing business; consequently pleasure is not pleasant.

He also showed that man was not born for himself, but for society; that the interests of the body are alone to be considered, and not those of the individual; and that a nation might be extremely happy, extremely powerful, and extremely rich, although every individual member of it might at the same time be miserable, dependent, and in debt. He regretted to observe that no one in the island seemed in the slightest degree conscious of the object of his being. Man is created for a purpose; the object of his existence is to perfect himself. Man is imperfect by nature, because if nature had made him perfect he would have had no wants; and it is only by supplying his wants that utility can be developed. The development of utility is therefore the object of our being, and the attainment of this great end the cause of our existence. This principle clears all doubts, and rationally accounts for a state of existence which has puzzled many pseudo-philosophers.

Popanilla then went on to show that the hitherto received definitions of man were all erroneous; that man is neither a walking animal, nor a talking animal, nor a cooking animal, nor a lounging animal, nor a debt-incurring animal, nor a tax-paying animal, nor a printing animal, nor a puffing animal, but a *developing animal*. Development is the discovery of utility. By developing the water we get fish; by developing the earth we get corn, and cash, and cotton; by developing the air we get breath; by developing the fire we get heat. Thus, the use of the elements is demonstrated to the meanest capacity. But it was not merely a material development to which he alluded; a moral development was equally indispensable. He showed that it was impossible for a nation either to think too much or to do too much. The life of man was therefore to be passed in a moral and material development until he had consummated his perfection. It was the opinion of Popanilla that this great result was by no means so near at hand as some philosophers flattered themselves; and that it might possibly require another half-century before even the most civilised nation could be said to have completed the destiny of the human race. At the same time, he intimated that there were various extraordinary means by which this rather desirable result might be facilitated; and there was no saying what the building of a new University might do, of which, when built, he had no objection to be appointed Principal.

In answer to those who affect to admire that deficient system of existence which they style simplicity of manners, and who are perpetually committing the blunder of supposing that every advance towards perfection only withdraws man further from his primitive and proper condition, Popanilla triumphantly demonstrated that no such order as that which they associated with the phrase 'state of nature' ever existed. 'Man,' said he, 'is called the masterpiece of nature; and man is also, as we all know, the most curious of machines; now, a machine is a work of art, consequently, the masterpiece of nature is the masterpiece of art. The object of all mechanism is the attainment of utility; the object of man, who is the most perfect machine, is utility in the highest degree. Can we believe, therefore, that this machine was ever intended for a state which never could have called forth its powers, a state in which no utility could ever have been attained, a state in which there are no wants; consequently, no demand; consequently, no supply; consequently, no competition; consequently, no invention; consequently, no profits; only one great pernicious monopoly of comfort and ease? Society without wants is like a world without winds. It is quite clear, therefore, that there is no such thing as Nature; Nature is Art, or Art is Nature; that which is most useful is most natural, because utility is the test of nature; therefore a steam-engine is in fact a much more natural production than a mountain.\*

---

\* The age seems as anti-mountainous as it is anti-monarchical. A late writer insinuates that if the English had spent their millions in levelling the Andes, instead of excavating the table-lands, society might

'You are convinced, therefore,' he continued, 'by these observations, that it is impossible for an individual or a nation to be too artificial in their manners, their ideas, their laws, or their general policy; because, in fact, the more artificial you become the nearer you approach that state of nature of which you are so perpetually talking.' Here observing that some of his audience appeared to be a little sceptical, perhaps only surprised, he told them that what he said must be true, because it entirely consisted of first principles.*

After having thus preliminarily descanted for about two hours, Popanilla informed his Majesty that he was unused to public speaking, and then proceeded to show that the grand characteristic of the social action † of the Isle of Fantaisie was a total want of development. This he observed with equal sorrow and surprise; he respected the wisdom of their ancestors; at the same time, no one could deny that they were both barbarous and ignorant; he highly esteemed also the constitution, but regretted that it was not in the slightest degree adapted to the existing want of society: he was not for destroying any establishments, but, on the contrary, was for courteously affording them the opportunity of self-dissolution. He finished by re-urging, in strong terms, the immediate development of the island. In the first place, a great metropolis must be instantly built, because a great metropolis always produces a great demand; and, moreover, Popanilla had some legal doubts whether a country without a capital could in fact be considered a State. Apologising for having so long

have been benefited. These monstrosities are decidedly useless, and therefore can neither be sublime nor beautiful, as has been unanswerably demonstrated by another recent writer on political æsthetics.—See also a personal attack on Mont Blanc, in the second number of the *Foreign Quarterly Review*, 1828.

* First principles are the ingredients of positive truth. They are immutable, as may be seen by comparing the first principles of the eighteenth century with the first principles of the nineteenth.

† This simple and definite phrase we derive from the nation to whom we were indebted during the last century for some other phrases about as definite, but rather more dangerous.

trespassed upon the attention of the assembly, he begged distinctly to state\* that he had no wish to see his Majesty and his fellow-subjects adopt these new principles without examination and without experience. They might commence on a small scale; let them cut down their forests, and by turning them into ships and houses discover the utility of timber; let the whole island be dug up; let canals be cut, docks be built, and all the elephants be killed directly, that their teeth might yield an immediate article for exportation. A short time would afford a sufficient trial. In the meanwhile, they would not be pledged to further measures, and these might be considered 'only as an experiment.'† Taking for granted that these principles would be acted on, and taking into consideration the site of the island in the map of the world, the nature and extent of its resources, its magnificent race of human beings, its varieties of the animal creation, its wonderfully fine timber, its undeveloped mineral treasures, the spaciousness of its harbours, and its various facilities for extended international communication, Popanilla had no hesitation in saying that a short time could not elapse ere, instead of passing their lives in a state of unprofitable ease and useless enjoyment, they might reasonably expect to be the terror and astonishment of the universe, and to be able to annoy every nation of any consequence.

Here, observing a smile upon his Majesty's countenance, Popanilla told the King that he was only a chief magistrate, and he had no more right to laugh at him than a parish constable. He concluded by observing that although what he at present urged might appear strange, nevertheless, if the listeners had been acquainted with the characters and cases of Galileo and Turgot, they would then have seen, as

---

\* Another phrase of Parliament, which, I need not observe, is always made use of in oratory when the orator can see his meaning about as distinctly as Sancho perceived the charms of Dulcinea.

† A very famous and convenient phrase this—but in politics *experiments* mean *revolutions*. 1828.

a necessary consequence, that his system was perfectly correct, and he himself a man of extraordinary merit.

Here the chief magistrate, no longer daring to smile, burst into a fit of laughter; and turning to his courtiers said, 'I have not an idea what this man is talking about, but I know that he makes my head ache: give me a cup of wine, and let us have a dance.'

All applauded the royal proposition; and pushing Popanilla from one to another, until he was fairly hustled to the brink of the lagoon, they soon forgot the existence of this bore: in one word, he was cut. When Popanilla found himself standing alone, and looking grave while all the rest were gay, he began to suspect that he was not so influential a personage as he previously imagined. Rather crest-fallen, he sneaked home; and consoled himself for having nobody to speak to by reading some amusing 'Conversations on Political Economy.'

## CHAPTER V.

POPANILLA was discomposed, but he was not discomfited. He consoled himself for the Royal neglect by the recollection of the many illustrious men who had been despised, banished, imprisoned, and burnt for the maintenance of opinions which, centuries afterwards, had been discovered to be truth. He did not forget that in still further centuries the lately recognised truth had been re-discovered to be falsehood; but then these men were not less illustrious; and what wonder that their opinions were really erroneous, since they were not his present ones? The reasoning was equally conclusive and consolatory. Popanilla, therefore, was not discouraged; and although he deemed it more prudent not to go out of his way to seek another audience of his sovereign, or to be too anxious again to address a public meeting, he nevertheless determined to proceed cautiously, but constantly, propagating his doctrines and proselytizing in private.

Unfortunately for Popanilla, he did not enjoy one advantage which all founders of sects have duly appreciated, and by which they have been materially assisted. It is a great and an unanswerable argument in favour of a Providence that we constantly perceive that the most beneficial results are brought about by the least worthy and most insignificant agents. The purest religions would never have been established had they not been supported by sinners who felt the burthen of the old faith; and the most free and enlightened governments are often generated by the discontented, the disappointed, and the dissolute. Now, in the Isle of Fantaisie, unfortunately for our revolutionizer, there was not a single grumbler.

Unable, therefore, to make the bad passions of his fellow-creatures the unconscious instruments of his good purposes, Popanilla must have been contented to have monopolised all the wisdom of the moderns, had he not, with the unbaffled wit of an inventor, hit upon a new expedient. Like Socrates, our philosopher began to cultivate with sedulousness the society of youth.

In a short time the ladies of Fantaisie were forced to observe that the fair sex most unfashionably predominated in their evening assemblages; for the young gentlemen of the island had suddenly ceased to pay their graceful homage at the altar of Terpsichore. In an Indian isle not to dance was as bad as heresy. The ladies rallied the recreants, but their playful sarcasms failed of their wonted effect. In the natural course of things they had recourse to remonstrances, but their appeals were equally fruitless. The delicate creatures tried reproaches, but the boyish cynics received them with a scowl and answered them with a sneer.

The women fled in indignation to their friendly monarch; but the voluptuary of nature only shrugged his shoulders and smiled. He kissed away their tears, and their frowns vanished as he crowned their long hair with roses.

'If the lads really show such bad taste,' said his Majesty, 'why I and my lords must do double duty, and dance with a couple of you at once.' Consoled and complimented, and crowned by a King, who could look sad? The women forgot their anger in their increasing loyalty.

But the pupils of Popanilla had no sooner mastered the first principles of science than they began to throw off their retired habits and uncommunicative manners. Being not utterly ignorant of some of the rudiments of knowledge, and consequently having completed their education, it was now their duty, as members of society, to instruct and not to study. They therefore courted, instead of shunned, their fellow-creatures; and on all occasions seized all opportunities of assisting the spread of knowledge. The voices of lecturing boys resounded in every part of the island. Their tones were so shrill, their manners so presuming, their knowledge so crude, and their general demeanour so completely unamiable, that it was impossible to hear them without delight, advantage, and admiration.

The women were not now the only sufferers and the only complainants. Dinned to death, the men looked gloomy; and even the King, for the first time in his life, looked grave. Could this Babel, he thought, be that empire of bliss, that delightful Fantaisie, where to be ruler only proved that you were the most skilful in making others happy! His brow ached under his light flowery crown, as if it were bound by the barbarous circle of a tyrant, heavy with gems and gold. In his despair he had some thoughts of leaving his kingdom and betaking himself to the mermaids.

The determination of the most precious portion of his subjects saved his empire. As the disciples of the new school were daily demanding, 'What is the use of dancing? what is the use of drinking wine? what is the use of smelling flowers?' the women, like prescient politicians, began to entertain a nervous suspicion that in time these sages might even presume to question the utility of that homage which, in spite of the Grecian Philosophers and the British Essayists, we have been in the habit of conceding to them ever since Eden; and they rushed again to the King like frightened deer. Something now was to be done; and the monarch, with an expression of countenance which almost amounted to energy, whispered consolation.

The King sent for Popanilla; the message produced a great sensation; the enlightened introducer of the new principles had not been at Court since he was cut. No doubt his Majesty was at last impregnated with the liberal spirit of the age; and Popanilla was assuredly to be Premier. In fact, it must be so; he was 'sent for;' there was no precedent in Fantaisie, though there might be in other islands, for a person being 'sent for' and not being Premier. His disciples were in high spirits; the world was now to be regulated upon right principles, and they were to be installed into their right places.

'Illustrious Popanilla!' said the King, 'you once did me the honour of making me a speech which, unfortunately for myself, I candidly confess, I was then incapable of understanding; no wonder, as it was the first I ever heard. I shall not, however, easily forget the effect which it produced upon me. I have since considered it my duty, as a monarch, to pay particular attention to your suggestions. I now understand them with sufficient clearness to be fully convinced of their excellence, and in future I intend to act upon them, without any exception or deviation. To prove my sincerity, I have determined to commence the new system at once; and as I think that, without some extension of our international relations, the commercial interest of this island will be incapable of furnishing the taxes which I intend to levy, I have determined, therefore, to fit out an expedition for the purpose of discovering new islands and forming relations with new islanders. It is but due to your merit that you should be appointed to the command of it; and further to testify my infinite esteem for your character, and my complete confidence in your abilities, I make you post-captain on the spot. As the axiom of your school seems to be that everything can be made perfect at once, without time, without experience, without practice, and without preparation, I have no doubt, with the aid of a treatise or two, you will make a consummate naval commander, although you have never been at sea in the whole course of your life. Farewell, Captain Popanilla!'

No sooner was this adieu uttered than four brawny lords of the bedchamber seized the Turgot of Fantaisie by the shoulders, and carried him with inconceivable rapidity to the shore. His pupils, who would have fled to his rescue, were stifled with the embraces of their former partners, and their utilitarianism dissolved in the arms of those they once so rudely rejected. As for their tutor, he was thrust into one of the canoes, with some fresh water, bread-fruit, dried fish, and a basket of alligator-pears. A band of mermaids carried the canoe with exquisite management through the shallows and over the breakers, and poor Popanilla in a few minutes found himself out at sea. Tremendously frightened, he offered to recant all his opinions, and denounce as traitors any individuals whom the Court might select. But his former companions did not exactly detect the utility of his return. His offers, his supplications, were equally fruitless; and the only answer which floated to him on the wind was, 'Farewell, Captain Popanilla!'

## CHAPTER VI.

NIGHT fell upon the waters, dark and drear, and thick and misty. How unlike those brilliant hours that once summoned him to revelry and love! Unhappy Popanilla! Thy delicious Fantaisie has vanished! Ah, pitiable youth! What could possibly have induced you to be so very rash? And all from that unlucky lock of hair!

After a few natural paroxysms of rage, terror, anguish, and remorse, the Captain as naturally subsided into despair, and awaited with sullen apathy that fate which could not be far distant. The only thing which puzzled the philosophical navigator was his inability to detect what useful end could be attained by his death. At length, remembering that fish must be fed, his theory and his desperation were at the same time confirmed.

A clear, dry morning succeeded the wet, gloomy night, and Popanilla had not yet gone down. This extraordinary suspension of his fate roused him from his stupor, and between the consequent excitement and the morning air he acquired an appetite. Philosophical physicians appear to have agreed that sorrow, to a certain extent, is not unfavourable to digestion; and as Popanilla began to entertain some indefinite and unreasonable hopes, the alligator-pears quickly disappeared. In the meantime the little canoe cut her way as if she were chasing a smuggler; and had it not been for a shark or two who, in anticipation of their services being required, never left her side for a second, Popanilla really might have made some ingenious observations on the nature of tides. He was rather surprised, certainly, as he watched his frail bark cresting the waves; but he soon supposed that this was all in the natural course of things; and he now ascribed his previous fright, not to the peril of his situation, but to his inexperience of it.

Although his apprehension of being drowned was now removed, yet when he gazed on the boundless vacancy before him, and also observed that his provisions rapidly decreased, he began to fear that he was destined for a still more horrible fate, and that, after having eaten his own shoes, he must submit to be starved. In this state of despondency, with infinite delight and exultation he clearly observed, on the second day, at twenty-seven minutes past three P.M., though at a considerable distance, a mountain and an island. His joy and his pride were equal, and excessive: he called the first Alligator Mountain, in gratitude to the pears; and christened the second after his mistress, that unlucky mistress! The swift canoe soon reached the discoveries, and the happy discoverer further found, to his mortification, that the mountain was a mist and the island a sea-weed. Popanilla now grew sulky, and threw himself down in the bottom of his boat.

On the third morning he was awakened by a tremendous roar; on looking around him he perceived that he was in a valley formed by two waves, each several hundred feet high. This seemed the crisis of his fate; he shut his eyes, as people do when they are touched by a dentist, and in a few minutes was still bounding on the ocean in the eternal canoe, safe but senseless. Some tremendous peals of thunder, a roaring wind, and a scathing lightning confirmed his indisposition; and had not the tempest subsided, Popanilla would probably have been an idiot for life. The dead and soothing calm which succeeded this tornado called him back again gradually to existence. He opened his eyes, and, scarcely daring to try a sense, immediately shut them; then heaving a deep sigh, he shrugged his shoulders, and looked as pitiable as a prime minister with a rebellious cabinet. At length he ventured to lift up his head; there was not a wrinkle on the face of ocean; a halcyon fluttered over him, and then scudded before his canoe, and gamesome porpoises were tumbling at his side. The sky was cloudless, except in the direction to which he was driving; but even as Popanilla observed, with some misgivings, the mass of vapours which had there congregated, the great square and solid black clouds drew off like curtains, and revealed to his entranced vision a magnificent city rising out of the sea.

Tower, and dome, and arch, column, and spire, and obelisk, and lofty terraces, and many-windowed palaces, rose in all directions from a mass of building which appeared to him each instant to grow more huge, till at length it seemed to occupy the whole horizon. The sun lent additional lustre to the dazzling quays of white marble which apparently surrounded this mighty city, and which rose immediately from the dark blue waters. As the navigator drew nearer, he observed that in most parts the quays were crowded with beings who, he trusted, were human, and already the hum of multitudes broke upon his inexperienced ear: to him a sound far more mysterious and far more exciting than the most poetical of winds to the most windy of poets. On the right of this vast city rose what was mistaken by Popanilla for an immense but leafless forest; but more practical men than the Fantaisian Captain have been equally confounded by the first sight of a million of masts.

The canoe cut its way with increased rapidity, and ere Popanilla had recovered himself sufficiently to make even an ejaculation, he found himself at the side of a quay. Some amphibious creatures, whom he supposed to be mermen, immediately came to his assistance, rather stared at his serpent-skin coat, and then helped him up the steps. Popanilla was instantly surrounded.

'Who are you?' said one.

'What are you?' asked another.

'Who is it?' exclaimed a third.

'What is it?' screamed a fourth.

'My friends, I am a man!'

'A man!' said the women; 'are you sure you are a real man?'

'He must be a sea-god!' said the females.

'She must be a sea-goddess!' said the males.

'A Triton!' maintained the women.

'A Nereid!' argued the men.

'It is a great fish!' said the boys.

Thanks to the Universal Linguist, Captain Popanilla, under these peculiar circumstances, was more loquacious than could have been Captain Parry.

'Good people! you see before you the most injured of human beings.'

This announcement inspired general enthusiasm. The women wept, the men shook hands with him, and all the boys huzzaed. Popanilla proceeded:—

'Actuated by the most pure, the most patriotic, the most noble, the most enlightened, and the most useful sentiments, I aspired to ameliorate the condition of my fellow-men. To this grand object I have sacrificed all that makes life delightful: I have lost my station in society, my taste for dancing, my popularity with the men, my favour with the women; and last, but, oh! not least (excuse this emotion), I have lost a very particular lock of hair. In one word, my friends, you see before you, banished, ruined, and unhappy, the victim of a despotic sovereign, a corrupt aristocracy, and a misguided people.'

No sooner had he ceased speaking than Popanilla really imagined that he had only escaped the dangers of sedition and the sea to expire by less hostile, though not less effective, means. To be strangled was not much better than to be starved: and certainly, with half-a-dozen highly respectable females clinging round his neck, he was not reminded for the first time in his life what a domestic bowstring is an affectionate woman. In an agony of suffocation he thought very little of his arms, although the admiration of the men had already, in his imagination, separated these useful members from his miserable body; and had it not been for some justifiable kicking and plunging, the veneration of the ingenuous and surrounding youth, which manifested itself by their active exertions to divide his singular garment into relics of a martyr of liberty, would soon have effectually prevented the ill-starred Popanilla from being again mistaken for a Nereid. Order was at length restored, and a committee of eight appointed to regulate the visits of the increasing mob.

The arrangements were judicious; the whole populace was marshalled into ranks; classes of twelve persons were allowed consecutively to walk past the victim of tyranny, corruption, and ignorance; and each person had the honour to touch his finger. During this proceeding, which lasted a few hours, an influential personage generously offered to receive the eager subscriptions of the assembled thousands. Even the boys subscribed, and ere six hours had passed since his arrival as a coatless vagabond in this liberal city, Captain Popanilla found himself a person of considerable means.

The receiver of the subscriptions, while he crammed Popanilla's serpent-skin pockets full of gold pieces, at the same time kindly offered the stranger to introduce him to an hotel. Popanilla, who was quite beside himself, could only bow his assent, and mechanically accompanied his conductor. When he had regained his faculty of speech, he endeavoured, in wandering sentences of grateful incoherency, to express his deep sense of this unparalleled liberality. 'It was an excess of generosity in which mankind could never have before indulged!'

'By no means!' said his companion, with great coolness; 'far from this being an unparalleled affair, I assure you it is a matter of hourly occurrence: make your mind quite easy. You are probably not aware that you are now living in the richest and the most charitable country in the world?'

'Wonderful!' said Popanilla; 'and what is the name, may I ask, of this charitable city?'

'Is it possible,' said his companion, with a faint smile, 'that you are ignorant of the great city of Hubbabub; the largest city not only that exists, but that ever did exist, and the capital of the island of Vraibleusia, the most famous island not only that is known, but that ever was known?'

While he was speaking they were accosted by a man upon crutches, who, telling them in a broken voice that he had a wife and twelve infant children dependent on his support, supplicated a little charity. Popanilla was about to empty part of his pocketfuls into the mendicant's cap, but his companion repressed his unphilosophical facility. 'By no means!' said his friend, who, turning round to the beggar, advised him, in a mild voice, to *work*; calmly adding, that if he presumed to ask charity again he should certainly have him bastinadoed. Then they walked on.

Popanilla's attention was so distracted by the variety, the number, the novelty, and the noise of the objects which were incessantly hurried upon his observation, that he found no time to speak; and as his companion, though exceedingly polite, was a man of few words, conversation rather flagged.

At last, overwhelmed by the magnificence of the streets, the splendour of the shops, the number of human beings, the rattling of the vehicles, the dashing of the horses, and a thousand other sounds and objects, Popanilla gave loose to a loud and fervent wish that his hotel might have the good fortune of being situated in this interesting quarter.

'By no means!' said his companion; 'we have yet much further to go. Far from this being a desirable situation for you, my friend, no civilised person is ever seen here; and had not the cause of civil and religious liberty fortunately called me to the water-side to-day, I should have lost the opportunity of showing how greatly I esteem a gentleman who has suffered so severely in the cause of national amelioration.'

'Sir!' said Popanilla, 'your approbation is the only reward which I ever shall desire for my exertions. You will excuse me for not quite keeping up with you; but the fact is, my pockets are so stuffed with cash that the action of my legs is greatly impeded.'

'Credit me, my friend, that you are suffering from an inconvenience which you will not long experience in Hubbabub. Nevertheless, to remedy it at present, I think the best thing we can do is to buy a purse.'

They accordingly entered a shop where such an article might be found, and taking up a small sack, for Popanilla was very rich, his companion inquired its price, which he was informed was four crowns. No sooner had the desired information been given than the proprietor of the opposite shop rushed in, and offered him the same article for three crowns. The original merchant, not at all surprised at the intrusion, and not the least apologising for his former extortion, then demanded two. His rival, being more than his match, he courteously dropped upon his knee, and requested his customer to accept the article gratis, for his sake. The generous dealer would infallibly have carried the day, had not his rival humbly supplicated the purchaser not only to receive his article as a gift, but also the compliment of a crown inside.

'What a terrible cheat the first merchant must have been!' said the puzzled Popanilla, as they proceeded on their way.

'By no means!' said his calm companion; 'the purse was sufficiently cheap even at four crowns. This is not Cheatery; this is Competition!'

'What a wonderful nation, then, this must be, where you not only get purses gratis but even well loaded! What use, then, is all this heavy gold? It is a tremendous trouble to carry; I will empty the bag into this kennel, for money surely can be of no use in a city where, when in want of cash, you have only to go into a shop and buy a purse!'

'Your pardon!' said his companion; 'far from this being the case, Vraibleusia is, without doubt, the dearest country in the world.'

'If, then,' said the inquisitive Popanilla, with great animation, 'if, then, this country be the dearest in the world; if, how ——'

'My good friend!' said his companion, 'I really am the last person in the world to answer questions. All that I know is, that this country is extremely dear, and that the only way to get things cheap is to encourage Competition.'

Here the progress of his companion was impeded for some time by a great crowd, which had assembled to catch a glimpse of a man who was to fly off a steeple, but who had not yet arrived. A chimney-sweeper observed to a scientific friend that probably the density of the atmosphere might prevent the intended volitation; and Popanilla, who, having read almost as many pamphlets as the observer, now felt quite at home, exceedingly admired the observation.

'He must be a very superior man, this gentleman in black!' said Popanilla to his companion.

'By no means! he is of the lowest class in society. But you are probably not aware that you are in the most educated country in the world.'

'Delightful!' said Popanilla.

The Captain was exceedingly desirous of witnessing the flight of the Vraibleusian Dædalus, but his friend advised their progress. This, however, was not easy; and Popanilla, animated for the moment by his natural aristocratic disposition, and emboldened by his superior size and strength, began to clear his way in a manner which was more cogent than logical. The chimney-sweeper and his comrades were soon in arms, and Popanilla would certainly have been killed or ducked by this superior man and his friends, had it not been for the mild remonstrance of his conductor and the singular appearance of his costume.

'What could have induced you to be so imprudent?' said his rescuer, when they had escaped from the crowd.

'Truly,' said Popanilla, 'I thought that in a country where you may bastinado the wretch who presumes to ask you for alms, there could surely be no objection to my knocking down the scoundrel who dared to stand in my way.'

'By no means!' said his friend, slightly elevating his eyebrows. 'Here all men are equal. You are probably not aware that you are at present in the freest country in the world.'

'I do not exactly understand you; what is this freedom?'

'My good friend, I really am the last person in the world to answer questions. Freedom is, in one word, Liberty: a kind of thing which you foreigners never can understand, and which mere theory can make no man understand. When you have been in the island a few weeks all will be quite clear to you. In the meantime, do as others do, and never knock men down!'

## CHAPTER VII.

'ALTHOUGH we are yet some way from our hotel,' remarked Popanilla's conductor, 'we have now arrived at a part of the city where I can ease you, without difficulty, from your troublesome burthen; let us enter here!'

As he spoke, they stopped before a splendid palace, and proceeding through various halls full of individuals apparently intently busied, the companions were at last ushered into an apartment of smaller size, but of more elegant character. A personage of prepossessing appearance was lolling on a couch of an appearance equally prepossessing. Before him, on a table, were some papers, exquisite fruits, and some liqueurs. Popanilla was presented, and received with fascinating complaisance. His friend stated the object of their visit, and handed the sackful of gold to the gentleman on the sofa. The gentleman on the sofa ordered a couple of attendants to ascertain its contents. While this computation was going on he amused his guests by his lively conversation, and charmed Popanilla by his polished manners and easy civility. He offered him, during his stay in Vraibleusia, the use of a couple of equipages, a villa, and an opera-box; insisted upon sending to his hotel some pineapples and some rare wine, and gave him a perpetual ticket to his picture-gallery. When his attendants had concluded their calculation, he ordered them to place Popanilla's precious metal in his treasury; and then, presenting the Captain with a small packet of pink shells, he kindly enquired whether he could be of any further use to him. Popanilla was loth to retire without his gold, of the utility of which, in spite of the conveniency of competition, he seemed to possess an instinctive conception; but as his friend rose and withdrew, he could do nothing less than accompany him; for, having now known him nearly half a day, his confidence in his honour and integrity was naturally unbounded.

'That was the King, of course?' said Popanilla, when they were fairly out of the palace.

'The King!' said the unknown, nearly surprised into an exclamation; 'by no means!'

'And what then?'

'My good friend! is it possible that you have no bankers in your country?'

'Yes, it is very possible; but we have mermaids, who also give us shells which are pretty. What then are your bankers?'

'Really, my good friend, that is a question which I never remember having been asked before; but a banker is a man who—keeps our money for us.'

'Ah! and he is bound, I suppose, to return your money when you choose?'

'Most assuredly!'

'He is, then, in fact, your servant: you must pay him handsomely, for him to live so well?'

'By no means! we pay him nothing.'

'That is droll; he must be very rich then?'

'Really, my dear friend, I cannot say. Why, yes! I—I suppose he may be very rich!'

''Tis singular that a rich man should take so much trouble for others!'

'My good friend! of course he lives by his trouble.'

'Ah! How, then,' continued the inquisitive Fantaisian, 'if you do not pay him for his services, and he yet lives by them; how, I pray, does he acquire these immense riches?'

'Really, my good sir, I am, in truth, the very last man in the world to answer questions: he is a banker; bankers are always rich; but why they are, or how they are, I really never had time to inquire. But I suppose, if the truth were known, they must have very great opportunities.'

'Ah! I begin to see,' said Popanilla. 'It was really very kind of him,' continued the Captain, 'to make me a present of these little pink shells: what would I not give to turn them into a necklace, and send it to a certain person at Fantaisie!'

'It would be a very expensive necklace,' observed his companion, almost surprised. 'I had no idea, I confess, from your appearance, that in your country they indulged in such expensive tastes in costume.'

'Expensive!' said Popanilla. 'We certainly have no such shells as these in Fantaisie; but we have much more beautiful ones. I should think, from their look, they must be rather common.'

His conductor for the first time nearly laughed. 'I forgot,' said he, 'that you could not be aware that these pink shells are the most precious coin of the land, compared with which those bits of gold with which you have recently parted are nothing; your whole fortune is now in that little packet. The fact is,' continued the unknown, making an effort to communicate, 'although we possess in this country more of the precious metals than all the rest of the world together, the quantity is nevertheless utterly disproportioned to the magnitude of our wealth and our wants. We have been, therefore, under the necessity of resorting to other means of representing the first and supplying the second; and, taking advantage of our insular situation, we have introduced these small pink shells, which abound all round the coast. Being much more convenient to carry, they are in general circulation, and no genteel person has ever anything else in his pocket.'

'Wonderful! But surely, then, it is no very difficult thing in this country to accumulate a fortune, since all that is necessary to give you every luxury of life is a stroll one morning of your existence along the beach?'

'By no means, my friend! you are really too rapid. The fact is, that no one has the power of originally circulating these shells but our Government; and if any one, by any chance, choose to violate this arrangement, we make up for depriving him of his solitary walks on the shore by instant submersion in the sea.'

'Then the whole circulation of the country is at the mercy of your Government?' remarked Popanilla, summoning to his recollection the contents of one of those shipwrecked *brochures* which had exercised so strange an influence on his destiny. 'Suppose they do not choose to issue?'

'That is always guarded against. The mere quarterly payments of interest upon our national debt will secure an ample supply.'

'Debt! I thought you were the richest nation in the world?'

'"Tis true; nevertheless, if there were a golden pyramid with a base as big as the whole earth and an apex touching the heavens, it would not supply us with sufficient metal to satisfy our creditors.'

'But, my dear sir,' exclaimed the perplexed Popanilla, 'if this really be true, how then can you be said to be the richest nation in the world?'

'It is very simple. The annual interest upon our debt exceeds the whole wealth of the rest of the world; therefore we must be the richest nation in the world.'

''Tis true,' said Popanilla; 'I see I have yet much to learn. But with regard to these pink shells, how can you possibly create for them a certain standard of value? It is merely agreement among yourselves that fixes any value to them.'

'By no means! you are so rapid! Each shell is immediately convertible into gold; of which metal, let me again remind you, we possess more than any other nation; but which, indeed, we only keep as a sort of dress coin, chiefly to indulge the prejudices of foreigners.'

'But,' said the perpetual Popanilla, 'suppose every man who held a shell on the same day were to ——'

'My good friend! I really am the last person in the world to give explanations. In Vraibleusia, we have so much to do that we have no time to think; a habit which only becomes nations who are not employed. You are now fast approaching the Great Shell Question; a question which, I confess, affects the interests of every man in this island more than any other; but of which, I must candidly own, every man in this island is more ignorant than of any other. No one, however, can deny that the system works well; and if anything at any time go wrong, why really Mr. Secretary Periwinkle is a wonderful man, and our most eminent conchologist. He, no doubt, will set it right; and if, by any chance, things are past even his management, why then, I suppose, to use our national motto, *something will turn up.*'

Here they arrived at the hotel. Having made every arrangement for the comfort and convenience of the Fantaisian stranger, Popanilla's conductor took his leave, previously informing him that his name was Skindeep; that he was a member of one of the largest families in the island; that, had he not been engaged to attend a lecture, he would have stayed and dined with him; but that he would certainly call upon him on the morrow.

Compared with his hotel the palace of his banker was a dungeon; even the sunset voluptuousness of Fantaisie was now remembered without regret in the blaze of artificial light and in the artificial gratification of desires which art had alone created. After a magnificent repast, his host politely inquired of Popanilla whether he would like to go to the Opera, the comedy, or a concert; but the Fantaisian philosopher was not yet quite corrupted; and, still inspired with a desire to acquire useful knowledge, he begged his landlord to procure him immediately a pamphlet on the Shell Question.

While his host was engaged in procuring this luxury a man entered the room and told Popanilla that he had walked that day two thousand five hundred paces, and that the tax due to the Excise upon this promenade was fifty crowns. The Captain stared, and remarked to the excise-officer that he thought a man's paces were a strange article to tax. The excise-officer, with great civility, answered that no doubt at first sight it might appear rather strange, but that it was the only article left untaxed in Vraibleusia; that there was a slight deficiency in the last quarter's revenue, and that therefore the Government had no alternative; that it was a tax which did not press heavily upon the individual, because the Vraibleusians were of a sedentary habit; that, besides, it was an opinion every day more received among the best judges that the more a man was taxed the richer he ultimately would prove; and he concluded by saying that Popanilla need not make himself uneasy about these demands, because, if he were ruined to-morrow, being a foreigner, he was entitled by the law of the land to five thousand a-year; whereas he, the exciseman, being a native-born Vraibleusian, had no claims whatever upon the Government; therefore he hoped his honour would give him something to drink.

His host now entered with the 'Novum Organon' of the great Periwinkle. While Popanilla devoured the lively pages of this treatise, he discovered that the system which had been so subtilely introduced by the Government, and which had so surprised him in the morning, had soon been adopted in private life; and although it was drowning matter to pick up pink shells, still there was nothing to prevent the whole commerce of the country from being carried on by means of a system equally conchological. He found that the social action in every part of the island was regulated and assisted by this process. Oyster-shells were first introduced; muscle-shells speedily followed; and, as commerce became more complicate, they had even been obliged to have recourse to snail-shells. Popanilla retired to rest with admiration of the people who thus converted to the most useful purposes things apparently so useless. There was no saying now what might not be done even with a nutshell. It was evident that the nation who contrived to be the richest people in the world while they were over head and ears in debt must be fast approaching to a state of perfection. Finally, sinking to sleep in a bed of eiderdown, Popanilla was confirmed in his prejudices against a state of nature.

## CHAPTER VIII.

SKINDEEP called upon Popanilla on the following morning in an elegant equipage, and with great politeness proposed to attend him in a drive about the city.

The island of Vraibleusia is one hundred and fifty miles in circumference, two-thirds of which are covered by the city of Hubbabub. It contains no other city, town, or village. The rest of the island consists of rivers, canals, and railroads. Popanilla was surprised when he was informed that Hubbabub did not contain more than five millions of inhabitants; but his surprise was decreased when their journey occasionally lay through tracts of streets, consisting often of capacious mansions entirely tenantless. On seeking an explanation of this seeming desolation, he was told that the Hubbabubians were possessed by a frenzy of always moving westward; and that consequently great quarters of the city are perpetually deserted. Even as Skindeep was speaking their passage was stopped by a large caravan of carriages and waggons heavily laden with human creatures and their children and chattels. On Skindeep inquiring the cause of this great movement, he was informed by one on horseback, who seemed to be the leader of the horde, that they were the late dwellers in sundry squares and streets situated far to the east; that their houses having been ridiculed by an itinerant ballad-singer, the female part of the tribe had insisted upon immediately quitting their unfashionable fatherland; and that now, after three days' journey, they had succeeded in reaching the late settlement of a horde who had migrated to the extreme west.

Quitting regions so subject to revolutions and vicissitudes, the travellers once more emerged into quarters of a less transitory reputation; and in the magnificent parks, the broad streets, the ample squares, the palaces, the triumphal arches, and the theatres of occidental Hubbabub, Popanilla lost those sad and mournful feelings which are ever engendered by contemplating the gloomy relics of departed greatness. It was impossible to admire too much the architecture of this part of the city. The elevations were indeed imposing. In general, the massy Egyptian appropriately graced the attic-stories; while the finer and more elaborate architecture of Corinth was placed on a level with the eye, so that its beauties might be more easily discovered. Spacious colonnades were flanked by porticoes, surmounted by domes; nor was the number of columns at all limited, for you occasionally met with porticos of two tiers, the lower one of which consisted of three, the higher one of thirty columns. Pedestals of the purest Ionic Gothic were ingeniously intermixed with Palladian pediments; and the surging spire exquisitely harmonised with the horizontal architecture of the ancients. But perhaps, after all, the most charming effect was produced by the pyramids, surmounted by weathercocks.

Popanilla was particularly pleased by some chimneys of Caryatides, and did not for a moment hesitate in assenting to the assertion of Skindeep that the Vraibleusians were the most architectural nation in the world. True it was, they had begun late; their attention as a people having been, for a considerable time, attracted to much more important affairs; but they had compensated for their tardy attention by their speedy excellence.\*

Before they returned home Skindeep led Popanilla to the top of a tower, from whence they had a complete view of the whole island. Skindeep particularly directed the Captain's attention to one spot, where flourished, as he said, the only corn-fields in the country, which supplied the whole nation, and were the property of one individual. So unrivalled was his agricultural science that the vulgar only accounted for his admirable produce by a miraculous fecundity! The proprietor of those hundred golden acres was a rather mysterious sort of personage. He was an aboriginal inhabitant, and, though the only one of the aborigines in existence, had lived many centuries, and, to the consternation of some of the Vraibleusians and the exultation of others, exhibited no signs of decay. This awful being was without a name. When spoken of by his admirers he was generally described by such panegyrical periphrases as 'soul of the country,' 'foundation of the State,' 'the only real, and true, and substantial being;' while, on the other hand, those who presumed to differ from those sentiments were in the habit of styling him 'the dead weight,' 'the vampire,' 'the night-mare,' and other titles equally complimentary. They also maintained that, instead of being either real or substantial, he was, in fact, the most flimsy and fictitious personage in the whole island; and then, lashing themselves up into metaphor, they would call him a meteor, or a vapour, or a great windy bubble, that would some day burst.

\* See a work which will be shortly published, entitled, 'The difference detected between *Architecture* and *Parchitecture*, by Sansovino the Second.'

The Aboriginal insisted that it was the common law of the land that the islanders should purchase their corn only of him. They grumbled, but he growled; he swore that it was the constitution of the country; that there was an uninterrupted line of precedents to confirm the claim; and that, if they did not approve of the arrangement, they and their fathers should not have elected to have settled, or presumed to have been spawned, upon his island. Then, as if he were not desirous of resting his claim on its mere legal merits, he would remind them of the superiority of his grain, and the impossibility of a scarcity, in the event of which calamity an insular people could always find a plentiful though temporary resource in sea-weed. He then clearly proved to them that, if ever they had the imprudence to change any of their old laws, they would necessarily never have more than one meal a day as long as they lived. Finally, he recalled to their recollection that he had made the island what it was, that he was their mainstay, and that his counsel and exertions had rendered them the wonder of the world. Thus, between force, and fear, and flattery, the Vraibleusians paid for their corn nearly its weight in gold; but what did that signify to a nation with so many pink shells!

## CHAPTER IX.

THE third day after his drive with his friend Skindeep, Popanilla was waited upon by the most eminent bookseller in Hubbabub, who begged to have the honour of introducing to the public a Narrative of Captain Popanilla's Voyage. This gentleman assured Popanilla that the Vraibleusian public were nervously alive to anything connected with discovery; that so ardent was their attachment to science and natural philosophy that voyages and travels were sure to be read with eagerness, particularly if they had coloured plates. Popanilla was charmed with the proposition, but blushingly informed the mercantile Mæcenas that he did not know how to write. The publisher told him that this circumstance was not of the slightest importance; that he had never for a moment supposed that so sublime a savage could possess such a vulgar accomplishment; and that it was by no means difficult for a man to publish his travels without writing a line of them.

Popanilla having consented to become an author upon these terms, the publisher asked him to dine with him, and introduced him to an intelligent individual. This intelligent individual listened attentively to all Popanilla's adventures. The Captain concealed nothing. He began with the eternal lock of hair, and showed how wonderfully this world was constituted, that even the loss of a thing was not useless; from which it was clear that Utility was Providence. After drinking some capital wine, the intelligent individual told Popanilla that he was wrong in supposing Fantaisie to be an island; that, on the contrary, it was a great continent; that this was proved by the probable action of the tides in the part of the island which had not yet been visited; that the consequence of these tides would be that, in the course of a season or two, Fantaisie would become a great receptacle for icebergs, and be turned into the North Pole; that, therefore, the seasons throughout the world would be changed; that this year, in Vraibleusia, the usual winter would be omitted, and that when the present summer was finished the dog-days would again commence. Popanilla took his leave highly delighted with this intelligent individual and with the bookseller's wine.

Owing to the competition which existed between the publishers, the printers, and the engravers of the city of Hubbabub, and the great exertions of the intelligent individual, the Narrative of Captain Popanilla's Voyage was brought out in less than a week, and was immediately in everybody's hand. The work contained a detailed account of everything which took place during the whole of the three days, and formed a quarto volume. The plates were numerous and highly interesting. There was a line engraving of Alligator Mountain and a mezzotint of Seaweed Island; a view of the canoe N.E.; a view of the canoe N.W.; a view of the canoe S.E.; a view of the canoe S.W. There were highly-finished coloured drawings of the dried fish and the bread-fruit, and an exquisitely tinted representation of the latter in a mouldy state. But the *chef-d'œuvre* was the portrait of the Author himself. He was represented trampling on the body of a boa constrictor of the first quality, in the skin of which he was dressed; at his back were his bow and arrows; his right hand rested on an uprooted pine-tree; he stood in a desert between two volcanoes; at his feet was a lake of magnitude; the distance lowered with an approaching tornado; but a lucky flash of lightning revealed the range of the Andes and both oceans. Altogether he looked the most dandified of savages, and the most savage of dandies. It was a sublime lithograph, and produced scarcely less important effects upon Popanilla's fortune than that lucky 'lock of hair;' for no sooner was the portrait published than Popanilla received a ticket for the receptions of a lady of quality. On showing it to Skindeep, he was told that the honour was immense, and therefore he must go by all means. Skindeep regretted that he could not accompany him, but he was engaged to a lecture on shoemaking; and a lecture was a thing he made it a point never to miss, because, as he very properly observed, 'By lectures you may become extremely well informed without any of the inconveniences of study. No fixity of attention, no continuity of meditation, no habits of reflection, no aptitude of combination, are the least requisite; all which things only give you a nervous headache; and yet you gain all the results of all these processes. True it is that that which is so easily acquired is not always so easily remembered; but what of that? Suppose you forget any subject, why then you go to another lecture.' 'Very true!' said Popanilla.

Popanilla failed not to remember his invitation from Lady Spirituelle; and at the proper hour his announcement produced a sensation throughout her crowded saloons.

Spirituelle was a most enchanting lady; she asked Popanilla how tall he really was, and whether the women in Fantaisie were as handsome as the men. Then she said that the Vraibleusians were the most intellectual and the most scientific nation in the world, and that the society at her house was the most intellectual and the most scientific in Vraibleusia. She told him also that she had hoped by this season the world would have been completely regulated by mind; but that the subversion of matter was a more substantial business than she and the Committee of Management had imagined: she had no doubt, however, that in a short time mind must carry the day, because matter was mortal and mind eternal; therefore mind had the best chance. Finally, she also told him that the passions were the occasion of all the misery which had ever existed; and that it was impossible for mankind either to be happy or great until, like herself and her friends, they were 'all soul.'

Popanilla was charmed with his company. What a difference between the calm, smiling, easy, uninteresting, stupid, sunset countenances of Fantaisie and those around him. All looked so interested and so intelligent; their eyes were so anxious, their gestures so animated, their manners so earnest. They must be very clever! He drew nearer. If before he were charmed, now he was enchanted. What an universal acquisition of useful knowledge! Three or four dukes were earnestly imbibing a new theory of gas from a brilliant little gentleman in black, who looked like a Will-o'-the-wisp. The Prime Minister was anxious about pin-making; a Bishop equally interested in a dissertation on the escapements of watches; a Field-Marshal not less intent on a new specific from the concentrated essence of hellebore. But what most delighted Popanilla was hearing a lecture from the most eminent lawyer and statesman in Vraibleusia on his first and favourite study of hydrostatics. His associations quite overcame him: all Fantaisie rushed upon his memory, and he was obliged to retire to a less frequented part of the room to relieve his too excited feelings.

He was in a few minutes addressed by the identical little gentleman who had recently been speculating with the three dukes.

The little gentleman told him that he had heard with great pleasure that in Fantaisie they had no historians, poets, or novelists. He proved to Popanilla that no such thing as experience existed; that, as the world was now to be regulated on quite different principles from those by which it had hitherto been conducted, similar events to those which had occurred could never again take place; and therefore it was absolutely useless to know anything about the past. With regard to literary fiction, he explained that, as it was absolutely necessary, from his nature, that man should experience a certain quantity of excitement, the false interest which these productions created prevented their readers from obtaining this excitement by methods which, by the discovery of the useful, might greatly benefit society.

'You are of opinion, then,' exclaimed the delighted Popanilla, 'that nothing is good which is not useful?'

'Is it possible that an individual exists in this world who doubts this great first principle?' said the little man, with great animation.

'Ah, my dear friend!' said Popanilla, 'if you only knew what an avowal of this great first principle has cost me; what I have suffered; what I have lost!'

'What have you lost?' asked the little gentleman.

'In the first place, a lock of hair——'

'Poh, nonsense!'

'Ah! you may say Poh! but it was a particular lock of hair.'

'My friend, that word is odious. Nothing is *particular*, everything is *general*. Rules are general, feelings are general, and property should be general; and, sir, I tell you what, in a very short time it must be so. Why should Lady Spirituelle, for instance, receive me at her house, rather than I receive her at mine?'

'Why don't you, then?' asked the simple Popanilla.

'Because I have not got one, sir!' roared the little gentleman.

He would certainly have broken away had not Popanilla begged him to answer one question. The Captain, reiterating in the most solemn manner his firm belief in the dogma that nothing was good which was not useful, and again detailing the persecutions which this conviction had brought upon him, was delighted that an opportunity was now afforded to gain from the lips of a distinguished philosopher a definition of what *utility* really was. The distinguished philosopher could not refuse so trifling a favour.

'Utility,' said he, 'is——'

At this critical moment there was a universal buzz throughout the rooms, and everybody looked so interested that the philosopher quite forgot to finish his answer. On inquiring the cause of this great sensation, Popanilla was informed that a rumour was about that a new element had been discovered that afternoon. The party speedily broke up, the principal philosophers immediately rushing to their clubs to ascertain the truth of this report. Popanilla was unfashionable enough to make his acknowledgments to his hostess before he left her house. As he gazed upon her ladyship's brilliant eyes and radiant complexion, he felt convinced of the truth of her theory of the passions; he could not refrain from pressing her hand in a manner which violated etiquette, and which a nativity in the Indian Ocean could alone excuse; the pressure was graciously returned. As Popanilla descended the staircase, he discovered a little note of pink satin paper entangled in his ruffle. He opened it with curiosity. It was 'All soul.' He did not return to his hotel quite so soon as he expected.

## CHAPTER X.

POPANILLA breakfasted rather late the next morning, and on looking over the evening papers, which were just published, his eyes lighted on the following paragraph:—

'Arrived yesterday at the Hôtel Diplomatique, His Excellency Prince Popanilla, Ambassador Extraordinary and Minister Plenipotentiary from the newly-recognised State of Fantaisie.'

Before his Excellency could either recover from his astonishment or make any inquiries which might throw any illustration upon its cause, a loud shout in the street made him naturally look out of the window. He observed three or four magnificent equipages drawing up at the door of the hotel, and followed by a large crowd. Each carriage was drawn by four horses, and attended by footmen so radiant with gold and scarlet that, had Popanilla been the late ingenious Mr. Keates, he would have mistaken them for the natural children of Phœbus and Aurora. The Ambassador forgot the irregularity of the paragraph in the splendour of the liveries. He felt triumphantly conscious that the most beautiful rose in the world must look extremely pale by the side of scarlet cloth; and this new example of the superiority of art over nature reminding him of the inferiority of bread-fruit to grilled muffin, he resolved to return to breakfast.

But it was his fate to be reminded of the inutility of the best resolutions, for ere the cup of coffee had touched his parched lips the door of his room flew open, and the Marquess of Moustache was announced.

His Lordship was a young gentleman with an expressive countenance; that is to say, his face was so covered with hair, and the back of his head cropped so bald, that you generally addressed him in the rear by mistake. He did not speak, but continued bowing for a considerable time, in that diplomatic manner which means so much. By the time he had finished bowing his suite had gained the apartment, and his Private Secretary, one of those uncommonly able men who only want an opportunity, seized the present one of addressing Popanilla.

Bowing to the late Captain with studied respect, he informed him that the Marquess Moustache was the nobleman appointed by the Government of Vraibleusia to attend upon his Excellency during the first few weeks of his mission, with the view of affording him all information upon those objects which might naturally be expected to engage the interest or attract the attention of so distinguished a personage. The 'ancien marin' and present Ambassador had been so used to miracles since the loss of that lock of hair, that he did not think it supernatural, having during the last few days been in turn a Fantaisian nobleman, a post-captain, a fish, a goddess, and, above all, an author, he should now be transformed into a plenipotentiary. Drinking, therefore, his cup of coffee, he assumed an air as if he really were used to have a Marquess for an attendant, and said that he was at his Lordship's service.

The Marquess bowed low, and the Private Secretary remarked that the first thing to be done by his Excellency was to be presented to the Government. After that he was to visit all the manufactories in Vraibleusia, subscribe to all the charities, and dine with all the Corporations, attend a *déjeûner à la fourchette* at a palace they were at present building under the sea, give a gold plate to be run for on the fashionable racecourse, be present at morning prayers at the Government Chapel, hunt once or twice, give a dinner or two himself, make one pun, and go to the Play, by which various means, he said, the good understanding between the two countries would be materially increased and, in a manner, established.

As the Fantaisian Ambassador and his suite entered their carriages, the sky, if it had not been for the smoke, would certainly have been rent by the acclamations of the mob. 'Popanilla for ever!' sounded from all quarters, except where the shout was varied by 'Vraibleusia and Fantaisie against the world!' which perhaps was even the most popular sentiment of the two. The Ambassador was quite agitated, and asked the Marquess what he was to do. The Private Secretary told his Excellency to bow. Popanilla bowed with such grace that in five minutes the horses were taken out of his carriage, and that carriage dragged in triumph by the enthusiastic populace. He continued bowing, and their enthusiasm continued increasing. In the meantime his Excellency's portrait was sketched by an artist who hung upon his wheel, and in less than half an hour a lithographic likeness of the popular idol was worshipped in every print-shop in Hubbabub.

As they drew nearer the Hall of Audience the crowd kept increasing, till at length the whole city seemed poured forth to meet him. Although now feeling conscious that he was the greatest man in the island, and therefore only thinking of himself, Popanilla's attention was nevertheless at this moment attracted by a singular figure. He was apparently a man: in stature a Patagonian, and robust as a well-fed ogre. His countenance was jolly, but consequential; and his costume a curious mixture of a hunting-dress and a court suit. He was on foot, and in spite of the crowd, with the aid of a good whip and his left fist made his way with great ease. On inquiring who this extraordinary personage might be, Popanilla was informed that it was THE ABORIGINAL INHABITANT. As the giant passed the Ambassador's carriages, the whole suite, even Lord Moustache, rose and bent low; and the Secretary told Popanilla that there was no person in the island for whom the Government of Vraibleusia entertained so profound a respect.

The crowd was now so immense that even the progress of the Aboriginal Inhabitant was for a moment impeded. The great man got surrounded by a large body of little mechanics. The contrast between the pale perspiring visages and lean forms of these emaciated and half-generated creatures, and the jolly form and ruddy countenance, gigantic limbs and ample frame, of the Aboriginal, was most striking; nor could any one view the group for an instant without feeling convinced that the latter was really a superior existence. The mechanics, who were worn by labour, not reduced by famine, far from being miserable, were impudent. They began rating the mighty one for the dearness of his corn. He received their attacks with mildness. He reminded them that the regulation by which they procured their bread was the aboriginal law of the island, under which they had all so greatly flourished. He explained to them that it was owing to this protecting principle that he and his ancestors, having nothing to do but to hunt and shoot, had so preserved their health that, unlike the rest of the human race, they had not degenerated from the original form and nature of man. He showed that it was owing to the vigour of mind and body consequent upon this fine health that Vraibleusia had become the wonder of the world, and that they themselves were so actively employed; and he inferred that they surely could not grudge him the income which he derived, since that income was, in fact, the foundation of their own profits. He then satisfactorily demonstrated to them that if by any circumstances he were to cease to exist, the whole island would immediately sink under the sea. Having thus condescended to hold a little parley with his fellow-subjects, though not fellow-creatures, he gave them all a good sound flogging, and departed amidst the enthusiastic cheering of those whom he had so briskly lashed.

By this time Popanilla had arrived at the Hall of Audience.

'It was a vast and venerable pile.'

His Excellency and suite quitted their carriages amidst the renewed acclamations of the mob. Proceeding through a number of courts and quadrangles, crowded with guards and officials, they stopped before a bronze gate of great height. Over it was written, in vast characters of living flame, this inscription:

TO
THE WISEST AND THE BEST,
THE RICHEST AND THE MIGHTIEST,
THE GLORY AND THE ADMIRATION,
THE DEFENCE AND THE CONSTERNATION.

On reading this mysterious inscription his Excellency experienced a sudden and awful shudder. Lord Moustache, however, who was more used to mysteries, taking up a silver trumpet, which was fixed to the portal by a crimson cord, gave a loud blast. The gates flew open with the sound of a whirlwind, and Popanilla found himself in what at first appeared an illimitable hall. It was crowded, but perfect order was preserved. The Ambassador was conducted with great pomp to the upper end of the apartment, where, after an hour's walk, his Excellency arrived. At the extremity of the hall was a colossal and metallic Statue of extraordinary appearance. It represented an armed monarch. The head and bust were of gold, and the curling hair was crowned with an imperial diadem; the body and arms were of silver, worked in the semblance of a complete suit of enamelled armour of the feudal ages; and the thighs and legs were of iron, which the artist had clothed in the bandaged hose of the old Saxons. The figure bore the appearance of great antiquity, but had evidently been often repaired and renovated since its first formation. The workmanship was clearly of different eras, and the reparations, either from ignorance or intention, had often been effected with little deference to the original design. Part of the shoulders had been supplied by the other, though less precious, metal, and the Roman and Imperial ornaments had unaccountably been succeeded by the less classic, though more picturesque, decorations of Gothic armour. On the other hand, a great portion of the chivalric and precious material of the body had been removed, and replaced by a style and substance resembling those of the lower limbs. In its right hand the Statue brandished a naked sword, and with its left leant upon a huge, though extremely rich and elaborately carved, crosier. It trampled upon a shivered lance and a broken chain.

'Your Excellency perceives,' said the Secretary, pointing to the Statue, 'that ours is a mixed Government.'

Popanilla was informed that this extraordinary Statue enjoyed all the faculties of an intellectual being, with the additional advantage of some faculties which intellectual beings do not enjoy. It possessed not only the faculty of speech, but of speaking truth: not only the power of judgment, but of judging rightly; not only the habit of listening, but of listening attentively. Its antiquity was so remote that the most profound and acute antiquarians had failed in tracing back its origin. The Aboriginal Inhabitant, however, asserted that it was the work of one of his ancestors; and as his assertion was confirmed by all traditions, the allegation was received. Whatever might have been its origin, certain it was that it was now immortal, for it could never die; and to whomsoever it might have been originally indebted for its power, not less sure was it that it was now omnipotent, for it could do all things. Thus alleged and thus believed the Vraibleusians, marvellous and sublime people! who, with all the impotence of mortality, have created a Government which is both immortal and omnipotent!

Generally speaking, the Statue was held in great reverence and viewed with great admiration by the whole Vraibleusian people. There were a few persons, indeed, who asserted that the creation of such a Statue was by no means so mighty a business as it had been the fashion to suppose; and that it was more than probable that, with the advantages afforded by the scientific discoveries of modern times, they would succeed in making a more useful one. This, indeed, they offered to accomplish, provided the present Statue were preliminarily destroyed; but as they were well assured that this offer would never be accepted, it was generally treated by those who refused it as a braggadocio. There were many also who, though they in general greatly admired and respected the present Statue, affected to believe that, though the execution was wonderful, and the interior machinery indeed far beyond the powers of the present age, nevertheless the design was in many parts somewhat rude, and the figure altogether far from being well-proportioned. Some thought the head too big, some too small; some that the body was disproportionately little; others, on the contrary, that it was so much too large that it had the appearance of being dropsical; others maintained that the legs were too weak for the support of the whole, and that they should be rendered more important and prominent members of the figure; while, on the contrary, there were yet others who cried out that really these members were already so extravagantly huge, so coarse, and so ungenteel, that they quite marred the general effect of a beautiful piece of sculpture.

The same differences existed about the comparative excellence of the three metals and the portions of the body which they respectively formed. Some admired the gold, and maintained that if it were not for the head the Statue would be utterly useless; others preferred the silver, and would assert that the body, which contained all the machinery, must clearly be the most precious portion; while a third party triumphantly argued that the iron legs which supported both body and head must surely be the most valuable part, since without them the Statue must fall. The first party advised that in all future reparations gold only should be introduced; and the other parties, of course, recommended with equal zeal their own favourite metals. It is observable, however, that if, under these circumstances, the iron race chanced to fail in carrying their point, they invariably voted for gold in preference to silver. But the most contradictory opinions, perhaps, were those which were occasioned by the instruments with which the Statue was armed and supported. Some affected to be so frightened by the mere sight of the brandished sword, although it never moved, that they pretended it was dangerous to live even under the same sky with it; while others, treating very lightly the terrors of this warlike instrument, would observe that much more was really to be apprehended from the remarkable strength and thickness of the calm and peace-inspiring crosier; and that as long as the Government was supported by this huge pastoral staff nothing could prevail against it; that it could dare all things, and even stand without the help of its legs. All these various opinions at least proved that, although the present might not be the most miraculous Statue that could possibly be created, it was nevertheless quite impossible ever to form one which would please all parties.

The care of this wonderful Statue was entrusted to twelve 'Managers,' whose duty it was to wind-up and regulate its complicated machinery, and who answered for its good management by their heads. It was their business to consult the oracle upon all occasions, and by its decisions to administer and regulate all the affairs of the State. They alone were permitted to hear its voice; for the Statue never spoke in public save on rare occasions, and its sentences were then really so extremely commonplace that, had it not been for the deep wisdom of its general conduct, the Vraibleusians would have been almost tempted to believe that they really might exist without the services of the capital member. The twelve Managers surrounded the Statue at a respectful distance; their posts were the most distinguished in the State; and indeed the duties attached to them were so numerous, so difficult, and so responsible, that it required no ordinary abilities to fulfil, and demanded no ordinary courage to aspire to, them.

The Fantaisian Ambassador, having been presented, took his place on the right hand of the Statue, next to the Aboriginal Inhabitant, and public business then commenced.

There came forward a messenger, who, knocking his nose three times with great reverence on the floor, a knock for each metal of the figure, thus spoke:

'O thou wisest and best! thou richest and mightiest! thou glory and admiration! thou defence and consternation! Lo! the King of the North is cutting all his subjects' heads off!'

This announcement produced a great sensation. The Marquess Moustache took snuff; the Private Secretary said he had long suspected that this would be the case; and the Aboriginal Inhabitant remarked to Popanilla that the corn in the North was of an exceedingly coarse grain. While they were making these observations the twelve Managers had assembled in deep consultation around the

Statue, and in a very few minutes the Oracle was prepared. The answer was very simple, but the exordium was sublime. It professed that the Vraibleusian nation was the saviour and champion of the world; that it was the first principle of its policy to maintain the cause of any people struggling for their rights as men; and it avowed itself to be the grand patron of civil and religious liberty in all quarters of the globe. Forty-seven battalions of infantry and eighteen regiments of cavalry, twenty-four sail of the line, seventy transports, and fifteen bombketches, were then ordered to leave Vraibleusia for the North in less than sixty minutes!

'What energy!' said Popanilla; 'what decision! what rapidity of execution!'

'Ay!' said the Aboriginal, smacking his thigh; 'let them say what they like about their proportions, and mixtures, and metals—abstract nonsense! No one can deny that our Government works well. But see! here comes another messenger!'

'O thou wisest and best! thou richest and mightiest! thou glory and admiration! thou defence and consternation! Lo! the people of the South have cut their king's head off!'

'Well! I suppose that is exactly what you all want,' said the innocent Popanilla.

The Private Secretary looked mysterious, and said that he was not prepared to answer; that his department never having been connected with this species of business, he was unable at the moment to give his Excellency the requisite information. At the same time, he begged to state that, provided anything he said should not commit him, he had no objection to answer the question hypothetically. The Aboriginal Inhabitant said that he would have no hypotheses or Jacobins; that he did not approve of cutting off kings' heads; and that the Vraibleusians were the most monarchical people in the world. So saying, he walked up, without any ceremony, to the chief Manager, and taking him by the button, conversed with him some time in an earnest manner, which made the stocks fall two per cent.

The Statue ordered three divisions of the grand army and a battering-train of the first grade off to the South without the loss of a second. A palace and establishment were immediately directed to be prepared for the family of the murdered monarch, and the commander-in-chief was instructed to make every exertion to bring home the body of his Majesty embalmed. Such an immense issue of pink shells was occasioned by this last expedition that stocks not only recovered themselves, but rose considerably.

The excitement occasioned by this last announcement evaporated at the sight of a third messenger. He informed the Statue that the Emperor of the East was unfortunately unable to pay the interest upon his national debt; that his treasury was quite empty and his resources utterly exhausted. He requested the assistance of the most wealthy and the most generous of nations; and he offered them as security for their advances his gold and silver mines, which, for the breadth of their veins and the richness of their ores, he said, were unequalled. He added, that the only reason they were unworked was the exquisite flavour of the water-melons in his empire, which was so delicious that his subjects of all classes, passing their whole day in devouring them, could be induced neither by force nor persuasion to do anything else. The cause was so reasonable, and the security so satisfactory, that the Vraiblousian Government felt themselves authorised in shipping off immediately all the gold in the island. Pink shells abounded, and stocks were still higher.

'You have no mines in Vraiblousia, I believe?' said Popanilla to the Aboriginal.

'No! but we have taxes.'

'Very true!' said Popanilla.

'I understand that a messenger has just arrived from the West,' said the Secretary to the Fantaisian Plenipotentiary. 'He must bring interesting intelligence from such interesting countries. Next to ourselves, they are

E E

evidently the most happy, the most wealthy, the most enlightened, and the most powerful Governments in the world. Although founded only last week, they already rank in the first class of nations. I will send you a little pamphlet to-morrow, which I have just published upon this subject, in which you will see that I have combated, I trust not unsuccessfully, the ridiculous opinions of those cautious statesmen who insinuate that the stability of these Governments is even yet questionable.'

The messenger from the Republics of the West now prostrated himself before the Statue. He informed it that two parties had, unfortunately, broken out in these countries, and threatened their speedy dissolution; that one party maintained that all human government originated in the *wants* of man; while the other party asserted that it originated in the *desires* of man. That these factions had become so violent and so universal that public business was altogether stopped, trade quite extinct, and the instalments due to Vraibleusia not forthcoming. Finally, he entreated the wisest and the best of nations to send to these distracted lands some discreet and trusty personages, well instructed in the first principles of government, in order that they might draw up constitutions for the ignorant and irritated multitude.

The Private Secretary told Popanilla that this was no more than he had long expected; that all this would subside, and that he should publish a postscript to his pamphlet in a few days, which he begged to dedicate to him.

A whole corps diplomatique and another shipful of abstract philosophers, principally Scotchmen, were immediately ordered off to the West; and shortly after, to render their first principles still more effective and their administrative arrangements still more influential, some brigades of infantry and a detachment of the guards followed. Free constitutions are apt to be misunderstood until half of the nation are bayoneted and the rest imprisoned.

As this mighty Vraibleusian nation had, within the last

half-hour, received intelligence from all quarters of the globe, and interfered in all possible affairs, civil and military, abstract, administrative, diplomatic, and financial, Popanilla supposed that the assembly would now break up. Some petty business, however, remained. War was declared against the King of Sneezeland, for presuming to buy pocket-handkerchiefs of another nation; and the Emperor of Pastilles was threatened with a bombardment for daring to sell his peppers to another people. There were also some dozen commercial treaties to be signed, or canvassed, or cancelled; and a report having got about that there was a rumour that some disturbance had broken out in some parts unknown, a flying expedition was despatched, with sealed orders, to circumnavigate the globe and arrange affairs. By this time Popanilla thoroughly understood the meaning of the mysterious inscription.

Just as the assembly was about to be dissolved another messenger, who, in his agitation, even forgot the accustomed etiquette of salutation, rushed into the presence.

'O most mighty! Sir Bombastes Furioso, who commanded our last expedition, having sailed, in the hurry, with wrong orders, has attacked our ancient ally by mistake, and utterly destroyed him!'

Here was a pretty business for the Best and Wisest! At first the Managers behaved in a manner the most undiplomatic, and quite lost their temper; they raved, they stormed, they contradicted each other, they contradicted themselves, and swore that Sir Bombastes' head should answer for it. Then they subsided into sulkiness, and at length, beginning to suspect that the fault might ultimately attach only to themselves, they got frightened, and held frequent consultations with pale visages and quivering lips. After some time they thought they could do nothing wiser than put a good face upon the affair; whatever might be the result, it was, at any rate, a victory, and a victory would please the vainest of nations: and so these blundering and blustering gentlemen determined to adopt the conqueror, whom they were at first weak enough to disclaim, then vile enough to bully, and finally forced to reward. The Statue accordingly whispered a most elaborate panegyric on Furioso, which was of course duly delivered. The Admiral, who was neither a coward nor a fool, was made ridiculous by being described as the greatest commander that ever existed; one whom Nature, in a gracious freak, had made to shame us little men; a happy compound of the piety of Noah, the patriotism of Themistocles, the skill of Columbus, and the courage of Nelson; and his exploit styled the most glorious and unrivalled victory that was ever achieved, even by the Vraibleusians! Honours were decreed in profusion, a general illumination ordered for the next twenty nights, and an expedition immediately despatched to attack the right man.

All this time the conquerors were in waiting in an anteroom, in great trepidation, and fully prepared to be cashiered or cut in quarters. They were rather surprised when, bowing to the ground, they were saluted by some half-dozen lords-in-waiting as the heroes of the age, congratulated upon their famous achievements, and humbly requested to appear in the Presence.

The warriors accordingly walked up in procession to the Statue, who, opening its mighty mouth, vomited forth a flood of ribbons, stars, and crosses, which were divided among the valiant band. This oral discharge the Vraibleusians called the 'fountain of honour.'

Scarcely had the mighty Furioso and his crew disappeared than a body of individuals arrived at the top of the hall, and, placing themselves opposite the Managers, began rating them for their inefficient administration of the island, and expatiated on the inconsistency of their late conduct to the conquering Bombastes. The Managers defended themselves in a manner perfectly in character with their recent behaviour; but their opponents were not easily satisfied with their confused explanations and their explained confusions, and the speeches on both sides grew warmer. At length the opposition proceeded to expel the administration from their places by force, and an eager scuffle between the two parties now commenced. The general body of spectators continued only to observe, and did not participate in the fray. At first, this *mêlée* only excited amusement; but as it lengthened some wisely observed that public business greatly suffered by these private squabbles; and some even ventured to imagine that the safety of the Statue might be implicated by their continuance. But this last fear was futile.

Popanilla asked the Private Secretary which party he thought would ultimately succeed. The Private Secretary said that, if the present Managers retained their places, he thought that they would not go out; but if, on the other hand, they were expelled by the present opposition, it was probable that the present opposition would become Managers. The Aboriginal thought both parties equally incompetent; and told Popanilla some long stories about a person who was chief Manager in his youth, about five hundred years ago, to whom he said he was indebted for all his political principles, which did not surprise Popanilla.

At this moment a noise was heard throughout the hall which made his Excellency believe that something untoward had again happened, and that another conqueror by mistake had again arrived. A most wonderful being galloped up to the top of the apartment. It was half man and half horse. The Secretary told Popanilla that this was the famous Centaur Chiron; that his Horseship, having wearied of his ardent locality in the constellations, had descended some years back to the island of Vraibleusia; that he had commanded the armies of the nation in all the great wars, and had gained every battle in which he had ever been engaged. Chiron was no less skilful, he said, in civil than in military affairs; but the Vraibleusians, being very jealous of allowing themselves to be governed by their warriors, the Centaur had lately been out of employ. While the Secretary was giving him this information Popanilla perceived that the great Chiron was attacking the combatants on both sides. The tutor of Achilles, Hercules, and Æneas, of course, soon succeeded in kicking them all out, and constituted himself chief and sole Manager of the Statue. Some grumbled at this autocratic conduct 'upon principle,' but they were chiefly connections of the expelled. The great majority, wearied with public squabbles occasioned by private ends, rejoiced to see the public interest entrusted to an individual who had a reputation to lose. Intelligence of the appointment of the Centaur was speedily diffused throughout the island, and produced great and general satisfaction. There were a few, indeed, impartial personages, who had no great taste for Centaurs in civil capacities, from an apprehension that, if he could not succeed in persuading them by his eloquence, his Grace might chance to use his heels.

## CHAPTER XI.

ON the evening of his presentation day his Excellency the Fantaisian Ambassador and suite honoured the national theatre with their presence. Such a house was never known! The pit was miraculously overflown before the doors were opened, although the proprietor did not permit a single private entrance. The enthusiasm was universal, and only twelve persons were killed. The Private Secretary told Popanilla, with an air of great complacency, that the Vraiblousian theatres were the largest in the world. Popanilla had little doubt of the truth of this information, as a long time elapsed before he could even discover the stage. He observed that every person in the theatre carried a long black glass, which he kept perpetually fixed to his eye. To sit in a huge room hotter than a glass-house, in a posture emulating the most sanctified Faquir, with a throbbing head-ache, a breaking back, and twisted legs, with a heavy tube held over one eye, and the other covered with the unemployed hand, is in Vraibleusia called a public amusement.

The play was by the most famous dramatist that Vrai-

bleusia ever produced; and certainly, when his Excellency
witnessed the first scenes, it was easier to imagine that he
was once more in his own sunset Isle of Fantaisie than in
the railroad state of Vraibleusia: but, unfortunately, this
evening the principal characters and scenes were omitted,
to make room for a moving panorama, which lasted some
hours, of the chief and most recent Vraibleusian victories.
The audience fought their battles o'er again with great
fervour. During the play one of the inferior actors was
supposed to have saluted a female chorus-singer with an
ardour which was more than theatrical, and every lady in
the house immediately fainted; because, as the eternal
Secretary told Popanilla, the Vraibleusians are the most
modest and most moral nation in the world. The male
part of the audience insisted, in indignant terms, that the
offending performer should immediately be dismissed. In
a few minutes he appeared upon the stage to make a most
humble apology for an offence which he was not conscious
of having committed; but the most moral and the most
modest of nations was implacable, and the wretch was
expelled. Having a large family dependent upon his exertions, the actor, according to a custom prevalent in Vraibleusia, went immediately and drowned himself in the
nearest river. Then the ballet commenced.

It was soon discovered that the chief dancer, a celebrated
foreigner, who had been announced for this evening, was
absent. The uproar was tremendous, and it was whispered
that the house would be pulled down; because, as Popanilla
was informed, the Vraibleusians are the most particular
and the freest people in the world, and never will permit
themselves to be treated with disrespect. The principal
chandelier having been destroyed, the manager appeared,
and regretted that Signor Zephyrino, being engaged to
dine with a Grandee of the first class, was unable to fulfil
his engagement. The house became frantic, and the terrified
manager sent immediately for the Signor. The artist, after
a proper time had elapsed, appeared with a napkin round
his neck and a fork in his hand, with which he stood some

moments, until the uproar had subsided, picking his teeth. At length, when silence was obtained, he told them that he was surprised that the most polished and liberal nation in the world should behave themselves in such a brutal and narrow-minded manner. He threatened them that he would throw up his engagement immediately, and announce to all foreign parts that they were a horde of barbarians; then, abusing them for a few seconds in round terms, he retired, amidst the cheerings of the whole house, to finish his wine.

When the performances were finished the audience rose and joined in chorus. On Popanilla enquiring the name and nature of this effusion, he was told that it was the national air of the Isle of Fantaisie, sung in compliment to himself. His Excellency shrugged his shoulders and bowed low.

The next morning, attended by his suite, Popanilla visited the most considerable public offices and manufactories in Hubbabub. He was received in all places with the greatest distinction. He was invariably welcomed either by the chiefs of the department or the proprietors themselves, and a sumptuous collation was prepared for him in every place. His Excellency evinced the liveliest interest in everything that was pointed out to him, and instantaneously perceived that the Vraibleusians exceeded the rest of the world in manufactures and public works as much as they did in arms, morals, modesty, philosophy, and politics. The Private Secretary being absent upon his postscript, Popanilla received the most satisfactory information upon all subjects from the Marquess himself. Whenever he addressed any question to his Lordship, his noble attendant, with the greatest politeness, begged him to take some refreshment. Popanilla returned to his hotel with a great admiration of the manner in which refined philosophy in Vraibleusia was applied to the common purposes of life; and found that he had that morning acquired a general knowledge of the chief arts and sciences, eaten some hundred sandwiches, and tasted as many bottles of sherry.

## CHAPTER XII.

The most commercial nation in the world was now busily preparing to diffuse the blessings of civilisation and competition throughout the native country of their newly-acquired friend. The greatest exporters that ever existed had never been acquainted with such a subject for exportation as the Isle of Fantaisie. There everything was wanted. It was not a partial demand which was to be satisfied, nor a particular deficiency which was to be supplied; but a vast population was thoroughly to be furnished with every article which a vast population must require. From the manufacturer of steam-engines to the manufacturer of stockings, all were alike employed. There was no branch of trade in Vraibleusia which did not equally rejoice at this new opening for commercial enterprise, and which was not equally interested in this new theatre for Vraibleusian industry, Vraibleusian invention, Vraibleusian activity, and, above all, Vraibleusian competition.

Day and night the whole island was employed in preparing for the great fleet and in huzzaing Popanilla. When at home, every ten minutes he was obliged to appear in the balcony, and then, with hand on heart and hat in hand, ah! that bow! that perpetual motion of popularity! If a man love ease, let him be most unpopular. The Managers did the impossible to assist and advance the intercourse between the two nations. They behaved in a liberal and enlightened manner, and a deputation of liberal and enlightened merchants consequently waited upon them with a vote of thanks. They issued so many pink shells that the price of the public funds was doubled, and affairs arranged so skilfully that money was universally declared to be worth nothing, so that every one in the island, from the Premier down to the Mendicant whom the lecture-loving Skindeep threatened with the bastinado, was enabled to participate, in some degree, in the approaching venture, if we should use so dubious a term in speaking of profits so certain.

Compared with the Fantaisian connection, the whole commerce of the world appeared to the Vraibleusians a retail business. All other customers were neglected or discarded, and each individual seemed to concentrate his resources to supply the wants of a country where they dance by moonlight, live on fruit, and sleep on flowers. At length the first fleet of five hundred sail, laden with wonderful specimens of Vraibleusian mechanism, and innumerable bales of Vraibleusian manufactures; articles raw and refined, goods dry and damp, wholesale and retail; silks and woollen cloths; cottons, cutlery, and camlets; flannels and ladies' albums; under waistcoats, kid gloves, engravings, coats, cloaks, and ottomans; lamps and looking-glasses; sofas, round tables, equipages, and scent-bottles; fans and tissue-flowers; porcelain, poetry, novels, newspapers, and cookery books; bear's-grease, blue pills, and bijouterie; arms, beards, poodles, pages, mustachios, court-guides, and bon-bons; music, pictures, ladies' maids, scrap-books, buckles, boxing-gloves, guitars, and snuff-boxes; together with a company of opera-singers, a band of comedians, a popular preacher, some quacks, lecturers, artists, and literary gentlemen, principally sketch-book men, quitted, one day, with a favourable wind, and amid the exultation of the inhabitants, the port of Hubbabub!

When his Excellency Prince Popanilla heard of the contents of this stupendous cargo, notwithstanding his implicit confidence in the superior genius and useful knowledge of the Vraibleusians, he could not refrain from expressing a doubt whether, in the present undeveloped state of his native land, any returns could be made proportionate to so curious and elaborate an importation; but whenever he ventured to intimate his opinion to any of the most commercial nation in the world he was only listened to with an incredulous smile which seemed to pity his inexperience, or told, with an air of profound self-complacency, that in Fantaisie 'there must be great resources.'

In the meantime, public companies were formed for

working the mines, colonizing the waste lands, and cutting the coral rocks of the Indian Isle, of all which associations Popanilla was chosen Director by acclamation. These, however, it must be confessed, were speculations of a somewhat doubtful nature; but the Branch Bank Society of the Isle of Fantaisie really held out flattering prospects.

When the fleet had sailed they gave Popanilla a public dinner. It was attended by all the principal men in the island, and he made a speech, which was received in a rather different manner than was his sunset oration by the monarch whom he now represented. Fantaisie and its accomplished Envoy were at the same time the highest and the universal fashion. The ladies sang *à la Syrene*, dressed their hair *à la Mermede*, and themselves *à la Fantastique*; which, by-the-bye, was not new; and the gentlemen wore boa-constrictor cravats and waltzed *à la mer Indienné*—a title probably suggested by a remembrance of the dangers of the sea.

It was soon discovered that, without taking into consideration the average annual advantages which would necessarily spring from their new connection, the profits which must accrue upon the present expedition alone had already doubled the capital of the island. Everybody in Vraibleusia had either made a fortune, or laid the foundation of one. The penniless had become prosperous, and the principal merchants and manufacturers, having realised large capitals, retired from business. But the colossal fortunes were made by the gentlemen who had assisted the administration in raising the price of the public funds and in managing the issues of the pink shells. The effect of this immense increase of the national wealth and of this creation of new and powerful classes of society was speedily felt. Great moves to the westward were perpetual, and a variety of sumptuous squares and streets were immediately run up in that chosen land. Butlers were at a premium; coach-makers never slept; card-engravers, having exhausted copper, had recourse to steel; and the demand for arms at the Heralds' College was so great that even the mystical genius of Garter was exhausted, and hostile meetings were commenced between the junior members of some ancient families, to whom the same crest had been unwittingly apportioned; but, the seconds interfering, they discovered themselves to be relations. All the eldest sons were immediately to get into Parliament, and all the younger ones as quickly into the Guards; and the simple Fantaisian Envoy, who had the peculiar felicity of taking everything *au pied du lettre*, made a calculation that, if these arrangements were duly effected, in a short time the Vraibleusian representatives would exceed the Vraibleusian represented; and that there would be at least three officers in the Vraibleusian Guards to every private. Judging from the beards and mustachios which now abounded, this great result was near at hand. With the snub nose which is the characteristic of the millionaires, these appendages produce a pleasing effect.

When the excitement had a little subsided; when their mighty mansions were magnificently furnished; when their bright equipages were fairly launched, and the due complement of their liveried retainers perfected; when, in short, they had imitated the aristocracy in every point in which wealth could rival blood: then the new people discovered with dismay that one thing was yet wanting, which treasure could not purchase, and which the wit of others could not supply—Manner. In homely phrase, the millionaires did not know how to behave themselves. Accustomed to the counting-house, the factory, or the exchange, they looked queer in saloons, and said 'Sir!' when they addressed you; and seemed stiff, and hard, and hot. Then the solecisms they committed in more formal society, oh! they were outrageous; and a leading article in an eminent journal was actually written upon the subject. I dare not write the deeds they did; but it was whispered that when they drank wine they filled their glasses to the very brim. All this delighted the old class, who were as envious of their riches as the new people were emulous of their style.

In any other country except Vraibleusia persons so

situated would have consoled themselves for their disagreeable position by a consciousness that their posterity would not be annoyed by the same deficiencies; but the wonderful Vraibleusian people resembled no other, even in their failings. They determined to acquire in a day that which had hitherto been deemed the gradual consequence of tedious education.

A 'Society for the Diffusion of Fashionable Knowledge' was announced; the Millionaires looked triumphantly mysterious, the aristocrats quizzed. The object of the society is intimated by its title; and the method by which its institutors proposed to attain this object was the periodical publication of pamphlets, under the superintendence of a competent committee. The first treatise appeared: its subject was NONCHALANCE. It instructed its students ever to appear inattentive in the society of men, and heartless when they conversed with women. It taught them not to understand a man if he were witty; to misunderstand him if he were eloquent; to yawn or. stare if he chanced to elevate his voice, or presumed to ruffle the placidity of the social calm by addressing his fellow-creatures with teeth unparted. Excellence was never to be recognised, but only disparaged with a look: an opinion or a sentiment, and the *nonchalant* was lost for ever. For these, he was to substitute a smile like a damp sunbeam, a moderate curl of the upper lip, and the all-speaking and perpetual shrug of the shoulders. By a skilful management of these qualities it was shown to be easy to ruin another's reputation and ensure your own without ever opening your mouth. To woman, this exquisite treatise said much in few words: 'Listlessness, listlessness, listlessness,' was the edict by which the most beautiful works of nature were to be regulated, who are only truly charming when they make us fool and feel themselves. 'Listlessness, listlessness, listlessness;' for when you choose not to be listless, the contrast is so striking that the triumph must be complete.

The treatise said much more, which I shall omit. It forgot, however, to remark that this vaunted nonchalance may be the offspring of the most contemptible and the most odious of passions: and that while it may be exceedingly refined to appear uninterested when others are interested, to witness excellence without emotion, and to listen to genius without animation, the heart of the Insensible may as often be inflamed by Envy as inspired by Fashion.

Dissertations 'On leaving cards,' 'On cutting intimate friends,' 'On cravats,' 'On dinner courses,' 'On poor relations,' 'On bores,' 'On lions,' were announced as speedily to appear. In the meantime, the Essay on Nonchalance produced the best effects. A *ci-devant* stock-broker cut a Duke dead at his club the day after its publication; and his daughter yawned while his Grace's eldest son, the Marquess, made her an offer as she was singing 'Di tanti palpiti.' The aristocrats got a little frightened, and when an eminent hop-merchant and his lady had asked a dozen Countesses to dinner, and forgot to be at home to receive them, the old class left off quizzing.

The pamphlets, however, continued issuing forth, and the new people advanced at a rate which was awful. They actually began to originate some ideas of their own, and there was a whisper among the leaders of voting the aristocrats old-fashioned. The Diffusion Society now caused these exalted personages great anxiety and uneasiness. They argued that Fashion was a relative quality; that it was quite impossible, and not to be expected, that all people were to aspire to be fashionable; that it was not in the nature of things, and that, if it were, society could not exist; that the more their imitators advanced the more they should baffle their imitations; that a first and fashionable class was a necessary consequence of the organisation of man; and that a line of demarcation would for ever be drawn between them and the other islanders. The warmth and eagerness with which they maintained and promulgated their opinions might have tempted, however, an impartial person to suspect that they secretly entertained some doubts of their truth and soundness.

On the other hand, the other party maintained that

Fashion was a positive quality; that the moment a person obtained a certain degree of refinement he or she became, in fact and essentially, fashionable; that the views of the old class were unphilosophical and illiberal, and unworthy of an enlightened age; that men are equal, and that everything is open to everybody; and that when we take into consideration the nature of man, the origin of society, and a few other things, and duly consider the constant inclination and progression towards perfection which mankind evince, there was no reason why, in the course of time, the whole nation should not go to Almack's on the same night.

At this moment of doubt and dispute the Government of Vraibleusia, with that spirit of conciliation and liberality and that perfect wisdom for which it had been long celebrated, caring very little for the old class, whose interest, it well knew, was to support it, and being exceedingly desirous of engaging the affections of the new race, declared in their favour; and acting upon that sublime scale of measures for which this great nation has always been so famous, the Statue issued an edict that a new literature should be invented, in order at once to complete the education of the Millionaires and the triumph of the Romantic over the Classic School of Manners.

The most eminent writers were, as usual, in the pay of the Government, and BURLINGTON, A TALE OF FASHIONABLE LIFE, in three volumes post octavo, was sent forth. Two or three similar works, bearing titles equally euphonious and aristocratic, were published daily; and so exquisite was the style of these productions, so naturally artificial the construction of their plots, and so admirably inventive the conception of their characters, that many who had been repulsed by the somewhat abstract matter and arid style of the treatises, seduced by the interest of a story, and by the dazzling delicacies of a charming style, really now picked up a considerable quantity of very useful knowledge; so that when the delighted students had eaten some fifty or sixty imaginary dinners in my lord's dining-room, and whirled some fifty or sixty imaginary waltzes in my lady's dancing-room, there was scarcely a brute left among the whole Millionaires. But what produced the most beneficial effects on the new people, and excited the greatest indignation and despair among the old class, were some volumes which the Government, with shocking Machiavelism, bribed some needy scions of nobility to scribble, and which revealed certain secrets vainly believed to be quite sacred and inviolable.

## CHAPTER XIII.

SHORTLY after the sailing of the great fleet the Private Secretary engaged in a speculation which was rather more successful than any one contained in his pamphlet on 'The Present State of the Western Republics.'

One morning, as he and Popanilla were walking on a quay, and deliberating on the clauses of the projected commercial treaty between Vraibleusia and Fantaisie, the Secretary suddenly stopped, as if he had seen his father's ghost or lost the thread of his argument, and asked Popanilla, with an air of suppressed agitation, whether he observed anything in the distance. Popanilla, who, like all savages, was long-sighted, applying to his eye the glass which, in conformity to the custom of the country, he always wore round his neck, confessed that he saw nothing. The Secretary, who had never unfixed his glass nor moved a step since he asked the question, at length, by pointing with his finger, attracted Popanilla's attention to what his Excellency conceived to be a porpoise bobbing up and down in the waves. The Secretary, however, was not of the same opinion as the Ambassador. He was not very communicative, indeed, as to his own opinion upon this grave subject, but he talked of making farther observations when the tide went down; and was so listless, abstracted, and absent, during the rest of their conversation, that it soon ceased, and they speedily parted.

The next day, when Popanilla read the morning papers, a feat which he regularly performed, for spelling the newspaper was quite delicious to one who had so recently learned to read, he found that they spoke of nothing but of the discovery of a new island, information of which had been received by the Government only the preceding night. The Fantaisian Ambassador turned quite pale, and for the first time in his life experienced the passion of jealousy, the green-eyed monster, so called from only being experienced by green-horns. Already the prominent state he represented seemed to retire to the background. He did not doubt that the Vraibleusians were the most capricious as well as the most commercial nation in the world. His reign was evidently over. The new island would send forth a Prince still more popular. His allowance of pink shells would be gradually reduced, and finally withdrawn. His doubts, also, as to the success of the recent expedition to Fantaisie began to revive. His rising reminiscences of his native land, which, with the joint assistance of popularity and philosophy, he had hitherto succeeded in stifling, were indeed awkward. He could not conceive his mistress with a page and a poodle. He feared much that the cargo was not well assorted. Popanilla determined to enquire after his canoe.

His courage, however, was greatly reassured when, on reading the second edition, he learned that the new island was not of considerable size, though most eligibly situate; and, moreover, that it was perfectly void of inhabitants. When the third edition was published he found, to his surprise, that the Private Secretary was the discoverer of this opposition island. This puzzled the Plenipotentiary greatly. He read on; he found that this acquisition, upon which all Vraibleusia was congratulated in such glowing terms by all its journals, actually produced nothing. His Excellency began to breathe; another paragraph, and he found that the rival island was, a rock! He remembered the porpoise of yesterday. The island certainly could not be very large, even at low water. Popanilla once more felt like a Prince: he defied all the discoverers that could ever exist. He thought of the great resources of the great country he represented with proud satisfaction. He waited with easy confidence the return of the fleet which had carried out the most judicious assortment with which he had ever been acquainted to the readiest market of which he had any knowledge. He had no doubt his mistress would look most charmingly in a barege. Popanilla determined to present his canoe to the National Museum.

Although his Excellency had existed in the highest state of astonishment during his whole mission to Vraibleusia, it must be confessed, now that he understood his companion's question of yesterday, he particularly stared. His wonder was not decreased in the evening, when the 'Government Gazette' appeared. It contained an order for the immediate fortification of the new island by the most skilful engineers, without estimates. A strong garrison was instantly embarked. A Governor, and a Deputy-Governor, and Storekeepers, more plentiful than stores, were to accompany them. The Private Secretary went out as President of Council. A Bishop was promised; and a complete Court of Judicature, Chancery, King's Bench, Common Pleas, and Exchequer, were to be off the next week. It is only due to the characters of courtiers, who are so often reproached with ingratitude to their patrons, to record that the Private Secretary, in the most delicate manner, placed at the disposal of his former employer, the Marquess Moustache, the important office of Agent for the Indemnity Claims of the original Inhabitants of the Island; the post being a sinecure, the income being considerable, and local attendance being unnecessary, the noble Lord, in a manner equally delicate, appointed himself.

'Upon what system,' one day enquired that unwearied political student, the Fantaisian Ambassador, of his old friend Skindeep, 'does your Government surround a small rock in the middle of the sea with fortifications, and cram it full of clerks, soldiers, lawyers, and priests?'

'Why, really, your Excellency, I am the last man in the

world to answer questions; but I believe we call it THE COLONIAL SYSTEM!'

Before the President, and Governor, and Deputy-Governor, and Storekeepers had embarked, the Vraibleusian journals, who thought that the public had been satiated with congratulations on the Colonial System, detected that the present colony was a job. Their reasoning was so convincing, and their denunciations so impressive, that the Managers got frightened, and cut off one of the Deputy-Storekeepers. The President of Council now got more frightened than the Managers. He was one of those men who think that the world can be saved by writing a pamphlet. A pamphlet accordingly appeared upon the subject of the new colony. The writer showed that the debateable land was the most valuable acquisition ever attained by a nation famous for their acquisitions; that there was a spring of water in the middle of the rock of a remarkable freshness, and which was never dry except during the summer and the earlier winter months; that all our outward-bound ships would experience infinite benefit from this fresh water; that the scurvy would therefore disappear from the service; and that the naval victories which the Vraibleusians would gain in future wars would consequently be occasioned by the present colony. No one could mistake the felicitous reasoning of the author of ' The Present State of the Western Republics!'

About this time Popanilla fell ill. He lost his appetite and his spirits, and his digestion was sadly disordered. His friends endeavoured to console him by telling him that dyspepsia was the national disease of Vraibleusia; that its connection with civil and religious liberty was indissoluble; that every man, woman, and child above fifteen in the island was a martyr to it; that it was occasioned by their rapid mode of despatching their meals, which again was occasioned by the little time which the most active nation in the world could afford to bestow upon such a losing business as eating.

All this was no consolation to a man who had lost his

appetite; and so Popanilla sent for a gentleman who, he was told, was the most eminent physician in the island. The most eminent physician, when he arrived, would not listen to a single syllable that his patient wished to address to him. He told Popanilla that his disorder was 'decidedly liver;' that it was occasioned by his eating his meat before his bread instead of after it, and drinking at the end of the first course instead of the beginning of the second; that he had only to correct these ruinous habits, and that he would then regain his tone.

Popanilla observed the instructions of the eminent physician to the very letter. He invariably eat his bread before his meat, and watched the placing of the first dish of the second course upon the table ere he ventured to refresh himself with any liquid. At the end of a week he was infinitely worse.

He now called in a gentleman who was recommended to him as the most celebrated practitioner in all Vraibleusia. The most celebrated practitioner listened with great attention to every particular that his patient had to state, but never condescended to open his own mouth. Popanilla was delighted, and revenged himself for the irritability of the eminent physician. After two more visits, the most celebrated practitioner told Popanilla that his disorder was 'unquestionably nervous;' that he had over-excited himself by talking too much; that in future he must count five between each word he uttered, never ask any questions, and avoid society; that is, never stay at an evening party on any consideration later than twenty-two minutes past two, and never be induced by any persuasion to dine out more than once on the same day. The most celebrated practitioner added that he had only to observe these regulations, and that he would speedily recover his energy.

Popanilla never asked a question for a whole week, and Skindeep never knew him more delightful. He not only counted five, but ten, between every word he uttered; and determining that his cure should not be delayed, whenever he had nobody to speak to he continued counting. In a few days this solitary computation brought on a slow fever.

He now determined to have a consultation between the most ominent physician and the most celebrated practitioner. It was delightful to witness the meeting of these great men. Not a shade of jealousy dimmed the sunshine of their countenances. After a consultation, they agreed that Popanilla's disorder was neither 'liver,' nor 'nervous,' but 'mind:' that he had done too much; that he had overworked his brain; that he must take more exercise; that he must breathe more air; that he must have relaxation; that he must have change of scene.

'Where shall I go?' was the first question which Popanilla had sent forth for a fortnight, and it was addressed to Skindeep.

'Really, your Excellency, I am the last man in the world to answer questions; but the place which is generally frequented by us when we are suffering from your complaint is Blunderland.'

'Well, then, to Blunderland let us go!'

Shortly before Popanilla's illness he had been elected a member of the Vraiblensian Horticultural Society, and one evening he had endeavoured to amuse himself by reading the following CHAPTER ON FRUIT.

## CHAPTER XIV.

THAT a taste for fruit is inherent in man is an opinion which is sanctioned by the conduct of man in all ages and in all countries. While some nations have considered it profanation or pollution to nourish themselves with flesh or solace themselves with fish, while almost every member of the animal creation has in turn been considered either sacred or unclean, mankind, in all climes and in all countries, the Hindoo and the Hebrew, the Egyptian and the Greek, the Roman and the Frank, have, in some degree, made good their boastful claim to reason, by universally

feeding upon those delightful productions of Nature which
are nourished with the dews of heaven, and which live for
ever in its breath.

And, indeed, when we consider how exceedingly refreshing at all times is the flavour of fruit; how very natural,
and, in a manner, born in him, is man's inclination for it;
how little it is calculated to pall upon his senses; and how
conducive, when not eaten to excess, it is to his health, as
well as to his pleasure; we must not be surprised that a
conviction of its excellence should have been one of those
few subjects on which men have never disagreed.

That some countries are more favoured in their fruit than
others is a fact so notorious that its notice is unnecessary;
but we are not therefore to suppose that their appetite for
it is more keen than the appetite of other nations for their
fruit who live in less genial climes. Indeed, if we were
not led to believe that all nations are inspired by an equal
love for this production, it might occasionally be suspected
that some of those nations who are least skilful as horticulturists evince a greater passion for their inferior growths
than more fortunate people for their choicer produce. The
effects of bad fruit, however, upon the constitution, and
consequently upon the national character, are so injurious
that every liberal man must regret that any people, either
from ignorance or obligation, should be forced to have recourse to anything so fatal, and must feel that it is the
duty of everyone who professes to be a philanthropist to
propagate and encourage a taste for good fruit throughout
all countries of the globe.

A vast number of centuries before Popanilla had the fortune to lose his mistress's lock of hair, and consequently to
become an ambassador to Vraiblousia, the inhabitants of
that island, then scarcely more civilised than their new
allies of Fantaisie were at present, suffered very considerably from the trash which they devoured, from that innate
taste for fruit already noticed. In fact, although there
are antiquaries who pretend that the Vraiblousians possessed some of the species of wild plums and apples even

at that early period, the majority of enquirers are disposed to believe that their desserts were solely confined to the wildest berries, horse-chestnuts, and acorns.

A tradition runs, that while they were committing these abominations a ship, one of the first ships that had ever touched at the island, arrived at the present port of Hubbabub, then a spacious and shipless bay. The master of the vessel, on being brought before the King (for the story I am recording happened long before the construction of the miraculous Statue), presented, with his right hand, to his Majesty, a small pyramidal substance of a golden hue, which seemed to spring out of green and purple leaves. His Majesty did not exactly understand the intention of this ceremony; but of course, like a true legitimate, construed it into a symbol of homage. No sooner had the King brought the unknown substance near to his eyes, with the intention of scrutinising its nature, than the fragrance was so delightful that by mistake he applied it to his mouth. The King only took one mouthful, and then, with a cry of rapture, instantly handed the delicacy to his favourite, who, to the great mortification of the Secretary of State, finished it. The stranger, however, immediately supplied the surrounding courtiers from a basket which was slung on his left arm; and no sooner had they all tasted his gift than they fell upon their knees to worship him, vowing that the distributor of such delight must be more than man. If this avowal be considered absurd and extraordinary in this present age of philosophy, we must not forget to make due allowance for the palates of individuals who, having been so long accustomed merely to horse-chestnuts and acorns, suddenly, for the first time in their lives, tasted Pine-apple.

The stranger, with an air of great humility, disclaimed their proffered adoration, and told them that, far from being superior to common mortals, he was, on the contrary, one of the lowliest of the human race; in fact, he did not wish to conceal it; in spite of his vessel and his attendants, he was merely a market-gardener on a great scale. This beautiful fruit he had recently discovered in the East, to which quarter of the world he annually travelled in order to obtain a sufficient quantity to supply the great Western hemisphere, of which he himself was a native. Accident had driven him, with one of his ships, into the Island of Vraibleusia; and, as the islanders appeared to be pleased with his cargo, he said that he should have great pleasure in supplying them at present and receiving their orders for the future.

The proposition was greeted with enthusiasm. The King immediately entered into a contract with the market-gardener on his own terms. The sale, or cultivation, or even the eating of all other fruits was declared high-treason, and pine-apple, for weighty reasons duly recited in the royal proclamation, announced as the established fruit of the realm. The cargo, under the superintendence of some of the most trusty of the crew, was unshipped for the immediate supply of the island; and the merchant and his customers parted, mutually delighted and mutually profited.

Time flew on. The civilisation of Vraibleusia was progressive, as civilisation always is; and the taste for pineapples ever on the increase, as the taste for pine-apples ever should be. The supply was regular and excellent, the prices reasonable, and the tradesmen civil. They, of course, had not failed to advance in fair proportion with the national prosperity. Their numbers had much increased as well as their customers. Fresh agents arrived with every fresh cargo. They had long quitted the stalls with which they had been contented on their first settlement in the island, and now were the dapper owners of neat depôts in all parts of the kingdom where depôts could find customers.

A few more centuries, and affairs began to change. All that I have related as matter of fact, and which certainly is not better authenticated than many other things that happened two or three thousand years ago, which, however, the most sceptical will not presume to maintain did not take place, was treated as the most idle and ridiculous fable by the dealers in pine-apples themselves. They said that they knew nothing about a market-gardener; that they were, and had always been, the subjects of the greatest Prince in the world, compared with whom all other crowned heads ranked merely as subjects did with their immediate sovereigns. This Prince, they said, lived in the most delicious region in the world, and the fruit which they imported could only be procured from his private gardens, where it sprang from one of the trees that had bloomed in the gardens of the Hesperides. The Vraibleusians were at first a little surprised at this information, but the old tradition of the market-gardener was certainly an improbable one; and the excellence of the fruit and the importance assumed by those who supplied it were deemed exceedingly good evidence of the truth of the present story. When the dealers had repeated their new tale for a certain number of years, there was not an individual in the island who in the slightest degree suspected its veracity. One more century, and no person had ever heard that any suspicions had ever existed.

The immediate agents of the Prince of the World could, of course, be no common personages; and the servants of the gardener, who some centuries before had meekly disclaimed the proffered reverence of his delighted customers, now insisted upon constant adoration from every eater of pine-apples in the island. In spite, however, of the arrogance of the dealers, of their refusal to be responsible to the laws of the country in which they lived, and of the universal precedence which, on all occasions, was claimed even by the shop-boys, so decided was the taste which the Vraibleusians had acquired for pine-apples that there is little doubt that, had the dealers in this delicious fruit been contented with the respect and influence and profit which were the consequences of their vocation, the Vraibleusians would never have presumed to have grumbled at their arrogance or to have questioned their privileges. But the agents, wearied of the limited sphere to which their exertions were confined, and encouraged by the success which every new claim and pretence on their part invariably experienced, began to evince an inclination to interfere in other affairs besides those of fruit, and even expressed their willingness to undertake no less an office than the management of the Statue.

A century or two were solely occupied by conflicts occasioned by the unreasonable ambition of these dealers in pine-apples. Such great political effects could be produced by men apparently so unconnected with politics as market-gardeners! Ever supported by the lower ranks, whom they supplied with fruit of the most exquisite flavour without charge, they were, for a long time, often the successful opponents, always the formidable adversaries, of the Vraibleusian aristocracy, who were the objects of their envy and the victims of their rapaciousness. The Government at last, by a vigorous effort, triumphed. In spite of the wishes of the majority of the nation, the whole of the dealers were one day expelled the island, and the Managers of the Statue immediately took possession of their establishments.

By distributing the stock of fruit which was on hand liberally, the Government, for a short time, reconciled the people to the change; but as their warehouses became daily less furnished they were daily reminded that, unless some system were soon adopted, the Islanders must be deprived of a luxury to which they had been so long accustomed that its indulgence had, in fact, become a second nature. No one of the managers had the hardihood to propose a recurrence to horse-chestnuts. Pride and fear alike forbade a return to their old purveyor. Other fruits there were which, in spite of the contract with the market-gardener, had at various times been secretly introduced into the island; but they had never greatly flourished, and the Statue was loth to recommend to the notice of his subjects productions an indulgence in which, through the instigation of the recently-expelled agents, it had so often denounced as detrimental to the health, and had so often discouraged by the severest punishments.

At this difficult and delicate crisis, when even expedients

seemed exhausted and statesmen were at fault, the genius of an individual offered a substitute. An inventive mind discovered the power of propagating suckers. The expelled dealers had either been ignorant of this power, or had concealed their knowledge of it. They ever maintained that it was impossible for pine-apples to grow except in one spot, and that the whole earth must be supplied from the gardens of the palace of the Prince of the World. Now, the Vraibleusians were flattered with the patriotic fancy of eating pine-apples of a home-growth; and the blessed fortune of that nation, which did not depend for their supply of fruit upon a foreign country, was eagerly expatiated on. Secure from extortion and independent of caprice, the Vraibleusians were no longer to be insulted by the presence of foreigners; who, while they violated their laws with impunity, referred the Vraibleusians, when injured and complaining, to a foreign master.

No doubt this appeal to the patriotism, and the common sense, and the vanity of the nation would have been successful had not the produce of the suckers been both inferior in size and deficient in flavour. The Vraibleusians tasted and shook their heads. The supply, too, was as imperfect as the article; for the Government gardeners were but sorry horticulturists, and were ever making experiments and alterations in their modes of culture. The article was scarce, though the law had decreed it universal; and the Vraibleusians were obliged to feed upon fruit which they considered at the same time both poor and expensive. They protested as strongly against the present system as its promulgators had protested against the former one, and they revenged themselves for their grievances by breaking the shop-windows.

As any result was preferable, in the view of the Statue, to the re-introduction of foreign fruit and foreign agents, and as the Managers considered it highly important that an indissoluble connection should in future exist between the Government and so influential and profitable a branch of trade, they determined to adopt the most vigorous measures to infuse a taste for suckers in the discontented populace. But the eating of fruit being clearly a matter of taste, it is evidently a habit which should rather be encouraged by a plentiful supply of exquisite produce than enforced by the introduction of burning and bayonets. The consequences of the strong measures of the Government were universal discontent and partial rebellion. The Islanders, foolishly ascribing the miseries which they endured, not so much to the folly of the Government as to the particular fruit through which the dissensions had originated, began to entertain a disgust for pine-apples altogether, and to sicken at the very mention of that production which had once occasioned them so much pleasure, and which had once commanded such decided admiration. They universally agreed that there were many other fruits in the world besides Pine-apple which had been too long neglected. One dilated on the rich flavour of Melon; another panegyrised Pumpkin, and offered to make up by quantity for any slight deficiency in *goût*; Cherries were not without their advocates; Strawberries were not forgotten. One maintained that the Fig had been pointed out for the established fruit of all countries; while another asked, with a reeling eye, whether they need go far to seek when a God had condescended to preside over the Grape! In short, there was not a fruit which flourishes that did not find its votaries. Strange to say, another foreign product, imported from a neighbouring country famous for its barrenness, counted the most; and the fruit faction which chiefly frightened the Vraibleusian Government was an acid set, who crammed themselves with Crab-apples.

It was this party which first seriously and practically conceived the idea of utterly abolishing the ancient custom of eating pine-apples. While they themselves professed to devour no other fruit save crabs, they at the same time preached the doctrine of an universal fruit toleration, which they showed would be the necessary and natural consequence of the destruction of the old monopoly. Influenced by these representations, the great body of the people openly joined the Crab-apple men in their open attacks. The minority, who still retained a taste for pines, did not yield without an arduous though ineffectual struggle. During the riots occasioned by this rebellion the Hall of Audience was broken open, and the miraculous Statue, which was reputed to have a great passion for pine-apples, dashed to the ground. The Managers were either slain or disappeared. The whole affairs of the kingdom were conducted by a body called 'the Fruit Committee;' and thus a total revolution of the Government of Vraibleusia was occasioned by the prohibition of foreign pine-apples. What an argument in favour of free-trade!

Every fruit, except that one which had so recently been supported by the influence of authority and the terrors of law, might now be seen and devoured in the streets of Hubbabub. In one corner men were sucking oranges, as if they had lived their whole lives on salt: in another, stuffing pumpkin, like cannibals at their first child. Here one took in at a mouthful a bunch of grapes, from which might have been pressed a good quart. Another was lying on the ground from a surfeit of mulberries. The effect of this irrational excess will be conceived by the judicious reader. Calcutta itself never suffered from a cholera morbus half so fearful. Thousands were dying. Were I Thucydides or Boccaccio, I would write pages on this plague. The commonwealth itself must soon have yielded its ghost, for all order had ceased throughout the island ever since they had deserted pine-apples. There was no Government: anarchy alone was perfect. Of the Fruit Committee, many of the members were dead or dying, and the rest were robbing orchards.

At this moment of disorganisation and dismay a stout soldier, one of the crab-apple faction, who had possessed sufficient command over himself, in spite of the seeming voracity of his appetite, not to indulge to a dangerous excess, made his way one morning into the old Hall of Audience, and there, groping about, succeeded in finding the golden head of the Statue; which placing on the hilt of his sword, the point of which he had stuck in the pedestal, he announced to the city that he had discovered the secret of conversing with this wonderful piece of mechanism, and that in future he would take care of the health and fortune of the State.

There were some who thought it rather strange that the head-piece should possess the power of resuming its old functions, although deprived of the aid of the body which contained the greater portion of the machinery. As it was evidently well supported by the sword, they were not surprised that it should stand without the use of its legs. But the stout soldier was the only one in the island who enjoyed the blessing of health. He was fresh, vigorous, and vigilant; they, exhausted, weak, and careless of everything except cure. He soon took measures for the prevention of future mischief and for the cure of the present; and when his fellow-islanders had recovered, some were grateful, others fearful, and all obedient.

So long as the stout soldier lived no dissensions on the subject of fruit ever broke out. Although he himself never interfered in the sale of the article, and never attempted to create another monopoly, still, by his influence and authority, he prevented any excess being occasioned by the Fruit toleration which was enjoyed. Indeed, the Vraibleusians themselves had suffered so severely from their late indiscretions that such excesses were not likely again to occur. People began to discover that it was not quite so easy a thing as they had imagined for every man to be his own Fruiterer; and that gardening was a craft which, like others, required great study, long practice, and early experience. Unable to supply themselves, the majority became the victims of quack traders. They sickened of spongy apricots, and foxy pears, and withered plums, and blighted apples, and tasteless berries. They at length suspected that a nation might fare better if its race of fruiterers were overseen and supported by the State, if their skill and their market were alike secured. Although, no longer being tempted to suffer from a surfeit, the health of the Islanders had consequently recovered, this was, after all, but a negative blessing, and they sadly missed a luxury once so reasonable and so refreshing. They sighed for an established fruit and a protected race of cultivators. But the stout soldier was so sworn an enemy to any Government Fruit, and so decided an admirer of the least delightful, that the people, having no desire of being forced to eat crab-apples, only longed for more delicious food in silence.

At length the stout soldier died, and on the night of his death the sword which had so long supported the pretended Government snapped in twain. No arrangement existed for carrying on the administration of affairs. The master-mind was gone, without having imparted the secret of conversing with the golden head to any successor. The people assembled in agitated crowds. Each knew his neighbour's thoughts without their being declared. All smacked their lips, and a cry for pine-apples rent the skies.

At this moment the Aboriginal Inhabitant appeared, and announced that in examining the old Hall of Audience, which had been long locked up, he had discovered in a corner, where they had been flung by the stout soldier when he stole away the head, the remaining portions of the Statue; that they were quite uninjured, and that on fixing the head once more upon them, and winding up the works, he was delighted to find that this great work of his ancestor, under whose superintendence the nation had so flourished, resumed all its ancient functions. The people were in a state of mind for a miracle, and they hailed the joyful wonder with shouts of triumph. The Statue was placed under the provisional care of the Aboriginal. All arrangements for its superintendence were left to his discretion, and its advice was instantly to be taken upon that subject which at present was nearest the people's hearts.

But that subject was encompassed with difficulties. Pine-apples could only be again procured by an application to the Prince of the World, whose connection they had rejected, and by an introduction into the island of those foreign agents, who, now convinced that the Vraibleusians could not exist without their presence, would be more arrogant and ambitious and turbulent than ever. Indeed, the Aboriginal feared that the management of the Statue would be the *sine quâ non* of negotiation with the Prince. If this were granted, it was clear that Vraibleusia must in future only rank as a dependent state of a foreign power, since the direction of the whole island would actually be at the will of the supplier of pine-apples. Ah! this mysterious taste for fruit! In politics it has often occasioned infinite embarrassment.

At this critical moment the Aboriginal received information that, although the eating of pine-apples had been utterly abolished, and although it was generally supposed that a specimen of this fruit had long ceased to exist in the country, nevertheless a body of persons, chiefly consisting of the descendants of the Government gardeners who had succeeded the foreign agents, and who had never lost their taste for this pre-eminent fruit, had long been in the habit of secretly raising, for their private eating, pine-apples from the produce of those suckers which had originally excited such odium and occasioned such misfortunes. Long practice, they said, and infinite study, had so perfected them in this art that they now succeeded in producing pine-apples which, both for size and flavour, were not inferior to the boasted produce of a foreign clime. Their specimens verified their assertion, and the whole nation were invited to an instant trial. The long interval which had elapsed since any man had enjoyed a treat so agreeable lent, perhaps, an additional flavour to that which was really excellent; and so enraptured and enthusiastic were the great majority of the people that the propagators of suckers would have had no difficulty, had they pushed the point, in procuring as favourable and exclusive a contract as the market-gardener of ancient days.

But the Aboriginal and his advisers were wisely mindful that the passions of a people are not arguments for legislation; and they felt conscious that when the first enthusiasm had subsided, and when their appetites were somewhat satisfied, the discontented voices of many who had been long used to other fruits would be recognised even amidst the shouts of the majority. They therefore greatly qualified the contract between the nation and the present fruiterers. An universal Toleration of Fruit was allowed; but no man was to take office under Government, or enter the services, or in any way become connected with the Court, who was not supplied from the Government depôts.

Since this happy restoration Pine-apple has remained the established fruit of the Island of Vraiblcusia; and, it must be confessed, has been found wonderfully conducive to the health and happiness of the Islanders. Some sectarians still remain obstinate, or tasteless enough to prefer pumpkin, or gorge the most acid apples, or chew the commonest pears; but they form a slight minority, which will gradually altogether disappear. The votaries of Pine-apple pretend to observe the characteristic effect which such food produces upon the feeders. They denounce them as stupid, sour, and vulgar.

But while, notwithstanding an universal toleration, such an unanimity of taste apparently prevails throughout the island, as if Fruit were a subject of such peculiar nicety that difference of opinion must necessarily rise among men, great Fruit factions even now prevail in Vraiblcusia; and, what is more extraordinary, prevail even among the admirers of pine-apples themselves. Of these, the most important is a sect which professes to discover a natural deficiency not only in all other fruits, but even in the finest pine-apples. Fruit, they maintain, should never be eaten in the state in which Nature yields it to man; and they consequently are indefatigable in prevailing upon the less discriminating part of mankind to heighten the flavour of their pine-apples with ginger, or even with pepper. Although they profess to adopt these stimulants from the great admiration which they entertain for a high flavour, there are, nevertheless, some less ardent people who suspect that they rather have recourse to them from the weakness of their digestion.

## CHAPTER XV.

As his Excellency Prince Popanilla really could not think of being annoyed by the attentions of the mob during his visit to Blunderland, he travelled quite in a quiet way, under the name of the Chevalier de Fantaisie, and was accompanied only by Skindeep and two attendants. As Blunderland was one of the islands of the Vraibleusian Archipelago, they arrived there after the sail of a few hours.

The country was so beautiful that the Chevalier was almost reminded of Fantaisie. Green meadows and flourishing trees made him remember the railroads and canals of Vraibleusia without regret, or with disgust, which is much the same. The women were angelic, which is the highest praise; and the men the most light-hearted, merry, obliging, entertaining fellows that he had met with in the whole course of his life. Oh! it was delicious.

After an hour's dashing drive, he arrived at a city which, had he not seen Hubbabub, he should have imagined was one of the most considerable in the world; but compared with the Vraibleusian capital it was a street.

Shortly after his arrival, according to the custom of the place, Popanilla joined the public table of his hotel at dinner. He was rather surprised that, instead of knives and forks being laid for the convenience of the guests, the plates were flanked by daggers and pistols. As Popanilla now made a point of never asking a question of Skindeep, he addressed himself for information to his other neighbour, one of the civilest, most hospitable, and joyous rogues that ever set a table in a roar. On Popanilla inquiring the reason of their using these singular instruments, his neighbour, with an air of great astonishment, confessed his ignorance of any people ever using any other; and in his turn asked how they could possibly eat their dinner without. The Chevalier was puzzled, but he was now too well bred ever to pursue an enquiry.

Popanilla, being thirsty, helped himself to a goblet of water, which was at hand. It was the most delightful water that he ever tasted. In a few minutes he found that he was a little dizzy, and, supposing this megrim to be occasioned by the heat of the room, he took another draught of water to recover himself.

As his neighbour was telling him an excellent joke a man entered the room and shot the joker through the head. The opposite guest immediately charged his pistol with effect, and revenged the loss. A party of men, well armed, now rushed in, and a brisk conflict immediately ensued. Popanilla, who was very dizzy, was fortunately pushed under the table. When the firing and slashing had ceased, he ventured to crawl out. He found that the assailants had been beaten off, though unfortunately with the total loss of all the guests, who lay lifeless about the room. Even the prudent Skindeep, who had sought refuge in a closet, had lost his nose, which was a pity; because, although this gentleman had never been in Blunderland before, he had passed his whole life in maintaining that the accounts of the disturbances in that country were greatly exaggerated. Popanilla rang the bell, and the waiters, who were remarkably attentive, swept away the dead bodies, and brought him a roasted potato for supper.

The Chevalier soon retired to rest. He found at the side of his bed a blunderbuss, a cutlass, and a pike; and he was directed to secure the door of his chamber with a great chain and a massy iron bar. Feeling great confidence in his securities, although he was quite ignorant of the cause of alarm, and very much exhausted with the bustle of the day, he enjoyed sounder sleep than had refreshed him for many weeks. He was awakened in the middle of the night by a loud knocking at his door. He immediately seized his blunderbuss, but, recognising the voice of his own valet, he only took his pike. His valet told him to unbar without loss of time, for the house had been set on fire. Popanilla immediately made his escape, but found himself surrounded by the incendiaries. He gave himself up for lost, when a sudden charge of cavalry brought him off in triumph. He was convinced of the utility of light-horse.

The military had arrived with such despatch that the fire was the least effective that had wakened the house for the whole week. It was soon extinguished, and Popanilla again retired to his bedroom, not forgetting his bar and his chain.

In the morning Popanilla was roused by his landlord, who told him that a large party was about to partake of the pleasures of the chase, and most politely enquired whether he would like to join them. Popanilla assented, and after having eaten an excellent breakfast, and received a favourable bulletin of Skindeep's wound, he mounted his horse. The party was numerous and well armed. Popanilla enquired of a huntsman what sport they generally followed in Blunderland. According to the custom of this country, where they never give a direct answer, the huntsman said that he did not know that there was any other sport but one. Popanilla thought him a brute, and dug his spurs into his horse.

They went off at a fine rate, and the exercise was most exhilarating. In a short time, as they were cantering along a defile, they received a sharp fire from each side, which rather reduced their numbers; but they revenged themselves for this loss when they regained the plain, where they burnt two villages, slew two or three hundred head of women, and bagged children without number. On their return home to dinner they chased a small body of men over a heath for nearly two hours, which afforded good sport; but they did not succeed in running them down, as they themselves were in turn chased by another party. Altogether, the day was not deficient in interest, and Popanilla found in the evening his powers of digestion improved.

After passing his days in this manner for about a fortnight, Popanilla perfectly recovered from his dyspepsia; and Skindeep's wound having now healed, he retired with regret from this healthy climate. He took advantage of the leisure moment which was afforded during the sail to enquire the reason of the disturbed state of this interesting country. He was told that it was in consequence of the majority of the inhabitants persisting in importing their own pine-apples.

## CHAPTER XVI.

ON his return to Hubbabub, the Chevalier de Fantaisie found the city in the greatest confusion. The military were marshalled in all directions; the streets were lined with field-pieces; no one was abroad; all the shops were shut. Although not a single vehicle was visible, Popanilla's progress was slow, from the quantity of shells of all kinds which choked up the public way. When he arrived at his hotel he found that all the windows were broken. He entered, and his landlord immediately presented him with his bill. As the landlord was pressing, and as Popanilla wished for an opportunity of showing his confidence in Skindeep's friendship, he requested him to pay the amount. Skindeep sent a messenger immediately to his banker, deeming an ambassador almost as good security as a nation, which we all know to be the very best.

This little arrangement being concluded, the landlord resumed his usual civility. He informed the travellers that the whole island was in a state of the greatest commotion, and that martial law universally prevailed. He said that this disturbance was occasioned by the return of the expedition destined to the Isle of Fantaisie. It appeared, from his account, that after sailing about from New Guinea to New Holland, the expedition had been utterly unable not only to reach their new customers, but even to obtain the slightest intelligence of their locality. No such place as Fantaisie was known at Ceylon. Sumatra gave information equally unsatisfactory. Java shook its head. Celebes conceived the enquirers were jesting. The Philippine Isles offered to accommodate them with spices, but could assist them in no other way. Had it not been too hot at Borneo, they would have fairly laughed outright. The Maldives and the Moluccas, the Luccadives and the Andamans, were nearly as impertinent. The five hundred ships and the judiciously-assorted cargo were therefore under the necessity of returning home.

No sooner, however, had they reached Vraibleusia than the markets were immediately glutted with the unsold goods. All the manufacturers, who had been working day and night in preparing for the next expedition, were instantly thrown out of employ. A run commenced on the Government Bank. That institution perceived too late that the issues of pink shells had been too unrestricted. As the Emperor of the East had all the gold, the Government Bank only protected itself from failure by bayoneting its creditors. The manufacturers, who were starving, consoled themselves for the absence of food by breaking all the windows in the country with the discarded shells. Every tradesman failed. The shipping interest advertised two or three fleets for firewood. Riots were universal. The Aboriginal was attacked on all sides, and made so stout a resistance, and broke so many cudgels on the backs of his assailants, that it was supposed he would be finally exhausted by his own exertions. The public funds sunk ten per cent. daily. All the Millionaires crashed. In a word, dismay, disorganisation, despair, pervaded in all directions the wisest, the greatest, and the richest nation in the world. The master of the hotel added, with an air of becoming embarrassment, that, had not his Excellency been fortunately absent, he probably would not have had the pleasure of detailing to him this little narrative; that he had often been enquired for by the populace at his old balcony; and that a crowd had perpetually surrounded the house till within the last day, when a report had got about that his Excellency had turned into steam and disappeared. He added that caricatures of his Highness might be procured in any shop, and his account of his voyage obtained at less than half-price.

'Ah!' said Popanilla, in a tone of great anguish, 'and all this from losing a lock of hair!'

At this moment the messenger whom Skindeep had despatched returned, and informed him with great regret that his banker, to whom he had entrusted his whole fortune, had been so unlucky as to stop payment during his absence. It was expected, however, that when his stud was sold a respectable dividend might be realised. This was the personage of prepossessing appearance who had presented Popanilla with a perpetual ticket to his picture gallery. On examining the banker's accounts, it was discovered that his chief loss had been incurred by supporting that competition establishment where purses were bought full of crowns.

In spite of his own misfortunes, Popanilla hastened to console his friend. He explained to him that things were not quite so bad as they appeared; that society consisted of two classes, those who laboured, and those who paid the labourers; that each class was equally useful, because, if there were none to pay, the labourers would not be remunerated, and if there were none to labour, the payers would not be accommodated; that Skindeep might still rank in one of these classes; that he might therefore still be a useful member of society; that, if he were useful, he must therefore be good; and that, if he were good, he must therefore be happy; because happiness is the consequence of assisting the beneficial development of the ameliorating principles of the social action.

As he was speaking, two gentlemen in blue, with red waistcoats, entered the chamber and seized Popanilla by the collar. The Vraibleusian Government, which is so famous for its interpretation of National Law, had arrested the Ambassador for high treason.

## CHAPTER XVII.

A PRISON conveyed the most lugubrious ideas to the mind of the unhappy Plenipotentiary; and shut up in a hackney-coach, with a man on each side of him with a cocked pistol, he formed the most gloomy conceptions of dark dungeons, confined cells, overwhelming fetters, black bread, and green water. He arrived at the principal gaol in Hubbabub. He was ushered into an elegantly furnished apartment, with French sash windows and a piano. Its lofty walls were entirely hung with a fanciful paper, which represented a Tuscan vineyard; the ceiling was covered with sky and clouds; roses were in abundance; and the windows, though well secured, excited no jarring associations in the mind of the individual they illumined, protected, as they were, by polished bars of cut steel. This retreat had been fitted up by a poetical politician, who had recently been confined for declaring that the Statue was an old idol originally imported from the Sandwich Isles. Taking up a brilliantly bound volume which reposed upon a rosewood table, Popanilla recited aloud a sonnet to Liberty; but the account given of the goddess by the bard was so confused, and he seemed so little acquainted with his subject, that the reader began to suspect it was an effusion of the gaoler.

Next to being a Plenipotentiary, Popanilla preferred being a prisoner. His daily meals consisted of every delicacy in season: a marble bath was ever at his service; a billiard-room and dumb-bells always ready; and his old friend, the most eminent physician and the most celebrated practitioner in Hubbabub, called upon him daily to feel his pulse and look at his tongue. These attentions authorised a hope that he might yet again be an Ambassador, that his native land might still be discovered, and its resources still be developed: but when his gaoler told him that the rest of the prisoners were treated in a manner equally indulgent, because the Vraibleusians are the most humane people in the world, Popanilla's spirits became somewhat depressed.

He was greatly consoled, however, by a daily visit from a body of the most beautiful, the most accomplished, and the most virtuous females in Hubbabub, who tasted his food to see that his cook did his duty, recommended him a plentiful use of pine-apple well peppered, and made him a present of a very handsome shirt, with worked frills and ruffles, to be hanged in. This enchanting committee generally confined their attentions to murderers and other victims of the passions, who were deserted in their hour of need by the rest of the society they had outraged; but Popanilla, being a foreigner, a Prince, and a Plenipotentiary, and not ill-looking, naturally attracted a great deal of notice from those who desire the amelioration of their species.

Popanilla was so pleased with his mode of life, and had acquired such a taste for poetry, pine-apples, and pepper since he had ceased to be an active member of society, that he applied to have his trial postponed, on the ground of the prejudice which had been excited against him by the public press. As his trial was at present inconvenient to the Government, the postponement was allowed on these grounds.

In the meantime, the public agitation was subsiding. The nation reconciled itself to the revolution in its fortunes. The *ci-devant* millionaires were busied with retrenchment; the Government engaged in sweeping in as many pink shells as were lying about the country; the mechanics contrived to live upon chalk and sea-weed; and as the Aboriginal would not give his corn away gratis, the Vraibleusians determined to give up bread. The intellectual part of the nation were intently interested in discovering the cause of the National Distress. One of the philosophers said that it might all be traced to the effects of a war in which the Vraibleusians had engaged about a century before. Another showed that it was altogether clearly ascribable to the pernicious custom of issuing pink shells; but if, instead of this mode of representing wealth, they had had recourse to blue shells, the nation would now have advanced to a state of prosperity which it had never yet reached. A third demonstrated to the satisfaction of himself and his immediate circle that it was all owing to the Statue having recently been repaired with silver instead of iron. The public were unable to decide between these conflicting opinions; but they were still more desirous of finding out a remedy for the evil than the cause of it.

An eloquent and philosophical writer, who entertains consolatory opinions of human nature, has recently told us that 'it is in the nature of things that the intellectual wants of society should be supplied. Whenever the man is required invariably the man will appear.' So it happened in the present instance. A public instructor jumped up in the person of Mr. Flummery Flam, the least insinuating and the least plausible personage that ever performed the easy task of gulling a nation. His manners were vulgar, his voice was sharp, and his language almost unintelligible. Flummery Flam was a provisional optimist. He maintained that everything would be for the best, if the nation would only follow his advice. He told the Vraibleusians that the present universal and overwhelming distress was all and entirely and merely to be ascribed to 'a slight over-trading,' and that all that was required to set everything right again was 'a little time.' He showed that this over-trading and every other injudicious act that had ever been committed were entirely to be ascribed to the nation being imbued with erroneous and imperfect ideas of the nature of Demand and Supply. He proved to them that if a tradesman cannot find customers his goods will generally stay upon his own hands. He explained to the Aboriginal the meaning of *rent*; to the mechanics the nature of *wages*; to the manufacturers the signification of *profits*. He recommended that a large edition of his own work should be printed at the public expense and sold for his private profit. Finally, he explained how immediate, though temporary, relief would

be afforded to the State by the encouragement of EMI-
GRATION.

The Vraibleusians began to recover their spirits. The
Government had the highest confidence in Flummery Flam,
because Flummery Flam served to divert the public
thoughts. By his direction lectures were instituted at the
corner of every street, to instil the right principles of politics into the mind of the great body of the people. Every
person, from the Managers of the Statue down to the chalk-
chewing mechanics, attended lectures on Flummery-Flam-
mism. The Vraibleusians suddenly discovered that it was
the great object of a nation not to be the most powerful, or
the richest, or the best, or the wisest, but to be the most
Flummery-Flammistical.

## CHAPTER XVIII.

THE day fixed for Popanilla's trial was at hand. The Prince
was not unprepared for the meeting. For some weeks
before the appointed day he had been deeply studying the
published speeches of the greatest rhetorician that flourished
at the Vraibleusian bar. He was so inflated with their
style that he nearly blew down the gaoler every morning
when he rehearsed a passage before him. Indeed, Popanilla looked forward to his trial with feelings of anticipated
triumph. He determined boldly and fearlessly to state the
principles upon which his public conduct had been founded,
the sentiments he professed on most of the important subjects which interest mankind, and the views he entertained
of the progress of society. He would then describe, in the
most glowing language, the domestic happiness which he
enjoyed in his native isle. He would paint, in harrowing
sentences, the eternal misery and disgrace which his ignominious execution would entail upon the grey-headed father,
who looked up to him as a prop for his old age; the
affectionate mother, who perceived in him her husband
again a youth; the devoted wife, who could never survive

his loss; and the sixteen children, chiefly girls, whom his death would infallibly send upon the parish. This, with an eulogistic peroration on the moral qualities of the Vraibleusians and the political importance of Vraibleusia, would, he had no doubt, not only save his neck, but even gain him a moderate pension.

The day arrived, the Court was crowded, and Popanilla had the satisfaction of observing in the newspapers that tickets for the best gallery to witness his execution were selling at a premium.

The indictment was read. He listened to it with intense attention. To his surprise, he found himself accused of stealing two hundred and nineteen Camelopards. All was now explained. He perceived that he had been mistaken the whole of this time for another person. He could not contain himself. He burst into an exclamation. He told the judge, in a voice of mingled delight, humility, and triumph, that it was possible he might be guilty of high treason, because he was ignorant of what the crime consisted; but as for stealing two hundred and nineteen Camelopards, he declared that such a larceny was a moral impossibility, because he had never seen one such animal in the whole course of his life.

The judge was kind and considerate. He told the prisoner that the charge of stealing Camelopards was a fiction of law; that he had no doubt he had never seen one in the whole course of his life, nor in all probability had any one in the whole Court. He explained to Popanilla, that originally this animal greatly abounded in Vraibleusia; that the present Court, the highest and most ancient in the kingdom, had then been instituted for the punishment of all those who molested or injured that splendid animal. The species, his lordship continued, had been long extinct; but the Vraibleusians, duly reverencing the institutions of their ancestors, had never presumed to abrogate the authority of the Camelopard Court, or invest any other with equal privileges. Therefore, his lordship added, in order to try you in this Court for a modern

offence of high treason, you must first be introduced by
fiction of law as a stealer of Camelopards, and then being
*in præsenti regio*, in a manner, we proceed to business by a
special power for the absolute offence. Popanilla was so
confounded by the kindness of the judge and the clearness
of his lordship's statement that he quite lost the thread of
his peroration.

The trial proceeded. Everybody with whom Popanilla
had conversed during his visit to Vraibleusia was subpœnaed
against him, and the evidence was conclusive. Skindeep,
who was brought up by a warrant from the King's Bench,
proved the fact of Popanilla's landing; and that he had
given himself out as a political exile, the victim of a tyrant,
a corrupt aristocracy, and a misguided people. But, either
from a secret feeling towards his former friend or from his
aversion to answer questions, this evidence was on the
whole not very satisfactory.

The bookseller proved the publication of that fatal volume
whose deceptive and glowing statements were alone sufficient to ensure Popanilla's fate. It was in vain that the
author avowed that he had never written a line of his own
book. This only made his imposture more evident. The
little philosopher with whom he had conversed at Lady
Spirituelle's, and who, being a friend of Flummery Flam,
had now obtained a place under Government, invented the
most condemning evidence. The Marquess of Moustache
sent in a state paper, desiring to be excused from giving
evidence, on account of the delicate situation in which he
had been placed with regard to the prisoner; but he referred
them to his former Private Secretary, who, he had no
doubt, would afford every information. Accordingly, the
President of Fort Jobation, who had been brought over
specially, finished the business.

The Judge, although his family had suffered considerably
by the late madness for speculation, summed up in the
most impartial manner. He told the jury that, although
the case was quite clear against the prisoner, they were
bound to give him the advantage of every reasonable

doubt. The foreman was about to deliver the verdict, when a trumpet sounded, and a Government messenger ran breathless into Court. Presenting a scroll to the presiding genius, he informed him that a remarkably able young man, recently appointed one of the Managers of the Statue, in consequence of the inconvenience which the public sustained from the innumerable quantity of edicts of the Statue at present in force, had last night consolidated them all into this single act, which, to render its operation still more simple, was gifted with a retrospective power for the last half century.

His lordship, looking over the scroll, passed a high eulogium upon the young consolidator, compared to whom, he said, Justinian was a country attorney. Observing, however, that the crime of high treason had been accidentally omitted in the consolidated legislation of Vraibleusia, he directed the jury to find the prisoner 'not guilty.' As in Vraibleusia the law believes every man's character to be perfectly pure until a jury of twelve persons finds the reverse, Popanilla was kicked out of court, amid the hootings of the mob, without a stain upon his reputation.

It was late in the evening when he left the court. Exhausted both in mind and body, the mischief being now done, and being totally unemployed, according to custom, he began to moralise. 'I begin to perceive,' said he, 'that it is possible for a nation to exist in too artificial a state; that a people may both think too much and do too much. All here exists in a state of exaggeration. The nation itself professes to be in a situation in which it is impossible for any nation ever to be naturally placed. To maintain themselves in this false position, they necessarily have recourse to much destructive conduct and to many fictitious principles. And as the character of a people is modelled on that of their Government, in private life this system of exaggeration equally prevails, and equally produces a due quantity of ruinous actions and false sentiment! In the meantime, I am starving, and dare not show my face in the light of day!'

As he said this the house opposite was suddenly lit up, and the words 'EMIGRATION COMMITTEE' were distinctly visible on a transparent blind. A sudden resolution entered Popanilla's mind to make an application to this body. He entered the Committee-room, and took his place at the end of a row of individuals, who were severally examined. When it was his turn to come forward he began to tell his story from the beginning, and would certainly have got to the lock of hair had not the President enjoined silence. Popanilla was informed that the last Emigration-squadron was about to sail in a few minutes; and that, although the number was completed, his broad shoulders and powerful frame had gained him a place. He was presented with a spade, a blanket, and a hard biscuit, and in a quarter of an hour was quitting the port of Hubbabub.

Once more upon the waters, yet once more!

As the Emigration-squadron quitted the harbour two large fleets hove in sight. The first was the expedition which had been despatched against the decapitating King of the North, and which now returned heavily laden with his rescued subjects. The other was the force which had flown to the preservation of the body of the decapitated King of the South, and which now brought back his Majesty embalmed, some Princes of the blood, and an emigrant Aristocracy.

What became of the late Fantaisian Ambassador; whether he were destined for Van Diemen's Land or for Canada; what rare adventures he experienced in Sydney, or Port Jackson, or Guelph City, or Goodrich Town; and whether he discovered that man might exist in too natural a state, as well as in too artificial a one, will probably be discovered, if ever we obtain Captain Popanilla's Second Voyage.

www.ingramcontent.com/pod-product-compliance
Lightning Source LLC
Chambersburg PA
CBHW030322020526
44117CB00030B/565